Anglo-Saxon Studies 50

OLD ENGLISH STUDIES AND ITS
SCANDINAVIAN PRACTITIONERS

Anglo-Saxon Studies

ISSN 1475-2468

General Editors
Andrew Rabin
John Hines
Catherine Cubitt

'Anglo-Saxon Studies' aims to provide a forum for the best scholarship on the Anglo-Saxon peoples in the period from the end of Roman Britain to the Norman Conquest, including comparative studies involving adjacent populations and periods; both new research and major re-assessments of central topics are welcomed.

Books in the series may be based in any one of the principal disciplines of archaeology, art history, history, language and literature, and inter- or multi-disciplinary studies are encouraged.

Proposals or enquiries may be sent directly to the editors or the publisher at the addresses given below; all submissions will receive prompt and informed consideration.

Professor Andrew Rabin, Department of English, Bingham Humanities 315, 2216 1st Street, University of Louisville, Louisville, KY 40292, USA

Professor Emeritus John Hines, School of History, Archaeology and Religion, Cardiff University, John Percival Building, Colum Drive, Cardiff, Wales, CF10 3EU, UK

Professor Catherine Cubitt, School of History, Faculty of Arts and Humanities, University of East Anglia, Norwich, England, NR4 7TJ, UK

Boydell & Brewer, PO Box 9, Woodbridge, Suffolk, England, IP12 3DF, UK

Recently published volumes in the series are listed at the back of this book

OLD ENGLISH STUDIES AND ITS SCANDINAVIAN PRACTITIONERS

NATIONALISM, AESTHETICS, AND SPIRITUALITY IN THE NORDIC COUNTRIES, 1733 TO 2023

Robert E. Bjork

D.S.BREWER

© Robert E. Bjork 2024

Some rights reserved. Without limiting the rights under copyright reserved above, any part of this book may be reproduced, stored in or introduced into a retrieval system, or transmitted, in any form or by any means (electronic, mechanical, photocopying, recording or otherwise)

The right of Robert E. Bjork to be identified as
the author of this work has been asserted in accordance with
sections 77 and 78 of the Copyright, Designs and Patents Act 1988

First published 2024
D. S. Brewer, Cambridge

ISBN 978-1-84384-726-7 (hardcover)
ISBN 978-1-84384-727-4 (paperback)

The eBook editions of this book are available under the Open Access Licence:
CC BY-NC-ND

Funding Body: The ASU Foundation at the Arizona State University

D. S. Brewer is an imprint of Boydell & Brewer Ltd
PO Box 9, Woodbridge, Suffolk IP12 3DF, UK
and of Boydell & Brewer Inc.
668 Mt Hope Avenue, Rochester, NY 14620-2731, USA
website: www.boydellandbrewer.com

A CIP catalogue record for this book is available
from the British Library

The publisher has no responsibility for the continued existence or accuracy of URLs for external or third-party internet websites referred to in this book, and does not guarantee that any content on such websites is, or will remain, accurate or appropriate

*For my daughter, Francesca, my best piece of poetry,
and for my wife, Gigi, my best friend*

Contents

List of Illustrations ix
List of Abbreviations and Citations xi

Introduction: The View from the North 1

Part 1: The Beginnings, 1733 to 1899

1. Old English Studies and the Politics of Philology in Eighteenth- and Nineteenth-Century Scandinavia 21
2. Myth of Spirit, Myth of Word in the Works of N. F. S. Grundtvig 49
3. Grundtvig's Vision of the Old English *Phoenix* 74

Part 2: The Flourishing, 1900 to 2023

4. Old English Studies in Twentieth- and Twenty-First Century Scandinavia 101

Part 3: The Continuing Interest: *Beowulf* and Translations of *Beowulf* and Other Old English Literature, 1733 to 2022

5. Scandinavian Approaches to *Beowulf* 139
6. Scandinavian Translations of *Beowulf* 178
7. Scandinavian Translations of Old English Literature other than *Beowulf* 217

Conclusion: A Truly Splendid Ruin 244

Works Cited 247

Acknowledgments 271

Appendix A: A Bibliography of Contributions to Old English Studies in the Scandinavian Languages, Finnish, and Neo-Latin Written in Scandinavia to 2023 273

Appendix B: A Bibliography of Translations of Old English Literature into the Scandinavian Languages, Finnish, Sámi, and Neo-Latin Written in Scandinavia to 2023   312

Index   325

Illustrations

Figures

1. Nicolai Frederik Severin Grundtvig, 1820. Oil on canvas, Christian Frederik Christensen. The Museum of National History at Frederiksborg. Photo: Kit Weiss. — 8
2. Grímur Jónsson Thorkelin, undated. Det Kgl. Bibliotek | Royal Danish Library. — 25
3. Bengt Erland Fogelberg, "Tor," 1845. Holger.Ellgaard, CC BY-SA 3.0 https://creativecommons.org/licenses/by-sa/3.0, via Wikimedia Commons. — 27
4. Hans Gram, 1754. Det Kgl. Bibliotek | Royal Danish Library. — 34
5. Jacob Langebek, 1751. National Gallery of Denmark (SMK Open). Public Domain. — 36
6. Joakim Skovgaard, "Kristus i de dødes rige," 1891–94. National Gallery of Denmark (SMK Open). Public Domain. — 65
7. N. F. S. Grundtvig, 1872. Photograph by Ad. Lønborg. Det Kgl. Bibliotek | Royal Danish Library. — 95
8. Keld Zeruneith, 2019. Photo by Suste Bonnén. Reprinted by permission. — 109
9. Fridtjof Nansen, 1890. Credit: Library of Congress, Prints & Photographs Division, LC-DIG-ggbain-03377. — 131
10. Ludvig Schrøder, 1894. Det Kgl. Bibliotek | Royal Danish Library. — 151
11. "Uhyret Grendel" 2012 by Gitte Skov. Reproduced by permission. — 191
12. Björn Collinder, 1957. Upplandsmuseet, Uppsala, Sweden, CC BY-SA 3.0. — 197
13. Johan Rudolf Dillström. Photo from obituary in *Laivastolehti*, number 6, June 1928. Public domain. — 209
14. Halldóra B. Björnsson, ca. 1963–65. Image courtesy of Þóra Björnsson. — 213
15. Suzanne Brøgger, 2019. Photo by Suste Bonnén. Reprinted by permission. — 218
16. Vibeke Vasbo, 2018. Image courtesy of Vibeke Vasbo. — 242

Illustrations

Map

1. Beowulf's route from Gotland, Sweden, to Stevns Klint, Denmark.   171

Music Examples

1. "Det var Kongen i Engelland."   10
2. "I Kveld."   64
3. "Grendel."   69
4. "Kong Hrodgar."   71
5. "Jeg gik mig ud."   93

The author and publisher are grateful to all the institutions and individuals for permission to reproduce the materials in which they hold copyright. Every effort has been made to trace the copyright holders; apologies are offered for any omission, and the publisher will be pleased to add any necessary acknowledgment in subsequent editions.

Abbreviations and Citations

Acad	*Academy*
ÆCHom	First Sunday in September: Godden 1979 260–67 *Ælfric's Catholic Homilies: The Second Series, Text*, EETS supplementary series 5 (London)
ÆGram	Grammar: Zupitza 1880 1–296 *Ælfrics Grammatik und Glossar*, Sammlung englischer Denkmäler 1 (Berlin); repr. with intro. by H. Gneuss, 1966
AfdA	*Anzeiger für deutsches Altertum*
AfNF	*Arkiv för Nordisk Filologi*
And	*Andreas*
APS	*Acta Philologica Scandinavica*
Arv	*Arv: Journal of Scandinavian Folklore*
AS	Anglo-Saxon
Ath	*Athenaeum*
Bede 3	Bede, *History of the English Church and Nation*, Book 3: Miller 1890–98, 152–252; *The Old English Version of Bede's Ecclesiastical History of the English People*, 4 vols., EETS 95, 96, 110, 111 (London) [repr. 1959–63]
Beibl	*Beiblatt zur Anglia*
Beo	*Beowulf*
ChristA,B,C	Christ A, B, C
ChrodR1	Langefeld 2003 163–343 *The Old English Version of the Enlarged Rule of Chrodegang: Edited together with the Latin Text and an English Translation*. Münchener Universitätsschriften, Texte und Untersuchungen zur Englischen Philologie, Band 26 (Frankfurt am Main)
ChronA	Bately 1986 1–100 *The Anglo-Saxon Chronicle: A Collaborative Edition. Vol. 3: MS. A* (Cambridge)
ChronC	O'Brien O'Keeffe 2001 14–123 *The Anglo-Saxon Chronicle: A Collaborative Edition. Vol. 5: MS. C* (Cambridge)
ChronD	Cubbin 1996 1–89 *The Anglo-Saxon Chronicle: A Collaborative Edition. Vol. 6: MS. D* (Cambridge).
ChronE	Irvine 2004 3–138 *The Anglo-Saxon Chronicle: A Collaborative Edition. Vol. 7: MS. E* (Cambridge).

CollGI 22	Liebermann 1894 414–15 "Aus Ælfrics Grammatik und Glossar," *Archiv* 92: 413–15 ; Ker 1957 356 *Catalogue of Manuscripts Containing Anglo-Saxon* (Oxford)
Conf 10.4	Ker 1959 275–77 "Three Old English Texts in a Salisbury Pontifical, Cotton Tiberius C.I," in P. Clemoes, ed., *The Anglo-Saxons, Studies ... Presented to Bruce Dickins* (London), 262–79
CP	Sweet 1871 24–467 *King Alfred's West-Saxon Version of Gregory's Pastoral Care* , 2 vols., EETS 45, 50 (London) [repr. 1958]
Dan	Daniel
DBL	*Dansk Biografisk Leksikon*
DS	*Danske Studier*
EETS	Early English Text Society
EGS	*English and Germanic Studies*
EHR	*English Historical Review*
El	Elene
ELH	*English Literary History*
ERNIE	*Encyclopedia of Romantic Nationalism in Europe* (https://ernie.uva.nl/viewer.p/21/56)
EStn	*Englische Studien*
Ex	Exodus
GenA,B	*Genesis A* and *Genesis B*
GgA	*Göttingische gelehrte Anzeigen*
GM	*Gentleman's Magazine*
GR	Stanley B. Greenfield and Fred C. Robinson, *A Bibliography of Publications on Old English Literature to the end of 1972* (Toronto, 1978). Available online at https://www.google.com/books/edition/A_Bibliography_of_Publications_on_Old_En/ZCtKAwAAQBAJ?hl=en&gbpv=1&d
GRM	*Germanisch-romanische Monatsschrift*
GS	*Grundtvig-Studier*
GuthA,B	*Guthlac A* and *B*
GV	*Grundtvigs værker* (http://www.grundtvigsværker.dk)
HIGI (Oliphant)	Oliphant 1966 21–208, corrected from MS *The Harley Latin–Old English Glossary*, Janua linguarum, series practica 20 (The Hague); with corrections by Schabram 1968 Review of Robert T. Oliphant, *The Harley Latin–Old English Glossary* in *Anglia* 86: 495–500, and Voss 1989 "Quinns Edition der kleineren Cleopatraglossare: Corrigenda und Addenda," *Arbeiten aus Anglistik und Amerikanistik* 14, 127–39

HomS 15	Fourth Sunday in Lent: Belfour 1909 50–58 *Twelfth-Century Homilies in MS. Bodley 343*, EETS 137 (London) [repr. 1962]
HomU 18	Blickling Homily no. 1: Morris 1874–80 3–13 *The Blickling Homilies*, 3 vols., EETS 58, 63, 73 (London) [repr. in 1 vol. 1967]
Husb	The Husband's Message
Iduna	*Iduna, en skrift för den nordiska fornålderens älskare*
JEGP	*Journal of English and Germanic Philology*
Josh	Joshua (London, British Library, MS Cotton Claudius B.IV): Crawford 1922 377–400 *The Old English Version of the Heptateuch*, EETS 160 (London); repr. with additions by N. R. Ker 1969
Jud	Judith
Jul	Juliana
KVHAA	Kungliga Vitterhets Historie och Antikvitets Akademien
LanM	*Les langues modernes*
LGRPh	*Literaturblatt für germanische und romanische Philologie*
Lit 4.3.1	Confessional Prayers (Cambridge, Corpus Christi College, MS 391): Hughes 1958–60 II, 14–15, *The Portiforium of St. Wulfstan*, 2 vols., Henry Bradshaw Society 89–90 (London)
LitZbl	*Literarisches Zentralblatt*
LS 35	Vitae Patrum: Assmann 1889 195–207 *Angelsächsische Homilien und Heiligenleben*, Bib. ags. Prosa 3 (Kassel); repr. with intro. by P. Clemoes (Darmstadt 1964)
LUÅ	*Lunds Universitets Årsskrift*
MÆ	*Medium Ævum*
Mald	"The Battle of Maldon"
MDutch	Middle Dutch
Met	The Meters of Boethius
MHG	Middle High German
MLR	*Modern Language Review*
Mt	Matthew
MtGI	The Rushworth Gospels (Mt): Skeat 1871–87 25–245 *The Four Gospels in Anglo-Saxon, Northumbrian, and Old Mercian Versions* (Cambridge) [repr. Darmstadt 1970]
NB	*Namn og Bygd*
Neophil	*Neophilologus*
NT	*Nordisk Tidsskrift*
NTfF	*Nordisk Tidsskrift för Filologi*
NTVKI	*Nordisk Tidsskrift för Vetenskap, Konst och Industri*

Abbreviations and Citations

OE	Old English
OHG	Old High German
ON	Old Norse/Icelandic
Or	*Orosius*, Book 4: Bately 1980 83–113 *The Old English Orosius*, EETS, supplementary series 6 (London).
OrW	*The Order of the World*
OSwed	Old Swedish
Pan	*The Panther*
Phoen	*The Phoenix*
PPs	*The Paris Psalter*
PsCaL	Canticles of the Psalter, London, Lambeth Palace, MS 427: Lindelöf 1909–14 235–57 *Der Lambeth-Psalter*, Acta societatis scientiarum Fennicae 35, i and 43, iii (Helsinki)
PsCaK	Canticles of the Psalter, Salisbury, Cathedral, MS 150: Sisam and Sisam 1959 285–308 *The Salisbury Psalter*, EETS 242 (London)
PsGID	Psalms, London, British Library, MS Royal 2 B.V.: Roeder 1904 1–274 *Der altenglische Regius-Psalter*, Studien zur englischen Philologie 18 (Halle)
PsGIG	Psalms, London, British Library, MS Cotton Vitellius E.XVIII: Rosier 1962 1–363 *The Vitellius Psalter*, Cornell Studies in English 42 (Ithaca)
PsGIH	Psalms, London, British Library, MS Cotton Tiberius C.VI: Campbell 1974 1–303 *The Tiberius Psalter* (Ottawa); corrections by Bierbaumer 1980 179–85 Review of A. P. Campbell, *The Tiberius Psalter* in *Anglia* 98: 179–85
RES	*Review of English Studies*
Rev germ	*Revue germanique*
Rid	*Riddles*
Sat	*Christ and Satan*
SBL	*Svensk Biografiskt Leksikon*
SBVS	*Saga-Book* (Viking Society for Northern Research)
Sea	*The Seafarer*
Seasons	*The Seasons for Fasting*
SN	*Studia Neophilologica*
SNF	*Studier i Nordisk Filologi*
SS	*Scandinavian Studies*
SSN	*Scandinavian Studies and Notes*
TfPP	*Tidsskrift för Philologi och Paedagogik*

Abbreviations and Citations

TLS	*Times Literary Supplement* (London)
UUÅ	*Uppsala Universitets Årsskrift*
VSLÅ	*Vetenskaps-societeten i Lund Årsbok*
WaldB	*Waldere*, Fragment II
Whale	*The Whale*
WHom 2	Matthew on the Last Days: Bethurum 1957 119–22 *The Homilies of Wulfstan* (Oxford)
WPol 2.1.2	"Institutes of Polity" (Cambridge, Corpus Christi College, MS 201): Jost 1959 40–164 *Die "Institutes of Polity, Civil and Ecclesiastical,"* Swiss Studies in English 47 (Bern)
YBVS	*Yearbook of the Viking Society*
ZfdPh	*Zeitschrift für deutsche Philologie*

Introduction: The View from the North

1. Background

The study of Old English (OE) literature effectively began in earnest in Scandinavia over 200 years ago,[1] and the contributions to the field in the languages of the North (and Neo-Latin produced in Scandinavia) now in 2023 number around 300 books, articles, and translations. Scandinavians produced, for example, the first edition of *Beowulf* in 1815,[2] the first and perhaps only transmutations of OE poems into church hymns in 1836,[3] the first edition and translation into any language of *The Phoenix* in 1840,[4] the first translation into any language of *Judith* in 1858,[5] the first translation into any language of "Bede's Death Song" in 1864,[6] one of the first statements in the world on the Celtic influence on OE literature in 1901,[7] and the first reference in the world to the connection between the Finnish god Pekko and Beow in *Beowulf* in 1910.[8] However, except for the initial item, the others and most of the remaining Scandinavian contributions are virtually unknown and inaccessible to students of early medieval England, who, even if they have studied Old Norse (ON), generally do not know Swedish, Danish, Norwegian, Icelandic, or Finnish. This book will help remedy the situation. In it, I analyze the background, context, and content of numerous items of scholarship in the Scandinavian languages that deal with OE language and literature. In addition, in two appendices, I offer complete bibliographies of both scholarship on OE literature produced in Scandinavia in the Scandinavian languages, Finnish, and Neo-Latin, and translations of OE literature into those languages. This book is timely as well, appearing as it does when Europe has started taking great interest in its subject matter for all of Europe, not just Scandinavia. The ERC

---

[1] Bradley points out that the early Scandinavian promoters of OE literature were indebted to some English precursors such as Sharon Turner, John Conybeare, and James Ingram, whose ideas for bringing OE literature to light never came to fruition: "'The First New-European Literature'," pp. 45–47.
[2] Thorkelin, *De Danorum*.
[3] Grundtvig, *Sang-Værk til den danske Kirke*, hymns 124, 158, 243, 244, 245, and 355. See chapter 2, below.
[4] Grundtvig, *Phenix-Fuglen*. See chapter 3, below.
[5] Nilsson, *Judith*.
[6] Kragballe, *Anglerfolkets Kirkehistorie*, p. xiv.
[7] Hansen, "Oldengelsk Litteratur," p. 6.
[8] Olrik, *Danmarks Heltedigtning*, II, pp. 254–55. See Fulk et al., *Klaeber's Beowulf*, p. 111, and Grant, "Beow in Scandinavia," p. 107, n. 7.

(European Research Council) recently awarded a €1.5 million starting grant over five years (2024–29) to the University of Leiden's project "Early Medieval English in Nineteenth-Century Europe: The Transnational Reception of Old English in the Age of Romantic Nationalism."[9] That project obviously adds currency to this one and perhaps also provides a much larger audience for it.

My purpose in writing this history is three-fold: first, the story has not yet been fully told, but should be.[10] The Scandinavians have had a unique affinity for and connection with the Anglo-Saxons and their literature since before the ninth century, as reflected in the deep-rooted Scandinavian influence on the English language, the likely influence of Viking Age poetry on OE verse, and the composition of Norse literature in early medieval England. The kinship between OE and ON, in fact, was probably mutually recognized at the time. One could deduce so, in any case, from two statements. One is found in the late thirteenth-century ON *Fornmanna sögur* that maintains that the Norse tongue "passed through Saxony, Denmark and Sweden, Norway and parts of England. And then these lands were called Gothland and the people, Gothonic."[11] The other comes in the mid-twelfth century in the ON *First Grammatical Treatise*. Englishmen, the author observes, use a modified Latin alphabet to write OE; "since we are of the same tongue, although there has been much change in one of them or some in both," he will do the same.[12] Changes in English include its indebtedness to the Scandinavians for several lexical, morphological, and syntactic innovations. Hundreds of ON loanwords, including items such as "window," "crawl," "law," "thrust," "sister," and place-names ending with ON suffixes ("-by," "-thwait," "-toft," "-dale," "-ey," "-scoe/-skew," and "-wath") enrich the lexicon; ON morphology such as in the third person plural pronoun "they," which replaced the native pronoun "hie," helped disambiguate the personal pronoun paradigm; and the syntax of things such as the reflexive "self" in both

---

[9] See https://thijsporck.com/emergence/.

[10] For partial explorations of this field, see especially Bjork, "Thorkelin's Preface"; "Nineteenth-Century Scandinavia" (revised as chapter 1 in the present book); "Grundtvig's Edition of *The Phoenix*" (revised as chapter 3 in the present book); and "On Grundtvig's Becoming a *Scop*"; Shippey and Haarder, *Beowulf*, items 2, 6, 8, 9, 14, 17, 27, 43, 60, 78, 85, 91, 92, and 116; Hall, "England, Denmark, America"; and Niles, *The Idea of Anglo-Saxon England*, pp. 204–15. See also section I of Appendix A in this book for a complete list of contributions to the field in English.

[11] "Gekk sú tunga um Saxland, Danmörk ok Svíþjóð, Noreg ok um nokkurn hluta Englands. En þá váru þessi lönd kölluð Goðlönd, en folkit Godjóð." *Fornmanna sögur*, XI, p. 412. Quoted on the title page of Schütte, *Vor folkegruppe Gottjod*, vol. 1.

[12] "alls vér erum einnar tungu, þó at görzk hafi mjök önnur tveggja eða nökkut báþar." Haugen, *First Grammatical Treatise*, pp. 12–13.

languages shows that the contact of the two tongues occasioned similar structural changes in both.[13] Lexical borrowing went both ways as well. The Old Danish word *gemsten* (precious stone) is borrowed from OE (*gimstan*),[14] and the word "Viking" itself seems to be an early loan from OE to ON, for example.[15] Given these linguistic facts, it is not far-fetched to propose, as some have done, that an "Anglo-Scandinavian" dialect was in use in Viking Age England.[16]

Regarding literature, the ON *Völundarkviða* may have arisen in Yorkshire;[17] the ON court poet Gunnlaugr ormstunga may have enjoyed the patronage of King Æthelred II (978–1016);[18] and the English court of King Cnut "was the most vibrant centre in the North for the production and performance of skaldic praise poetry" during Cnut's twenty-year reign in England (1016–35).[19] Cnut patronized eight poets. Four more – including Gunnlaugr ormstunga – were supported by other patrons before Cnut, and another three enjoyed patronage from others than Cnut during the eleventh century.[20] The Anglo-Scandinavian literary connection, latent until the eighteenth century, gave rise to a considerable body of scholarly work that offers a distinctive view of OE literature, a view that (as Kemp Malone [1889–1971] suggested over eighty years ago) every scholar of early medieval England should apprehend.[21]

Second, this history sheds light on the cultural and national geography of OE scholarship and on the current ramifications of that geography. Although it was the work of a Danish scholar rather than an English one that brought the treasure trove of OE literature to light in 1830, few scholars are aware of that fact. In his *Bibliotecha Anglo-Saxonica. Prospectus and Proposals of a subscription for the publication of the most valuable Anglo-Saxon Manuscripts illustrative of the early poetry and literature of our Language, most of which have never yet been printed* (London, 1830, 1831), N. F. S. Grundtvig (1783–1872),[22] however, laid out ambitious plans for making OE literature

---

[13] For a full discussion, see Miller, *External Influences on English*, pp. 91–147, and Pons-Sanz, *The Lexical Effects of Anglo-Scandinavian Linguistic Contact on Old English*.
[14] Gammeltoft and Holck, "Gemsten and other Old English Pearls," p. 133.
[15] See Grønvik, "Ordet norr. *Víkingr* m." See also Hødnebø, "Hvem var de første vikinger?" pp. 3–5.
[16] Frank, *The Etiquette of Early Northern Verse*, p. xxvii.
[17] McKinnell, "The Context of *Völundarkviða*."
[18] Lawson, *Cnut: The Danes in England in the Early Eleventh Century*, p. 6.
[19] Frank, "A Taste for Knottiness," p. 197. For a fuller discussion, see Bjork, "Scandinavian Relations."
[20] Thornbury, *Becoming a Poet*, pp. 248–49.
[21] Malone, "Grundtvig as *Beowulf* Critic," p. 130.
[22] For a brief biography of the great OE scholar, mythologist, historian, pastor, hymn writer, and politician, see Holm, *The Essential Grundtvig*, pp. 15–22.

more widely known. Those plans had their genesis early in the century and were first made public in 1817 in Grundtvig's article on "The Battle of Brunanburh," which I deal with below. There Grundtvig laments the paucity of editions of OE texts, stating,

> There lie the many noteworthy writings in the Angles' tongue, lie only, it seems, waiting for the flames that shall release them from their prison and unite them with their brothers and sisters, yes; in prison, in sinful fetters they lie with their fathers' spirit; not even one of the children of the Angles understands their language, not one, as far as we know, understood it for seven centuries ... it has long grieved me so deeply to stare at those locked cabinets, not simply because I know that they hide great treasures and suspect that they hide even more than any of us knows, but especially because it is downright pitiful to see such madness as is rampant among the people who boast of holding the fathers' spirit in honor while they diminish it ... [23]

He also promises a better edition of *Beowulf* than what was provided in Grímur Jónsson Thorkelin's first edition of the poem in 1815.

That improved edition is presumably included in his *Prospectus*. The ten-volume work Grundtvig proposed would contain two volumes devoted to *Beowulf*, a third to Cædmon's *Genesis*, a fourth to miscellaneous poems chiefly from *The Exeter Book*, three volumes to Layamon's *Brut*, and three more to the OE homilies. The resultant publication could have formed the basis for all future work on OE literature. The second printing of the *Prospectus* in 1831 lists the names of 38 subscribers, including the King of England, the Archbishop of Canterbury, Joseph Bosworth, and the Advocates Library in Edinburgh, and Grundtvig was incorrectly told that the list had grown by June 1831 to over 70.[24] But growing simultaneously with that list was resentment of Grundtvig among certain members of the Society of Antiquaries in London. The reason for that resentment could have been, at least partially, Grundtvig's seriously misjudging his audience by prefacing his plan with statements such as this:

---

[23] "Hist ligge de mange mærkelige Skrifter paa Anglers Tungemaal, ligge kun, som det synes, for at oppebie Luerne der skal løse dem af Fængselet og forene dem med deres Sødskende, ja; i Fængsel, i syndige Lænker ligge de med Fædrenes Aand, ikke een af Anglernes Børn forstaaer deres Tungemaal, ikke een, saavidt man veed, forstod det giennem syv Aarhundreder ... men længe har det græmmet mig saa inderlig, at stirre paa de lukkede Skabe, ei blot fordi jeg veed de skjule store Kostbarheder, og ahner at de skjule meer end nogen af os veed, men især fordi det ret er ynkeligt at see paa slig en Vanvid som den der gaaer i Svang hos, det Folk der praler af at holde Fædres Aand i Ære, mens de tage den af Dage ..." "Om Bruneborg-Slaget," pp. 69–70. Unless otherwise noted, all translations in this book are my own.

[24] Rønning, "Grundtvig og den oldengelske literatur," p. 131.

Introduction: The View from the North

> The slightest reflection will teach us, that, without due attention to Anglo-Saxon literature, we can neither estimate nor understand the importance or the progress of that of the present day ... But this seems to have been altogether overlooked [in England], and this ancient treasury has been regarded as a dunghill, where, because the pearls do not lie exposed and obvious to every passing eye, they have been thought not worth seeking ... [It is] astonishing that a nation, so acute and enlightened as the English, should have chanced to overlook a source from whence they might have derived both credit and profit to themselves. [If] this Anglo-Saxon literature, far from being the dull and stupid trash which some English writers of no small name have chosen to suppose, should [be worth] ... the attention and admiration of cultivated minds, it may be no fantastic hope of mine, perhaps, that England will one day regret the neglect and unkindness she has shown to her high-born and honourable kinsmen, and atone for it by "one stride equal to many mincing steps."[25]

Among the resentful, for example, was Sir Frederic Madden (1801–73), who became aware of Grundtvig's plan in August 1829, and wrote in his diary that the plan fulfilled "will be a disgrace to England."[26] Grundtvig abruptly learned the result of the rising resentment on 7 June 1831, when he visited his publisher in London and was told that the English themselves had taken over the publication of OE literature and had produced a new prospectus, which would quickly attract 42 subscribers, most of whom were from the 38 subscribers to Grundtvig's original plan.[27] Thus Grundtvig was unceremoniously booted out of the mainstream of OE studies, never to return.[28] John Kemble (1807–57), writing to Jakob Grimm (1785–1863) in January 1842, thirteen years after Grundtvig's ejection, elaborates on the resentment and revises the history:

> With regard to Grundtwig, I dare say he is a man of knowledge, but he is a great rogue. The coolness with which he abuses us for taking *his* work out of his hands is exemplary. I beg for your information to

---

[25] *N. F. S. Grundtvig's Transcriptions of the Exeter Book*, pp. 3–4.
[26] Quoted in Toldberg, "Grundtvig og de engelske Antikvarer," p. 281. See also Gurteen, who expressed a similar sentiment almost 70 years later in 1896: "We acknowledge, though not without shame, that this second revival of Anglo-Saxon learning is due to the genius of foreigners ... [but] the descendants of the Anglo-Saxons have awakened to the fact that the language and literature of their ancestors is worthy of the attention of scholars, and that they will not allow other nations, although kindred, to carry off the palm in this particular." *The Epic of the Fall of Man*, p. 20.
[27] Rønning, "Grundtvig og den oldengelske literatur," pp. 131 and 134.
[28] For full details, see Toldberg, "Grundtvig og de engelske Antikvarer" and Rønning, "Grundtvig og den oldengelske literatur."

tell you that Grundtwig stole the plan & even the name of his undertaking from *Thorpe*, who mentioned it in Copenhagen to G[rundtwig] two years before he came to England, and mentioned it to many other people besides. There were actual proposals for a subscription & c., when to our infinite surprise *Grundtwig* came to England, put the thing into the hands of a bookseller & published a prospectus. After this piece of treachery, especially as we do not look upon the Dane as so very competent as he himself imagines, Thorpe & I certainly had no scruple whatever in proceeding with our own views, Thorpe publishing Cædmon, I Beowulf & c., as it suited our own convenience to do.[29]

In his preface to his *Phenix-Fuglen* (The Phoenix Bird) in 1840, and to which Kemble was probably referring in his letter to Grimm above, Grundtvig reports on his third, fateful trip to England in June 1831. He writes that:

people openly regarded and treated me as a Danish Viking who, following the example of my dear forefathers, wished to enrich both myself and Denmark with England's treasures, and my publisher came close to coming right out and saying that he didn't dare have anything more to do with me lest he be branded a traitor.[30]

And so, as R. W. Chambers phrased it, "the *editio princeps* of the *Exeter Book* was to be the work of a more humdrum scholar, Benjamin Thorpe," rather than the arrogant but extremely gifted rogue, Nicolai Frederik Severin Grundtvig.[31] (For more on the conflict between Grundtvig and the British, see chapter 3.)

Third, a history such as this one elucidates how and why the aesthetic appreciation of OE literary texts actually began in Denmark in the early nineteenth century, not in England in the early twentieth. Many modern scholars routinely assume that that appreciation started in 1936 with J. R. R. Tolkien's famous essay, "*Beowulf*: The Monsters and the Critics." I show instead that N. F. S. Grundtvig's broad influence and his emphasis on the centrality of metaphor in productive thought both radically differentiates

---

[29] Kemble and Grimm, *A Correspondence*, pp. 220–21.
[30] "man aabenbar betragtede og behandlede mig som en Dansk Viking, der, after mine kiære Forfædres Exempel, vilde berige baade mig selv og Danmark med Englands Skatte, og Boghandleren var nær ved reent ud at sige, han ikke turde befatte sig mere med mig, for ikke at stemples til en Landsforræder," *Phenix-Fuglen*, p. 11.
[31] Chambers, "Modern Study of the Poetry of the Exeter Book," p. 35. Bradley echoes this sentiment in saying that "nineteenth-century Anglo-Saxon scholarship is unquestionably the poorer for being denied both the textual-critical experience and the interpretative flair, which Grundtvig did not manage to deliver to the world in an edition of the Exeter Book": *N. F. S. Grundtvig's Transcriptions of the Exeter Book*, p. 12.

the great Danish scholar from his German and English rationalist contemporaries and goes far in explaining why Scandinavian scholarship on OE literature is distinctive.

2. Methods

To give you a sense of what this book contains, I look briefly in this Introduction at some Danish, Swedish, Icelandic, and Norwegian articles and books from 1817 to 1987. Besides being in the Scandinavian languages, these items have one other thing in common (and this is the main point of this book): they participate to varying degrees in two traditions of Scandinavian scholarship on OE literature – nationalism, beginning with Romantic Nationalism in Europe in the eighteenth and nineteenth centuries, and an appreciation of the aesthetics of OE poetry that precedes J. R. R. Tolkien's 1936 breakthrough on *Beowulf* by decades. Grundtvig once again takes the lead in this regard in his 1815 review of the first edition of *Beowulf*. In it, he states that the poem

> is so unique of its kind that I dare not classify it with any of the poems we have from the North's ancient times, for in its plan and execution one traces genuine artistry ... It is a beautiful, tastefully ordered and ornamented whole ... in every way Beowulf's spiritual monument of molten gold which shines from headland far away over the sea and announces to the watchful eye of the steersman the glory of the Sea-Goth ... [32]

We can see both of these traditions in full bloom in Grundtvig's earliest excursion into OE literature apart from *Beowulf* in his 1817 article on "The Battle of Brunanburh," a poem from *The Anglo-Saxon Chronicle* that may owe much to the skaldic court poetry tradition of Viking Age England.[33] The battle itself was of sufficient interest to Scandinavians that it takes up chapters 52 to 55 of *Egils saga Skalla-Grímssonar*.[34] Grundtvig's article begins with a scholarly essay on the OE poem, then moves to Grundtvig's heroic ballad in its honor, then ends with an "Echo" or "Reverberation" poem reflecting on the OE poet, on Grundtvig, and on the Danish ballad composed by Grundtvig. In the essay, Grundtvig describes the importance of the battle to the English, the nature and content of the poem, and the inadequacies of Henry of Huntingdon's ca. 1133 and Edmund Gibson's 1692 Latin translations of it. He also lambasts the English for neglecting

---

[32] Busbee, "A Few Words," p. 29.
[33] Townend, "Pre-Cnut Praise-Poetry."
[34] Livingston, *The Battle of Brunanburh*, pp. 68–81.

Figure 1. Nicolai Frederik Severin Grundtvig, 1820.

poetry blessed with a glorious spirit and infused with a spiritually alive mother tongue, concluding by saying:

> were my voice powerful enough to travel across the sea and penetrate the ears of the English, then I would shout at, implore, beseech them, both for the human race's and their own sake, to look seriously back, discern the tongue of their fathers, learn to understand it, and strive to appropriate for themselves the spirit, the soul, from those distant days.[35]

---

[35] "var min Røst mægtig til at dønne over Havet og trænge ind i Anglernes Øren, da vilde jeg raabe, bede, besværge dem, dog for Menneske-Slægtens og deres egen Skyld alvorlig at see sig tilbage, løse Fædrenes Tunger, lære at forstaae dem, og stræbe at tilegne sig Aanden fra de gamle Dage." "Om Bruneborg-Slaget," p. 72.

Introduction: The View from the North

He then rounds off his essay with a scholarly, accurate, and literal prose translation of the poem together with numerous textual notes correcting Henry of Huntingdon and Gibson. Before offering his own rendition of "Brunanburh," however, Grundtvig states the following about the scholarly accuracy of his literal rendition:

> Thus may the poem's words be interpreted, but the poem is not translated or "Danished" in that way at all. It just lies there like a corpse for raven and wolf, its spirit gone. I will try now to recapture that spirit and let it speak as well as it can in my Danish tongue without uttering anything other than what the old scald would have. And that, as you know, is what I call translating poetry.[36]

To make the poem better than it was, to release its soul and allow it to live again in Danish, Grundtvig offers us a 29-line stanza poem in one of the three main forms of the medieval Nordic ballad, that of a four-line stanza followed by a refrain (the other two are two-line stanzas, one with terminal refrain, one with medial and terminal refrain).[37] The "Danishing" in this folk ballad is again accurate insofar as Grundtvig deletes little from and adds little to the narrative content of the OE. But the ballad form he employs reincarnates the poem (*verbum cantus factum est*) in an ancient yet contemporary guise, a popular and familiar guise. So thoroughly Nordic and balladic is this poem, in fact, that it can actually be sung. James Massengale, Emeritus Professor of Scandinavian Studies and a musicologist at UCLA, analyzed the meter and form of the original Danish for me and fit the ballad to a known balladic tune, that of one of the "King Diderik" ballads. We cannot prove that this tune is what Grundtvig had in mind for Brunanburh, but we know that it could have been. Volume 5 of the collected Danish ballads from the Middle Ages in which it appears was published in 1814. Stanza 1 with music is reproduced below,[38] as are stanzas one to three with English translations.

---

[36] "Saaledes maa da Rimets Ord udtydes, men dermed er i mine Tanker Rimet ingenlunde oversat eller fordansket, det ligger som et Liig til Ravn og Ulv, og *Aanden* er borte, denne vil jeg nu søge at gribe og lade tale saa godt den kan med min danske Tunge, uden at udsige Andet end den gamle Skjald, og det er, som man veed, hvad jeg kalder at *oversætte Digte*." "Om Bruneborg-Slaget," p. 78.

[37] For a discussion of the medieval Scandinavian ballad, see Colbert, "The Medieval Ballad." Pp. 61–63 focus on *kæmpeviser*, "heroic ballads."

[38] Possible music to accompany N. F. S. Grundtvig's "Kæmpevise om Bruneborg-Slaget" (Heroic Ballad about the Battle of Brunanburh) from his "Om Bruneborg-Slaget og et Riim i den Anledning." Lightly adapted and simplified melody courtesy of James Massengale, UCLA, from Nyerup and Rahbek, *Udvalgte Danske Viser fra Middelalderen*, p. 18, no. 3.

Example 1. "Det var Kongen i Engelland."

Det var Kongen i Engelland,
Paa guldet saa gad han ej spare,
Det var Herren, Kong Adelstan,
Ham fulgte de Grever i Skare.
Udødelig Ære ved Bruneborg de Ædlinger have
sig vundet.

Edmund Ædling og Adelstan,
De Sønner af Edvard saa kjække,
Hjelm og Skjolde de skar som Vand,
Thi helte saa vare de begge.
Udødelig Ære ved Bruneborg de Ædlinger have
sig vundet.

Herlig var deres Høvdingsfærd,
De Æbler af ædelig Stamme,
Mur om Land deres Heltesværd,
Saa Fjenderne bleve til Skamme.
Udødelig Ære ved Bruneborg de Ædlinger have
sig vundet.

There was a king in England,
with gold he chose not to be spare,
that was the lord, King Adelstan,
the earls followed him in a troop.
Undying honor at Brunanburh for themselves
the nobles have won.

Edmund the noble and Adelstan,
those sons of Edward so brave,
helmet and shield like water they hewed,
for heroes both were they.
Undying honor at Brunanburh for themselves
the nobles have won.

> Glorious was their chieftain's raid,
> those apples from noble tree,
> a wall around land their heroic sword,
> so their enemies were put to shame.
> Undying honor at Brunanburh for themselves
> the nobles have won.

The style here is Danish Baroque and is directed at the common man, at anyone who reads and can sing Danish. Grundtvig clearly popularizes the poem in the best sense of that word, infusing it with a Danish spirit brought further to life by the incessant pounding of the balladic refrain (twenty-nine iterations of "Udødelig Ære ved Bruneborg de Ædlinger have sig vundet" have their effect). In the "Efterklang" (After Ring or Echo Poem) that follows the "Danishing" of the poem, Grundtvig, as a Nordic scald comparable to the OE *scop*, reflects on the OE poem and his balladic rendition of it. The "Echo Poem" is Grundtvig's creation, the first instance of which appeared in 1815 in his *Heimdall*. There, "Efterklang" follows "Norne-Giæst," a fairly faithful translation of a selection from *Olav Tryggveson's Saga*, and represents Grundtvig's poetic and personal response to a text from the past, which has specific historical and typological relevance to the present.[39] In the "Echo Poem" for "The Battle of Brunanburh," the central metaphor is of Grundtvig as a bell founder, digging up precious ore to be melted down and shaped into a bell to ring throughout Denmark. The OE alliterative poem thus moves from the ancient pages of *The Anglo-Saxon Chronicle* to the contemporary pages of Grundtvig's journal *Dannevirke*, first in a rough-hewn, lifeless prose translation – the precious ore from the past – and then in a modern Danish folk ballad. From there, it moves to the living society of Grundtvig's Denmark, where it can be sung in its new, living form in Danish.

Purely, relentlessly nationalistic, to be sure, but this ballad also demonstrates the second tradition and an essential premise that Grundtvig was to voice definitively twenty-three years later in his preface to his edition of the OE *Phoenix* (see chapter 3). There he articulates the credo that the philological is secondary and much inferior to the aesthetic appreciation of a given text: for Grundtvig philology, the study of the word, should give way to pneumatology, the study of the spirit. This belief by one of the giants of nineteenth-century philology had its definite impact, I believe, on Scandinavian scholarship on OE and ensured that it reached the insights that Tolkien would reach, more than sixty years before Tolkien. Ludvig Schrøder's symbolic reading of *Beowulf*, which does precisely that, appeared in 1875 (see chapter 5).

---

[39] http://www.grundtvigsværker.dk/tekstvisning/14200/0#{%220%22:0,%22v0%22:0,%22k%22:4} and Holm, *Historie og efterklang*, especially p. 31.

Aesthetic interest in OE poetry appears in two other examples from the nineteenth century. I begin with a rapid glance at the first translation into any language of *Judith*. Lars Gabriel Nilsson (1833–99) was the Swede responsible for this act when he studied under three friends of Grundtvig (George Stephens [1813–95], Peder Munch [1810–63], and C. R. Unger [1817–97]) at the University of Copenhagen. In 1858, Nilsson's master's thesis, "Judith, Fragment af ett fornengelskt Qväde" (Judith: Fragment of an Old English Poem), was published. In it, he uses the text of the poem by Benjamin Thorpe (1782–1870) from his *Analecta Anglo-Saxonica* of 1834 to create a literary translation that is implicitly based on the Grundtvigian notion that the spirit of the original is more important than its surface. His method is to render the text freely instead of literally into Swedish in a facing-page translation, and he employs "rhythmic prose" instead of alliteration because prose has exerted great power over the language for a long time and is therefore more appropriate than poetry for a contemporary audience.[40] In addition to the OE text opposite his translation, he appends a glossary to allow readers to decide for themselves how well he has accomplished his task. Here are the first few lines of *Judith* with my English translation of them followed by Nilsson's Swedish translation with my English translation of them. You will see that Nilsson creates a modern Swedish prose narrative out of the OE original:

> ... tweode gifena,
> in ðis ginnan grunde;
> heo þær þa gearwe funde
> mund byrd æt þam mæran þeoðne,
> þa heo ahte mæste þearfe
> hyldo þæs hehstan Deman.[41]

> Hon ej tviflade på framgång
> i denna vida värld;
> hon skulle lätt finna hjelp
> hos den allsmägtige Försten,
> då hon hade största behof
> af den högste Domarna nåd.[42]

> ... doubted gifts
> in this spacious earth;
> she there then easily found
> protection from the famous prince

---

[40] *Judith*, p. 3.
[41] Ibid., p. 4
[42] Ibid., p. 5.

when she most had need
of grace from the highest Judge.

She didn't doubt success
in this wide world;
she would easily find help
from the all-powerful Prince
when she had the greatest need
of the high Judge's favor.

It is worth noting here that Nilsson also had a philological interest in OE as manifested in his publishing an OE Grammar in 1866–70[43] and an OE reader in 1871[44] that few if any OE specialists know exist.

The Dane Frederik Hammerich (1809–77) gives even louder and more explicit voice to Grundtvigianism in his *De episk-kristelige Oldquad hos de gothiske Folk* (Christian Narrative Poetry among the Gothic People) published in 1873. A theologian and historian at the University of Copenhagen whose childhood home was marked by Moravian piety and Danish patriotism, Hammerich often listened as a schoolboy to Grundtvig preach and eventually became a close friend. He also took a long trip abroad in the 1830s, beginning with Sweden and Norway, and returned a keen Scandinavian because of the close relationship he observed among the Scandinavian languages and cultures.[45] Grundtvig's spirit clearly lived on in his friend's work.

Hammerich's book is Grundtvigian in scope, first of all. It embraces OE, Old Saxon, Old High German, and ON literature; it puts those literatures into a European context (i.e., Syrian, Greek, Latin, and French); and it contains the text and an alliterative verse translation of parts of "The Dream of the Rood," a translation of "The Grave," and selected translations from everything from "Cædmon's Hymn" and the biblical verse paraphrases and elegies to the "Meters of Boethius," "The Ruthwell Cross," *Genesis A and B, Exodus, Daniel, Christ and Satan, Judith, Christ I, Andreas, Guthlac B, The Phoenix,* "Soul and Body II," "The Seafarer," and "The Wife's Lament" interspersed throughout a discussion of the poems. The book is Grundtvigian in spirit, second of all. Like Grundtvig, Hammerich believed that scholarly work on ancient history and languages opens the door to a new spiritual world in the present.[46] But scholarship was not enough. He also saw an inextricable link between a literary text's form and its soul, and lavished great care on his translations to make

---

[43] *Anglosaxisk (fornengelsk) grammatika,* parts 1 and 2.
[44] *Anglosaxisk (fornengelsk) läsebok för Nybegynnare.*
[45] Lindhardt, "Frederik Hammerich."
[46] *De episk-kristelige Oldquad,* p. 1.

them vibrant and relevant to his contemporaries. These translations, he states, absorbed more of his time than any other aspect of his book, and he explains in some detail what problems one faces in creating literary translations of the OE poems.[47]

From 1927 to 1962, Stefán Einarsson (1897–1972) was Professor of Icelandic at Johns Hopkins University, where he distinguished himself as one of the premier scholars in the world of Icelandic language and literature. He authored over 500 books and articles, including a comprehensive, authoritative history of Icelandic literature for the American-Scandinavian Foundation and a substantial introduction to modern Icelandic.[48] In 1936, he published an article on "Widsith" motivated at least in part by love of country "[i]n these patriotic times" ([á] þessum þjóðræknistímum)[49] before the advent of WWII. In that article, he briefly deals with "Waldere," "Deor," "The Finnsburg Fragment," and *Beowulf* before turning at length to "Widsith" and offering a complete Icelandic translation of that poem at the end of the article. All five OE heroic poems are important, but, more than any other, "Widsith" shows just how popular heroic tales were in the period during which it was composed. Einarsson intends to demonstrate its value, "especially its connection to ON and Icelandic stories and poems."[50] The first is the poem's resemblance to the ON *kappatöl* ("list of heroes"), the popular genre of poetry in which the poet lists characters from Icelandic literature, chiefly the *Íslendingasögur*; the second is the poem's being a catalogue poem resembling the name catalogues in Snorri's *Edda*; and the third is the poem's beginning with words reminiscent of Odin's in "The Lay of Vafðrúðnir," stanza 52:[51]

> Much have I travelled,
> much have I tried,
> much have I put the gods to the test.[52]

A fourth connection first noticed by Grundtvig is Widsith-Víðförull's resemblance to Norna-Gestr, who "had been with all the famous kings from Völsung to King Ólafr Tryggvason and eventually dies there at 300 years old."[53] Víðförull, too, has been with numerous heads of state (the

---

[47] Ibid., pp. 7–10.
[48] *A History of Icelandic Literature* and *Icelandic: Grammar, Texts, Glossary*. For an overview of Einarsson's life, see Liberman, *Studies in Germanic Philology*, pp. iii–vi and ix–xlii.
[49] Einarsson, "Wídsíð = Víðförull," p. 184.
[50] "einkum samhengi þess við norrænar eða íslenzkar sagnir og kvæði." Ibid., p. 170.
[51] Ibid., p. 171.
[52] Calder et al., *Sources and Analogues*, p. 172.
[53] "hafði verið með öllum frægum konungum frá Völsungum til Ólafs konungs

poems list 71 kings and 81 nations or ethnic groups) who lived between the third and sixth centuries.[54] Einarsson continues his study of the connections between "Widsith" and the Nordic tradition mainly by referring to Kemp Malone's 1936 edition of the poem and by recommending readers to other noteworthy work: R. W. Chambers' 1912 edition, Rudolf Much's 1925 contributions to a commentary on the poem, Karl Sundén's 1929 Swedish translation of the poem, and Gudmund Schütte's *Oldsagn om Godtjod* (1907) and *Vor Folkegruppe: Gottjod* (1926), translated into English as *Our Forefathers I–II* (1929–33).[55] Finally, before offering his own Icelandic translation of "Widsith," Einarsson expresses the hope that Icelanders will translate the four other OE heroic poems, especially *Beowulf*.[56] That hope was never fulfilled, except in the case of *Beowulf*. Halldóra B. Björnsson's illustrated *Bjólfskviða* was published posthumously in 1983.

We move finally in this brief survey to the late twentieth and early twenty-first centuries with a glance at a collection of OE poetry in translation, the only such collection ever to come out of Norway: *Vers fra vest: gammelengelske dikt i utvalg* (Verse from West: A selection of OE poetry, 1987) by Arthur O. Sandved (1931–2021). Professor of English at the University of Oslo (1963–96) and a skilled linguist and translator, Sandved dedicated much of his career to translating important medieval and Early Modern English literary works into Norwegian:[57] the selection of OE poetry (1987),[58] Langland's *Piers Plowman* (1990),[59] Milton's *Paradise Lost* (1993 and 2005),[60] Shakespeare's *Henry VI* (1996),[61] Julian of Norwich's *Revelations of Divine Love* (2000),[62] selections from Chaucer's *The Canterbury Tales* (2002),[63] Milton's *Paradise Regained* (2005),[64] selections from Malory (2007),[65] and Shakespeare's *Henry VIII* (2013)[66] and *King Lear* (2013).[67] Sandved's 1981 article[68] containing his translation of "The Dream of the

---

Tryggvasonar og deyr þar að lokum 300 ára gamall." "Widsið = Víðförull," p. 172.
[54] Ibid., p. 172.
[55] Ibid., p. 184.
[56] Ibid., p. 184.
[57] Elsness, "Minnetal om Arthur Olav Sandved."
[58] *Vers fra vest.*
[59] *Peter Plogman.*
[60] *Det tapte paradis.*
[61] *Kong Henrik VI.*
[62] *Visjoner av Guds kjærlighet.*
[63] *Canterbury-fortellingene: i utdrag.*
[64] *Det gjenvundne paradis.*
[65] *Kong Arthur og hans riddere.*
[66] *Kong Henrik VIII.*
[67] *Kong Lear.* Sandved also translated Fielding's *Joseph Andrews* into Norwegian.
[68] Sandved, "Drømmen om Kristi Kors."

Rood" started his interest in assembling a collection of OE poetry when he was surprised to find that the only OE poem that had been translated into Norwegian was *Beowulf*, once into Nynorsk (New Norwegian) in 1929 by Henrik Rytter (1877–1950) and once into *Riksmål* (Dano-Norwegian written language) in 1976 by Jan W. Dietrichson (1927–2019).[69] Because Danes and Swedes already had access to a good deal of OE poetry via translations into their mother tongues, it was time for Norwegians to have access to those treasures as well.[70]

Vers fra vest begins with a foreword (pp. 5–8) in which Sandved states his reasons for selecting the poems he does (literary merit, historical importance, and having come from contact between the Anglo-Saxons and Scandinavians)[71] and a general introduction (pp. 11–27) in which he writes a good overview of the history, extent, themes, and characteristics of OE poetry and then offers a few words (pp. 27–30) about his theory of translation. He then offers introductions to and *Riksmål* translations of "Cædmon's Hymn," "Bede's Death Song," "The Ruin," "The Wanderer," "The Seafarer," "The Dream of the Rood," and "The Battle of Brunanburh" as well as introductions to and prose translations of *Genesis B*, *Judith*, and "The Battle of Maldon" (in addition, he appends to the book an introduction to and translations of fourteen Middle English lyrics). The main goal of a translation, Sandved states, is to create reactions in the reader of a translation that are comparable to the reactions of the original audience. That sometimes means replicating some of the poetic features of the original text such as alliteration, archaic diction, and variation but without making the translation sound too foreign or strange. In his translation, for example, Sandved uses alliteration extensively but not in the same systematic way as in the original texts. He also uses somewhat archaic diction and style as well as variation. "But there are strict limits to what can be tolerated of that by modern Norwegian before the style will feel long-winded and ponderous."[72] As for form, Sandved chooses what seems most appropriate to the text at hand. "The Battle of Maldon" and *Judith*, for example, have freer forms in prose than do more lyrical or elegiac items such as "The Ruin" or "The Seafarer."[73] "Maldon" in Sandved's rendition begins thus:

---

[69] *Vers fra vest*, p. 5.
[70] Ibid., p. 5.
[71] Ibid., pp. 4–5.
[72] "[M]end et er trange grenser for hva som kan tales av dette i moderne norsk uten at stilen vil føles omstendelig og overlesset." Ibid., p. 29.
[73] Ibid., pp. 29–30.

> Han bød så de unge hærmenn å sende hestene bort, drive dem avsted,
> og rykke frem til fots, stole på sin styrke, sin manndom og sitt mot.[74]
>
> He then bade the young warriors to send the horses away, drive them off, and move forward on foot, trust in their strength, their manhood and their courage.

The style is chronicle-like, moving forcefully ahead but still adorned by alliteration on "h" in "*H*an bød så de unge *h*ærmenn å sende *h*estene bort" and by alliteration on "s" in "*s*tole på *s*in *s*tyrke, *s*in manndom og *s*itt mot." Sandved also uses the archaic "hærmenn" for "warriors" instead of the modern "krigere." "The Ruin," on the other hand, reads like this:

> Storslagne disse byggverk av sten,
> men nu lagt i grus av den mektige skjebne;
> byens bygningere ligger i ruiner,
> kjempers byggverk brytes ned og smuldrer bort.[75]
>
> Impressive these structures of stone,
> but now reduced to rubble by mighty fate;
> the city's buildings lie in ruins,
> the giants' structures are broken down and crumble away.

"S" alliteration graces the first line and ties it to the second ("grus" and "skjebne") as well as "b" alliteration in the third and fourth lines. And Sandved has introduced a more focused variation ("byggverk," "byens bygningere," "kjempers byggverk") than obtains in the original OE, which reads:

> Wrætlic is þes weal-stan, wyrde gebræcon;
> burg-stede burston, brosnað enta geweorc.
>
> Wondrous is this wall stone; disastrous events have shattered it;
> the fortified cities have broken apart, the work of giants decays.[76]

Recreating the aesthetic experience of the original audience for the modern one is not the same as transforming the original into a modern Danish poem in native balladic form. In line with translation theory in the West, in fact, Grundtvig's "Danishing" of poems would be classified as the "extraneous" approach to form "usually associated with radical stylistic alteration."[77] Sandved's would be classified as the "analogical"

---

[74] Ibid., p. 109.
[75] Ibid., p. 41.
[76] Bjork, *Old English Shorter Poems*, pp. 118–19.
[77] Kelly, *The True Interpreter*, p. 188.

approach, which "seeks to frame the translation in a form whose function is the same as that of the original."[78] In the first instance, nationalism predominates; in the second, it is negligible. The secondary literature supporting Sandved's introductions and translations is all in English, without a single item of Scandinavian scholarship except his own article on "The Dream of the Rood" being referenced,[79] and the brief intra-Scandinavian reference to the competition among Norwegians, Swedes, and Danes noted above is quaint at most.

All of the scholars and translators touched on here, as well as others such as Niels Lund,[80] Andreas Haarder,[81] Halldóra Björnsson,[82] Frands Herschend,[83] Keld Zeruneith,[84] and Suzanne Brøgger,[85] are keeping OE literature alive in Scandinavia through their work on and their translations into their native languages of OE texts. Since 1976 there have been three collections of OE poetry in Danish translation (1983, 1991, 1996);[86] one each in Norwegian (1987) and Swedish (1991);[87] three Danish translations of *Beowulf* (1983, 1984 [reprint 2001], 2018);[88] two Norwegian translations of *Beowulf* (1976, 1999);[89] one Swedish revision of a translation first published in 1889 (2022);[90] one Icelandic (1983);[91] one Finnish (1999);[92] and one Sámi translation of a prose retelling of *Beowulf* for children (2019).[93] What this work and these translations mean in the aggregate seems clear. The nationalistic motivation for studying and promoting OE poetry has diminished in Scandinavia in the twenty-first century, but both it and the aesthetic motivation – the pneumatological or spiritual motivation – definitely linger on. Both motivations have a history, to which we will now turn.

---

[78] Ibid., p. 198.
[79] *Vers fra vest*, pp. 6–7.
[80] *Ottar og Wulfstan. To rejsebeskrivelser fra vikingatiden.*
[81] *Sangen om Bjovulf.*
[82] *Bjólfskviða.*
[83] Herschend, "Striden i Finnsborg."
[84] *De sidste tider.*
[85] Translations in Zeruneith, *De sidste tider*, pp. 317–32.
[86] Noack, *Menneskevordelse og korsdød* and *Helvedstorm og Himmelfart*, and Lund, *Sangen om slaget ved Maldon.*
[87] Sandved, *Vers fra vest* and Hansson, *Slaget ved Maldon.*
[88] Wilmont, *Bjowulf*; Haarder, *Sangen om Bjovulf*; Zeruneith, *Beowulf.*
[89] Dietrichson, *Beowulf-kvadet*, and Bringsværd, *Beowulf.*
[90] Gräslund, *Beowulf.*
[91] Björnsson, *Bjólfskviða.*
[92] Pekonen and Tolley, *Beowulf.*
[93] McGuinne, *Beowulf.*

PART 1

THE BEGINNINGS, 1733 TO 1899

1

Old English Studies and the Politics of Philology in Eighteenth- and Nineteenth-Century Scandinavia

The Anglo-Scandinavian literary connection mentioned briefly in the Introduction was renewed in England in the sixteenth, seventeenth, and eighteenth centuries, chiefly in the scholarly community, which had increasing access to important Scandinavian texts.[1] The first edition of Saxo Grammaticus's *Gesta Danorum* (Deeds of the Danes) was published in Paris in 1514, and Olaus Magnus's *Historia de gentibus septentrionalibus* (History of the Northern Peoples) followed from Rome in 1555. A host of other important Scandinavian texts subsequently appeared internationally between 1636 and 1702. Learned readers had access to Snorri Sturluson's *Heimskringla*, editions of the Old Norse (ON) legendary sagas and runes, summaries of material related to the Orkneys, an Icelandic grammar, basic Icelandic dictionaries, and the *Poetic Edda*, with its evidence that "old northern 'barbarians' had developed a coherent system of ethics, a mythological system, and an artful tradition of poetic composition."[2]

In the nineteenth century, British interest in all things Scandinavian – particularly Icelandic – expanded exponentially, as Andrew Wawn has impressively documented in his *The Vikings and the Victorians*. People were enlightened and moved by English translations of the *Poetic Edda*,[3] for example, and *Heimskringla*[4] and *Njal's Saga*;[5] by Sir Walter Scott, whose hugely influential novel *The Pirate* (1822) gives a vivid account of Viking life;[6] and by English translations or popularized forms of Esaias Tegnér's *Frithiof's Saga*[7] (1820–25), the Swedish epic poem built on the ON *Friðþjófs saga*. The Vikings were everywhere in the past and present of Gregorian

---

[1] This chapter is a revised and expanded version of my "Nineteenth-Century Scandinavia and the Birth of Anglo-Saxon Studies." Reprinted with permission of the University Press of Florida.
[2] Wawn, *The Vikings and the Victorians*, pp. 17–18.
[3] Ibid., chapter 7.
[4] Ibid., chapter 4.
[5] Ibid., chapter 6.
[6] Ibid., chapter 3. See also Leersen, *National Thought in Europe*, pp. 202–03.
[7] Ibid., chapter 5.

and Victorian England,[8] and N. F. S. Grundtvig (1783–1872) was one of them. On his first trip to England, he was a vacationing, unthreatening one, as he himself describes it in 1839:

> The first summer I was in England – for like the first Danish Vikings, I only made summer expeditions to the Thames to store up for the winter – the first summer, Englishmen regarded me as a half-mad poet who had gotten the crazy idea that there lay great treasure in the old, barbaric scrolls, which they really laughed at seeing me sit and rummage through daily and told me with a self-important air that there was nothing there.[9]

No. They – both scholars and laypeople – thought nothing was there. Daines Barrington, the exception to the rule, implicitly laments the situation in his preface to his 1773 translation of the ninth-century Old English (OE) translation of Orosius's Latin world history (*Historiae aduersum paganos*, fifth century), stating that "[t]here are so few who concern themselves about Anglo-Saxon literature that I have printed the work chiefly for my own amusement, and that of a few antiquarian friends."[10] John Bosworth in 1823, on the other hand, promotes the situation in describing OE poetry "as an artificial and mechanical thing, cultivated by men chiefly as a trade" that should not be confused "with those delightful beauties which we call poetry."[11] An observation made by one of Thomas Hughes's characters in a novel published in 1859 seems to characterize a more general nineteenth-century attitude: "Yes, people sneer at the Old English chronicles now-a-days, and prefer the Edda, and all sorts of heathen stuff, to them."[12]

In Scandinavia, interest in its past glory was keen as well, and had been since the thirteenth century.[13] That interest increased through the centuries and reached new heights in the seventeenth century with the

---

[8] For the full extent of the presence of ON poetry and saga during the period, see Wawn, "Early Literature of the North."

[9] "Den første Sommer, jeg var i England–thi ligesom de første danske Vikinger gjorde jeg kun Sommertog til Themsen og pakkede mig før Vinter–altsaa den første Sommer betragtede Engelskmanden mig som an halvgal Poet, der havde faaet den Grille, at der laa store Skatte begravede i de gamle barbariske Skroller, som de ordentlig lo ad at se mig sidde daglig og rode i, og fortalte mig med en vigtig Mine, der var ingen Ting." Repr. in Johansen and Høirup, *Grundtvigs Erindringer og Erindringer om Grundtvig*, pp. 70–71.

[10] Quoted in Adams, *Old English Scholarship*, p. 106.

[11] Bosworth, *The Elements of Anglo-Saxon Grammar*, p. 212.

[12] In *The Scouring of the White Horse or, The long vacation ramble of a London clerk and what became of it: and the ashen faggot: a tale for Christmas*, p. 37. Quoted in Wawn, *The Vikings and the Victorians*, p. 183.

[13] Clunies Ross and Lönnroth, "The Norse Muse," pp. 8–10.

development of Scandinavian Gothicism, which originated in Sweden and promoted the nationalistic idea that the Gothic tribes that defeated the Romans in late antiquity came originally from Sweden. Sweden, therefore, was one of the most ancient countries in Europe and "possessed a culture that was at least as venerable and glorious as that of the Romans."[14] The great Swedish runologist and father of Swedish grammar Johannes Bureus (1568–1652), most prominently championed the idea and even proposed replacing the Latin alphabet in Sweden with the runic.[15] The idea never took hold, and neither did August Strindberg's over 200 years later to replace the study of Latin in schools with the study of Icelandic.[16] A milder form of Scandinavian Gothicism was also practiced in Denmark during Bureus's time, although its major proponent there, Ole Worm (1588–1654), professor of Latin, Greek, physics, and medicine at the University of Copenhagen, sought to prove that ON poetic language and runes originated in Denmark, not Sweden.[17]

Then came the Nordic Renaissance,[18] which brought a renewed awareness of Nordic culture in Western Europe from ca. 1750 to ca. 1800. Nordic myth, sagas, poetry, and runes were viewed on a par with Latin and Greek myth and poetry,[19] and the primitive aspects of Norse poetry – "wild, passionate, and sublime"[20] – captured the imagination. The first Swedish novel, Jacob Mörk's and Anders Törngren's *Adalriks och Giöthildas äfwentyr* (Adalrik's and Giothilda's Adventure, 1742–44), for instance, is partially based on episodes from the *Heimskringla*.[21] Language reformers were also at work for patriotic reasons during the eighteenth century in Scandinavia. For instance, in Sweden, Jesper Swedberg (1653–1735), one of the most prominent figures in the Swedish Church of his day and father of the mystic Emmanuel Swedenborg (1688–1772), published long lists of foreign words and expressions that should be replaced by Swedish equivalents in order to purify the language;[22] and in Denmark, J. S. Sneedorff (1724–64) helped promote a purified Danish stripped as much as possible of foreign influences in his periodical *Den patriotiske Tilskuer* (The Patriotic Spectator, 1761–63).[23]

---

[14] Ibid., p. 11.
[15] Enoksen, *Runor*, pp. 182–84.
[16] Mjöberg, *Drömmen om sagatiden*, vol. 2, p. 21. Although not supplanting Latin, Icelandic began being taught in the nineteenth century in schools in Norway and continues to this day. See Mjöberg, "Romanticism and Revival," p. 236.
[17] Clunies Ross and Lönnroth, "The Norse Muse," p. 11.
[18] The pioneering work in this field is Blanck, *Den nordiska renässansen*.
[19] Clunies Ross and Lönnroth, "The Norse Muse," pp. 14–18.
[20] Ibid., p. 15.
[21] Lönnroth and Delblanc, *Den Svenska Litteraturen*, p. 24.
[22] Bexell, "Swedberg."
[23] Haugen, *The Scandinavian Languages*, p. 397.

Romantic Nationalism (ca. 1800 to ca. 1870) focused the attention even more, with its emphasis on the earliest literature of a language group being the earliest expression of the nation itself. It started in Denmark around 1800, in Sweden around 1810, and in Norway and Iceland in the 1830s and was associated with a nationalistic revival in each country.[24] When the Norwegian constitution was ratified on 17 May 1814 in Eidsvoll, Norway, in fact, among the assembly delegates, known as "the Eidsvoll men," the coupling of the dream of the saga period with the possibility of a national awakening was self-evident and central. They even looked on Peder Claussen's Danish translation of *Heimskringla* (*Snorre Sturlesøns Norske Kongers Chronica* [Snorri Sturluson's Chronicle of the Norwegian Kings, 1633]) as a kind of Norwegian *Magna Carta*.[25] Despite the Scandinavians' veneration of their own literary heritage, however, there was no sneering at the OE chronicles in Scandinavia, where the whole of OE literature was increasingly held in high regard, and not just by N. F. S. Grundtvig.

The history of OE studies in Scandinavia winds through certain complex and tumultuous political realities of the eighteenth and nineteenth centuries – especially Napoleonic ones between 1795 and 1815 – as well as reactions to those realities by Scandinavians. During the earliest period, the cradle of OE studies in Scandinavia, the political climate in Scandinavia was stormy.[26] Before Napoleon, for example, Sweden was plagued by recurrent internal strife and imperiled by a Danish–Russian alliance leading to a war with Russia in 1789; after the advent of Napoleon, all of Scandinavia was in jeopardy, either from him, his allies, or his enemies. Denmark was threatened by England (which was then allied to Sweden) and successfully repelled an English naval attack in 1801, but suffered grievously from another onslaught six years later. In 1807, Copenhagen was besieged once more as a result of the British belief that Denmark would help Napoleon exclude all British goods from import to Europe. Grímur Jónsson Thorkelin (1752–1829), in fact, who had ventured to England from 1785 to 1791 for the express nationalistic purpose of "examin[ing] and transcrib[ing] every manuscript that could shed light on Danish history,"[27] claimed that he would have published his edition and translation of *Beowulf* in 1807 instead of 1815 had not "the city of

---

[24] Clunies Ross and Lönnroth, "The Norse Muse," p. 20.
[25] Mjöberg, *Drömmen om sagatiden*, vol. 1, p. 224.
[26] The following sketch of Scandinavian history is based on Mjöberg, *Drömmen om sagatiden*, vol. 1, pp. 207–39. See also Olesen and Kouri, *The Cambridge History of Scandinavia*, and Derry, *A History of Scandinavia*. Mjöberg touches on many of his findings in his two-volume *Drömmen om sagatiden* in his "Romanticism and Revival."
[27] "inspiciendi, tractandi, et exscribendi omnia, qvæ rebus Danicis lucem affere possent manuscripta." Bjork, "Thorkelin's Preface," pp. 300–01.

Figure 2. Grímur Jónsson Thorkelin, undated.

Copenhagen, ancient home of riches, thrice renowned in cruel war," sunk in flames, as he paraphrases *the Aeneid* in his preface to his 1815 first edition of the poem.[28] His scholarship, wrote Thorkelin, sank along with Copenhagen, and only "love of country" and the monetary and moral support of his patron allowed him to bring it back again.[29]

Sweden, meanwhile, had more of its own troubles. England was its only ally; it was at odds with Denmark–Norway (a well-established tradition, but this time because of Denmark's alliance with Russia); Russia invaded Finland in 1808, and the Swedes had lost that region, which had been theirs for 600 years, by 1809. The same year, a new constitution was set up.[30] Then followed revolution, the abdication of King Gustav IV Adolf, and a new truce with Denmark. Everything was in turmoil.

Norway, too, was in a precarious position, especially after Denmark's aligning itself with Napoleon after the 1807 British attack on Copenhagen. Norway disapproved of Danish foreign policy, but because it was under Danish rule at the time (as were Iceland, Greenland, the Faeroe Islands, and the duchies of Schleswig and Holstein),[31] its disapproval did not lessen the

---

[28] "Divum antiqva domus sævo ter incluta bello / Havnia." Ibid., pp. 308–09.
[29] "amor patriæ." Ibid., pp. 310–11.
[30] This constitution lasted until 1975, becoming the "oldest written constitution still in force in Europe." Derry, *A History of Scandinavia*, p. 216.
[31] Denmark was one of two Nordic states during this period, the other being Sweden. The Kingdom of Sweden included Finland, Swedish Pomerania, and

oppressive effect that the British hunger blockade on the Danes had on the Norwegians. When Jean Baptiste Jules Bernadotte, Napoleon's marshal to Sweden, became the successor to the Swedish throne and then took part in the allied victory over Napoleon, Denmark gave up Norway to Sweden through the treaty of Kiel in January 1814. The Norwegians, though, were disgruntled about this act, since they had not been directly involved in it. They developed a new constitution as a consequence, and had hardly begun reveling in their new-found freedom and solidarity when Norway put itself under the rule of Bernadotte. Bernadotte, however, approved the new constitution anyway, thus preserving Norwegian freedoms.

The reaction to all this political tumult and uncertainty and to the rampant expansionism of Napoleon was, of course, nationalism, the glorification of the Fatherland. While nationalism manifests itself in such acts as establishing new constitutions, it also has its effect in many other areas such as architecture, design, theater, music, art, and sculpture.[32] Furniture, porcelain, silverware, pewterware, and textiles, for example, were created in forms inspired by the ON style and spirit.[33] Patriotic songs were also composed and sung throughout Scandinavia,[34] as were the twenty-four songs from Tegnér's *Fritiofs saga*, which had been set to music by the Swedish-Finnish composer Bernhard Henrik Crusell (1775–1838). In Norway, Edvard Grieg wrote music for one of Bjørnstjerne Bjørnson's Viking plays, *Sigurd Jorsalfar*, and began writing an opera about Olaf Tryggvason as well.[35] After Sweden lost Finland to Russia in 1809, representing the world of the Norse gods and Sweden's most ancient history in art became one way of coping with the humiliation and pain. An exhibition of such art in 1818 inaugurated a new era in Sweden that would thrive to the end of the nineteenth century.[36]

In addition, nationalism also found one of its most forceful and compelling articulations in imaginative literature. Although Finland itself plays no direct role in OE studies in Scandinavia, what took place there epitomizes a more general Scandinavian response. The separation of Finland from Sweden and its incorporation into Russia as an autonomous grand duchy by 1809 was traumatic for both Sweden and Finland. In Finland, the urge to find a national identity emerged most powerfully in the work of Elias Lönnrot (1802–84), a physician, writer, and professor of

---

St. Barthélemy island in the Caribbean. See Nordstrom, *Scandinavia Since 1500*, p. 165.

[32] See Mjöberg, *Drömmen om sagatiden*, vol. 2, chapter I, and on architecture see Lane, *National Romanticism and Modern Architecture*.
[33] Mjöberg, *Drömmen om sagatiden*, vol. 2, p. 8.
[34] For a comprehensive survey, consult Enefalk, *En patriotisk drömvärld*.
[35] Mjöberg, "Romanticism and Revival," p. 236.
[36] See Stenroth, *Gudar eller människor*.

Figure 3. Bengt Erland Fogelberg, "Tor," 1845.

the Finnish language, who compiled two large literary works out of the oral poetry of the Finns, *Kalevala* (Land of Kaleva, 1835–36; second edition 1849) and the *Kanteletar taikka Suomen Kansan Wanhoja Lauluja ja Wirsiä* (Kanteletar or old songs and ballads of the Finnish people, 1840–41).[37] The first of these – 22,795 lines in fifty poems in the definitive edition of 1849[38] – became almost instantly regarded as Finland's national epic and has served the needs of artists, writers, politicians, businessmen and women, educators, and others in promoting Finland's identity. The impact of it and the *Kanteletar* on the arts and scholarship and politics in Finland, where its publication day (28 February) is still a national holiday, "has been enormous and still awaits systematic analysis and assessment."[39]

In Denmark, Adam Oehlenschläger (1779–1850) and N. F. S. Grundtvig responded to the two British sieges by reaching back into the Viking Age for inspiration. Both had already been moving strongly in the direction of Romantic Nationalism, Oehlenschläger with his *Nordiske Digte* (Nordic

---

[37] Branch, "Finnish Oral Poetry," p. 3.
[38] Ibid., p. 4.
[39] Ibid., p. 33.

Poems, 1807) and Grundtvig with his *Nordens Mytologi* (Nordic Mythology, 1808).[40] Oehlenschläger – then deemed the leading Danish author and later in 1829 honored as the "King of Nordic Poetry"[41] – penned three poisoned poems against the British in which, for instance, he says that "Oldtids Aand og Oldtids Ære" (the past's spirit and the past's glory)[42] are rekindled by the Danish deeds of the present, and Thor actually awakens to inspire the Danish and Norwegian warriors with the fire of ancient heroism.[43] Grundtvig – who became a member of the Danish Constitutional Assembly in 1849[44] – has Valhalla opening to welcome the brave naval officer Peter Villemoes, slain like a dauntless Viking by the British, in his "Drapa om Villemoes" (The Heroic Poem of Villemoes, 1808).[45]

The Swedes responded with the same righteous fury (and fear) to the loss of Finland as the Danes did to the assaults from England. Pehr Henrik Ling, for example, wrote an allegorical poem (1810) about the loss, in which the Viking king Gylfe (Sweden) sits on a burial mound mourning his dead love, Aura (Finland).[46] Esaias Tegnér wrote his anti-Russian "Svea" (subtitled "Pro patria") in response to the situation as well. In that poem, the poet's glorious Viking forefathers rise from their graves to applaud Swedish soldiers who recapture Finland.[47] In such writers as Ling and Tegnér, Swedish nationalism was being redirected and rejuvenated. It actually began in a flamboyant way in the Middle Ages, and continued in the Renaissance with independence from Denmark. From a linguistic point of view, it was institutionalized in 1786 when the Swedish Academy was established to preserve the purity of the national language and to compile a historical dictionary. The 37-volume *Svenska Akademiens ordbok* (SAOB) (the Swedish Academy's Dictionary) started to be published in 1898 and was completed in 2019. It is the Swedish equivalent of the *Oxford English Dictionary*, the *Deutsches Wörterbuch*, and the Dutch *Woordenboek Der Nederlandsche Taal* (Dictionary of the Netherlandic Language).[48]

The Norwegian situation was more complicated than the Danish or Swedish because Norway was still part of Denmark and subject to the strict censorship rules of *Tvillingrigerne* (the Twin Realms). Possibly for

---

[40] Rossel, "From Romanticism to Realism," pp. 187–88.
[41] Gerven, "Oenlenschläger."
[42] Quoted in Mjöberg, *Drömmen om sagatiden*, vol. 1, p. 209.
[43] Ibid.
[44] Holm, *The Essential Grundtvig*, p. 11.
[45] Mjöberg, *Drömmen om sagatiden*, vol. 1, p. 211. See also Mjöberg, "Romanticism and Revival," p. 233.
[46] Mjöberg, *Drömmen om sagatiden*, vol. 1, p. 216.
[47] Mjöberg, "Romanticism and Revival," p. 233.
[48] Haß, "The Germanic Languages," p. 475.

that reason and certainly for others, no important literary works were produced in Norway between 1800 and 1830, a golden age for literature in Sweden and Denmark.[49] But Norwegian nationalism had already been engendered among members of "Det Norske Selskab" (the Norwegian Society), founded in Copenhagen in 1772. Those members "created and consolidated a Norwegian national consciousness, which did not appear in its full flowering until after the dissolution of the Danish-Norwegian union in 1814."[50] In the meantime, wanting a freedom and independence they had not possessed since the Middle Ages, the Norwegians clung above all to *Heimskringla*, the ON book about ancient Norwegian kings and glory that took its place next to the Bible in most Norwegian homes.[51]

Amidst the striking literary reactions to political chaos and threat come the somewhat more restrained reactions of historians and philologists. Less fired by the flames of Hyperborean Apollo (to use Thorkelin's phrase for the god of poetry in the extreme north) than poets, perhaps, they nevertheless manifest the same kind of patriotic feeling. All over Europe, the Napoleonic wars and the rise of Romanticism had their effect on people's worldviews. Joep Leersen outlines the main changes between the eighteenth and nineteenth centuries relative to nationalism:

> Nationalism emerges in the nineteenth century from eighteenth-century roots: Herder's belief in the individuality of nations, Rousseau's belief in the sovereignty of the nation, a general discourse of national peculiarities and "characters". What changes from the eighteenth century to the nineteenth is this:
>
> 1. an unprecedented imperial campaign mounted by Napoleon and fiercely resented outside France; this turns eighteenth-century notions of tyranny and liberty from a power imbalance within the state (between rulers and governed) into one of power imbalance between states (between occupier and occupied);
> 2. the rise of Romantic idealism which sees national character as a spiritual principle, a "soul", rather than a set of peculiarities;
> 3. the Romantic belief that a nation's culture, and in particular its language, are the manifestation of its soul and essence;
> 4. the historicist belief that all culture must be seen as an organic tradition linking generations across centuries.[52]

---

[49] Naess, "Norwegian Literature 1800–1860," p. 83.
[50] Naess, "Holdberg and the Age of Englightenment," p. 77.
[51] Mjöberg, *Drömmen om sagatiden*, vol. 1, p. 224.
[52] Leersen, *National Thought in Europe*, pp. 125–26.

There is a long tradition of appropriative, nationalistic historical writing in Scandinavia, including Saxo Grammaticus's *Gesta Danorum* (ca. 1208) in which Saxo glorifies Danish history to justify Denmark's being a Baltic power. Denmark, in fact, compares favorably with the Roman Empire for Saxo, and any accomplishment in the latter could be equaled in the former.[53] Saxo is followed by somewhat less restrained reflections on the past such as those by the Swede Ericus Olai in his *Chronica regni Gothorum* (1460s), which promotes the thesis that the Swedes (*götar* or Geats) descend from the Goths of antiquity.[54] His identification of the two had been articulated before in 1434 by Nils Ragvaldsson, who found support for his view both in native Swedish sources and in learned ones such as Jordanes, the sixth-century Roman historian who wrote about the Goths, and Isidore of Seville, the seventh-century Hispano-Roman scholar and archbishop of Seville.[55] The Gothicism of Olai's *Chronica* had in turn great impact on later authors such as Johannes Magnus, who elaborates Isidore of Seville's idea that the Swedes descend directly from Gog and Magog of the Old Testament in his *Historia de omnibus gothorum suedonumque regibus* (History of all the Kings of the Goths and Swedes, 1554).[56] The Dane Hans Svaning in his *Refutatio calumniarum cuiusdam Ioannis Magni* (Refutation of the False Claims of one Johannes Magnus, 1561), on the other hand, seeks to prove that the Goths originated in Denmark, not Sweden, and that only Danes therefore can claim to descend from them. Similarly, Erasmus Laetus in his *Res Danicæ* (1574) tries to show that the Danes have roots in the Cimbrian (southern Bavarian) and Gothic past, the Swedes only in the Gothic,[57] and in 1679, the Swede Olof Rudbeck published the most ambitious work of Swedish Gothicism, his *Atland, eller Manheim* (Atlantis or the Home of Mankind). This "enormous work of misguided but influential research"[58] asseverated that all languages demonstrably descend from a Swedish original and that Sweden (i.e., Atlantis) is the birthplace of European culture, including Greek and Roman.[59] After moving through the slightly maniacal speculations of Rudbeck, the tradition of historical writing settles into the more empirically based, but still nationalistic, studies of the Age of Reason.

---

[53] Colbert, "The Middle Ages," p. 11.
[54] Johannesson, *The Renaissance of the Goths*, p. 85.
[55] Michell, "The Middle Ages," p. 46. On the tension between Sweden and Spain in claiming to have been founded by the Goths, see Leerssen, *National Thought in Europe*, p. 38.
[56] Johannesson, *The Renaissance of the Goths*, p. xviii.
[57] Skovgaard-Petersen, "The Literary Feud," p. 115.
[58] Clunies Ross and Lönnroth, "The Norse Muse," pp. 12–13.
[59] Larson, "The Reformation and Sweden's Century as a Great Power," pp. 92–93.

Philologists embed national spirit first in the titles of many of their works on OE language and literature. Thorkelin's title is a prime example in its boldly proclaiming that *Beowulf* is a Danish, not an English, poem; the epic merely comes to us in the OE dialect: *De Danorum rebus gestis seculi III & IV: Poëma Danicum dialecto Anglo-Saxonica* (Of Events Concerning the Danes in the Third and Fourth Centuries: A Danish Poem in the Anglo-Saxon Dialect). The original poem is Danish or ON,[60] and the epic "that had been absent for more than a thousand years returned to its country of origin"[61] when Thorkelin brought his transcripts back to Denmark. Other prime examples are the various titles of works by Grundtvig. In 1819, he titled his selection of translations from *Beowulf* "Stykker af Skjöldung-Kvadet eller Bjovulfs Minde" (Fragments of the Scylding Song or Beowulf's Memorial), but he is subtler on other occasions. He labeled his important 1817 review of Thorkelin "Om Bjovulfs Drape" or "Concerning the [implied Old Norse or Northern European] Heroic Praise Poem of Beowulf" and titled his 1820 translation *Bjowulfs Drape* but appended a subtitle: "Et Gothisk Helte-Digt fra forrige Aar-tusinde af Angelsaxisk paa Danske Rim" (A Gothic Epic Poem from the Previous Millennium Rendered from Anglo-Saxon into Danish Rhyme). In his introduction to the translation, he further reinforces Nordic provenance by stating, "if I am right, then the poem is also beyond question elevated, a very Thor of a poem, to which Iceland itself cannot find the like."[62] He then transmutes the subtitle in his 1841 review of Thorkelin, Kemble, Leo, and Ettmüller to reaffirm the poem's Northern European provenance: "Bjovulfs Drape eller det Oldnordiske Heltedigt" (The Heroic Praise Poem of Beowulf or the Old Nordic [Northern European] Epic Poem). Concluding his review with particular criticism of John Kemble (who regarded the poem as English) and Heinrich Leo (who regarded it as German) and further affirmation of the poem's provenance, Grundtvig observes that "it is both an honour and a profit to the North that foreigners find powerful resistance, when they set themselves up as judges of the Nordic condition, which they do not know and defenders of the Nordic spirit, which they do not understand."[63] Grundtvig naturally does know, however, and does understand. He makes the final transformation of the subtitle in his second, improved edition of his translation published in 1865: *Bjovulvs-Drapen, et høinordisk heltedigt, fra Anguls-Tungen fordansket* [Beowulf's Heroic Praise Poem, a High Nordic Epic Poem Danished from the Language of Angul]. "Gothic" had become too much associated with Germany by this time, so Grundtvig

---

[60] Shippey, "Kemble, *Beowulf*," p. 68.
[61] "in patriam una Epos, qvod suum olim fuerat, post plus qvam mille annos postliminio rediit." Bjork, "Thorkelin's Preface," pp. 300–01.
[62] Shippey and Haarder, *Beowulf*, p. 160.
[63] Ibid., p. 245.

narrows his focus on the High North; and "Anglo-Saxon" changes to the language of the legendary founder of the Anglo-Saxons, Angul, brother of Dan, the legendary founder of Denmark.

The change in Grundtvig's subtitle clearly reflects his Romantic Nationalism.[64] As *Beowulf* speedily gained stature as a major early Germanic text, more Germanic tribes tried to lay claim to it. Kemble, writes Grundtvig, was "pulling at all the oars to move Gothland to Angeln," and Leo was "sparing no effort to squeeze, if possible, the whole of Scandinavia into the 'Cimbric peninsula', which he sees as part of the great 'Germania'."[65] Leo, who naturally viewed OE as a German (not Danish) dialect,[66] would be the first of four German scholars to think *Beowulf* was "dasz älteste *deutsche* ... Heldengedicht,"[67] and Grundtvig had a reputation, by his own account, "for being almost as bitter an enemy of the Germans as of the Romans" for their tendency to want to make everything, such as poems and the Scandinavian languages, German.[68]

But Grundtvig had another nationalistic reason for altering the subtitle in his 1841 review. He hoped, namely, that *Beowulf* would

> instantly attract the attention of all Nordic, and especially Danish, scholars, and, as soon as it became readable in the mother tongue [i.e., in Grundtvig's Danish translation], be found in all homes and become a reader for all children, yes, become for Scandinavia in a small way what the *Iliad* and the *Odyssey* were for the Greeks.[69]

Grundtvig concludes by stating that indifference to "such a treasure trove" is "truly a crystal clear testimony to how horribly unnatural we have become in placing Latin above our mother tongue."[70]

---

[64] On the broad impact of Grundtvig's nationalism, see Hall et al., *Building the Nation*.
[65] Shippey and Haarder, *Beowulf*, p. 245.
[66] Stanley, *The Search for Anglo-Saxon Paganism*, pp. 5–7.
[67] Haarder, *Beowulf: The Appeal of a Poem*, p. 20 note 10, lists the other three scholars: J. P. E. Gerverus (1848), Karl Simrock (1859), P. Hoffmann (1893), and G. Paysen Petersen (1904). Note that one of the original reviewers of Thorkelin's edition, Nicholaus Outzen, in 1816 also argues that the poem is German. See Shippey and Haarder, *Beowulf*, pp. 123–31. On the proto-Nazi claim on *Beowulf* for the German people, see Osborn "Bruder's *Beowulf*." On the German reception history of *Beowulf*, see Baatz, *Beowulf in Deutschland*.
[68] Broadbridge and Jensen, *A Grundtvig Anthology*, p. 99.
[69] "Strax tiltrække sig alle Nordiske og da især Danske *Lærdes* Opmærksomhed, og, saasnart det blev læseligt paa Modersmaalet, findes i alle Huse og blive Læsebog for alle Børn, ja, blive for Norden, efter fattig Leilighed, hvad *Iliaden* og *Odysseen* var for *Grækerne*." "Bjovulfs Drape," p. 482.
[70] "Saadant et *Dannefee* er ret et soleklart Vidnesbyrd om, hvor rædsom *unaturlige* vi er blevne ved at sætte *Latinen* over *Modersmaalet*." Ibid.

Titles do or can imply nationalistic sentiment, but philological studies, grammars, prefaces to collections of texts, and random comments interspersed throughout the literature frequently make the nationalism explicit. In pre-Napoleonic Scandinavia, we find the love of country seen as early as the Middle Ages bubble to the surface in works embracing OE language or literature. This is the case with the first four Scandinavian texts ever published that pertain to OE studies. They were produced in 1733, 1751, 1772, and 1787, the first by Andreas Bussæus or Anders Buss (1669–1735). Born in Norway, fatherless at age seven, and rather corpulent,[71] Bussæus was a philologist, historian, and lawyer, who became barrister of the supreme court in Denmark in 1710 and mayor of Helsingør in 1718. In 1733, he published the first complete edition of Ári Þorgilsson's *Íslendingabók* (Book of the Icelanders)[72] together with Latin translation and notes,[73] to which he appended the OE *Periplus Otheri, Halgolando-Norvegi, ut et Wulfstani* (Voyages of Ohthere and Wulfstan) from the OE *Orosius*, also together with Latin translation and notes. The Latin translation was reprinted from Christopher Ware's 1678 edition of John Spelman's *The Life of Ælfred the Great*. During a visit to Wessex and the court of King Alfred the Great, the ninth-century Norwegian chieftain or wealthy seafarer Ohthere told the story of three voyages in Scandinavia, which were recorded in OE. This account and the account of an Englishman or Frisian named Wulfstan of his journey into the Baltic have obvious interest for Scandinavians and are suitably appended to what is essentially a national history of Iceland. In his greeting to the reader, Bussæus asserts that all that he offers in his book is "for the glory and profit of the fatherland."[74]

Hans Gram (1685–1748) was a historian, philologist, professor of Greek, twice vice chancellor of the University of Copenhagen, patriot, and famous both in Denmark and Europe for his capacious learning, which evidences itself in the earliest yoking we have of OE and one of the Scandinavian languages.[75] In "Prøve af Danske Ord og Talemaader, af det Engel-Saxiske Sprog forklarede" (Sampling of Danish Words and Expressions Clarified by the Anglo-Saxon Language, 1751), Gram gives shape to an idea that will influence many subsequent Danish scholars. He maintains that language is an integral part of a nation's history. One needs it not only to "understand those documents that pertain thereto, but also to be able to decide about the origin of its people

---

[71] Meier, "Bussæus, Andreas."
[72] Titled *Arii Thorgilsis filii, cognomento Froda id est Multiscii, Schedae, seu Libellus de Is-landia, Islendinga-Bok dictus.*
[73] Paulli, "Andreas Bussæus."
[74] "in patriae gloriam et emolumentum." Bussæus, *Periplus Otheri*, "Lecturo salute."
[75] Paulli, "Hans Gram."

Figure 4. Hans Gram, 1754.

and inhabitants or its relationship to other nations."[76] Icelandic has been accepted as Old Danish (128), he writes, but there is a language older than Icelandic that can help us understand modern Danish even better: OE, a tongue which "on the one hand our old forefathers from southern Jutland and on the other their neighboring Saxons, whom people have since called Holsteiners, brought with them to Britain."[77] Gram examines 117 Danish words and phrases, from "Aand" (ON ønd, mistakenly designated OE, "spirit")[78] to "Øl" (OE *ealu*, "ale" or "beer"), and observes that they "have been [in use] among the ancient Saxons and Jutlanders long before they come to appear in any Icelandic text."[79] In his review of the first edition of *Beowulf* in 1815, however, Grundtvig agrees that OE is more like Danish than Icelandic, but "one must strongly remember to give up the illusion that Danish grew out of Icelandic, which Gram claimed in vain, but which history and healthy reflection contradict, and which a thorough study of the Norse languages utterly destroys ..."[80]

Our next adventurer into OE studies, Jacob Langebek (1710–75), was left without either parent at age seventeen; Hans Gram took him into his household about eight years later. Langebek had been interested in the history of the Denmark from the beginnings of his studies at the University of Copenhagen, where he learned Old Icelandic, OE, French, and German as supplements to his already very strong Latin. Gram gave Langebek access not only to his home but also to his considerable library of books and manuscripts and arranged for an amanuensis position for him at the Royal Library, which helped Langebek advance a plan that he had been formulating from early in his career: a monumental edition of the sources of Danish history.[81] That plan was eventually realized when he became the Danish National Archivist, working with a massive collection

---

[76] "Forstaae de Skrifter, som dertil hører, men endogsaa til at kunde dømme om dets Folkes og Indbyggeres Herkomst, eller dets Slegtskab med andre Nationer." Gram, "Prøve," p. 127.
[77] "Til deels vore gamle Forfædre fra Synder-Jylland, till deels deres Naboer Saxerne, som man siden har kaldet Holster, bragte over med sig til Britannien." Ibid., p. 129.
[78] On "Aand," Gram observes "At Spiritus og Anima ogsaa i Engel-Saxiske Skrifter kaldes Ond beviser Hickesius in *Grammatic. Anglo-Saxon. & Moeso-Gothica*, pag. 118" (that spirit and anima are also called *ond* in Anglo-Saxon writings Hickes shows in *Institutiones*, p. 118). The *Institutiones*, however, that Gram refers to ends at p. 114 and is followed by an Icelandic grammar with separate pagination, Runólfur Jónsson's *Grammatica Islandica rudimenta*. In the Icelandic glossary on p. 119, not p. 118, *ønd* is glossed as "anima."
[79] "Har været [i Brug] hos de ældgamle Saxer og Iyder, længe førend de ere komme i noget Islandsk Skrift at staae." Gram, "Prøve," p. 130.
[80] Busbee, "A Few Words," p. 31.
[81] Bech, "Jacob Langebek."

Figure 5. Jacob Langebek, 1751.

of documents having anything at all to do with Denmark, Norway, and provinces, the *Scriptores rerum Danicarum medii ævi* (Danish Historians of the Middle Ages), including documents in OE. Volume one contains a genealogy from *The Anglo-Saxon Chronicle* (pp. 6–9), volume two, "The Voyages of Ohthere and Wulfstan" (pp. 106–23) and "The Battle of Brunanburh" (pp. 412–22), and volume five, miscellaneous OE material (pp. 1–231). Of *Beowulf,* and anticipating the reaction but not the stridency of Grundtvig about the lack of English editions of OE poetry, he states, "I am surprised that none of the scholars of England has taken the trouble to edit a work of such antiquity, which would infinitely gratify both his own people on account of the poetry, and ours on account of its history."[82] Langebek was definitely serving his own people in the *Scriptores* and is unequivocal both in his title and in his preface about what moved him to his enterprise: "Glory and love of my country, both of which seem wholly at risk in whatever part of our land you turn, have given me stimulus."[83] Langebek's patriotism, as keen as Gram's, seems to have roots running deeper into Danish history than the fifteenth century, when predominantly German-speaking Holstein became a Danish duchy. He comes close to apologizing for some small items "written in the inferior Saxon tongue"[84] that have crept into his work, a disdain that may harken back to ninth-century nationalism and the building of the Dannevirke (Danes' Bulwark). The walls in southern Denmark were raised, according to an entry for the year 808 in the Frankish annals, *Annales regni Francorum*, to protect the kingdom from the Saxons.[85] In a very real sense, OE scholarship in the eighteenth century was a kind of Dannevirke, protecting and preserving national linguistic and literary boundaries against the Germans. The fortification grew stronger in the nineteenth century.

Rasmus Nyerup (1759–1829) is my last eighteenth-century example. Head of the Royal Library and professor of literary history,[86] he was devoted to his teacher Peter Frederik Suhm (1728–98), a figure largely forgotten today but a central intellectual in eighteenth-century Denmark. Besides being a remarkable book collector, Suhm was "a dramatist, a translator, a journalist and critic, a political commentator, and, finally, a historian," who eventually published a 14-volume history of Denmark.[87] He was also a nationalist and proponent of Scandinavianism, as reflected in his writing several short stories or novellas based on early Danish and Scandinavian history, in which his ON characters are depicted as eighteenth-century Europeans[88] and in which he sometimes contrives some pretty improbable scenes. In *De Tre Venner* (The Three Friends), for example, he has fifteen fishermen sing the *Völuspá* from the *Poetic Edda* "as a sea shanty."[89] Suhm's *Symbolæ ad Literaturam Teutonicam Antiquorem* (Contributions to Ancient Teutonic Literature), one of the earliest collections of Old High German (OHG) texts, is a serious work of scholarship,

---

[82] Shippey and Haarder, *Beowulf*, p. 77.
[83] "Gloria & amor patriæ meæ, qvi uterqve, in qvamcunqve etiam partem systema nostrum vertas, periclitari admodum videtur, mihi stimulos addidit." Langebek, *Scriptores*, vol. 1, p. iv.
[84] "In lingva Saxonica inferiori scripta." Langebek, *Scriptores*, vol. 1, p. vi.
[85] Glob, *Denmark*, p. 275.
[86] Jørgensen and Petersen, "R. Nyerup."
[87] Mitchell, "The Age of Englightenment," p. 152.
[88] Blanck, *Den nordiska renässansen*, p. 218.
[89] Mjöberg, "Romanticism and Revival," p. 230.

however, yet still informed by Suhm's nationalist impulses. In Nyerup's preface to the book, he echoes some of Suhm's concerns as well as Hans Gram's, making nationalism a clear motivator for studying OE. It is absolutely certain, he writes, that the origin of Danish should not be sought solely in the Icelandic dialect:

> It appears that three languages once held sway in the northern and western regions of Europe sprung from one and the same mother and differing among themselves solely by dialect: Franco-Theotiscan [Old High German], Anglo-Saxon, and Gothic. The name Gothic signifies that language from which in the course of time flowed Danish, Swedish, Norwegian, and Icelandic. Both the other dialects, Anglo-Saxon and Franco-Theotiscan, prove of remarkable use for scrutinizing and studying the antiquity and origins of our language, and Anglo-Saxon, polished and cultivated with great learning from the most ancient times, supplies written memorials that are numerous, distinguished, and more ancient than the Icelandic.[90]

Note here and in Gram that the simplifications of the *Stammbaum* model for the development of the Germanic languages (i.e., dividing the language group into branches) serve an unconscious ideological purpose. The ancient Franco-Theotiscan and Anglo-Saxon (now called West Germanic) branches both explain and legitimate the younger Gothic (North Germanic) branch. Scandinavian dedication to OE thus grows as the philological Dannevirke rises.

In post-Napoleonic Scandinavia we find even more intense expressions of love of country stretching from 1815 to 1885. Thorkelin, for example, writing at the beginning of the century in 1815, expresses a kind of simplicity as well as a dependence on the work of Hans Gram. Obviously having formulated his ideas long before Napoleon caused him so much grief, he says this about the language and origin of *Beowulf*:

---

[90] "Plane et unice ex Islandica dialecto peti non debere, nec posse. Obtinuere scilicet olim in septentrionalibus et occidentalibus Europæ regionibus tres fere, ut videtur, lingvæ, ab una eademqve matre prognatæ, et sola dialecto inter se discrepantes, Franco-theotisca, Anglosaxonica, et Gothica. Gothico nomine fas est insignire illam, ex qva tractu temporis fluxere Danica, Svecica, Norvegica, Islandica. Ambas reliqvas dialectos, Anglosaxonicam et Franco-theotiscam, insignem in antiqvitatibus et originibus lingvæ nostræ perscrutandis excolendisqve præstare utilitatem, inde intelligitur, qvod illa, ab antiqvissimis inde temporibus magno studio exculta et expolita, monumenta suppeditet, ut longe multa et egregia, ita Islandicis antiqviora." Nyerup, preface to Suhm, *Symbolæ*, pp. v–vi.

By Hercules! I am astounded that Hickes attributed to the Anglo-Saxons a song that poured forth from the Danish bard, fired by the flame of hyperborean Apollo

 . . . . Obviously he does not remember that the language spoken by the English before William I had been common to three peoples of the north – all called by one name, "Danes" – who spoke slightly different dialects of the same tongue. This fact is as clear as the light of day, even if no other authority could be found for it. For our epic plainly teaches that the Anglo-Saxon idiom is actually Danish, a language cultivated and kept pure even to this day by the inhabitants of Iceland, who dwell almost beyond the path of the sun.[91]

The clear light of Thorkelin's day would have had a different luster in Germany, where the OE idiom was actually considered to be German. "The German language," wrote Count Friedrich Leopold zu Stolberg, "became the language of England, and remained fairly pure."[92] As amusing as Thorkelin's and Stolberg's views may seem today, they point to an important fact: OE comes from a period of linguistic history relatively close to when the proto-Germanic mother tongue from which the modern Germanic languages descend was in use. Though later, OHG and ON do as well, and so all three are fairly mutually intelligible. Take, for example, the first few lines of Ælfric's "The Letter of Christ to Abgarus" (Blessed are you, Abgar, who believes in me when you see me not).

> Eadig eart þu, Abgar,
> þu þe gelyfost on me,
> þonne þu me ne gesast. (OE)
>
> Sæll ertú, Abgarus,
> er þu eins um trúir,
> þótt þú sjálfan mik
> sæir aldreigi. (ON)

---

[91] "Igitur hercle miror Hickesium Anglosaxonibus tribuisse carmen, qvod vates Danus Appolinis hyperborei igne calefactus fudit … Eqvidem non bene meminit lingvam, qva ante Wilhelmum I. utebantur Angli, fuisse communem tribus septentrionis populis, qvi vocati uno nomine Dani, omnes ore eodem dialectice solummodo differente loqvebantur. Hujus si vel aliunde auctoritas nulla peti posset, plena sane hic in aprico cubat. Epos etenim hoc, qvale id nunc habemus, evidenter docet, idioma Anglosaxonicum esse revera Danicum, qvod Islandi extra solis vias fere jacentes hodiedum servant purum, et studiose colunt." Bjork, "Thorkelin's Preface," pp. 302–03.

[92] Quoted in Stanley, *Search*, p. 5.

Abagarus du bist selig
dz du an mich gelobest
vnd mich nicht gesehen hast. (19th-century German)[93]

One can easily see by comparing these three versions of the prayer how an early Danish or German scholar might confuse parallels among OE, ON, and OHG with parenthood of one of those languages over another. "OE," observes Hans F. Nielsen, "has more exclusive (and active) parallels in common with ON than with any of the other [Germanic] languages except OFris, which suggests that pre-ON and pre-OE were once in immediate contact (or that there was a Scandinavian element among the fifth-and-sixth century invaders)."[94] In 1705, George Hickes, in chapter 21 of the OE grammar included in his *Thesaurus*, adumbrated Nielsen's observation by classifying OE poetic language as Dano-Saxon. And in 2014, Joseph Embley Emonds and Jan Terje Faarlund argued that Middle English descends from North Germanic (i.e., ON), not West Germanic, in their *English: The Language of the Vikings*. OE, like Gothic, simply died out.

Frederik Hammerich (1809–77), Grundtvig's friend and follower, displays in his *De episk-kristelige oldkvad hos de gotiske folk* (The Ancient Christian Epic Among the Gothic People, 1873) his piety in his selection of OE, ON, OS, OHG, and other "Gothic" texts; his nationalism or, more precisely, Scandinavianism in gathering those texts in one Danish volume; and his aesthetic appreciation of those texts inspired by Grundtvig. "We have gone through the most important poems," he states in the last chapter of the book. "They sounded in our ear like birdsong far away on a spring morning after rain, like sweet chirping upon chirping, where one cannot easily distinguish the individual's – the thrush's, the starling's – melodies."[95] Whether OE is the thrush and ON is the starling or vice versa, the point is that beautiful melodies emerge from all the Gothic languages, which are, in a sense, one. Hammerich's treatment of OE texts comprises close to half his book, which contains the text and an alliterative verse translation of parts of "The Dream of the Rood" (pp. 15–20), a translation of "The Grave" (pp. 92–93), and selected translations from, for example, "Cædmon's Hymn," "The Ruthwell Cross," *Genesis A* and *B*, *Exodus*, *Daniel*, *Christ and Satan*, *Judith*, *Christ I*, *Andreas*, *Guthlac B*, *The Phoenix*, "Soul and Body II," and "Meters of Boethius" interspersed throughout a

---

[93] Stephens, *Tvende Old-Engelske Digte*, pp. 17, 41, 70–71.
[94] *Old English and the Continental Germanic Languages*, p. 258. See also Robinson, *Old English and Its Closest Relatives*, especially chapter 10, and Fulk, *A Comparative Grammar*.
[95] "Vi har gennemgået de vigtigste kvad. De lød i vort øre som fuglesang langt borte en forårsmorgen efter regn, som sødt kvidder i kvidder, hvor man ikke let kan skelne den enkeltes, drosselens, stærens, melodier." *Oldkvad*, p. 171.

discussion of the poems (pp. 13–96). He expresses some Grundtvigian surprise, however, at English deafness to the distant melodies: "Englishmen, whose Anglo-Saxon (Old English) heritage is far richer in Christian epics than any other Gothic people, have taken on a strangely cool attitude toward it."[96] For hundreds of years, Hammerich claims, they have resented the fact that their cultural life began with the Scandinavians, and that has made them "blind to their rich heritage,"[97] as they "greatly underestimate the remnants from their antiquity."[98] Hammerich, as J. R. Hall points out, "is the first to suggest that the account of Satan's fall and the temptation of man in the poem now known as *Genesis B* owes something to book II, *De originali peccato*, of *Carmina de spiritalis historiae gestis*, by Alcimus Avitus."[99]

Two other Scandinavian scholars, both editing the same texts by Ælfric, one writing in Latin in 1835, the other in Danish in 1853, offer the standard Gramian justifications for studying OE but add a couple of twists. Ludvig Christian Müller (1806–51), a minister and gifted linguist, translated the New Testament from Greek into Hebrew as a student, received a scholarship from Rasmus Rask to go to Iceland to learn Icelandic, tutored Hans Christian Andersen, and later became a tutor for Grundtvig's sons.[100] He promoted Grundtvig's ecclesiastical and popular views and in 1835 published a collection of OE texts. He begins his preface to his *Collectanea Anglo-Saxonica*[101] with the bold statement that "No obsolete Germanic dialect is more distinguished today than Anglo-Saxon."[102] But, he argues, OE and Old Icelandic poetry represent the whole range of Nordic literature, a literature revealing a race not inferior to the Romans in its thinking, feeling, or writing. Furthermore, he writes, "the tongue itself finally about which we are speaking sheds so much light on the tongues of the Icelanders, Danes, Germans, and English that it must be judged worthy for that reason alone to be snatched from oblivion."[103]

---

[96] "Engelskmændene, hvis angelsaksiske (oldengelske) arv er langt rigere på kristelig epik, end noget andet gotisk folks, har stillet sig underlig koldsindigt lige over for denne." Ibid., p. 2.
[97] "Det er en gennem hundreder af år næret fordom, at Englands kulturliv begynder med Normannerne, som har gjort Engelskmænd blinde for den rige fædrenearv." Ibid., p. 3.
[98] "stærkt undervurdere lævningerne fra sin oldtid." Ibid.
[99] Hall, "England, Denmark, America," p. 446.
[100] Engberg, "Ludvig Christian Müller."
[101] *Collectanea Anglo-Saxonica maximam partem nunc primum edita et vocabulario illustrata* (Copenhagen, 1835).
[102] "Nulla dialectus Germanica hodie obsoleta insignior est quam Anglo-Saxonica." Ibid., p. iii.
[103] "Lingua denique ipsa, de qua loquimu, tantam Islandorum, Danorum,

He, "being a Dane, [has] concluded that a language so closely related to ours should be cultivated."[104]

More than promoting the OE language, however, Müller offers in his book a mini first edition of prose and poetry inspired by Grundtvig and his defunct *Prospectus*, including Ælfric's "The Letter of Christ to Abgarus," the "Vindicta Salvatoris," Ælfric's homily "Dominica III in Quadragesima," "Maxims I," "Maxims II," "The Battle of Brunanburh," "The Battle of Maldon," *Riddles* 5 (shield) and 43 (book or Bible), and "Christ I," lines 1–29. After crediting the memory of Rasmus Rask for urging him on in this endeavor, Müller makes his indebtedness to the living clear:

> Grundtvig has urged [this], three times having set out to England, who brought back the richest spoils. Obstructed by occupational concerns, he was unable to make these things available to the public himself, but he wished and was able to help me strive for the same thing. The codices described by him no less than his advice were at hand for me, by which being supported, I attacked the matter; I edited these items, which hopefully prepare the way for writings of greater moment.[105]

The *Collecteana Anglo-Saxonica* thus served an explicit linguistic as well as a subtler, intrinsic political or personal purpose for both Müller and Grundtvig. Again, however, Grundtvig was stymied. Benjamin Thorpe's *Analecta Anglo-Saxonica: A Selection in Prose and Verse from A-S Authors of Various Ages; with a Glossary* appeared in 1834, a year before Müller's collection did, and contains numerous OE texts edited for the first time.

George Stephens (1813–95), being an Englishman turned Dane, agrees with Müller about the linguistic importance of OE. After marrying in 1834, and deeply interested in finding evidence of the origin of English in the so-called Skando-Saxon (Dano-Saxon for Hickes), he and his new bride moved to Stockholm. There he immersed himself in Swedish and the language and culture of the North, editing and translating numerous old northern texts and runic inscriptions. He ultimately became a major force in those areas of research. He remained in Stockholm until 1851, when he took a position at the University of Copenhagen, where he taught

---

Germanorum et Anglorum linguis lucem affundit, ut vel hanc solam ab causam digna sit judicanda, quæ oblivion eripiatur." Ibid.

[104] "Natione Danus linguam colendam existimavi nostræ affinem." Ibid., p. iv.

[105] "hortatus est *Grundtvig*, ter in Angliam profectus, qui spolia retulit ditissima. Occupationibus impeditus cum illa publici juris facere ipse nequiret, me eadem molientem juvare et potuit et voluit. Codices ab eo descrlpti non minus quam consilia mihi præsto erant, quibus sublevatus rem aggressus sum; hæcce edidi, quæ ut viam muniant scriptis majoris momentum in votis est." Ibid., pp. iv–v.

and conducted research until 1893.[106] In his *Tvende Old-Engelske Digte med Oversættelser og Tillæg* (Two Old English Poems with Translations and Supplements, 1853), he generates both a more complicated edition than Müller's and a more convoluted brand of nationalism. He dedicates the book to Grundtvig, "Great as Priest, Poet, Patriot, Greatest as the Unwearied Champion of the Northern Mother-Tongue," and reprints Müller's texts as poetry (Ælfric's "Letter of Christ to Abgarus" from *Lives of the Saints* and his homily on the third Sunday in Lent) that Grundtvig "first transcribed and made known by himself," as Stephens phrases it in his dedication. Together with these texts are translations of them into English, Danish (by C. J. Brandt, a doctoral student at the University of Copenhagen), and ON (by Gísli Brynjlfsson, a stipendiary scholar at the University of Copenhagen) as well as original translations in Old Danish, Old Swedish (OSwed), MHG, German, and Dutch.

Including such a panoply of languages is meant to affirm international brotherhood: one of the most important developments in recent times, Stephens feels, is the growing spirit of community among Denmark, Norway, Sweden, and England, partially because of a mutual recognition of common roots. The work of philologists reinforces that idea, according to Stephens:

> The English are now eagerly studying the Nordic languages in order to understand their own, and Danes learn with satisfaction that sumptuous OE (i.e., Anglo-Saxon) in a sense may be called a West Danish dialect from the 5th and 6th centuries within which the peculiarities that now distinguish the Scandinavian languages (passive form in sk or s, enclitic definite article, etc.) had developed to a certain extent ...[107]

Linguists, claims Stephens, recognize that the sound system of English has preserved more ON features than has Danish, and that many ON words and expressions "extinct in Denmark are in lively use among the common people of England."[108] Small wonder, then, that the old water route between Denmark and England – "det stolte Vikinge-Stræde" (the proud Viking Street) – has been traversed once more. OE, "de Danskes Modersmaal" (the mother tongue of the Dane), has such great simplicity, such striking usefulness, that it understandably came to supplant first

---

[106] Dehn-Nielsen, "George Stephens."
[107] "Englænderen begynder nu ivrigt at studere de nordiske Folkesprog for at kunne forstaae sit eget, og Danskeren lærer med Velbehag, at det rige Old-Engelske (Angel-Saxiske) i en vis Forstand maa kaldes en Vest-Dansk Mundart fra det 4de og 5te Aarhundrede, inden de Egenheder, som nu udmærke de skandinaviske Sprog (Passiv-Formen paa sk eller s, Post-Artikeln m. fl.) havde udviklet sig i nogen Grad ..." Stephens, *Tvende Digte*, p. 1.
[108] "Uddöde i Danmark, ere i frisk Brug iblandt Englands Almue." Ibid.

Latin and then French as the universal language. Stephens concludes: "That such an illustrious future was decided by Providence for a branch of the Nordic people, whose cradle was west Denmark (northern and southern Jutland) and Norway ... is a thought that cannot help but rouse every Northman, each and every Danish man."[109] This small edition of two texts thus became one of Stephens' several attempts to promote his philological and political interests, which consisted of four parts:

> (i) all that was best in British life, letters, and language was based on old northern values; (ii) a common culture had united the islands of and islands bordering the north Atlantic from the third century onwards; (iii) the most authentic extant texts from that unified old north were runic inscriptions; (iv) texts exhibiting the "folk-tungs" [dialects] of old northern English stand closer to the early common "Anglo-Scandic" language than do those texts that survive only in the standardized "book dialects of Alfredian Wessex and Saga Age Iceland."[110]

By far the most sophisticated statements about why Scandinavians should engage in OE studies seem to come at the beginning and toward the end of the nineteenth century. Rasmus Rask (1787–1832), although a frail and sickly child, turned into one of the most powerful and influential scholars in Europe. He conducted research in Sweden, Finland, Russia, India, and Persia, spoke twenty-five languages, published widely about and in several languages,[111] and is considered the founder of modern linguistics in Scandinavia.[112] Grundtvig, in his poem titled "Rasmus Christian Rask" that he penned just days after Rask's death, writes:

> So his epitaph shall witness
> "He broke ground where he came by,
> and to follow in his footsteps
> honour be to all who try.
> He came down from reindeer lands
> and encamped with elephants!"[113]

---

[109] "At denne glimrende Fremtid af Forsynet er bestemt en nordisk Folkestamme, hvis Vugge var Vest-Danmark (Nörre- og Sönder-Jylland) og Norge ... er en Tanke, som ikke kan andet end röre hver Nordbo, hver dansk Mand." Ibid., p. 2.
[110] Wawn, "Early Literature of the North," p. 280. For more on Stephens, see Wawn, *The Vikings and the Victorians*, pp. 132–34 and chapter 8 and Eriksson, "George Stephens."
[111] Broadbridge, *Living Wellsprings*, p. 369. See also Wolf, "Thorkelin and Rask," pp. 117–23.
[112] Haugen, *First Grammatical Treatise*, p. 2.
[113] Broadbridge, *Living Wellsprings*, p. 292.

In his dedicatory letter to Johan Bülow (patron also of Thorkelin and Grundtvig) for *Angelsaksisk Sproglære, tilligemed en kort Læsebog* (1817; trans. as *A Grammar of the Anglo-Saxon Tongue, with a Praxis*, 1830), Rask reveals a nationalistic bias that probably has its philosophic roots in the works of Storm and Stress writers such as Johann Gottfried Herder (1744–1803), who emphasized the importance of concentrating on language and poetry in order to recover a nation's culturally distinct, glorious past.[114] That distinctive identity had to be "founded in the language and oral literature of the ordinary, nonliterate people."[115] But Rask's nationalism also participates in the pan-Scandinavian penchant in imaginative literature for setting heathen cult and Christian faith in opposition.[116] In this pairing, heathenism frequently has the upper hand; Christianity sometimes does, as in Grundtvig after 1810;[117] and sometimes the two balance each other, as in Grundtvig's "Maskeradeballet i Danmark 1808" (The Masquerade Ball in Denmark, 1808), where he states that Odin and Christ are "begge Sønner af Alfader" (both sons of the All-Father), who represents "a higher Christian consciousness that subsumes the Nordic."[118]

> High Odin! White Christ!
> Settled is your dispute,
> Both sons of the All-Father.
> With our Cross and our sword,
> We consecrate your pyre here,
> You both have loved our father. [119]

Rask's sympathies seem to fall with the heathens. Writing to Bülow, Rask quotes first from "Lunden ved Jægerspriis" (The Grove at Jægerspriis, 1788), a poem by Christen Andersen Lund (1763–1833) celebrating the spirit of the Nordic heroic past that was forgotten after the advent of Christianity. Both poem and poet, until now utterly forgotten, were well-enough known at the time that neither needed to be identified by Rask and the poem could be excerpted in a standard school reader.[120] "More than eight hundred years have elapsed," Rask begins, since the time:

---

[114] See Wilson, *Folklore*, pp. 28–31.
[115] Branch, "Finnish Oral Poetry," p. 5.
[116] See Mjöberg, *Drömmen*, 1: 107–207.
[117] Ibid., 1: 155–62.
[118] Broadbridge, *Living Wellsprings*, p. 361.
[119] Ibid., 1: 112. "Høje Odin! Hvide Krist! / Slettet ud er Eders Tvist, / Begge Sønner af Alfader. / Med vort Kors og med vort Sværd, / Vies Eder Baalet her, / Begge elskte I vor Fader," GV "Maskeradeballet i Danmark," pp. 19–20.
[120] Knud Lyne Rahbek, *Dansk Læsebog og Exempelsamling til de lærde Skolers Brug*, vol. 1 (Copenhagen, 1818), pp. 184–86.

da gamle Norden vendte bort sit Öje
med hellig Gru fra Fædres Hvilehöje,
og Munkens Messe dövede den Sang
der fordum höjt om Nordens Kjæmpe klang.[121]

when the ancient North turned its eye
with righteous horror from the Father's lofty place of rest,
and the priest's mass muffled the song
that once was raised about the Nordic warrior.

It was then, Rask states, that the country was thrown into disarray, its customs transformed, its language corrupted; that was when national power began to falter.[122] Although the country sank into barbarism and thralldom, it was saved by the Reformation and the resultant birth of scholarship, which allowed Danes to turn to ancient books "to purify and adorn our language as well as zealously seek its original sources."[123] Seeking the sources of Danish justifies Rask's project: "Our modern mother tongue as well as our ancient history can gain so much light from Anglo-Saxon that it is well worth dragging it from the darkness and describing it in Danish."[124] For Rask, it seems, OE language and literature were the loftiest expressions, in a pure Herderian sense, of the Danish soul. To recover them was to recover Danish national identity.

Rask's *A Grammar of the Anglo-Saxon Tongue* is known to just about all OE scholars, but his highly charged, polemical dedicatory epistle has not been. Thorpe published his English translation of the grammar in 1830 but did not include the epistle. He did, however, include Rask's lengthy introduction, which, among other things, establishes the importance of studying OE for Scandinavians, so Rask's nationalism was not entirely effaced. That effacement took place later, as the impulse to claim OE as specifically English seems to have taken full control. From the third edition of 1879, Thorpe eliminates Rask's introduction as well, explaining the alteration thus: "The Grammar, as originally published, was obnoxious to at least one objection, which, in the present edition, will not be found – it was, perhaps, too Scandinavian, owing, no doubt, to the very natural bias of its author."[125] Thorpe's own bias caused him to suppress Rask's valuable letter and expunge his introduction, steal Grundtvig's ideas for

---

[121] Rask, *Angelsaksisk Sproglære*, p. i.
[122] Ibid., p. ii.
[123] "At rense og pryde vort Sprog, samt opsöge med Iver dets Kilder i deres förste Udspring." Ibid., p. iv.
[124] "Vort nuværende Modersmaal saavel som vor gamle Historie kan ogsaa af Angelsaksisken vinde saa meget Lys, at denne vel fortjente at fremdrages af Mörket og skildres paa Dansk." Ibid., pp. iv–v.
[125] Thorpe, preface to Rask's *Grammar*, pp. iii–iv.

a library of OE texts, and become a prime mover in the mounting English antipathy toward the Scandinavian interest in OE studies. J. M. Kemble likewise reveals his bias in the following statement at the beginning of his 1840 study of Anglo-Saxon runes:

> These preliminary remarks will not be without service in assisting to explain why my interpretations of certain Anglo-Saxon Runic monuments differ toto coelo from those of the learned Danes, who have been so obliging as to attempt to decypher them for us; and to save them this trouble in the future, is partly the intention of this paper; especially as there seems to have been a sort of tacit understanding in this country, that the labour and the honour might just as well be left to them; in the propriety of which view it is difficult to concur.[126]

Frederik Rønning (1851–1929) did not take an interest in runic monuments, but he did study Nordic philology at Odense University, took a half-year of OE at the British Museum in 1880, and received his doctoral degree in 1883 after writing a dissertation on *Beowulf*. He wrote extensively about Grundtvig and his work, including a four-volume biography (1907–14). He also wrote biographical works on Rasmus Rask (1887) and Rasmus Nyerup (1898).[127] Writing on "Den oldengelske digtning" (OE Poetry) at the end of the century in 1885,[128] Rønning reflects a more modest kind of nationalism than Rask and a more balanced view of paganism and Christianity. Because, says Rønning, the language and literature of the northern peoples are distinct from those of other geographic areas – Herder seems in the background here – "the study of OE poetry will therefore always be of great value for us Northern dwellers."[129] In OE literature we have "an important source for the illumination of our own ancient past."[130] *Beowulf*, for example, "in its original form arose in Scandinavia, probably in southern Sweden"[131] and manifests distinctly Nordic characteristics. Beowulf's fighting Grendel without weapons is one of these; the poem's verse form itself is another.[132] In Christian literature, where "den hvide Krist" (the white Christ) is described in terms previously reserved for "den stærke Thor" (the powerful Thor), Rønning sees his Nordic heritage. The Nordic (as opposed to the generally Germanic)

---

[126] *Anglo-Saxon Runes*, pp. 9–10.
[127] Petersen, "F. Rønning."
[128] *Historisk Månedsskrift for Folkelig og Kirkelig Oplysning* 4 (1885), 1–36.
[129] "Studiet af den oldengelske digtning vil derfor altid være af stor betydning for os Nordboer." Rønning, "Digtning," p. 2.
[130] "En vigtig kilde til oplysning om vor egen oldtid." Rønning, "Digtning," p. 2.
[131] "I sin oprindelige skikkelse er opstået i Norden, og rimeligvis i Sydsverrig." Ibid., p. 2.
[132] Ibid., pp. 8 and 9, respectively.

view of life as a battle reveals itself in both Christ and his apostles. "Christ is the great hero, who bursts the gates of hell, and his apostles are the loyal warriors who surround their chieftain."[133] All these distinctive features of OE, Rønning argues, demand that it be learned by Scandinavians.

Clearly Müller and Stephens, Rask and Rønning illustrate how varied, but essentially similar, the Scandinavian promotion of OE studies can be. These philologists and others, as Leersen phrases it, "stood with one leg in the field of literature and learning, with another in the arena of politics and its emerging institutions. They were in large measure the go-betweens, the transmitting agents, from one sphere to the other."[134] Grundtvig had no peers in this realm and stands at the center of the whole history of OE studies both in Denmark and the rest of Scandinavia. His contributions and influence deserve much fuller exploration.

---

[133] "Kristus er den store helt, der sprænger Helvedes porte, og hans apostler er de trofaste kæmper, der slår kreds om deres høvding." Ibid., p. 5.
[134] Leersen, *National Thought in Europe*, p. 185.

2

Myth of Spirit, Myth of Word in the Works of N. F. S. Grundtvig

OE poetry (seventh to eleventh centuries), comprising some 30,000 lines of verse in four manuscript volumes (*The Exeter Book, The Junius Codex, The Vercelli Book,* and *The Beowulf Manuscript*), is the largest and earliest body of surviving Germanic poetry. It is also one of the oldest bodies of poetry of any of the vernacular languages in Europe. It is a unique case, offering a broad, yet still fragmentary, view into a distant era. So important is one of the four volumes mentioned above, in fact, that UNESCO put it on its "Memory of the World Register" in 2016. *The Exeter Book* "is one of only four surviving major poetic manuscripts in [the Old English] vernacular … Since it is the largest and probably the oldest of them, and since its contents are not found in any other manuscript, it can claim to be the foundation volume of English literature, one of the world's principal cultural artefacts."[1]

Grundtvig intimated the magnitude and cultural importance of this body of literature early in his career in 1817, when he lamented the paucity of editions of it, as had Hans Gram, Jakob Langebek, and Peter Frederik Suhm (1728–98) before him.[2] He intimated the significance of *The Exeter Book* as well and transcribed it during his trips to England in the summers of 1830 and 1831 in preparation for the edition he planned to produce of it.[3] That edition would have occupied much of volume four of the collection of Old English (OE) texts described in his *Prospectus* but was blocked by the Society of Antiquaries from publication along with the rest of the collection, as we have seen. Grundtvig began his transcribing work in July 1830 during a trip to Exeter, continued it back in London and then in Copenhagen, and then filled in the missing parts of the transcription in the summer of 1831 in the British Museum, which

---

[1] Flood, "UNESCO lists Exeter Book."
[2] Grundtvig, draft letter to King Frederik VI, Christmas Eve 1828. Cited in Bradley, *N. F. S. Grundtvig's Transcriptions of the Exeter Book,* p. 5.
[3] Bradley outlines "the considerable breadth" of Grundtvig's transcriptions of and annotated material on OE literature well beyond *The Exeter Book* that the Grundtvig Arkiv in the Royal Library, Copenhagen, contains. "'The First New-European Literature'," p. 45.

had received *The Exeter Book* on loan from Exeter Cathedral by special dispensation to make a transcription of it.[4]

Apart from OE literature's being the foundation of English literature, Grundtvig regarded it as having much greater significance. He regarded it as the foundation of all modern European literature, as being "the first new-European literature,"[5] bringing the pagan past into fruitful, enlivening contact with the Christian present. "Cædmon's Hymn," one of the earliest OE poems, if not the earliest, offers a prime example:

> Nu sculon **h**erigean / **h**eofonrices weard
> [Now must we praise / the Guardian of the heaven-kingdom,]
> **m**eotodes **m**eahte / and his **m**odgeþanc
> [the Measurer's might / and his mind-thought,]
> **w**eorc **w**uldorfæder / swa he **w**undra gehwæs
> [the work of the Glory-Father, / when he each of wonders,]
> ece drihten / or **o**nstealde
> [eternal Lord, / established the beginning.]
> He **æ**rest sceop / **eo**rðan bearnum
> [He first created / for the sons of earth]
> **h**eofon to **h**rofe, / **h**alig scyppend;
> [heaven as a roof, / the holy Creator;
> þa **m**iddangeard, / **m**oncynnes weard,
> [then middle-earth / the Guardian of mankind,]
> ece drihten, / æfter teode
> [the eternal Lord / afterwards created]
> firum foldan / frea ælmihtig.[6]
> [for men earth, / the Ruler almighty.]

Here we have the essential features of Old Germanic verse established hundreds of years before the seventh century. Alliteration (marked in bold) binds each line together across a strong medial caesura (marked with a forward slash), and the poem depends on variation and traditional vocabulary, two standard features of classic OE poetry. The initial epithet for God, "Guardian of the heaven-kingdom," becomes "Measurer," "Glory-Father," "eternal Lord," "holy Creator," "Guardian of mankind," "eternal Lord," and "Ruler almighty." Here we also have a central tenet of the Judeo-Christian tradition expressed through variation, namely the ineffability of God. No one term for YAHWEH or "I am who I am" can capture the expansiveness and majesty of God's being. This seemingly simple poem, then, becomes a profound blending of pagan, vernacular poetic technique and Christian or Judeo-Christian message,

---

[4] Ibid., pp. 8–12.
[5] "den *første* nyeuropæiske Literatur." *Phenix-Fuglen*, p. 11.
[6] O'Donnell, *Cædmon's Hymn*, p. 208.

transplanted by Gregory the Great in the late sixth century, Grundtvig observes, "from Italy to England and thereby from the Romance to the Gothic circle of languages."[7]

Grundtvig saw the same confluence in *Beowulf* and dozens of other OE texts, including homilies, as S. A. J. Bradley has masterfully documented.[8] A very practical demonstration of Grundtvig's having internalized all the OE material that he collected can be seen in the two OE poems he himself composed during his lifetime. They were attached to his two major publications on *Beowulf*, his translation of the poem from 1820 and his edition of it from 1861. The first of these poems is 98 lines long, with all but 24 of those lines coming from original OE texts, both poetry and prose. The other 24 lines Grundtvig created himself. Here is the poem, followed by a table that shows the depth and breadth of Grundtvig's indebtedness to the OE tradition in composing his own OE verse.

1	Hwæt we Gar-Dena	Lo, we of the Spear-Danes
	In gear-dægum	in days of yore
	Þeod-Scyldinga	of the people-Scyldings
	Þrym gefrunon	have heard the glory,
5	Hu þa æþelingas	how the nobles,
	Ellen-rofe	the braves ones,
	And hira beod-geneatas	and their table companions,
	Bil-wite rincas	the pure warriors
	On Dene-mearce	in Denmark
10	Mærþa gefremedon.	performed glorious deeds.
	And hie ne ealle fornam	And the terrible deadly attack
	Ærran mælum	in former times
	Feorh-bealu frecne	did not take them all
	Folce to ceare:	as a sorrow to the people:
15	Freodoric siteþ	Frederik[9] sits
	On fæder-stole	on the paternal throne,
	Gumena baldor	the protector of men.
	Þæt is god cyning.	That is a good king.
	Swylcum gifeþe biþ	To such a one will be granted
20	Þæt he Grendles cynn	that he will put an end
	Denum to dreame	as a joy to the Danes
	Dæda getwæfe.	to the deeds of the kin of Grendel.
	A þone sinc-gyfan	Always around that treasure-giver

[7] "fra Italien til Engeland, og dermed fra den Romantiske til den Gothiske Sprog-Kreds." Grundtvig, *Christendomens Syvstjerne*, p. iv.
[8] "'The First New-European Literature.'"
[9] Frederik VI, king of Denmark 1808–39.

	Ymbe-scinon	shone
25	Witena betstan	the best of counselors,
	Wis-fæste eorlas	wise men,
	Monige swylce	many such
	On Middan-gearde	in middle earth.
	Swylc Bilof is	Such is Bülow,[10]
30	Byre æþelinga	the son of nobles,
	Se þe wæs wide-ferhþ	he who was for a long time
	Worda gemyndig	mindful of the words
	Þara þe se snotra spræc	that the prudent one spoke,
	Sunu Ecgþeowes:	the son of Ecgtheow:
35	Unc æghwylc sceal	"Each of us must
	Ende gebidan	await the end
	Worolde-lifes	of life in the world;
	Wyrce se þe mote	achieve he who can
	Domes ær deaþe	fame before death;
40	Þæt biþ driht-guman	that will be best for an
	Unlifigendum	unliving retainer
	Æfter selest.	afterwards."
	Uton geferan swa	Let us bring it about thus
	Frome gesiþas	bold companions
45	Þæt on us gladie	that on us will shine
	Gleaw-ferhþ hæleþ	the wise-hearted man
	Bilof se goda	Bülow the good,
	Se þe us beagas geaf	he who gave us rings,
	Se þe wordum and weorcum	he who in words and in works
50	Wægde and hwette	moved and urged
	Ripiende rincas	the ripening and skilled in mysteries
	And run-cræftige.	warriors.
	Forþan sceal on uferan dægum	Therefore in later days must
	Ealde and geonge	many old and young
55	Scopas and witan	poets and wise men mention the fame
	Scyldinga-bearna	of Scylding children
	Beorna beah-gyfan	of the ring-giver of men
	Blonden-feaxes	of the
	Mærþo gemænan	grey-haired one,
60	Monig oft cweþan:	often say:

[10] Johan Bülow, Grundtvig's patron.

	Þæt te suþ ne norþ	that neither south nor north
	Be sæm tweonum	between two seas
	Ofer eormen-grund	over the spacious ground
	Oþer nænig	no one else
65	Rond hæbbendra	of shield-bearers and
	Reade beagas	golden-red rings owners
	Leofra nære	was more beloved
	On lif-dægum	in his life days
	Eallum duguþe	to all the troop
70	Dena-cynnes	of the kin of the Danes
	Þara þe on wil-siþ	of those who on the wished-for journey
	Wægas ofer-sohton	over-taxed the waves,
	Beornas on blancum	men on horses [ships],
	Bocera-meres.	of the sea of scholars.
75	Secge ic Engla-frean	I say thanks to the all powerful
	Alwealdan þanc	lord of the Angles (or Angels)
	Þæs þæt ic moste	because I was able
	Mæran to willan	by the will of the famous one
	Discas of beorge	to carry
80	Deore maþmas	plates out from the burial mound, dear treasures
	Ut-geferian	
	Swylce æt eorþan-fæþm	that in the bosom of the earth
	Þusend wintra	for a thousand winters
	Þær eardodon.	there had remained.
85	Gewyrce se þe mote	Make he who can
	Witig of golde	wise of gold
	Heafodes-hyrste	a head ornament
	Harum rince	with hoary treasure
	Swa þæt he wlite-beorht	so that he, radiantly bright,
90	Þonne westan gyt	when in the west
	Hadre scineþ	heaven's candle
	Heofones-candel	still shines clear,
	Glitnie blonden-feax	the grey-haired one glitters
	Under gyldnum beage	under the golden ring
95	Oþ þæt him of earde	until his soul from the earth
	Ellor hwyrfe	turns elsewhere
	Sawol secean	to seek
	Soþ-fæstra dom.[11]	the judgment of the righteous.

---

[11] Grundtvig, *Bjowulfs Drape*, pp. xvi–xxii. The translation is mine, reprinted from

Line #	Sources for Grundtvig's 1820 OE Poem with Modern Line Numbers[12]
1	*Beo* 1a
2	*Beo* 1b
3	*Beo* 2a, 1019a
4	*Beo* 2b
5	*Beo* 3a
6	*Beo* 340a, 358a, 1787b, 3063a; *GenA,B* 1117, 1779, 1844, 1873, 2033; *And* 349, 408, 1139, 1390; *Jul* 382; *Pan* 40; *Rid* 22 17; *Jud* 107, 141; *WaldB* 11; *ÆGram* 49.6; *Josh* 1.6, 1.7, 1.9
7	beod-geneatas: *Beo* 343a, 1713b
8	bil-wite: *LS* 10.1, 2.23; *Mt* 11.29; *CP* 1134 (35.237.18), 1135 (35.237.19); *PsGlH* 1342 (85.5); *PsGlG* 1350 (85.5); *PsGlD* 1149 (75.10), 1348 (85.5); *MtGl* 282 (10.16)
9	Dene-mearce: *Or* 0126 (1.16.19), 0128 (1.16.23); *ChronC* 0175 (108.1), 0717 (1019.1), 0723 (1023.1); *ChronE* 0995 (1036.3)
10	*Sea* 0020 (80)
11–12	Inspired from *Beo* 2236b–2237a
13	*Beo* 2537a
14	Grundtvig
15	Grundtvig
16	Grundtvig
17	*GenA,B* 0840 (2694)
18	*Beo* 11b
19	*Beo* 299b
20	Grundtvig
21	Grundtvig
22	getwæfe: *Beo* 479b, 1433b, 1658a, 1763b, 1908a; *GenA,B* 0020 (51); *Ex* 0035 (116); *ChristA,B,C* 0278 (984); *Husb* 0006 (24)
23	sinc-gyfan: *Beo* 1012a, 1342a, 2311a; *ChristA,B,C* 0122 (458); *GuthA,B* 0397 (1351); *Mald* 0090 (277)
24	ymbe-scinon: *ÆCHom11,35* 0017 (261.27); *HomU* 18 0038 (87)
25	Grundtvig
26	Grundtvig
27	Grundtvig

---

my "On N. F. S. Grundtvig's Becoming an Old English *Scop*," pp. 29–32.

[12] From Bjork, "On N. F. S. Grundtvig's Becoming an Old English *Scop*," pp. 34–38.

28	"on Middan-gearde" is a common dative construction in the corpus, but it occurs in *Beo* specifically at 2996a. "middan-geard" occurs elsewhere in *Beo* at 504a, 751b, 75b, 1771b
29	Grundtvig
30	Grundtvig
31	wide-ferhþ: *Beo* 702a, 937b, 1222a; *GenA,B* 0306 (903); *Dan* 0120 (405); *ChristA,B,C* 0043 (162), 0160 (581); *GuthA,B* 0186 (600), 0198 (670); *Jul* 0062 (221); *OrW* 0014 (57); *Rid 39* 0004 (7), 0008 (20)
32	*PPs* 0376 (76.9), and probably 0883 (104.37) as well
33	Grundtvig
34	*Beo* 1550b, 2367b, 2398b
35	Probably *Beo* 1386a given the following lines
36–42	*Beo* 1386b–1389b
43	Grundtvig
44	Grundtvig
45	*PsCaK* 0063 (65.17)
46	*GenA,B* 0378 (1150)
47	"se goda": *Beo* 205a, 355a, 675a, 758a, 1190b, 1518a, 2944b, 2949ª
48	Possibly from *Beo*, specifically lines 1719b, 2635b, or 3009b
49	*Beo* 1833a; possibly *Sat* 0083 (216); *ChristA,B,C* 0259 (910), 0340 (1232); *GuthA,B* 0189 (618), 0238 (790); *Whale* 0016 (82); *Seasons* 0011 (71); *HomS 15* 0037 (80); *ChrodR1* 0378 (37.10); *Conf 10.4* 0002 (4); *WPol 2.12* 0029 (35)
50	wægde: From "wægan?" *Bede 4* 0790 (33.382.32); *HlGl (Oliphant)* 3177 (F270)
	hwette: *Beo* 490b; *Rid 11* 0002 (3); *Ægram* 1061 (166.13); *LS 35* 0143 (338); *PsCaI* 0105 (76.41); *CollGl 22* 0018 (18), 0023 (23)
51	ripiende: probably from "ripian," but the only occurrence in the corpus of a present participle is "ripende" in *ÆCHom II* 0018 (319.28), which could also come from "ripan" or "repan"
52	run-cræftig: *Dan* 0214 (733)
53	uferan dægum: *Beo* 2392a; *WHom 2* 0002 (31); *Or 4* 0103 (5.90.15)
54	A common phrase in the corpus. It occurs precisely in this case and order in *PPs* 1606 (148.12). "geongum ond ealdum" occurs in *Beo* at 72a
55	Grundtvig

56	Grundtvig
57	Line appears in *El* 0040 (99) and 0329 (1197), "beorna beag-gifa" and "beorna beag-gifan" respectively. "Beag-gyfan" appears in *Beo* at 1102a
58	blonden-feaxes: *Beo* 1594b, 1791a, 1873a, 2962a; *GenA,B* 0729 (2341), 0810 (2602)
59–65	*Beo* 857–859 and 861a
66	Grundtvig
67	*ChronA* 0257 (753.33); *ChronC* 019810 (755.33), 0658 (1014.3); *ChronD* 0131 (755.28), 0661 (1014.5); *ChronE* 0396 (755.28)
68	Specifically occurs in *El* 0136 (432); *PPs* 1124 (118.17), 1486 (139.8). But also occurs in a few other instances with other prepositions and sometimes a possessive pronoun, as in *Whale* 0014 (71) "in hira lif-dagum." Accusative plural "lif-dagas" appears in *Beo* at 793a, 1622a
69	Grundtvig
70	Grundtvig
71	wil-siþ: *Beo* 216a; *And* 0325 (1046); *Bede 3* 0322 (13.200.4); *ChristA,B,C* 0007 (18)
72	ofer-sohton: *Beo* 2686a "ofer-sohte"
73	*Beo* 856a
74	Grundtvig
75	engla-frean: *El* 0358 (1307)
76	*Beo* 928b
77	Probably from *Beo* 2797a "þæs þe ic moste"
78	*HomU 26* 0081 (243); *Conf 10.4* 0023 (65); *Lit 4.3.1* 0004 (6)
79	Grundtvig
80	*Beo* 2236a
81	*Beo* 3130b "ut geferedon"
82	eorþan-fæðm: *ChristA,B,C* 0319 (1141); *Phoen* 0120 (482)
83–84	*Beo* 3050
85	Grundtvig
86	Grundtvig
87	Grundtvig
88	harum: *Beo* 1678a
89	wlite-beorht: *Beo* 93a; *GenA,B* 0041 (129), 0062 (187), 0075 (218), 0495 (1555), 0538 (1726), 0557 (1800); *Met* 0320 (25.1)
90	Grundtvig
91	*Beo* 1571b

92	heofones-candel: *Ex* 0034 (111); *And* 0075 (243). "rodores candel" in *Beo* at 1571a
93	glitnie: From "glitinian." The infinitive appears in *Beo* at 2758a. This particular conjugation only appears in *HomU 16* at 0013 (12).
	blonden-feax: see note for line 58
94	*Beo* 1163a
95	Fairly common words, but possibly from *Beo* 56 "aldor of earde – oþþæt him eft onwoc" given the following line
96	*Beo* 55b; also *Jud* 0031 (11)
97–98	*Beo* 2820

This list is simply stunning in scope and attests to Grundtvig's intense interest in OE literature. The reason for that intense interest – so intense that he as good as memorized the entirety of *Beowulf*[13] and virtually became an OE *scop* to compose his own OE poems – is complex. It relates to his connected views on Church history, on how history and other "texts" can and should be read, and on how language works within the continuum of history. All three of these areas need some explication.

First, Church history. Grundtvig was deeply engaged in the Book of *Revelation* from early in his career and in 1810 began to "Danish" it in hexameter verse. He got to just chapter 8 of the twenty-two chapters, but by this time the beginnings of his historical vision had already taken root.[14] In chapters 1 to 3 of the Book of *Revelation*, St. John the Divine introduces us to the mystery of the seven stars that he saw being held by "one like a son of man, clothed with a long robe and with a golden girdle round his breast" and surrounded by seven lampstands (1:13).[15] John falls as though dead at his feet, and the "one like a son of man" says to him:

> Now write what you see, and what is and what is to take place hereafter. As for the mystery of the seven stars which you saw in my right hand, and the seven golden lampstands, the seven stars are the angels of the seven churches and the seven lampstands are the seven churches. (1:19–20)

The seven churches of Asia Minor are Ephesus (*Revelation* 2:1–7), Smyrna (*Revelation* 2:8–11), Pergamum (*Revelation* 2:12–17), Thyatira (*Revelation*

---

[13] Grundtvig, *Beowulfes Beorh*, p. xviii.
[14] Balslev, *Christenhedens Syvstjerne*, p. 259.
[15] *The Oxford Annotated Bible*, p. 1492. All quotations from the Revised Standard Version of the English Bible are from this edition.

2:18–29), Sardis (*Revelation* 3:1–6), Philadelphia (*Revelation* 3:7–13), and Laodicea (*Revelation* 3:14–22). To subsequent readers of the Bible, however, the literal churches easily bear an additional three levels of Augustinian meaning stacked on top of the literal. On the allegorical level, they represent all churches; on the moral level, they signify the individual; and on the highest level, the anagogical or mystical or spiritual, the seven churches represent the seven phases in the spiritual history of the Church from about 96 CE, the time of the writing of *Revelation*, to Doomsday.

As early as 1810, Grundtvig included himself among the historicist interpreters of the seven churches, which he felt "reflect the course of history as far as each church corresponds to the seven 'principal nations' which, according to Grundtvig, shape world history from the birth of Christ to the Day of Judgment."[16] He wrote an epic-length poem elaborating this view in the late 1850s. *Christenhedens Syvstjerne* (Christianity's Seven Stars) consists of a lengthy introduction and 833 seven-line stanzas divided into seven songs, each devoted to a 300-year period in Church history. The first church or Ephesus represents the Hebraic period; the second or Smyrna, the Greek; the third or Pergamum, the Roman; the fourth or Thyatira, the Anglo-Saxon; the fifth or Sardis, the German; the sixth or Philadelphia, the Nordic (in the broadest sense, including the English); and the seventh or Laodicea, which had not yet taken place, the Indian. OE literature was a crucial area of study for Grundtvig because of the prominent place in Church history that the Anglo-Saxon church played. It supplanted the Roman church and adumbrated the Protestant Reformation and the Nordic church as well, having, for example, sent the missionaries Willibrord to Christianize the Frisians and Winfred (Boniface) to Christianize the Germans.[17] Sardis, or the fifth church, stands for the Protestant Reformation, whose works would be completed in the phase represented by Philadelphia. The Anglo-Saxons were thus the first of the Germanic-speaking peoples who constituted the fourth principal people to carry out God's plan in "universal history," a term that Grundtvig borrowed from Friedrich Schiller (1759–1805).[18] The other two are the Germans and the Scandinavians, and the three peoples preceding the Germans are the Jews, the Greeks, and the Romans.[19]

For Grundtvig, the seven messages to these churches not only sketch out the spiritual history of the Church but also point to the seven great reformers of the Church central to each historical phase. The fourth

---

[16] Broadbrige and Jensen, *A Grundtvig Anthology*, p. 89.
[17] Vind, *Grundtvigs historiefilosofi*, p. 316.
[18] Holm, *Historie og efterklang*, p. 16.
[19] Vind, *Grundtvigs historiefilosofi*, p. 617.

reformer, aligned with Thyatira, was Bede (or possibly Cædmon);[20] the fifth, aligned with Sardis, was Martin Luther; and the sixth, aligned with Philadelphia, was not yet known, but Grundtvig believed that he himself – an acknowledged Cædmon figure in his time[21] and considered by some in the mid-twentieth century to be on a par with Luther[22] – was his forerunner.[23] This belief informed and motivated much if not all of Grundtvig's work, and only with that fact in mind and the fact that Pastor Grundtvig's primary purpose in life was to serve God[24] can we fully comprehend his excursions into OE studies. Nationalism was a major reason for Grundtvig's studying OE language and literature, to be sure, but Grundtvig's nationalism actually expands to embrace "the Nation of God," to paraphrase St. Augustine, and the whole history of the Christian Church, and, thus to explain the world's, and Denmark's and Grundtvig's, place in it.

So the second and intimately related item to the first that bears more scrutiny is how Grundtvig reads history. We have already had a glimpse of the way he reads the Book of *Revelation*. The assurance he finds in that reading of the centrality of both himself and Denmark in the history of the Church gives rise to a typological view of Danish and Nordic myth, literature, and history. Nordic myth and literature, for example, anticipates the Christian myth that replaced it. For the trinity of Odin, Thor, and Freyja, for instance, we get the real Trinity of the Father, the Son, and the Holy Ghost, and for Odin's gallows and Thor's hammer, we get the Cross. In Nordic history in the broad sense, Cædmon, who introduced to the world the new-European literature, can be said to foreshadow Grundtvig, Denmark's prophet, who "stands as a sign for a time of flowering in the North."[25] This typological or mythical view, as I loosely call it, was validated for Grundtvig both by *Revelation* 2–3, where the sixth reformer of the Church was foretold, and by 1 Cor. 13:9–12, where the opacity of the present and the relative lucidity of the future were likewise foretold ("for we know in part and we prophesy in part [9] ... we see through a glass, darkly; but then face to face [12]"). This typological view reveals

---

[20] Ibid., p. 314.
[21] In a letter dated 20 February 1876, the Swedish poet Viktor Rydberg described Grundtvig as "en väsentligen ursprunlgit kraft, en Cædmon i vårt århundrade" (a considerable original power, a Cædmon in our century). Quoted in Mjöberg, *Drömmen*, II, p. 53, and Nielsen, "Grundtvig set fra Sverige," p. 19.
[22] Nielsen, "Grundtvig set fra Sverige," p. 28. See also Holm, "The Luther of Denmark."
[23] Holm, *Historie og efterklang*, p. 18.
[24] Holm, *The Essential Grundtvig*, p. 64.
[25] "stander som et Tegn / For en Blomster-Tid I Norden," quoted from Grundtvig's *Paaske-Lilien* in Holm, *Historie og efterklang*, p. 129.

itself dramatically in and helps determine the form of Grundtvig's work on "The Battle of Brunanburh," *Beowulf*, and *The Phoenix*. It embodies, for one thing, a doctrine of redemptive progress that moves from the literal OE text to its reincarnation in Grundtvig's Danishing of it and finally to the echo poem reflecting on the present state of the text in the modern, Danish world, and moving us into the future.[26]

The typological view also embodies a deep-rooted nationalism that emphasizes the centrality of the Germanic languages, especially Danish, in universal history, where the Danes enjoyed being one of God's chosen people.[27] As soon as the biblical or Christological typology developed by the Church Fathers – the science of studying how real historical figures in the Old Testament such as Adam, Isaac, Moses, and Jonah prefigured the historical Christ[28] – moved to sacramental typology, which asserted the connection of events in the Old Testament, such as the Flood or the Crossing of the Red Sea, to the sacraments of the Church, such as baptism, the gate was open for exploiting typology's conjunctive power. From a mere tool for observing historical reiterations and thereby establishing the intimate relationship between the Old Testament and the New, it was elevated to an allegorical or symbolic plane. From validating the historical unity of scripture, it could be pushed to show the unity of scripture with things outside of scripture, such as the sacraments or national histories. By connecting Denmark's history and language with the Bible in this way, Grundtvig connected them to the divine.

The third and last item to consider is how Grundtvig thought language works. He believed deeply in the creative power of "the living word" (*det levende ord*), a concept that Grundtvig first mentions in an unpublished document from 1811,[29] which is grounded in belief in the Logos, a belief shared by Heraclitus, the authors of the Old and New Testaments, and OE poets. Heraclitus, for example, considered the Logos to be universal reason that both governs and permeates the world, and Old Testament authors refer to its creative powers (Wisdom 18:14–16; 2 Samuel 15:10; Isaiah 55:11; Jeremiah 23:29).[30] The doctrine of the Logos continues in the New Testament, where it becomes identified with Christ: "in the beginning was the word and the word was with God and the word was God," John 1:1). While the doctrine undergirds Grundtvig's understanding of Scripture, his notion of "the living word" has even broader implications for both his own language and his own poetry as they participate in the typological dance of universal history. The "word," he wrote in 1817, is the highest

---

[26] "fører os ind i fremtiden." Holm, *Historie og efterklang*, p. 137.
[27] Holm, *Historie og efterklang*, p. 19.
[28] Auerbach, "Figura," p. 29.
[29] Vind, *Grundtvigs historiefilosofi*, p. 102.
[30] Cross and Livingstone, *Oxford Dictionary of the Christian Church*, s.v. "Logos."

expression of human life, and without it there could be no progress or history.[31] Furthermore, for Grundtvig, the salvific truth of John 1:14 ("the word was made flesh") at once remains constant and transmutes into "the word was made song." For it is the articulated word, the living word, liberated from the deadening confines of script, that carries the greatest force of all. Grundtvig expounds on this matter in his introduction to the 1832 edition of his *Nordens Mytologi eller Sindbilled-Sprog* (Nordic Mythology or Symbolic Language), where he observes that the difference between word and script is as enormous as that between life and death.

> But] ... life is not propagated by the dead but by the living. Life profits as little by dead words as by dead fish; as little by blunt quills as by pointed pens of steel; as little by shadowy word as by shadowy people ... Should the reader, however, by a stroke of good fortune discover the secret, which Latin conceals but which we reveal every time we open our mouth, namely, that the word belongs in the mouth and not in the pen and that ideas and emotions, faith and "*Anskuelse*" [points of view] are expressed orally, not manually, and in brief and precise, clear and living, expressive, informative, and propagating manner, should the reader have taken this giant step out of the grave, then he would see immediately and without my prodding what a wonderful light is shed on our human living.[32]

The spirit (*spiritus*) resides in the word and when literal breath (*spiritus*) gives voice to it, it lives once more. Grundtvig's inspiration for these ideas comes, as it did for Rasmus Rask, as we saw in chapter 1, from German philosophy, primarily in the works of Johann Gottfried Herder. In his *Ideen zur Philosophie der Geschichte der Menschheit* (Ideas on the Philosophy of Human History), Herder asserts that language is,

> apart from the genesis of living beings, perhaps the greatest creation on earth ... A breath from our mouth becomes the picture of the world, the model of our thoughts and feelings in the soul of another. On a moving breeze, all that human beings on earth have ever thought, wanted, did, and will do depends: because we would all still be running around in the forests if this divine breath hadn't breathed on us and floated like a magic sound on our lips. The whole history of mankind with all the treasures of its tradition and culture is nothing but a consequence of this resolved divine mystery.[33]

---

[31] Quoted in Vind, *Grundtvigs historiefilosofi*, p. 102.
[32] *Selected Writings*, p. 28.
[33] "ausser der Genesis lebendiger Wesen vielleicht das grösseste der Erdeschöpfung... . Ein Hauch unsres Mundes wird das Gemälde der Welt, der Typus unsrer Gedanken und Gefühle in des andern Seele. Von einem

Herder's understanding of the primacy of language, of the living word, made a profound impression on Grundtvig. In his worldview, the word is inextricably bound to the spirit, which speaks through the word, and to history itself, through which the living word works.[34]

Grundtvig, then, certainly believed passionately in the power of "the living word." He also believed in the revelatory nature of poetry, discourse sent by God, and, within poetry, he discerned three levels. Earthly poetry deals with the sensible world, and historical poetry deals with the movements of the spirit within the sensible world. *Lyspoesi*, luminous poetry, states Grundtvig, "clarifies the Word and the history thereof and the Voice of the word and the nature thereof, what one calls poetry in the first instance and music in the second, the context of history and the harmony of nature, both as effects of the almighty word of God."[35] The word in luminous poetry becomes yet more luminous when accompanied by music. Grundtvig explains this further:

> Song, as the birds show us, is the most natural of all arts, also art in its nature: the expression of the pure truth, the sound of the creative word, that flaps towards heaven and calls plaintively to the Word from which it is separated. Every time a bird sings, it is as if it wanted to remind us that in humanity the great meeting [of word and song] comes to pass and that there the holy reunification takes place.[36]

Grundtvig put these insights as well as those concerning theology and history into extremely practical use in his *Sang-Værk til den danske Kirke* (Song Work for the Danish Church, 1836–37). He was a hugely prolific

---

bewegten Lüftchen hangt alles ab, was Menschen je auf der Erde menschliches dachten, wollten, taten und tun werden: denn alle liefen wir noch in Wäldern umher, wenn nicht dieser göttliche Otem uns angehaucht hätte und wie ein Zauberton auf unsern Lippen schwebte. Die ganze Geschichte der Menschheit ist also mit allen Schätzen ihrer Tradition und Kultur ist nichts als eine Folge dieses aufgelösten göttlichen Ratsels." Quoted in Vind, *Grundtvigs historiefilosofi*, pp. 105–06.

[34] Ibid., pp. 108, 110.

[35] "Lys-Poesien skal da først forklare *Ordet* og Historien af det, og dernæst *Røsten* og (af) Naturen af den, først hvad Man kalder Poesien og dernæst Musiken: Historiens Sammenhæng og Naturens Harmoni begge som Virkninger af det almægtige *Guds-Ord*." Quoted in Holm, *Historie og efterklang*, p. 105.

[36] "Sang, det sige Fuglene os, er den naturligste af alle Konster, altsaa Konsten i sin Natur: Udtrykket af den rene Sandselighed, Skaber-Ordets vingede Lyd, der flagrer mod Himlen og kalder smeltende paa Ordet hvorfra det er adskilt. Hvergang Fuglen synger os over Hovedet, da er det som om den fødle, og vilde minde os om at i Mennesket er det store møde kommet i Stand, og at der skal den hellige Gienforening gaae for sig." Quoted in Ibid., pp. 105–06.

and continuously popular hymn and song writer and composed some 1,600 of them during his lifetime,[37] thus abundantly demonstrating his belief that word and song have their great reunification in humanity. Of the 754 hymns in the current Danish hymnal, 271 are by Grundtvig;[38] several of the 601 songs in the *Folkehøjskolens sangbog* (Folk High School's Song Book), which in 2020 was in its nineteenth edition since 1894, are also by him.

The 401 songs in the *Sang-Værk*, however, distinguish themselves from the rest in their adhering to and illustrating Grundtvig's view of the development of Church history from the first iteration of it to Grundtvig's day.[39] To represent the Anglo-Saxon Church, he transmutes parts of three OE poems into six church hymns in volume one of his *Sang-Værk*. Hymn 124 is a free rendition or adaptation of antiphon 1 in *The Advent Lyrics*; hymn 158, a Christmas hymn, is a free rendition of antiphons 8 and 9 but with "a long stretch of congruities"[40]; hymn 243 is a free rendition of *Christ and Satan*, lines 398–596 (the Harrowing of Hell);[41] hymn 244 is a verse paraphrase of parts of *Christ II*;[42] hymn 245 is a rendition of *Christ II*, lines 720–44 (the six leaps of Christ); and hymn 355 is a rendition of *Christ II*, lines 600 ff., where Christ is the sun and the Church, the moon.[43] Take hymn 243 on the Harrowing of Hell as an example. Here are lines 398–404 of *Christ and Satan*, juxtaposed with my literal translation below them:

Hwearf þa to helle hæleða bearnum,
meotod þurh mihte; wolde manna rim,
fela þusenda, forð gelædan
up to eðle. þa com engla sweg,
dyne on dægred; hæfde drihten seolf
feond oferfohten. Wæs seo fæhðe þa gyt
open on uhtan, þa se egsa becom.[44]

To hell, then, to the children of men, the
Measurer turned through might; he wanted
to lead forth a number of men, many thousands,

[37] Holm, *The Essential Grundtvig*, p. 128.
[38] Lawson, "N. F. S. Grundtvig."
[39] Vind, *Grundtvigs historiefilosofi*, p. 43.
[40] "en lang række overensstemmelser." Noack, "Den oldengelske digtning," p. 149.
[41] For a full English translation, see Broadbridge, *Living Wellsprings*, pp. 94–97. For a discussion of hymns 243, 244, and 245 and their relationship to the OE poems that inspired them, see Bradley, "Grundtvig's *I Kveld*."
[42] For a full English translation, see Broadbridge, *Living Wellsprings*, pp. 106–08.
[43] Noack, "Den oldengelske digtning," p. 150.
[44] Finnegan, *Christ and Satan*, pp. 80–81.

up to their homeland. Then came the sound of
angels, a din at dawn of day; the Lord himself
had vanquished the enemy. The violence was still
ongoing in the early morning when the fearful event
came.

What Grundtvig said of the literal translation of "The Battle of Brunanburh" he would have said of my translation: it lies there dead like a corpse for the raven and wolf to gnaw on. He would then have Danished the translation to infuse it with its original spirit and power. Here are the first four lines where he begins that process together with the 2015 translation of them:[45]

I Kvæld blev der banket paa Helvedes Port,
Saa dundrer den rullende Torden,
Herolden var stærk og Hans Bukskab fuldstort,
Thi lyttede Alt under Jorden!

This night came a knocking at the portals of Hell
as loud as the rolling of thunder;
the Herald was strong and his message immense,
all souls under earth heard in wonder.

The music for this hymn looks like this:[46]

Example 2. "I Kveld."

An intriguing fact about this OE poem's being transmogrified into a Danish hymn is that the hymn in turn was reincarnated by the artist Joakim Skovgaard (1856–1933) in his "Christ in the Realm of the Dead" ("Kristus i de dødes rige," 1891–94), which is currently in Statens Museum for Kunst in Copenhagen. The original OE text, which is dead to most people because they cannot read the language, thus becomes accessible, at least in part, to both the voices and the eyes of the Danish people. We will see this phenomenon reversed in chapter 5 in the work of Henry Larsen, where the hymn brings him back to the original OE text.

---

[45] Broadbridge, *Living Wellsprings*, p. 94.
[46] Song 456 in Madsen et al., *Folkehøjskolens sangbog*. Melody by T. Laub, 1922.

Myth of Spirit, Myth of Word in the Works of N. F. S. Grundtvig

Figure 6. Joakim Skovgaard, "Kristus i de dødes rige," 1891–94.

Grundtvig's translation of *Beowulf* participates in the same vision of the living word and its enhancement through music as well as in Grundtvig's view on universal history, where *Beowulf* came to play a central role.[47] His first mention of the poem appears in *Nordens Mytologi* of 1808, where he expresses great enthusiasm for Thorkelin's forthcoming edition of the poem:

> It has been remarked before that we actually only have Nordic poems about the Volsunger and the Niflunger (Gjukunger), but both over these and especially over the Skjoldungs and Skilfings a glorious light will surely rise when State Counselor Thorkelin (oh, please, soon!) makes a glorious memorial for himself by publishing the Anglo-Saxon poem he has at hand and thereby satisfies the growing longing that burns among the friends of the old North.[48]

---

[47] Vind, *Grundtvigs historiefilosofi*, p. 172.
[48] "Det er før bemærket, at Vi kun om Volsunger og Niflunger (Gjukunger) have egenlig nordiske Digte, men saavel over disse som især over Skjoldunger og Skilfinger vil udentvivl opgaa et herligt Lys, naar Hr. Justitsraad Thorkelin (o

Grundtvig's first encounter with the poem comes in 1815, when Thorkelin's edition finally appeared. Grundtvig was bitterly disappointed in it, and among the many unflattering things he said about it in print, he wondered if Thorkelin had devoted even two weeks to learning OE before undertaking the project.[49] Grundtvig then "Danished" the first 52 lines of the poem in 1817[50] and produced a complete translation in 1820.[51] He followed that with a substantial essay on the poem in 1841,[52] his own scholarly edition of it in 1861,[53] and his slightly revised translation in 1865.[54]

For Grundtvig, *Beowulf* was a lifetime preoccupation because it offers confirmation of his views on Church and human history and on language functioning within history. It was the "missing link" that tied Denmark's and the North's ancient history with development of the mainstream of universal history from Babel, Hellas, and Rome, the most decisive factor being that the Nordic Anglo-Saxons adopted Christianity early. In their earliest poetry, "Hebraic poetry was transferred to a Nordic mother tongue – long before Luther."[55] As an expression of pan-Scandinavianism and the notion of a unified northern people, *Beowulf* affirms Denmark's place in the history of the Church (where it is central in the sixth phase) even as it provides what Grundtvig calls in 1817 "a visible, collective picture of the whole of history."[56] "Skjold," for example, is "the country's gracious father, and the Danish people are dear to him and faithfully devoted"[57]; Beowulf incorporates within himself all the virtues of heroism and stands at least occasionally in a typological relationship with Christ and perhaps even Grundtvig; and the monsters express through their horrific acts all the evil and death in the world, anything that hinders spiritual development. Grendel could even signify the Catholic Church, the Latin

---

gid dog snart!) sætter sig et glandsfuldt Mindesmærke ved at udgive det angelsaksiske Digt, Han har under Haand, og derved tilfredstiller den voksende Længsel, der brænder hos gamle Nordens Venner." *Nordens Mytologi* (1808), p. 130, note 81.

[49] "Et par Ord," pp. 951–52.
[50] Cooley, "Grundtvig's First Translation from *Beowulf*."
[51] *Bjowulfs Drape*.
[52] "Bjovulfs Drape eller det Oldnordiske Heltedigt."
[53] *Beowulfes Beorh*.
[54] *Bjovulvs-Drapen*.
[55] "den hebræiske poesi overført til et nordisk modersmål – længe før Luther." Vind, *Grundtvigs historiefilosofi*, p. 172.
[56] "synligt, sammentrængt Billede of hele Historien." "Om Bjovulfs Drape," p. 273.
[57] "den Landets milde Fader, og det ham kiærlig, tro hengivne danske Folk." Ibid., p. 219.

Letter Troll that we will meet in the next chapter and that Grundtvig had so often railed against. In his edition of *Beowulf* from 1861, he calls the poem an instrument for "enlightenment of life" (*livsoplysning*) and his edition a means of awakening the "spirits of the people" by appealing directly to "the hearts of the people."[58] That direct appeal occurs through language that is suffused with "the power of the spirit of the people,"[59] which moves the reader to a "living connection with the world-historical life of the old Angles."[60]

To accomplish his goal of infusing the living word into his 1820 translation of *Beowulf*, Grundtvig first uses verse forms and rhythms familiar to his audience, just as we have seen him do in his rendition of "The Battle of Brunanburh" and his hymns for the Danish Church. In *Beowulf*, the major verse type is *Knittelvers*, the verse couplet that typifies both the Danish rhymed chronicles and ballads. But he also uses unmistakable ballad forms and folksong. Second, to make the living word fly yet higher, he clearly had familiar melodies in mind for many parts of the translation, as subsequent publications verify. An 1872 collection of historical songs gathered by H. Nutzhorn and L. Schrøder (*Historiske sange*), for example, includes thirteen passages from Grundtvig's translation with notes on what melodies should accompany them. The chart below summarizes that information.

---

[58] "Folke-Aander," "Folke-Hjerterne," *Beowulfes Beorh*, p. xxiv.
[59] "Folke-Aandens Kraft," *Beowulfes Beorh*, p. xxvii.
[60] "levende Sammenhæng med den gamle Anglers verdenshistoriske Liv," *Beowulfes Beorh*, p. xxiv.

Song number and first line from Nutzhorn and Schrøder, *Historiske sange*, pp. 75–96.	From song number in Grundtvig's 1820 translation.	Suggested melody in *Historiske sange*, pp. 75–96.
39 Grændel han ypped med Hrodgar en kiv	3	Barnekow[61] or "Der vanker en ridder mellen grönne træer"[62]
40 Det var Gote-helten bold	4	Barnekow or "Danevang ved grönne bred"
41 "Kong Hrodgar!" sagde helten	5	Improvise á la Barnekow or "Vift stolt på Kodans bølge"
42 Ej sprang med kæmpefølge	7	Barnekow
43 Gloende fra top til tå	8	Barnekow
44 Mer ej mindes jeg nu med sorg	9	Barnekow
45 For dagens lys det kom nu brat	11	Barnekow
46 Ej Bjovulv var i hallen med	11	Barnekow
47 Bjovulv gik med spejderöje	12	Barnekow or "Unge genbyrdsliv"
48 Bjovulv sprang i samme stund	12	Barnekow or "Danevang ved grönne bred"
49 Midlertid de vise mænd	12	Barnekow or "Dansker født ved bølgen blå"
50 Med almagt troner ærens drot	13	Barnekow or "Det er et land så kosteligt"
51 Se, jeg gammel er og grå	13	Barnekow or "Danevang ved grönne bred"

Before Howard Hanson in 1925 composed his choral work, "Lament for Beowulf";[63] before Ezra Pound in 1928 after hearing a performance of

---

[61] Christian Barnekow (1837–1913) was a Danish composer whose numerous melodies for historical songs were widely known. He wrote the melodies for songs 39, 40, 41, 42, 43, and for "Danerkongen for Øje stod." See *Sange fra Nordens Sagnhisorie af N.F.S. Grundtvig*, part 1.
[62] To listen to the melody for this and other Danish songs listed here, go to https://ugle.dk/sange.html.
[63] See Bjork "The Reception History of *Beowulf*," pp. 6–10, for a discussion of

the songs of the Hebrides decided that *Beowulf* should be sung to one of those songs;[64] before John C. Pope in 1942 published his *Rhythm of Beowulf*, where he uses musical notation to chart the meter of the poem; before Thomas Cable in 1974 produced his *The Meter and Melody of Beowulf*, where he postulates the melodic basis of meter in the poem; and before Benjamin Bagby's musical performances of the poem beginning in 1990, Grundtvig intuited the happy union of word and music in *Beowulf*. For example, in the first song listed above, we find Grendel starting his feud with Hrothgar. Here's the first stanza of Grundtvig's translation:

> Grændel, han yppet med Hrodgar en kiv
> Han rased med list og med lue:
> mangen god kæmpe da misted sit liv,
> og danemænd måtte vel grue.

> Grendel, he picked a quarrel with Hrothgar,
> he raged with cunning and hate;
> many a good warrior then lost his life,
> and the Danes must well have been in dread.

One of the possible melodies for this song is "Der vanker en ridder" (There Wanders a Knight) by C. E. F. Weyse. Here is the music for the first stanza:[65]

Example 3. "Grendel."

This melody comes from a well-known Danish folksong, the text for which was written by Ludvig Johan Heiberg (1791–1860). Because of the story

---

    musical adaptations and interpretations of *Beowulf*.
[64] "The Music of Beowulf."
[65] Nutzhorn, *Melodierne til Sangbog*, no. 268, adapted by James Massengale, who notes the details he changed. 1) Upbeat (eighth note on d) omitted; 2) an upbeat (sixteenth note on d) added in measure 2; 3) an upbeat (eighth note on a) omitted, measure 4. He notes further that the accent pattern for the word "danemænd" appears slightly awkward (one would prefer two sixteenths plus an eighth note), but subsequent strophes imply that the above is the accentual pattern intended by Grundtvig.

that folksong tells, it is worth quoting in full, with my English translation of it following the text:

> Der vanker en Ridder mellem grønne Træer,
> Roser og yndelige Blommer.
> Der synger en Drossel, han står den så nær,
> med kviddren den hilser Skærsommer.
>
> Han lytter med List imellem grønne Træer,
> Roser og yndelige Blommer.
> Han grubler og støtter sig tavs til sit Sværd,
> Mens Fuglen den hilser Skærsommer.
>
> Nu åbner en Jomfru Vinduet mod de Træer,
> roser og yndelige Blommer.
> Som Fuglen hun synger, han står hende nær,
> Da føler hans Barm, det er Sommer.
>
> Da spirer hans Håb alt som de grønne Træer,
> Roser og yndelige Blommer.
> Han skuer den Elskte, hun er ham så kær,
> Han hilser sit Håb i Skærsommer.

> There wanders a knight among green trees,
> roses and lovely flowers.
> There sings a thrush; he's so close to it;
> with chirping it greets midsummer.
>
> He listens with feeling among green trees,
> roses and lovely flowers.
> He ponders and leans silently on his sword
> while the bird greets midsummer.
>
> Now a maiden opens the window to the trees,
> roses and lovely flowers.
> Like the bird she sings; he stands near her;
> Then his bosom feels, it is summer.
>
> Then sprouts his hope just like the green trees,
> roses and lovely flowers.
> He looks at his beloved; she is to him so dear;
> he greets his hope in midsummer.

The familiar tune for this poem would have called to mind its romantic, sentimental content as the listener responded to Grundtvig's translation and pondered Grendel, whose monstrosity is undercut by its juxtaposition to the folksong.

The melody for Beowulf's first meeting with Hrothgar in song 5 of Grundtvig's translation and song 41 in the Nutzhorn and Schrøder list, on the other hand, brings other emotions to mind. Grundtvig's text for the first stanza reads:

"Kong Hrodgar!" sagde Helten,	"King Hrothgar!" said the hero,
"hilsæl og mange tak!	greetings and many thanks!
I salen og i felten	In the hall and in the field
jeg tjæner Higelak;	I serve Hygelac;
hans frænde jeg mon være	his kinsman, yes, I am
og tjæner i hans gård	and serve in his court
hel mangen dåd med ære	a great many deeds with honor
jeg drev i ungdomsår.	I performed in my youth.

And the melody for Grundtvig's words looks like this:[66]

Example 4. "Kong Hrodgar."

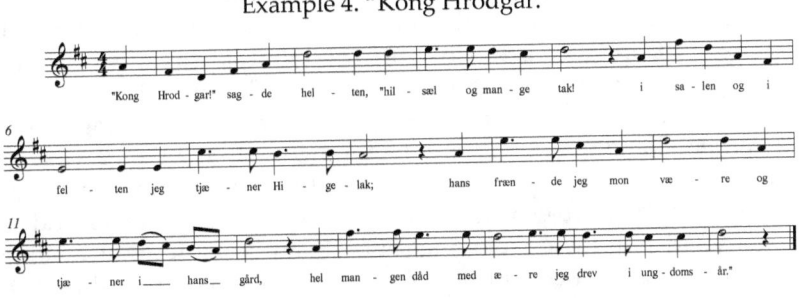

This comes from B. S. Ingemann's (1789–1862) salute to the Danish flag, the Dannebrog, which was written in 1807 and set to music in 1817 by Rudolph Bay (1791–1856). Ingemann's patriotic text, penned as the British were bombarding Copenhagen, exudes the steely resolve of the Danes to persevere, as the first stanza attests:

Vift stolt på Kodans bølge
blodrøde Dannebrog!
Din glans ej nat skal dølge,
ej lynet dig nedslog.
Du over helte svæved,
som sang i dødens favn,

---

[66] Nutzhorn, *Melodierne til Sangbog*, no. 309, adapted to Grundtvig's text by James Massengale.

dit lyse kors har hævet
til himlen Danmarks navn.

Waft proudly on the Baltic's wave
bloodred Dannebrog!
Your splendor the night shall not conceal;
the lightning did not strike you down.
You flapped above heroes,
who sang in death's embrace;
your bright cross has raised
to heaven Denmark's name.

The melody to this song would have called to the listener's mind brave Danish soldiers resolved to protect the homeland even unto death. No irony inheres in its juxtaposition to the resolute Beowulf, of course.

As we have seen in Grundtvig's multiple excursions into OE literature, his scholarship on the subject – as philologically precise and innovative and groundbreaking as it may be – is really only the kernel, the quiescent worm (to look forward to his work on the mythical Phoenix), of a coherent program. That program is one of fulfilling biblical prophecy, of creating worldly prophecy by seeing ancient Nordic (including OE) texts as foreshadowing the sixth stage of the Church in Denmark, of viewing language as sacramental and giving vibrant, winged voice to the living word. This program may seem eccentric, even inimical to our contemporary way of conducting rational, objective, empirical research. But we do Grundtvig – this major voice in the development of OE studies, a founding father of modern Denmark, an educational reformer venerated around the world and honored alongside Gandhi in progressive schools in India[67] – a great disservice if we ignore it. S. A. J. Bradley sagely observes that Grundtvig

> experienced Anglo-Saxon poetry as it was composed to be experienced – as a religious experience which would truly feed the religious and spiritual life. If such subjective enthusiasm, such personalization of scholarship, was distasteful to the English antiquarian establishment, he was nonetheless one of the most dynamic respondents of any time to Anglo-Saxon culture viewed in historical retrospect, a remarkable phenomenon in nineteenth-century European culture, drawing upon a genuine insight into the Anglo-Saxon literary mentality.[68]

Grundtvig's dynamic response to OE verse informs his *Sang-Værk til den danske Kirke*, his translation of *Beowulf*, and his work on "The Battle of Brunanburh." That article foreshadows in an almost typological way his

---

[67] Holm, *The Essential Grundtvig*, pp. 192, 204.
[68] "'The First New-European Literature'," p. 70.

edition of the OE *Phoenix*. Here we have figure and fulfillment. Looking at Brunanburh, we see through a glass darkly; looking at the *Phoenix* edition, we see face to face. The rough-hewn structure of the Brunanburh article (scholarly introduction including a literal translation and the statement on the dead letter followed by the ballad embodying the living word then by the echo poem) emerges flawless in his edition of a major poem from *The Exeter Book*. In some ways, that edition is his most significant achievement in the field of OE studies and deserves more attention than it has received.

3

Grundtvig's Vision of the Old English *Phoenix*

The Phoenix – the magnificent mythical bird from antiquity that lives for 500 to 600 years, at least according to one legend, dies, is consumed in flame, and then rises triumphant from its own ashes in a kind of virgin birth – was regarded by many Christian authors, from Pope Clement I (35–99 CE) and Tertullian (155–220 CE) to Grundtvig, as a symbol of Christ and His Resurrection.[1,2] Grundtvig saw broader applications of the myth than just the religious as well. In a lecture delivered on 13 July 1838, he observed that it embraces humankind's ideal of its own great destiny:

> [T]his Phoenix, which every morning in its earthly paradise greeted the rising sun with heavenly song, is the symbol of the human spirit in its highest flight and most natural activity... So when the myth ends with the ashes being rolled together into an egg, from which the sun hatches a living creature, first, to be sure, in the form of the smallest worm, but then nevertheless growing and developing from the morning dew into a bird in its father's likeness, with his voice and with the right of inheritance to the beautiful fatherland, to which, fully-grown and accompanied by all the birds of the forest it returns in joy and triumph, I cannot but see in this an image of modern times as encouraging as it is striking, in which learning up to now was undeniably a bookworm that only wanted to gnaw on the monuments of the beautiful song of the Bird of Antiquity ... and I thought I could feel within myself how the worm began to be transformed into a tiny bird. And since that time I see this change taking place wherever the sprit was present in olden days, and I consider my attitude to you now, gentlemen, to be just such a transformation through which the bookworm endeavours to shed its skin ...[3]

The Phoenix myth is perfect for Grundtvig's multiple purposes. First and foremost, it sheds its bright light on the period of history that includes the introduction of printing, the voyages of discovery, and the

---

[1] This chapter is a revised and expanded version of my "N. F. S. Grundtvig's 1840 Edition of the Old English *Phoenix*." Portions of it were also used in my Introduction. Reprinted with permission of the University of Toronto Press.
[2] Cross and Livingstone, *Oxford Dictionary of the Christian Church*, s.v. "Phoenix."
[3] Broadbridge and Jensen, *A Grundtvig Anthology*, pp. 98–99.

Reformation, the period that Grundtvig calls "the Age of the New Year," characterized by development, change, and renewal. That age would lead to the rise of universal-historical knowledge that explains what went before and clarifies what lies ahead: antiquity corresponds to the Phoenix in its prime; the Middle Ages to the Phoenix building its funeral pyre and then being consumed on it; and the Age of the New Year to its rising from its own ashes into the present of Grundtvig's day.[4] Second, the myth encapsulates within itself the discipline of typology, one of Grundtvig's prime means of interpreting history. The real and historical Phoenix bird anticipates the reborn Phoenix that comes after it, and the two lend veracity to one another through their mirror-like connection. Third, the myth embodies Grundtvig's central concept of "the living word." The bird itself is "the King of songbirds,"[5] the most perfect and glorious of birds; and the singing is a perfect, revivifying song that transcends all others[6] and transforms "the living word" into "the winged word."[7]

Grundtvig adopted the Phoenix as a symbol for rebirth and renewal early in his career. In 1815, he launched his periodical *Dannevirke* (earthwork of the Danes, 1815–21), named after the system of fortifications begun in the seventh century along the neck of the Cimbrian peninsula to protect against invaders from the south. They were still there. Grundtvig's aim with this publication, which he single-handedly filled with poems and essays on historical and religious themes, was to promote "a revival of faith and a regeneration of national life."[8] In the first volume of the periodical in a poem of the same name, "Dannevirke," Grundtvig uses the Phoenix as a symbol of that regeneration in stanza 27, where the bird rises from its "triumphant ashes."[9]

In an even more patriotic, nationalistic gesture that harkens back to outrage over the English bombardment of Copenhagen in 1807, Grundtvig uses the Phoenix symbol again in his poem "Phønix-Gaarden" (The Phoenix Courtyard). The central building of the University of Copenhagen (founded in 1479) along with many other public buildings had been destroyed in the onslaught, and the university had had to carry out its

---

[4] Vind, *Grundtvigs Historiefilosofi*, pp. 349–51.
[5] "Den Sangfugles Drot." "Fugel Fønix" 1840 in *N.F. S. Grundtvigs Poetiske Skrifter* 6, p. 297.
[6] "Fugle-kvidder" (1840) in Bågøs and Nørregård, eds., *Nordiske Fædrelands-sange og Folkesange* (Copenhagen, 1873), no. 46, repr. in *N. F. S. Grundtvigs Poetiske Skrifter* 6, pp. 361–62.
[7] "det vingede Ord." "Pheniksfuglen," stanza 2, Grundtvig and Christensen, *Poetiske Skrifter* 8, p. 58.
[8] Broadbridge and Jensen, *A Grundtvig Anthology*, p. 19.
[9] "Aske seierrig." "Dannevirke," stanza 26. http://www.grundtvigsværker.dk/tekstvisning/8551/0#{%220%22:0,%22k%22:0}.

work since then in temporary locations around the city. In 1836, however, a new central building was completed and inaugurated to great fanfare, with members of the royal family attending the dedication ceremony. Grundtvig wrote his poem to celebrate the occasion.[10] In it, the Phoenix is "born like a winged word,"[11] rising from the ashes of the bombardment as the University of Copenhagen.[12] In two other poems on the Phoenix in 1840, Grundtvig reflects on the nature of the bird in one and on his edition of the Old English (OE) poem dedicated to it in the other.[13] His use of the Phoenix symbol is by far the most fully realized in his edition of the OE poem.

Four years after the appearance of "Phønix-Gaarden," Grundtvig published *Phenix-Fuglen*, the first full edition and first complete translation into any language of the major poem from *The Exeter Book*.[14] His other work on the Phoenix is generally attached to a specific event or occasion; this one is motivated by multiple occasions and events. Twenty-five years before this publication, for example, a coronation took place in 1815, that of King Frederik VI of Denmark (1768–1839; reigned over Denmark 1808–39 and over Norway 1808–14); 1815 also saw the emergence from Danish soil of the first edition of *Beowulf* – flawed though it was – which thus began a new epoch in OE studies that "ever since rises more and more clearly like a phoenix from its own ashes."[15] Grundtvig himself also began his work in OE studies in 1815 by publishing the first part of his translation of *Beowulf*,[16] the whole of which appeared five years later.[17] Thus, the year 1840 marked Grundtvig's silver anniversary in the field and was again a coronation year, this time for King Christian VIII (1786–1848; reigned

---

[10] Pedersen, "Indledning til 'Phønix-Gaarden'," 1.
[11] "Fødtes som et vinget Ord," stanza 13.
[12] Pedersen, "Indledning til 'Phønix-Gaarden'," 3.1.
[13] Pedersen, "Indledning til *Phenix-Fuglen*," 1.
[14] *Phenix-Fuglen: et Angelsachsisk Kvad, førstegang udgivet med Indledning, Fordanskning og Efterklang* (The Phoenix-Bird: An Anglo-Saxon Lay, Published for the First Time, with Introduction, Danish Translation and Echo Poem, 1840). Lines 1–27 of the poem were first published and translated into Latin and English by Conybeare in "Account of an Anglo-Saxon Paraphrase of the Phoenix." Conybeare also offers a transcription and Latin translation of lines 81b–84.
[15] "der siden stedse klarere opstaaer som en Phenix af sin Aske." *Phenix-Fuglen*, p. 9.
[16] Ibid., p. 9. See Grundtvig, "Et Par Ord." This review of Grímur Thorkelin's first edition of *Beowulf* from 1815 contains Grundtvig's free-verse translation of lines 1–52 and is reprinted in Cooley, "Grundtvig's First Translation from *Beowulf*."
[17] *Phenix-Fuglen*, p. 9. See *Bjowulfs Drape*. Between Grundtvig's first translation from the poem and his complete translation of it came "Stykker af Skjøldung-Kvadet," which is a rendition of lines 53–319 (through the coastguard episode).

1839–48). The first edition of *Beowulf* came out of Denmark in 1815; the first edition of what Grundtvig considered to be another major OE text should come out of Denmark in 1840, this year of national celebration, as well. In addition, although Grundtvig does not say so, the new king's ascension to the throne was particularly important because it began a relatively halcyon period for Grundtvig, who was admired and favored both by the king and the Crown Princess Caroline Amalie.[18]

In addition to these motivations for editing and translating *The Phoenix*, Grundtvig had at least one other that was a bit more personal. As discussed in chapter 1, Grundtvig was eager in 1830 to embark on an ambitious publication project of OE material that he laid out in his *Prospectus*, but was thwarted from doing so. He could at least fittingly and symbolically resuscitate part of that plan in 1840 by issuing to the world *The Exeter Book*'s chief resurrection allegory. The work thus becomes more than just scholarship: it is an intricate blending of Grundtvig's nationalistic, aesthetic, religious, and scholarly interests.

The 71-page book consists of eight parts: a dedication page, a dedicatory poem (pp. 5–8), a preface (pp. 9–14), an introduction (pp. 15–22), the OE text (pp. 23–43), the Danish translation (pp. 44–63), an "echo of the ballad" (pp. 63–70), and a concluding seven-stanza lyric (pp. 70–71).[19] The text itself and much of the introduction – what we would now consider the most scholarly and valuable parts of the book – actually contain the least interesting material. The text, for example, which is based entirely on Grundtvig's transcriptions of *The Exeter Book*, is relatively conservative but imperfect by his own admission. On p. 14 of the preface, he acknowledges that his edition is based on his transcription and that a close comparison of it with the original manuscript would surely reveal some errors.[20]

As was the custom at the time, Grundtvig arranges the poem in half-lines, and he prints the OE poet's direct source for the poem, Lactantius's *De Ave Phoenice*, directly beneath the first 758 of them.[21] He seems to try to preserve the structure of the original, inserting Roman numerals to substitute for the spaces and large capitals that the scribe uses to indicate where

---

[18] See chapter 4, "Unexpected Fulfillment, 1839–58," pp. 67–83, in Allchin, *N. F. S. Grundtvig*.
[19] Dedicatory poem, translation, "Echo," and concluding lyric reprinted in Grundtvig, *N. F. S. Grundtvigs poetiske Skrifter* 6, pp. 297–366.
[20] For a detailed study of the transcriptions, see Bradley, *N. F. S. Grundtvig's Transcriptions of the Exeter Book*.
[21] *Phenix-Fuglen*, pp. 23–35. Conybeare first identified Lactantius as the possible Latin source for part I of the poem in "Account of an Anglo-Saxon Paraphrase of the Phoenix." Grundtvig uses Rudolph Johannes Frederik Henrichsen's edition of Lactantius in *Pröveskrift om Phenix-Mythen (De Phoenicis Fabula)* (Copenhagen, 1825/1827). For the current state of Latin source studies for the poem, see Gorst, "Latin Sources of the Old English *Phoenix*."

each fitt begins, but he inexplicably divides the poem into seven, not eight fitts, joining manuscript fitts 5 (lines 350–453) and 6 (lines 424–517) into one. Otherwise, his divisions follow those of the manuscript precisely. Except for Muir (*The Exeter Anthology*), the subsequent standard English editions (Krapp and Dobbie, *The Exeter Book*, and Blake, *The Phoenix*) do not indicate the fitt divisions in the text itself at all and thus, with Grundtvig, lose the obvious symbolic value of the number eight, the medieval number of baptism, resurrection, and eternity,[22] and Grundtvig preserves the manuscript readings in fifteen places where subsequent editors have emended the text.[23] He does not, however, preserve either þ or ð consistently, so he substitutes ð for þ with only a handful of exceptions throughout the text, and he substitutes a for o almost without fail. While he prefers ð to þ, he also always replaces manuscript o with Þ.[24] The text also displays sporadic misreadings of letters,[25] two letter omissions, and one letter addition.[26] All such blemishes are, of course, minor ones that do not substantially affect the reliability of the edition. But slightly more serious problems do occur. Grundtvig omits one word (*oo*, 50 [= 25b]) and one half-line (*heafde onbrygdeð*, 282 [= 143b]), misreads eight words,[27] and inserts line breaks incorrectly nine times.[28] As an *editio princeps*

---

[22] For a full explication of the ramifications of number symbolism in the manuscript and poem, see Stevick, "Mathematical Proportions and Symbolism in 'The Phoenix'" and "The Form of *The Phoenix*."

[23] At half-lines 142 (MS *gehongene*), 144 (MS *wuniað*), 229 (MS *holm wræce*), 265 (MS *winsumra*), 306 (MS *rene*; Grundtvig suggests *grene* in a note), 307 (MS *fugla*; Grundtvig suggests *fugel*), 391 (MS *gewæs*; Grundtvig suggests *gehwæs*), 610 (MS *bregden*), 645 (MS *somnað*), 681 (MS *wefiað*), 739 (MS *fille*), 812 (MS *ageald*), 886 (MS *we*), 1024 (MS *liges*; Grundtvig suggests *lifes*), and 1169 (MS *eadwelan* but *-an* is altered in MS to *-um*). At half-line 330, Grundtvig misreads MS *syrwara* for *fyrwara* and preserves that misreading but notes that the former makes more sense in context than the latter.

[24] At half-lines 169, 546, 659, 668, 891, 1137, 1175, 1208, and 1262.

[25] At half-lines 15 (i for e), 52, 1206 (e for a), 52 (o for e), 79, 852 (a for ea), 82, 1095 (j for i), 86, 423, 1196 (u for a), 97, 847 (o for eo), 123, 971 (ð for d), 160 (e for o), 174, 563, 721, 912 (a for e), 221, 330 (f for s), 247 (g for h), 276, 1201 (th for ht), 319, 446 (e for a), 409, 575, 603 (æ for a), 536, 980, 1248, 1268 (d for þ or ð), 466 (i for o), 479 (ll for l), 485, 778, 1345 (æ for e), 533, 885 (a for u), 592, 630, 707, 1159, 1331 (e for i), 628 (o for u), 664 (ea for a), 944 (y for i), 1089 (r for s), 1112 (i for ie), 1161 (i for y), 1173 (u for e).

[26] Letter omissions: half-line 267 (m), 1347 (t); letter additions: half-line 303 (m).

[27] At half-lines 135 (*þingum* for *þragum*), 318 (*midlum* for *mid him*), 437 (*lænan* for *lænne*), 459 (*þam* for *þære*), 490, 492, 1156 (*him* for *hi*), 1105 (*hram werig* for *hrawerig*).

[28] At half-lines 212–13, 272–73, 281–82, 326–27, 522–23, 532–33, 748–49, 808–09, and 812–13. These errors have occurred despite Grundtvig's hoping "to have divided lines with a little better measure than the English Anglo-Saxonists have

based on a transcription instead of the original manuscript, however, *Phenix-Fuglen* deserves respect.

Like the text, the introduction contains fairly standard material. Grundtvig briefly examines how the Phoenix myth is treated by the Hebrews, Pliny, Tacitus, Herodotus, Hesiod, Ovid, Claudian, Artemidorus, and in the poem attributed to Lactantius, which he claims offers us the most complete treatment of the myth.[29] But permeating that standard scholarly survey and following it comes Grundtvigian polemic about the nature and importance of figurative language and its resurrection in the nineteenth century. That seemingly extraneous, topical matter offers us the key to the entire book as both valuable cultural artifact and aesthetic unity. As Grundtvig sagely observed in his introduction to *Nordens Mytologi* in 1832, "poetry will have to become scholarly for scholarship to become poetic."[30]

Grundtvig's circuitous, associative argument basically turns on two central and inter-related concepts: the biblical and Augustinian notion that derives from 2 Corinthians 3:6 of the supremacy of a text's spirit to its literal expression ("the letter killeth, but the spirit giveth life"); and the idea of the history of the individual, of the nation, of the world, and of the race being contracted into the Phoenix myth. Figurative language or the spirit, Grundtvig believes, had sunk into oblivion during the Middle Ages and remained there since the Reformation in 1536 because of the strictures of what he terms "the Latin School."[31] Protestantism "in its one-sidedness became the denial of the spirit,"[32] the affirmation of the letter, and it is only in the present century, "which will easily win the name of 'the resurrection from the dead,'" that a period of renewal for figurative language has arisen.[33] Grundtvig's century is "a lovely period of transition, transition namely from the yard of the worm to the bird's nest, or from the slough of the worm to the bird's wing, from the spirit destroying ABC to the spirit illuminating figurative language, or from the dead letter to the living word."[34]

---

yet managed" ("at have afdeelt Linierne med lidt bedre Takt end de Engelske Angelsachser endnu har erhvervet sig," p. 14).

[29] *Phenix-Fuglen*, pp. 15–17.
[30] "Poesin maa blive videnskabelig, for at Vidskaben kan blive poetisk." Quoted in Haarder, *Beowulf*, p. 61.
[31] "Latinskolen," *Phenix-Fuglen*, p. 15.
[32] "i sin Eensidighed blev Aands-Fornægtelse." Ibid., p. 21.
[33] "der sagtens vil vinde Navn af 'Opstandelsens fra de Döde'." Ibid., p. 15.
[34] "en deilig Overgangs-Tid, paa Overgangen nemlig fra Orme-Gaarden til Fugle-Buret, eller fra Orme-Hammen til Fugle-Vingen, fra den aandsfortærende ABC til det aandsoplysende Billed-Sprog, eller fra den döde Bogstav-Skrift til det levende Ord." Ibid., p. 20.

The period we are in transition from Grundtvig calls the "bookworm period"[35] or period of excessive adherence to the letter, and the "bookworm creature"[36] has held sway in it for 300 years. The creature, which he also calls the spirit-devouring, spirit-destroying "Latin letter creature," stood "in hostile opposition to both Bible, Spirit and Mother Tongue."[37] Scholars schooled in that period and subject to that creature, therefore, insisted on interpreting the Hebrew word *kol*, which can mean either "Phoenix" or "sand" in Job 29:18 and Psalms 103:5, not as the former but as the latter because of "the spiritlessness whereby they regarded the figurative language of antiquity." Even if they were compelled to admit the presence of the bird in scripture, they would still try to offer a rational interpretation of its constant rebirth, which would only mean "that it changed plumage like other birds"[38] or nothing more "than a certain period of revolution of the planets." These "dwarves under the Parnassus" continue in the present day, amusing themselves "with making up riddles and dark speeches about present, obvious, and crystal-clear things while all the major poets strive in figurative language to give us a living conception of the invisible and distant." To the dwarves, "the eternal truths of the almanac are both much more important and more poetic than the whole of human life with all its vagaries, its entrance and exit, longing and hope."[39]

But the Phoenix is more than a bird, and when it is liberated from the literal-minded, Grundtvig points out, we see its relevance to all facets of human existence. We see with the Egyptians that it symbolizes the immortality of the soul, with the Church Fathers that it offers us "a beautiful prototype both of the Lord's Resurrection and of ours," and with the OE poet that it is the human spirit itself.[40] We also see that the bookworm period, lamentable though it may seem, was necessary. During it the

---

[35] "Bogorme-Tid." Ibid., p. 22.
[36] "Bogorme-Væsen." Ibid., p. 20.
[37] "Latinske Bogstav-Væsen, der stod i fiendtlig Modsætning baade til Bibel, Aand og Modersmaal." Ibid., p. 21.
[38] "den Aandlöshed, hvormed man betragtede Oldtidens Billed-Sprog ... at han skiftede Fier som andre Fugle." Ibid., p. 16.
[39] "end en vis Omlöbs-Tid af Planeterne ... Dværgene under Parnasset ... med at lave Gaader og mörke Taler af nærværende, öiensynlige og soleklare Ting, medens alle Hoved-Skjaldene stræbe i Billed-Sprog at give os en levende Forestilling om det Usynlige og Fraværende ... Almanakkens evige Sandheder er baade langt vigtigere og mere poetiske end hele Menneske-Livet med alle dets Omskiftelser, dets Indgang og Udgang, Længsel og Haab." Ibid., p. 18.
[40] "et deiligt Forbillede baade paa Herrens Opstandelse og paa vores." Ibid., pp. 18–19. Bradley points out in "'Stridige Stykker snild jeg forbandt'" that here Grundtvig defines himself "as heir to the Fathers and the Christian Anglo-Saxon poets," p. 99.

Phoenix worm developed out of the ashes of its father before being reborn as the Phoenix once more. Grundtvig explains the process thus:

> The phoenix myth would always illustrate the great course even if the spirit of man, because of his sins, should be found too weak for completing it. The paradise bird, one might say, surveyed its wondrous course and prophesied truly about it but after its decline could only show the way, not follow it; but where one around the New Year has come far enough to see this and speak sensibly about it, the rebirth and resurrection must have taken place to a certain degree after all, *philology may have developed into pneumatology* [my emphasis], hair-splitting risen to presence of mind; for just as little as the worm knows the bird's way, so little can the mere bookworm talk sensibly about the course of the spirit ...[41]

Grundtvig explains, furthermore, that if the Phoenix, king of the songbirds, is the natural symbol of the spirit, the history of the Phoenix is an image of the history of the human spirit as reflected in both the individual and the race, in both Denmark and the whole world.[42] Only three conditions are required for that history to reach fruition: "the memory of a lost glory and the longing for its renewal ... deep respect for the Bible as the holy inheritance of the great spirit, and ... love of the mother tongue as the only living tool for the spirit."[43] In Denmark in 1840, all these conditions coalesced, particularly in King Christian VIII and N. F. S. Grundtvig.

With the basic principles in mind from Grundtvig's introduction, we return now to the first page of *Phenix-Fuglen* to begin seeing how Grundtvig uses the Phoenix myth's identification with universal history as the structural basis for his book and how he simultaneously transmutes philology into pneumatology.

---

[41] "saa altid vilde Phenix-Mythen afbilde den store Löbebane, om end Menneske-Aanden, for sine Synders Skyld, skulde findes for svag til at fuldende den. Paradis-Fuglen, maatte man da sige, overskuede sin vidunderlige Bane, og spaaede sandt om den, men kunde efter sit Fald kun vise Retningen, ei fölge den; men hvor man i Nyaarstiden er kommet saavidt at see det og tale forstandig derom, der maa Gienfödelsen og Opstandelsen dog alt i en vis Grad have fundet Sted, maa Philologien have udviklet sig til Pneumatologi, Ordklöveriet hævet sig til Aandsfatning; thi ligesaalidt som Ormen kiender Fuglens Vei, ligesaalidt kan den blotte Bogorm tale forstandig om Aandens Bane." *Phenix-Fuglen*, p. 20.

[42] Ibid., pp. 19, 22.

[43] "Mindet af en forsvundet Herlighed og Længsel efter fornyelse deraf ... dybe Ærbödighed for Bibelen, som den store Aands hellige Efterladenskab ... Kiærligheden til Modersmaalet, som det eneste levende Redskab for Aanden." Ibid., p. 21.

The dedication reads simply, "To His Danish Majesty, Heir of the Scyldings, King Christian VIII, as a portent of good fortune is dedicated in his coronation year the lay of *The Phoenix*."[44] Two of Grundtvig's primary concerns reside in this simple declaration. First, in his public offering of his scholarship and art to the most public of all figures, Grundtvig affirms the national and historical importance of both. Second, in his allusion to the Scylding dynasty, he affirms the continuity of Danish national history from Dan, the eponymous founder of Denmark mentioned by Saxo Grammaticus in book 1 of *Gesta Danorum*, to Dan's grandson Scyld, the eponymous founder of the Scyldings mentioned in the prologue to *Beowulf*, to Christian VIII, the new Danish king. Grundtvig reinforces this notion in the dedicatory poem and amplifies it in the preface to the book and the "echo" poem when he refers to *The Phoenix* as "Angul's ancient lay."[45] "The Danes trace their beginnings from Dan and Angul,"[46] Saxo informs us, the latter also being the first ruler of the Angles, and so Danish and English history meaningfully coalesce in the OE language and in the poem.

From the broad, public, and relatively uncomplicated perspective of the dedication, we move to the dedicatory poem, likewise broadly public in perspective but specifically incorporating both Grundtvig himself and his art, and that art is considerable. Grundtvig is regarded as one of Denmark's greatest poets, perhaps the greatest,[47] and he lavishes great care on this 17-stanza poem. Each stanza consists of six lines rhyming ababcc, lines 1, 3, 5, and 6 containing ten syllables each, lines 2 and 4, nine. The poem's initial two stanzas form a paradigm of Danish and universal history, of royal death and rebirth, of anguished silence transformed to joyous song, that the rest of the poem fleshes out. They read:

---

[44] "Den Danske Majestæt / Skjoldungers Arving / Kong Christian den Ottende / tilegnes / som / Lykke-Varsel / i / Kronings-Aaret / Phenix-Kvadet."

[45] "Anguls Oldkvad," "Anguls-Kvadet," *Phenix-Fuglen*, pp. 9, 64. Grundtvig also uses Angul in the title of his second, revised edition of his translation of *Beowulf* in 1865. The first edition in 1820 was titled *Bjowulfs Drape. Et Gothisk Helte-Digt fra forrige Aartusinde af Angelsaxisk paa Danske Rim* (The Heroic Poem of Beowulf: A Gothic Heroic Poem from the Previous Millennium in Danish verse from the Anglo-Saxon). The 1865 title, *Bjovulvs-Drapen, et høinordisk Heltedigt, fra Anguls-Tungen fordansket* (The Heroic Poem of Beowulf: A High Nordic Heroic Poem translated into Danish from Angul's Tongue), more clearly brings the poem into the provenance of Denmark and Danish prehistory. On Grundtvig's tendentious use of titles, see chapter 1.

[46] *Saxo Grammaticus: The History of the Danes, Books I–IX*, ed. Hilda Ellis Davidson, trans. Peter Fisher (Bury St. Edmunds, 1979), p. 14.

[47] Borum, *Danish Literature*, pp. 34–37, and *Digteren Grundtvig*, p. 9.

Kongen döde under Vinters Hjerte,
Med Naturen bar vi alle sorg,
Dyb var altid Dannekvindens Smerte,
Som i Hytten , saa paa Kongeborg,
Og paa Jorden findes ei de Helte,
Som ved Hjerte-Sorg jo maae hensmelte.

Kongen lever ved Midsommers-Tide,
Med Naturen smile vi paany,
Danske Aasyn er som Bögens blide,
Let sig klarer deres Pandesky;
Og naar Frygt ei Munden paa os binder,
Glædens Bæk i Frydesang udrinder.

The king died beneath the heart of winter,
with Nature bore we all our sorrow,
deep always the pain of the Danish woman,
alike in cottage as in castle royal,
and on earth is not found those heroes
who with their heartache would not have to melt away.

The king lives in the midsummer time,
with Nature smile we once again,
the Danish countenances are like the beech's mild,
their furrowed brows quickly clear;
and when dread our mouth no longer binds,
the brook of delight flows forth in joyful song.

Stanzas 3 through 7 move us through Danish history, from the unnamed but paronomastically present Scyld Scefing in the distant past to the new king, standing "with the Scylding crown on,"[48] in the present (stanza 3). Scyld, the nameless "spirit [that] died," the "child-angel" with "wings wide as the shield of the land of Dan," was borne out to sea, but "the spirit's death on earth ... is just a torpid state" (stanza 4).[49] The spirit hovers above the crown, "popular song in child-like tones sweet" (stanza 5)[50]; it alone can create life, for "the power of life," in an obvious pun on *spiritus*, "is in breathing" (stanza 6).[51] Only the word is the spirit's equal,

---

[48] "med Skjoldung-Kronen paa." *Phenix-Fuglen*, p. 5.
[49] "Aanden döde ... Barne-Englen ... Vingebreed som Dane-Markens Skjold ... Aanders Dͺd paa Jord er dog kun Dvale." Ibid., p. 6.
[50] "Folkesang i Barne-Tone söd." Ibid.
[51] "Livskraften er i Aandedrættet." Ibid.

sharing with it "all his achievement and praise, / as a queen shares the honor of the king" (stanza 7).[52]

Stanza 8 brings Christian VIII, the spirit, and Scyld Scefing together as Grundtvig expresses his wish that "the spirit will rule freely in your kingdom" where false spirits will never defeat "Denmark's child-angel,"[53] where the king's "true queen, the mother tongue, / who has been enslaved now for 300 years," will shine once more (stanza 9).[54] Christian VIII is Denmark's hope (stanza 10), and Grundtvig's hope for Denmark's good fortune "bloomed in the shadow of death, / enthroned in my bosom like a king" (stanza 11).[55] Grundtvig used to sing of Balder but now "clearly intones of a Phoenix-age" (stanza 12)[56] that was not entirely fulfilled during Frederik VI's reign (stanza 13).

In stanzas 14 through 16, Christian VIII and Grundtvig seem significantly to merge. The child-angel who was Scyld Scefing in stanza 4 and reincarnated as Christian VIII in stanza 8 matures as "the angel in Denmark," who can be either Christian VIII or Grundtvig and scald-like sings (stanza 14),[57] then "Denmark's angel," who as a truthful spirit becomes yet more truthful (stanza 15),[58] and finally "Denmark's angel" once more, enjoined to "embrace tenderly our mother tongue, his bride" (stanza 16).[59] In the concluding stanza, the ambiguity of these stanzas resolves itself into a clear, unequivocal paean to the king, who has become one with Denmark's spirit, language, and song (and, perhaps, with Grundtvig):

> Hil Dig da, Kong Christian! med Din Krone,
> Med Dit Folk og med Dit Time-Glar!
> Danmarks Aand! sid herlig paa Din Throne!
> Modersmaal! giör Loven mild og klar!
> Folkesang! udbryd fra alle Munde!
> Overstem alt Gny og Glam i Lunde!

> Hail to you, King Christian! With your crown,
> with your people, and with your hourglass!
> Denmark's Spirit! Sit grand upon your throne!

---

[52] "al hans Daad og Priis, / Som en Dronning deler Kongens Ære." Ibid.
[53] "I sit Rige Aanden herske frit! ... Danmarks Barne-Engel." Ibid.
[54] "ægte Dronning, Modersmaalet, / Som har trællet nu trehundred Aar." Ibid., p. 7.
[55] "blomstred selv i Dödens Skygge, / Throned mig i Barmen som en Drot." Ibid.
[56] "Toner klart nu om en Phenix-Alder." Ibid.
[57] "Engelen i Danevange." Ibid., p. 8.
[58] "Danmarks Engel." Ibid., p. 8.
[59] "Favne ömt vort Modersmaal, sin Brud!" Ibid., p. 8.

Mother tongue! Make the law mild and clear!
Folksong! Burst forth from every mouth!
Outvoice all din and baying in the groves!

Perspective narrows in the dedicatory poem even as it becomes more complex, and it narrows still more in the preface to *Phenix-Fuglen*. Here Grundtvig focuses almost exclusively on himself, the "genuine Kämpe [warrior] ... heaving up masses of historic labour with the energy of Thor," as two of his contemporaries phrase it,[60] and intoning "with barbaric eloquence about the beauty and unfortunate lot of Anglo-Saxon literature," as he himself does.[61] To explain to his public his "seeming infidelity"[62] to OE studies over the past several years, Grundtvig recounts his journeys to England and their aftermath. When he ventured to London the first time in 1829 and made known his interest in OE literature, he was greeted with patronizing smiles and scholarly assurances "that what I raised to the skies as an Elf Queen was an old, wrinkled witch" deserving the scorn of "Hume, Warton, and other gentlemen of the finest classical education."[63] Grundtvig says that he retorted that the English were ignorant of what they had and were handing over "the historical and poetic Queen of the new Europe" to the Danes, who were "her weak but loyal knights."[64] When he returned to England the second time in 1830, he was taken more seriously, and the publishers Black, Young, and Young asked him to formulate his *Prospectus*. Sensing, therefore, that his initial abrasiveness had worked to good effect, he continued the strategy in trying to raise interest in (and subscriptions to) the project. Among other things, for instance, he declared, "If I were an English instead of a Danish poet and historian, I'd want to address my fatherland in the words of the 'immortal bard'":

And duller shouldst thou be than the fat weed
That rots itself in ease on Lethe wharf,
Wouldst thou not stir in this. [*Hamlet* I.v.33–35][65]

---

[60] Howitt, *The Literature and Romance of Northern Europe*, p. 152.
[61] "med barbarisk Veltalenhed over den Angel-Sachsiske Literaturs Skiönhed og ulykkelige Skiæbne." *Phenix-Fuglen*, p. 10.
[62] "tilsyneladende Utroskab." Ibid., pp. 9, 12.
[63] "at hvad jeg löftede til Skyerne som en Ælve-Dronning, var en gammel rynket Hex ... Hume, Warton, og andre Gentlemen af den fineste Classiske Dannelse." Ibid., p. 10.
[64] "det ny Europas Historiske og Poetiske Dronning ... svage men trofaste Riddere." Ibid.
[65] "'Dersom jeg var en Engelsk, istedenfor en Dansk, Digter og Historiker, da vilde jeg tiltale mit Fædreneland med den 'udödelige Sangers' Ord:

Such marketing ploys stir neither the dull nor the swift, however, so it came as a surprise only to Grundtvig that he was treated as a marauding Viking, not a liberating hero, when he sailed to England for the third time in 1831. "The publication of the important and valuable remains of the first new-European literature" had understandably become a matter of honor for England and could not possibly be handed over to a foreigner.

> As this was exactly what I had wanted from the beginning, I was not hard to console (although it was a little impertinent of a certain man [Benjamin Thorpe] to say that the publication of an Old English library was his profound idea that I had come upon by chance and wanted now to destroy him with by completing), and I have therefore sat by very patiently and watched how they have published one part after the other of the work that I had announced.[66]

After the appearance of Thorpe's edition of *Cædmon's Metrical Paraphrase of Parts of the Holy Scriptures* in 1832 and Kemble's of *Beowulf* in 1835, Grundtvig laments, "the English Anglo-Saxonists barely seem to know that I exist."[67] He consoles himself, however, in knowing that he was the first to transcribe *The Exeter Book* and that he is willing and able to produce an edition of *Beowulf* that will both save Denmark's honor from the shame of Thorkelin's edition and rescue the poem from the clutches of Caesar Lexicographicus and Caesarina Grammatica into which the English have thrust it.[68]

With the next two and central sections of the book, we reach the final narrowing of perspective in *Phenix-Fuglen*: scholarship nationalized and set in balanced contrast with the imagination in the introduction and

---

Dorskere er du end Urten, som raadner
Paa Fedme-Jords-Bredden af Lethe i Mag,
Vil du dig ei röre endnu'." Ibid., p. 11.
Grundtvig had been making such inflammatory statements for years. In "Om Bruneborg-Slaget," for example, we have seen him lambast the English for ignoring their ancient heritage and adumbrate his 1830 *Prospectus* by urging them to look seriously back to the language and spirit and texts of the Anglo-Saxons. See also Grell, *England og Grundtvig*, pp. 14, 17, 24.

[66] "Udgivelsen af de vigtige og dyrebare Levninger af den förste nyeuropæiske Literatur ... Da nu dette netop var, hvad jeg fra Begyndelsen havde önsket, blev jeg ikke vanskelig at tröste, (skiöndt det var lidt nærgaaende af en vis Mand at fortælle, at Udgivelsen af et Angelsachsisk Bibliothek var hans dybe Idee, som jeg tilfældigviis havde opsnappet og vilde nu ödelægge ham ved at udföre) og jeg har derfor siddet meget taalmodig og seet paa, hvordan man udgiver den ene Deel efter den anden af Værket, jeg bebudede," *Phenix-Fuglen*, pp. 11–12.
[67] "de Engelske Angelsachsere knap synes vide, jeg er til." Ibid., p. 12.
[68] Ibid., pp. 12–13.

then pure philology, unaffected by national, philosophical, aesthetic, or personal concerns, in the edited text. The text is the worm of the OE poem (and the book) created by the bookworm creature, Grundtvig, and from it rises his free Danish translation just as the OE poem seems to rise Phoenix-like from the ashes of the Latin original running directly beneath it. Grundtvig implies, in fact, the metaphorical transmutation of the Latin into the OE when he states in his introduction that on the Lactantian poem "the Anglo-Saxons built where we see the new Phoenix develop as a worm out of the old one's ashes."[69] And he creates a similar ambiguity that points to the identification of the OE text with the worm when he states that scholars of the day are "very angry about that worm, which here comes to daylight."[70] Grundtvig states earlier that the OE poem itself "steps forth here for the first time into the light of day" and "now comes to light."[71]

Grundtvig's translation of *The Phoenix* is even more complex and impressive than his dedicatory poem. It consists of 152 stanzas of nine lines each in feminine rhyme for a total of 1,368 lines, a mere fifteen lines longer than the 1,353 half-lines of the original. The rhyme scheme for each stanza is an intricate aabccbdde but, amazingly, no one stanza uses identical combinations of rhyming sounds to replicate the scheme. In the first three stanzas, for example, the pattern takes this shape: aabccbdde, ffghhgiij, and kklmmlnno. The a-rhyme ("-leden") is not used again until stanza 92 ("Eden") but is followed there by "Vei" for the b-rhyme instead of "Land"; the f-rhyme ("Luften") does not appear again until stanza 73 ("Luften") but is followed by "Öe" for the g-rhyme instead of "-elig"; and the k-rhyme ("Vinger") does not show up again until stanza 85 ("bringer") but is followed by "Ord" for the l-rhyme instead of "Port."[72] The very

---

[69] "byggede Angel-Sachsiske, hvor vi see den ny Phenix udvikle sig af den Gamles Aske som en Orm." Ibid., p. 17.
[70] "meget vrede paa den 'Orm,' som her kommer for Dagen." Ibid., p. 18.
[71] "træder her förste Gang for Lyset," "nu kommer for Lyset." Ibid., pp. 13, 15.
[72] The stanzas containing a rhyme in the a-line that is repeated as the a-line rhyme in other stanzas are as follows (with subsequent stanzas in parentheses): 31 Sangen (28), 39 Midte (14), 71 Hjörne (55), 72 Skove (4), 73 Luften (2), 74 side (21), 81 Sove-Kammer (23, 44, 49), 85 bringer (3), 102 brænder (46), 103 Tanker (41, 43, 63, 64), 108 svinde (33, 88), 110 grue (84), 112 Fromme (95, 109), 113 Fenix-Reden (1, 92), 114 opsvinger (3, 85), 116 Mange (67), 118 Öre (90), 120 Grave (86, 93), 121 Brystet (26), 122 Döde (25, 48, 98), 123 tilbage (9, 27, 53, 94, 117), 124 Fenix-Fuglen (19, 29), 126 Sjæle (104), 130 Glandsen (32), 136 Ære (59, 66, 80), 138 Sale (134), 144 Fenix-Livet (16, 60, 119), 145 bygger (125), 146 Helgen-Folket (6, 97), 147 fredes (42, 75, 77, 132, 141), 148 histoppe (7), and 150 Höie (105).

rhyme scheme thus seems to symbolize the Phoenix: it is ever changing but constantly the same.

The poetic form gives the translation its modern Danish plumage, the outward manifestation of the risen Phoenix. Inwardly, the bird remains essentially identical. Grundtvig keeps it so by retaining the core story of the poem with its narrative components in approximately the same order as the original, but he occasionally contracts material where the OE poet expands it and expands where the OE poet contracts. To describe the tree in which the Phoenix dwells, for instance, the OE poet uses eight half-lines:

þær he heanne beam	there the lofty tree
on holt-wuda	in the wood
wunað and weardað,	he occupies and inhabits,
wyrtum fæstne,	fast in its roots,
under heofum hrofe,	under the vault of heaven,
þone hatað men	that men on earth
fenix on foldan	call phoenix
of þæs fugles naman (339-346)	from the bird's name.

Grundtvig conveys the same sense in two lines in stanza 24: "I Palmens Krone / der er hans Throne" (in the palm's crown, there is his throne). In addition, by specifying the tree as a palm as Lactantius does, Grundtvig also deftly injects into his translation the dual meaning of the Greek word for Phoenix (Phoenix and palm) that is contained in the OE and that he briefly discusses in his introduction. When Grundtvig wants to emphasize a thought in the OE, on the other hand, he does so. The blessed and the angels praise God in twenty half-lines in the OE (1241–61), for example, but do so in twenty-seven lines in Grundtvig's translation (stanzas 136–38). And the concluding ninety-one half-lines of the original become 126 lines in the translation as Grundtvig magnifies his glorification of the Father.

The first two stanzas of Grundtvig's translation, juxtaposed to his edition of the original OE and my translations of both, amply exemplify his technique:

In eastern parts,
and far from here,
there is a land,
famous in songs,
not known by many
who can be found,
widely renowned
for warmth and
    mildness
and beauty.

Crystal clear is the air,
and sweet is the smell
inexpressible,
where fair from the sea

the island lifts itself
unequalled,
as the favored work,
as the monument
of the almighty's hand.

(1) I Österleden,
og langveis heden,
der er et Land,
berömt i Sange,
skiöndt ei af Mange
det findes kan,
navnkundigt vide
for Luun og Blide,

og Deilighed.

(2) Speilklar er Luften,
og söd er Duften,
usigelig,
hvor faur af Söen

sig hæver Öen,
ulignelig,
som Yndlings-Værket,
som Mindes-Mærket
af Almagts Haand.

I have heard
that far from here
in eastern parts is
the noblest of lands
known to men;
the region of earth
across the world isn't
accessible to many

of rulers,

but it is removed
by the Maker's might
from evil-doers.
Beautiful is all the
    plain,
joyfully blessed
with the sweetest
smells of earth;
unique is that island.

Hæbbe ic gefrungnen,
þæt te is feor heonan,
east-dælum in,
æðelest londa,
firum gefræge;
nis se foldan-sceat
ofer middan-geard
mongum gefere

folc-agendra,

ac he afyrred is
þurh Meotodes meaht
mán-fremmendum.
wlitig is se wong eall

wynnum geblissad,
mid þam fægristum
foldan stencum;
ænlic is þæt iglond.

In the book's penultimate section, the 59-stanza "Dansk Efterklang" (Danish echo), Grundtvig moves still further away from the worm of the original OE. He echoes his translation by employing its stanzaic pattern and by repeating its last stanza as the echo's last, but he also allows themes and motifs from the introduction and translation, as well as extra-textual reflections on Nordic myth, to reverberate throughout the entire text. The resulting structure is a fairly amorphous one, governed primarily, it seems, by association or by the echoes any one topic generates in Grundtvig's mind. The poem opens simply with birdsong:

Naar Dagen gryer,	When day breaks
i blanke Skyer	in the bright clouds
ved Sommers-Tid,	in the summertime,
af Fugle-Munde	from the mouths of birds
da fyldes Lunde	the groves are filled
med Kviddren blid,	with gentle chirping,
og Sange möde	and songs meet
hver Morgen-Röde	every dawn
i Tusindtal.	by the thousands.

After this initial stanza, however, Grundtvig offers five more that are only loosely attached to each other and touch on such matters as the rarefied nature of the Phoenix's song and the Danishness of the rider on Odin's horse. Then, with stanza 7, a semi-linear and familiar argument starts taking shape. Grundtvig mentions the OE *Phoenix* specifically as "Angul's lay," which, "on the vellum leaf," is only ashes from the Phoenix's pyre.[73] A new Phoenix has begun to rise from those ashes in Denmark and to fly on delicate wings across the Danish countryside, providing remedy for the spirit of the folk (stanzas 8–11). It is a Christian Phoenix, of course, and one dedicated to the old ways (the ship Skíðblaðnir that bore the life of the folk is rechristened "Humility" in stanza 14) and the mother tongue. She is immolated on the Phoenix's pyre in stanza 23 and replaced by "a robber's voice / only at home in the grave."[74] "Then the popular voice / sank fully into oblivion / in Denmark" as "everything in the North / completely famous / from sepulchral Latin / to hell torment / became quickly doomed."[75]

---

[73] "Anguls-Kvadet, / paa Kalvskinds-Bladet." *Phenix-Fuglen*, p. 64.
[74] "en Röver-Stemme, / i Grav kun hjemme." Ibid., p. 66.
[75] "Da Folke-Stemme / gik reent ad Glemme / i Danevang ... Alt i Norden / fuldvidt berömt, / af Grav-Latinen / til Helved-Pinen / blev rask fordömt." Ibid.

Grundtvig's Vision of the Old English Phoenix

We know what's coming now. The bookworm Grundtvig who appears in stanza 33 tries to drive the Roman blight from the land in stanzas 39 through 44:

dit Lys er Mörke,	your light is dark,
og Luft din Störke,	your substance, air,
og Lögn dit Liv.	falsehood is your life.
...	...
jeg dig nedmaner,	I exorcise you,
du Kirke-Raner,	you church stealer
ved Korsets Fod,	at the foot of the cross,
du Grav-Latiner,	you sepulchral Latinist,
du Præste-Piner,	you priest tormentor,
du Bogstav-Trold!	you letter troll!

Grundtvig concludes by trying to rouse his countrymen and women to affirm the Fatherland and the mother tongue and by extolling Denmark's manifest virtues, virtues very much akin to those of the island in the east where the Phoenix has its home. In Denmark, for instance, the lamb entrusts itself to the lion (stanza 52); disputes settle themselves over mead and wine (stanza 53); goodness exudes warmth, and evil, coldness (stanza 54). In Danish books, you can easily find what you seek, and in Danish women, fidelity has its safest home (stanza 55). The days of Scyld and Dan should return, then, "for the joys of life, / and peace-loving deeds," for "the mother of the beech tree," and for Christian VIII.[76]

As the reverberations from the "echo" subside in its climactic "Hallelujah," *Phenix-Fuglen* ends in its beginning in relative serenity. The concluding seven-stanza poem directed, as was the opening poem, to the newly crowned king is brief enough to quote in full along with my literal and inadequate translation of it. Both are followed by the music to which the poem was sung:[77]

Jeg gik mig ud en Sommerdag at höre
Fuglesang, som Hjertet kunde röre,
I de dybe Dale,
Mellem Nattergale,
Og de andre Fugle smaa, som tale.

---

[76] "for Livets Glæder, / og fredsæl Daad ... for Bögens Moder." Ibid., p. 70.
[77] The melody used here was first published in 1814 in Nyerup and Rahbek, *Udvalgte Danske Viser*, pp. lxxiv–v.

Der sad paa Kvist en lille Fugl i Lunden,
Södt den sang i Sommer-Morgenstunden,
I de grönne Sale,
Mellem Nattergale,
Sang saa klart, som Nogen kunde tale.

Paa Straale-Krandsen og paa Engle-Rösten
Kiendte jeg den sære Fugl fra Östen,
Paradisets Svale,
Som af Vinter-Dvale
Vaagned op til Sang i grönne Sale.

I Graadens Dal var Glædens Röst begravet,
Sangens Soel gik ned i Tone-Havet,
Löst var Styrkens Belte,
Blege alle Helte,
Hjertet maatte i et Suk hensmelte.

Dog leved op Höisangen efter Döden,
Tone-Havet födte Morgenröden,
Og i Sole-Glandsen,
Under Straale-Krandsen,
Let gik over Bölge Havfru-Dandsen.

Hilsæl, vor Drot! hilsæl i Danevangen!
Daglig her nu voxer Phenix-Sangen,
Fugl og Sang tillige,
Og alt som de stige,
Blomstrer med Dit Septer Danmarks Rige.

Omton da nu det Danske Konge-Sæde,
Fuglesang, som röre kan og glæde:
Phenix-Sang, oprunden
Sært i Böge-Lunden,
Morgenröde-Sang med Guld i Munden![78]

I went out one summer day to hear
Birdsong that could touch the heart,
In the deep valleys
Among the nightingales
And the other small birds that speak

There on a branch in the grove a little bird sat
Sweetly it sang in the summer morning,

---

[78] *Phenix-Fuglen*, pp. 70–71.

Grundtvig's Vision of the Old English Phoenix

In the green halls
Among the nightingales,
Sang as clearly as anyone could speak.

By its halo and angelic voice
I knew the singular bird from the East,
The swallow of Paradise
That from winter torpor
Awakened to song in green halls.

Buried in the valley of tears, the voice of happiness,
The song's sun set in the sea of sound,
Loosed was the belt of strength,
Pale all heroes went,
The heart had to melt away in a sigh.

But after death the solemn song revived,
The sea of sounds gave birth to the dawn,
And in the sunshine,
Under the halo,
Lightly the mermaid dance passed over the wave.

Hail, our king! Hail in Denmark!
Daily here now the Phoenix-song grows,
Bird and song alike,
And already as they rise,
Denmark's kingdom blossoms with your scepter.

Surround in sound now the royal seat,
Birdsong that can move and delight:
Phoenix-song, come
Singularly from the beech grove,
Dawn-song with gold in its mouth!

Example 5. 5. "Jeg gik mig ud."

An elegant simplicity graces this poem as the "little bird" in stanza 1 becomes the "swallow of Paradise" in stanza 3 then metamorphoses further in stanzas 4 and 5 from the "song's sun" to "solemn song," "dawn," and "mermaid dance." Simultaneously, the new and unnamed king is identified with bird, song, and dawn. In this lyric, the relatively separate elements in the dedicatory and echo poems – individual, king, Danish people, folksong, and Phoenix – are completely integrated in an utterance only partially topical, only partially tied to the historical context. The Phoenix has finally flown. Philology has become pneumatized.

With a lyrical flourish, *Phenix-Fuglen* ends as more than a mere edition of an OE poem and Grundtvig as more than a mere scholarly editor. He actually becomes the Phoenix in the course of the book, and the book becomes an embodiment of a coherent view of history and the place of the Angles and Saxons and the Danes in it even as it celebrates a new era of the spirit in Denmark. The edition's movement through eight parts, in fact, seems at least partially to symbolize Grundtvig's goal of incorporating the individual into "a greater community – linguistically into the community of the native language, nationally into the community of history, socially into the community of society, ecclesiastically into the community of the congregation and religiously into the community of evangelical Christianity."[79] The book also represents a rebirth of Grundtvig's own work in OE studies, although his interest had not waned over the years. After *Phenix-Fuglen*, he produced additional Phoenix poems from 1840 to 1853, as we have seen, a substantial essay on and brief discussion of *Beowulf* in 1841 and 1844 respectively,[80] his own long-desired, long-promised edition of the poem in 1861, and the second, improved edition of his translation of it in 1865.[81] To the end of his life, Grundtvig remained committed to OE studies. He died on 1 September 1872, but three days before his demise, he was still so keenly engaged in the field that he asked his friend Frederik Hammerich to read him John Earle's recent translation of "The Ruin."[82] Grundtvig knew the poem well, of course, and remarked to Hammerich that it brings to mind the whole of OE literature, itself "a truly splendid ruin." That was the last time Hammerich was to see Grundtvig "in this life."[83] To the end of his life as well, Grundtvig championed the mother tongue and his beloved Denmark, "where the

---

[79] Flemming Lundgreen-Nielsen, "Grundtvig and Romanticism" in Thodberg and Thyssen, *N. F. S. Grundtvig: Tradition and Renewal*, p. 41.
[80] "Bjovulfs Drape eller det Oldnordiske Heltedigt"; *Brage-Snak om Græske og Nordiske Myther og Oldsagn for Damer og Herrer*, pp. 322ff.
[81] *Beowulfes Beorh; Bjovulvs-Drapen.*
[82] Earle, "An Ancient Saxon Poem."
[83] "en rigtig stolt Ruin"; "i dette Liv." Johansen and Høirup, *Grundtvigs Erindringer og Erindringer om Grundtvig*, p. 263. For an English translation of Hammerich's

Figure 7. N. F. S. Grundtvig, 1872.

spirit always lives in the chamber of the heart and teaches the little elves to use their sweet voices for songs that are worthy of them."[84] *Phenix-Fuglen* is such a song.

Grundtvig's edition of *The Phoenix*, like much of his other work, did not, in its entirety, rise to prominence in OE studies either in Denmark or abroad. There was only one review (in German) of the edition, which focused primarily on the importance of the OE poem in the history of the Church,[85] and since then only editors of the OE poem appear to have referred to it with a couple of exceptions.[86] George Stephens based his 1844 metrical translation on Grundtvig's OE text, not on his translation, which

---

"Min sidste Samtale med Grundtvig" (My Last Conversation with Grundtvig), see Bradley, "'A Truly Proud Ruin'," pp. 161–62.

[84] "hvor Aanden altid boer i Hjerte-Kamret og lærer Smaa-Alferne at bruge deres söde Stemmer til Sang, som er dem værd." *Phenix-Fuglen*, p. 22.

[85] Rudelbach.

[86] Ludvig Ettmüller, C. W. M. Grein, Albert S. Cook, George Philip Krapp and

the bookwormish Stephens dismissed as "a very loose, meaningless, sentimental paraphrase,"[87] and Frederik Hammerich used Grundtvig's OE text as the basis for his 1873 Danish translation of lines 1–84.[88] Like Stephens, he did not use Grundtvig's rendering, which he considered "rewriting, free 'Danishing,' as [Grundtvig] himself phrases it, not translation; such a peculiar approach cannot be of service for anyone else. Of all the translations, for my part I have found Thorpe's the most useful."[89]

In the twentieth century, references to Grundtvig's edition were even more sparse. Stener Grundtvig, for example, quoted from p. 10 of the preface to the edition in his 1920 introduction to Grundtvig's letters to his wife during his trips to England,[90] and Steen Johansen and Henning Høirup in 1948 quoted pp. 10–12 of the preface in their *Grundtvigs Erindringer og Erindringer om Grundtvig*.[91] Grundtvig's two other major OE projects before his death – his 1861 edition of *Beowulf* and his 1865 revised translation of it – suffered a similar fate. The former is referred to almost entirely for its presentation of the OE text of the poem, and the latter has been virtually ignored and denigrated. On reading the first part of that translation published in 1815, for instance, Thorkelin cried out,

---

Elliott Van Kirk Dobbie, Norman F. Blake, and Bernard J. Muir all refer to Grundtvig's edition either to accept or reject some of his suggested readings.

[87] Stephens, "The King of the Birds," p. 257.
[88] Hammerich, *De episke-kristelige Oldkvad*, pp. 75–78.
[89] "omdigtning, fri fordanskning, som han selv kalder det, ingen oversættelse; en så egendommelig natur kan ikke gjøre tjæneste som våbenbærer for en anden. Af alle oversættelser har jeg for min del fundet Thorpes mest brugbar." Ibid., p. 8.
[90] Stener Grundtvig, *N. F. S. Grundtvigs Breve til hans Hustru under Englandsreiserne 1829–1831*, p. vii.
[91] pp. 73–75. See also R. W. Chambers, who mentions the importance of Grundtvig's edition in "Modern Study of the Poetry of the Exeter Book," p. 35; Borum, who assesses the edition's place in Grudtvig's poetic corpus in *Digteren Grundtvig*, pp. 83–85; Haarder, who mentions the edition in "Grundtvig and the Old Norse Cultural Heritage," p. 73; Pope, who notes the edition's existence in "The text of a damaged passage in the Exeter Book," p. 140; Schjørring, who examines the importance of the Phoenix myth in Grundtvig's work in "Om Fugl Fønix motivet," pp. 383–97; Bradley, who touches on various aspects of the edition in "'The First New-European Literature'," pp. 46–47, 50. "'Stridige Stykker snild jeg forbandt'," pp. 97–102, and "The Recovery of England's 'skrinlage fortid'," pp. 142–43; Chase, "True at Any Time," pp. 512–13, who points to two important statements about myth in the edition. In the late twentieth and early twenty-first centuries, Grundtvig's translation has been read with sympathy. John D. Niles, for example, observed that, in it, Grundtvig "let his own voice merge with that of the Anglo-Saxon poet so as to achieve a passionate nobility of expression that could have a transformative effect on his readers": *The Idea of Anglo-Saxon England*, p. 212. See also Jørgensen, "Reconstructing the Past and the Poet," and Zeruneith, *De siste tider*, p. 282, note 121, who merely notes that Grundtvig translated the poem into Danish in 1840.

"What a translation! What madness!"[92] While aesthetics in Scandinavian scholarship in OE studies remained an interest beyond the nineteenth century, it took a back seat to philology. Pneumatology, however, did not remain entirely behind with Grundtvig. It seems to have been carried on or reconstituted by one of the earliest twentieth-century Scandinavian scholars interested in OE subjects, Vilhelm Grønbech (1873–1948).

---

[92] Quoted in Bradley, "Det er vad jeg kalder," p. 37.

PART 2

THE FLOURISHING, 1900 TO 2023

4

Old English Studies in Twentieth- and Twenty-First-Century Scandinavia

Well over 80 percent of the work touching on Old English (OE) subjects and published in the Scandinavian languages appears in the twentieth and twenty-first centuries, and the variety of topics that work addresses is vast, making the choosing of a methodology for discussing it complicated. Creating a fluent historical account of developments in the field from 1900 to 2023 is one possible approach, but that presupposes a coherence and continuity in the history that does not quite exist. Another approach, the one adopted here, I borrow from Stanley B. Greenfield and Fred C. Robinson's *A Bibliography of Publications on Old English Literature to the End of 1972* (GR). The 6,550 items in that bibliography are arranged into three sections on general works on OE literature, OE poetry, and OE prose, with each section being broken down further into sub-categories. The following discussion is organized similarly, then by the rubrics supplied by GR, and then by country within those rubrics, which move from "Studies in Historical, Linguistic, and Cultural Subjects" to increasingly narrow topics until reaching the individual texts themselves. This chapter concerns OE literature generally, while chapters 5 and 6 below deal with Scandinavian approaches to and translations of *Beowulf* and chapter 7, with Scandinavian translations of OE literature other than *Beowulf*. A complete bibliography of contributions in the Scandinavian languages to OE studies is contained in appendices A and B of this book.

1. Studies in Historical, Linguistic, and Cultural Subjects (with a direct bearing on the Literature)

Denmark is the sole Scandinavian country in this category. We begin with Vilhelm Grønbech's spectacular four-volume *Vor Folkeæt i Oldtiden* (Our Peoples in Antiquity). It appeared in 1909–12 and was translated into English by William Worster as *The Culture of the Teutons* (1931) and into German by Ellen Hoffmeyer as *Kultur und Religion der Germanen* (1937–39). It is a substantial and important work by an important scholar who has been compared in intellectual impact to Grundtvig in the international community.¹ Although there is not a direct line of descent from the latter to the former, the two men shared some interesting characteristics. Grundtvig was, among other things, a preacher; Grønbech was, among other things, a professor of religion and church organist; Grundtvig was conversant with multiple ancient and modern languages and studied OE with the internationally known linguist Rasmus Rask; Grønbech was conversant with multiple ancient and modern languages and studied OE with the internationally known linguist Otto Jespersen (1860–1943);² Grundtvig was a celebrated poet; Grønbech was both a poet and novelist, though far less prolific and far less celebrated than Grundtvig;³ both Grundtvig and Grønbech believed in the power of myth;⁴ and, most importantly for our purposes, both thinkers believed in the importance of a scholar's immersing themselves in the culture they study. As we have seen, Grundtvig practiced dynamic equivalence in translating OE texts and even transformed himself into an OE poet to produce spiritually faithful, pneumatological translations into Danish of OE texts.⁵ Similarly, Grønbech in 1922 explained both his method of conducting research and the responsibility that a researcher has, which is "to live in the culture or the person he wants to describe until the unfamiliar thoughts spring forth from his own comprehensive understanding"⁶ as familiar ones in the present day.

Grønbech applies this method in his *The Culture of the Teutons*. The work is Grundtvigian in scope, dealing as it does with the language and literature of all the major Germanic peoples: Scandinavians, mainland Germans, and Anglo-Saxons to whose words and poetry – such as *Beowulf*, "The Rune Poem," and gnomic verse – he refers dozens of times throughout his study.⁷ By looking at single words such as "peace," "honor," "luck," and "soul," and what they meant in all their fullness in the original culture, Grønbech could explore larger subjects such as "Death and Immortality," "The Realm of the Unhappy Dead," "The Structure of the Clan," "Name and Inheritance," "Play and Vow," and "The Gods." Because of the anisomorphism of languages, the word "frith" (peace), or "freod" in OE, for example, embraces a range of meanings in the original languages not

---

1   Mitchell, "Vilhelm Grønbech, Synthesist," p. 318.
2   Hvidtfeldt, "Grønbech."
3   Mitchell, "Vilhelm Grønbech, Synthesist," pp. 319 and 321.
4   Ibid., p. 323.
5   Bjork, "Grundtvig the Old English *Scop*."
6   "Det er forskerens pligt at leve sig ind i den kultur eller det menneske han vil skildre, til de fremmede tanker springer frem af hans egen helhedsforståelse." Quoted in Hvidtfeldt, "Grønbech."
7   Grønbech, *The Culture of the Tuetons*: references to *Beowulf* throughout beginning at p. 35; "Rune Poem," p. 133; gnomic verse, p. 136.

embraced by comparable words in modern target languages into which it is translated. The "frith" that Hrothgar gives to Beowulf in line 1707a after Beowulf has killed Grendel and his mother brings affection and obligation along with it; the "frith" that a woman bestows, on the other hand, "glows with passion" for the Northmen.[8] On the reality of death, Grønbech observes that it is not much like our own, which embraces our own realities:

> We do not find, among our forefathers, any fear of the ending of life. They passed with a laugh of defiance through the inevitable, we are told; or they faced the thought of an earthly ending with a convinced indifference, plainly showing that they did not attach great importance to that event.[9]

Grønbech's concentrating on the psychology and spirit of the early Germanic peoples as revealed in their language and literature allowed him to open their world to us as had not been done before.[10] Worster's translating Grønbech's groundbreaking study into English allowed it to reach an international audience as it would not have otherwise.

Other historical and cultural studies in Danish on OE topics during the twentieth and twenty-first centuries have tended to be much more restricted in scope than Grønbech's. Four historians have focused on some aspect of the history of Denmark and used OE material to help substantiate their arguments. Possessed by a raging energy, driven by a violent temper, raised in a Grundtvigian and nationalistic home, and twice incarcerated by the Nazis for his work against them during the German occupation of Denmark during WWII,[11] the historian Vilhelm la Cour (1883–1974) traces the Danes back to 4000 BCE[12] in his contribution to volume one of *Det danske Folks Historie: Skrevet af danske Historikere* (The Danish People's History, written by Danish Historians, 1927 – note that titles continue to be important).[13] In doing so, he affirms the strong historical connection between Denmark and England because the Angles and Jutes came from what is now Denmark and the Saxons from an area contiguous with Denmark to the south. The Angles, for example, came from the region between Flensborg Fjord and Sli (or the southern part of Schleswig), as attested by OE documents from "Widsith" to Bede's

---

[8] Ibid., p. 35.
[9] Ibid., p. 190. For a great deal more on this concept, see Shippey, *Laughing Shall I Die*.
[10] Grønbech cites *Beowulf* from Holder, not Grundtvig, and the rest of OE poetry from Wülcker, *Bibliothek*.
[11] Kjersgaard, "Vilh. la Cour."
[12] "Vort Folks Oprindelse," p. 263.
[13] Ibid., especially pp. 276–327.

Ecclesiastical History,[14] and the Jutes came from Jutland to inhabit Kent, according once again to Bede. Hengest was among those Jutes.[15] La Cour does not promote a closer connection between the Danes and English, however, such as that supposedly affirmed by Saxo Grammaticus. Saxo begins his great history of the Danes, writes la Cour, by stating that the Danes trace their beginning back to Dan and Angul, sons of Humbli, who were both founders of and guides for the Danish people:

> It is said that the historical background for Saxo's account of the two brothers is Canute the Great's time, when Denmark and England were united under one ruler and when Danes and Angles (Englishmen) felt more closely connected to each other than to any other people. But this explanation does not touch on the most essential point. It is not England that Saxo is thinking of at all in the first place. "From one of them, Angul," he says, "the Angle people are descended according to legend; he named the landscape that he ruled after himself ... , and when his descendants later occupied Britain, they separated the island from its old name and gave it a new one instead, namely their own homeland." It is, therefore, the Schleswig Angel and nothing else that is associated with Angul's person, and although his descendants took dominion in England and transferred the name to it, it is nevertheless the fact that he and his brother are in effect the descendants of the Danes that has captured Saxo's attention.[16]

Such clear-sightedness typifies la Cour's scholarly work, and he uses it in his frequent judicious references to "Widsith"[17] and *Beowulf*[18] as well as his two references to "The Rune Poem"[19] and one to an Anglo-Saxon genealogy[20] to

---

[14] Ibid., pp. 276–77.
[15] Ibid., p. 305.
[16] "Det er sagt, at den historiske Baggrund for Sakses Beretning om de to Brødre er Knud den Stores Tid, da Danmark og England var forenet under een Hersker, og da Daner og Angler (Englændere) følte sig næmere knyttede til hinanden end til noget andet Folkeslag. Men denne Forklaring rammer ikke det væsentligste. Det er slet ikke England, Sakse i første Række tænker paa. 'Fra den ene af dem,' siger han, 'Angul, skal efter Sagnet Anglerfolket nedstamme; han gav det Landskap, han raadede, Navn efter sig selv ... , og da hans Efterkommere siden indtog Britannien, skilte de Øen ved dens gamle Navn og gav den et nyt i Stedet, nemlig deres eget Hjemlands.' Det er altsaa det slesvigske Angel og intet andet some forbindes med Anguls Person, og selv om hans Efterkomere tog Herredømmet i England og overførts Navnet dertil, er det dog den Kendsgerning, at han og Broderen staar som Danernes Ætmænd, der har fanget Sakses Sind." Ibid., p. 307.
[17] Ibid., pp. 276, 301–02, 311, 319, 321, and 323.
[18] Ibid., pp. 280, 311, 313ff., 323–27.
[19] Ibid., pp. 280 and 311.
[20] Ibid., p. 301.

bolster his meticulous account of the Danish people. His other contributions to OE studies center on *Beowulf* and its relationship to Denmark.[21]

Writing in the same 1927 volume on Danish history (written by Danish historians) as does la Cour is Johannes C. H. R. Steenstrup (1844–1935), Professor of History at the University of Copenhagen 1882–1917 and a Danish romantic nationalist specializing in medieval law. He was also interested in broad and untraditional topics such as women's history, the relationship between nature and culture, and historiography. His studies of Danish place-names and works on legal history were groundbreaking.[22] In the final section of his contribution to *The Danish People's History*, Steenstrup outlines the meaning for England of Danish settlement and governance, basing his view on numismatics (for the reigns of Harald I Harefoot and Hardicanute), placenames, "The Battle of Brunanburh," and the Norse influence on OE legal terminology.[23] Another historian affiliated with the University of Copenhagen (from 1947 to 1968) was Erik Kroman (1892–1982), who combined dialect studies and historical linguistics with the study of early Danish history, as in his 1976 book *Det Danske Rige i den Ældre Vikingetid* (The Danish Kingdom in the Earlier Viking Age). He focused in particular on his discussion of Danish settlements in England, where place-names tell such an intriguing story, as Steenstrup also saw.[24] But AS historical sources likewise tell an intriguing story for part of Danish history. Among others, these for Kroman include Bede's *Ecclesiastical History*, the *Annales Lindisfarnenses et Dunelmenses*, Asser's *Life of Alfred*, and *The Anglo-Saxon Chronicle*,[25] which has interested Scandinavian scholars ever since Jakob Langebek in 1772[26] and which Kroman finds particularly useful for Viking history, both in England and on the continent, where relevant historical sources are so scarce.[27]

Niels Lund (1939–), likewise affiliated with the University of Copenhagen as Emeritus Professor of Medieval History and likewise interested in the Vikings, published two books on the Viking connection between Denmark and England. In the first, *De danske vikinger i England:*

---

[21] "Lejrestudier," *DS* 17 (1920), 49–67; "Lejrestudier: Mindesmærkerne," *DS* 18 (1921), 147–66 ; "Lejrestudier: Navnet," *DS* 21 (1924), 13–22 ; and "Skjoldungefejden," *DS* 23 (1926), 147–56.

[22] Tiemroth, "Johannes Steenstrup."

[23] Steenstrup, "Harald Harefod," pp. 432–37.

[24] Kroman, *Det Danske Rige*, pp. 137–55.

[25] Ibid., pp. 36–41.

[26] Langebek, *Scriptores*, vol. 1, pp. 6–9. See also Steenstrup, *Normannerne*, especially vols. 2 (1878) and 3 (1882), and "Harald Harefod og Hardeknud 1035–42," pp. 363–66, 370–77, 414–37; Brynildsen, "Om tidsregningen i Olav den Helliges Historie," especially chapter 7, pp. 66–73 and 80; Jónsson, "Um Erík blóðöx"; and Schiern, "Om Navnet Lodbrog."

[27] Kroman, *Det Danske Rige*, p. 37.

Røvere og bønder (The Danish Vikings in England: Robbers and Farmers, 1967), Lund acknowledges that nationalism continues to play at least a small role in the study of the Viking period, even though it does not rise to the level of Romantic Nationalism that we have seen at work during the nineteenth century in Scandinavia. Because the Viking period, however, represents the only Great Power Period in Danish history, it is naturally regarded with some favor by Danes and other Scandinavians.[28] "Our cruel ancestors, the wild Vikings, had not been blessed for long in Valhalla," he writes, " – or in God's heaven, of course, since many of them were baptized – before they were held up as a model for later generations. The romantic idea of the Vikings that we still cultivate when given the chance arose very quickly."[29] Basing his argument on sources such as *The Anglo-Saxon Chronicle, Domesday Book, The Kalendar of Abbot Samson of Bury St. Edmunds*, and place-name studies, he de-romanticizes the Vikings, noting that much of their luster vanishes on closer examination. "They were hardly as wild, cruel, or all-conquering as we thought."[30]

In the twenty-first century, Brian Patrick McGuire (1946–) continued the trend of focusing on Denmark in his 2008 *Da Himmelen kom nærmere: Fortællinger om Danmarks kristning 700-1300* (When Heaven Came Closer: Stories of the Christianization of Denmark 700–1300), the second edition of which appeared a year later in 2009. McGuire, an American turned Dane whose mother was a high school teacher and whose father was publicity director for the San Francisco 49ers,[31] moved in 1970 to Denmark, which he has made his home ever since. He is currently Emeritus Professor of Medieval History at Roskilde University Center. In chapters 2 and 3 of his book, McGuire focuses on *Beowulf* to help us understand the Danes' transition from heathenism to Christianity and then elaborates by looking at the first AS missionary to Denmark, St. Willibrord (658–735). Without mentioning Kevin Kiernan's hypothesis that the date of composition of *Beowulf* is the same as the date of its sole manuscript from the early eleventh century,[32] McGuire advances a similar theory regarding the poem's late origins. Although heathen in content, the poem was written

---

[28] *De danske vikinger*, pp. 7–8.
[29] "Vore grumme forfædre, de vilde vikinger, havde ikke længe været salige i Valhal--eller i Guds himmel, menge af dem blev jo døbt--førend de blev hold op som forbillede for senere generationser. Den vikingeromantik, som vi stadig dyrker, når lejlighed gives, opstod meget hurtigt." Ibid., p. 7.
[30] "De var knap så vilde, grumme eller altbesejrende, som vi har troet." Ibid., p. 97. Lund furthers this thesis in his 1997 *De hærger og de brænder: Danmark og England i Vikingetiden* (They Ravage and They Burn: Denmark and England in the Viking Period).
[31] McGuire, *Min amerikanske Barndom*, p. 18.
[32] *Beowulf and the Beowulf Manuscript*.

by a Christian during the reign of Canute the Great (1014–35) when both England and Denmark were under one ruler, and it illustrates a heroic mentality moving from its heathen roots to its Christian flowering in Northern Europe.[33] Some Danes turning back to their old heathen gods for consolation after the depredations of Grendel is one instance of the transitional nature of the epic, as are the various assurances given that Beowulf's coming to the aid of the Danes is by the will of God, the Christian God being understood. Beowulf, therefore, becomes to some degree a Christ figure sent to save the Danish people.[34] He is so both in his fight against Grendel and that against Grendel's mother, especially when he emerges alive from the mere as Christ did alive from the tomb.[35] He is much less so in his fight against the dragon that finally kills him. Nevertheless, in the person of Beowulf we find a heathen hero showing the way toward a new and better and Christian world.[36]

2. OE Literature: Surveys, Critical Analyses

a. Denmark

The Danish study of OE literature in the twentieth century began with the publication in 1901 of *Illustreret Verdens-Litteraturhistorie* (The Illustrated History of World Literature), volume three. In an essay on "Oldengelsk Litteratur," Adolf Hansen (1850–1908) – distinguished historian of English literature[37] and translator into Danish of poets such as Shelley, Tennyson, Arnold, and Swinburne[38] as well as of *Beowulf*[39] – contextualizes OE literature within Danish and English history during the Migration Period, much as Fredrik Rönning had done in his 1885 Danish survey of OE poetry.[40] The Germanic tribes coming to the British Isles drove the Celts to the peripheries of the region and brought with them their native heathen literature and its traditions. But those traditions were eventually influenced by Celtic ones; Hansen's assertion of this premise is one of the first in the history of OE studies.[41] Hansen states that

---

[33] *Da Himmelen kom nærmere*, pp. 40–41.
[34] Ibid., pp. 42–44.
[35] Ibid., p. 47.
[36] Ibid., p. 52.
[37] Hansen, *Engelsk Litteraturhistorie*.
[38] Hansen, *Oversatte engelske Digte*.
[39] Hansen, *Bjovulf*.
[40] Rönning, "Den oldengelske digtning," pp. 1–2.
[41] Henry Morley seems to be the first, in 1873, in his *A First Sketch of English Literature*. For the most recent work on the topic, see Wright, *The Irish Tradition*, and Ireland, *The Gaelic Background*.

it is easy to see which of these two [peoples] had the best prospect of becoming the Conqueror. The ancient Bard of the Celts, Ossian, sang of his people: "They went out to battle, but they always fell." They were unfit to form the foundation of a great and victorious nation. But they were perfectly suited to contribute valuable spiritual elements of a fine and beautifying kind to such a nation.[42]

He further observes that "as time passed, in addition to the influence that gradually took place through the blending of the races, English literature in many different ways drew material and inspiration from Celtic sources."[43]

Hansen does not elaborate on the notion of Celtic influence on OE literature, but as he surveys the aesthetic characteristics of OE poetry, including the use of kennings, variation, and war and treasure and nature imagery, he does note that later English literature is grounded in OE and thus affirms a continuity in the history of English literature. OE poets' depictions of sea voyages, as seen in *Beowulf* and "The Seafarer," for instance, we hear echoed in Shakespeare's *Pericles* and *The Tempest* and in Dickens' *David Copperfield*, in Byron's "Childe Harold," and in "Swinburne in our day, when he puts the waves' own long rocking into the rhythms he writes about them."[44] There are therefore some distinct features of OE poetry "from which later English poetry rises as from a foundation of uncut granite."[45]

The most recent exploration of OE literature in Danish is by Keld Zeruneith (1941–), Emeritus Reader at the University of Copenhagen and member of the Royal Danish Academy of Sciences and Letters. Zeruneith is a poet, literary critic, historian, and prolific author, well known in Old Norse (ON) studies for his work on the sagas and in modern literary studies for his biographies of three famous Danish poets; he is equally well known in Classical Studies for *The Wooden Horse: The Liberation of the Western Mind, from Odysseus to Socrates* (2007; original Danish 2002), for which he won Denmark's most prestigious literary award, the Søren Gyldendal Prize, in

---

[42] "det er let at se, hvem af disse to der havde mest Udsigt til at blive Sejrherre. Kelternas gamle Oldtidsbarde Ossian sang om sit Folk: 'De drog ud til Kampen, men de faldt altid.' De vare lidet skikkede til at danne Grundvolden for en stor og sejrende Nation. Men de egnede sig ypperligt til at tilføre en saadan Nation værdifulde Aandselementer af fin og forskønnende Art." Hansen, "Oldengelsk Litteratur," p. 6.

[43] "Og alt som Tiden skred, har--foruden Paavirkning gennem Raceblandningen, som efterhanden fandt Sted--paa mange forskelige Maader engelsk Litteratur hentet Stof og Inspiration fra keltiske Kilder." Ibid., p. 6.

[44] "Swinburne i vore Dage, naar han lægger Bølgernes egen langlige Vuggen ind i de Rytmer, han skriver om dem." "Oldengelsk Litteratur," p. 13.

[45] "fra hvilken den senere engelske Digtning hæver sig som fra en Grundvold af utilhugget Granit." Ibid., p. 16.

Figure 8. Keld Zeruneith, 2019.

2004.[46] Zeruneith brings his considerable breadth of scholarly and linguistic expertise and depth of poetic and psychological insight and knowledge to bear upon OE studies in *De sidste tider: Hedenskab heroisme kristendom: en angelsaksisk overgangshistorie* (The Last Times: Paganism Heroism Christianity: An Anglo-Saxon Transitional History, 2017).

He begins his foray into OE literature with two simple but profound observations: 1) OE poetry is first and foremost a poetry of the soul,[47] and 2) created as it was during a time of upheaval, it says a great deal about problems we face today, such as existential angst, melancholy, and a feeling of alienated homelessness arising from the radical changes occurring in the world and in our value systems.[48] The poetry's power derives from its transitional nature, its syncretic amalgamation of Germanic verse form with Christian content. Both the person of Guthlac and the poems about him are emblematic of this syncretism. Guthlac, the Anglo-Saxon warrior, is transformed into St. Guthlac, the warrior of the Lord, and his Christian story is told in OE verse form, with all its alliterative resonance and heroic trappings, as the saint engages in single combat with the devil.[49] Zeruneith touches on a number of OE texts as he fleshes out his thesis, including "The Franks Casket," the poems of Cynewulf and

---

[46] Anon., "Keld Zeruneith."
[47] *De sidste Tider*, p. 15.
[48] Ibid., p. 16.
[49] Ibid., p. 27.

Cædmon, "Widsith," the elegies (especially "The Wanderer" and "The Seafarer"), the biblical paraphrases, and, most prominently, *Beowulf*, to which Zeruneith devotes about one third of his book (see chapter 5 below for his book-length development of his views on *Beowulf*). All in all, Zeruneith's study is a stimulating apology for OE poetry in the modern world, not just in Denmark.

b. Sweden

Although Sweden has not produced a survey of OE literature per se in the twentieth and twenty-first centuries, the work of one scholar, Ernst Kock (1864–1943), could be viewed as such a survey in the aggregate, albeit more of a textual-critical than a literary survey. Kock's biographer, Erik Rooth, describes Kock in his private life as a lovable, loyal, entertaining human being, a *homo ludens* and skilled sailor, who loved playing all kinds of games including cards and chess and billiards and who was also an accomplished musician, especially on the violin.[50] His playfulness occasionally impinged on his professional life as a Germanic philologist, as when he titled one of his works to fit the volume in which it was included. "Jubilee Jaunts and Jottings: 250 Contributions to the Interpretation and Prosody of Old West Teutonic Alliterative Poetry" formed part of a Festschrift volume of *Lunds Universitets Årsskrift* to celebrate the 250th anniversary – *Jubileum* – of the founding of Lund University, where he was Professor of German.

As a practitioner of descriptive syntax and textual criticism, however, Kock was deadly serious and is considered on a par with the notable Germanic philologists Eduard Sievers and Andreas Heusler in his remarkable ability to work across the old Germanic languages and in his finely tuned ear for Nordic verse and style.[51] With great precision and speed, he produced a wide range of publications on Old West Germanic alliterative poetry in which he considered the West Germanic languages as a unit and therefore found connections among the literatures that were previously unrecognized. The chief of these publications (which touch on various aspects of over forty OE poems) are "Jubilee Jaunt and Jottings" (1918), "Interpretations and Emendations of Early English Texts" (1904, 1918, 1919, 1920, 1921, 1922, 1923), *Fornjermansk forskning* (1922), "Plain Points and Puzzles, 60 Notes on OE Poetry" (1922), and "Notationes Norroenæ: Anteckningar till Edda och Skaldediktning" (1923). The last item, which contains 197 notes in which Kock frequently cites OE in his discussion of ON poetry, has had the most impact.

---

[50] Rooth, "Ernst Kock."
[51] Ibid.

3. OE Poetry: Studies of Themes and Topics

a. Denmark

With the first study of a major theme in OE literature in Denmark in the twentieth century, we again meet N. F. S. Grundtvig, this time through the person of Henry Vincent Christian Larsen (1860–1936). He was a rural dean and parish minister in the Roskilde diocese from 1907 to 1930, published several essays in Church and theological journals, was a poet and active in *Danmarks Provstforening* (Denmark's Union of Rural Deans), and loved his Church, his country, and his home. He died in his chair behind the podium in church while waiting to deliver a eulogy at his wife's funeral. A service for both her and him was held a few days later, presided over by his son.[52]

Larsen's love of country, of Christ, and of Grundtvig is made plain in his *Krist og Satan: nogle Blade af gammel kristelig Digtning særlig hos Angelsakserne (Cædmon)* (Christ and Satan: Some Remnants of Ancient Christian Poetry, Especially Among the Anglo-Saxons [Cædmon]), published in 1903. The eleven-chapter, 240-page book's frontispiece is a photo of Joakim Skovgaard's (1856–1933) "Kristus i de dødes rige," (Christ in the Realm of the Dead, 1891–94), which was inspired by Grundtvig's hymn 243 in his *Sang-Værk*, "I Kvæld blev der banket paa Helvedes Port," which itself is a paraphrase of lines 398–596 of the OE *Christ and Satan* on the Harrowing of Hell (see chapter 2 above). Larsen moves from Grundtvig's Danish hymn back to the original OE text itself along with works ascribed to Cædmon, such as "The Dream of the Rood." Before getting to those, Larsen rehearses how the concept of Christ's journey came to be, beginning with I Peter 3:18–4:6 and the apocryphal *Gospel of Nicodemus*, and then summarizes theological opinion on the concept, from Irenæus, Clement of Alexandria, and Tertullian to Martin Luther and Grundtvig.[53]

Grundtvig's hymn, which because of its power and beauty ("Kraft og Skønhed")[54] Larsen regards as the premier hymn in any language about Christ's descent into the underworld, is Grundtvig's best-known statement on the subject. Larsen devotes a chapter to examining it. For example, he identifies the herald in the first stanza as John the Baptist (34) and points out echoes from *Proverbs*, *Psalms*, *Völuspá*, and *Vafþrúðnismál* in the third as Christ makes his descent to deliver the message of salvation to the many children of Adam who died before His advent:[55]

---

[52] Nedergaard, *Dansk Præste og Sognhistorie*, p. 274.
[53] *Krist og Satan*, pp. 14–32.
[54] Ibid., p. 13.
[55] Ibid., pp. 34–35.

> He walks over fire-coals as light as a bird,
> With lizards and dragons He clashes;
> the viper he crushes, the Hell-wolf He binds,
> as downward the great chasm crashes.[56]

Eve appears in the hymn, acknowledges her culpability for committing the first sin, but is released from the bondage of Satan and death as a rainbow – the symbol of the pact between God and all living souls after the Flood – forms around her head. As she is embraced by the glory of God, the demons sink yet deeper into the abyss in stanza 17, and Christ and his new disciples rise to heaven. Christ's descent into hell is thus a blessed event for Christians because it shows Christ's conquering death, and it affirms salvation for all believers, even those who died before He was born.[57]

To some, Grundtvig's hymn could also be dangerous. Bjørnstjerne Bjørnson (1832–1910), the first Norwegian author to win the Nobel Prize in Literature (1903), is said to have become a Freethinker because of it and, for him, its indictment of the idea of eternal punishment.[58] Because of that indictment, in fact, the very concept of the Harrowing of Hell was controversial, especially in Norway,[59] so Larsen wanted to return to the OE poem to try to ascertain how it might have sounded to the original audience.[60] He begins by translating, recounting, and discussing great portions of *Genesis A* and *Genesis B* up to the birth of Cain and Abel and thereby Satan's battle against God in heaven and on earth as a prelude to his battle against Christ in the underworld. As he does so, Larsen notes how the OE poem reflects certain Anglo-Saxon cultural norms such as the *comitatus* in which God functions as the chieftain or king and His angels as his thanes.[61] He also adapts his own method of translation for a Scandinavian audience by employing the ON *fornyrðislag* meter, a loose, irregular version of which he claims Cædmon originally used.[62] And he points out similarities between the OE paraphrases of *Genesis* and Milton's *Paradise Lost*,[63] similarities arising from a blind Milton's having listened to those paraphrases with the help of his friend Francis Junius (1591–1677).[64]

---

[56] Broadbridge, *Living Wellsprings*, p. 95. Broadbridge offers a translation of the entire hymn on pp. 94–97.
[57] Larsen, *Krist og Satan*, pp. 36–40.
[58] Ibid., p. 41.
[59] Ibid., pp. 44–46.
[60] Ibid., p. 46.
[61] Ibid., p. 104.
[62] Ibid., p. 101.
[63] E.g., ibid., pp. 108, 110, 112, 113, and 130–34.
[64] Ibid., p. 134.

As for *Christ and Satan*, no other song, claims Larsen, was as beloved by the Anglo-Saxons as that work. It depicts Christ as a glorious, powerful hero who also treats Adam and Eve with mercy. The depiction of Eve, furthermore, indicates the Anglo-Saxons' noble view of women, a view "doubly natural, moreover, for a monk-poet who had found shelter and retreat, understanding and appreciation in Hilda's monastery."[65] Grundtvig's use of the OE poem demonstrates both what he had learned from the Anglo-Saxons and how he managed to create a coherent narrative out of the fragmentary work.[66] Cædmon follows Christ, the King of Victory,

> into the fortress of the strong, into the kingdom of death and the devil, and describes how the second Adam lays it waste, frees the prisoners of death, and leads them up with him – home to his Father's House with the multitude! Only then is Paradise actually regained for Adam and his family. Only then has the woman's seed crushed the serpent's head. Only then can the angels of heaven rejoice over the salvation of sinners.[67]

Larsen concludes his study by surveying a range of Old Germanic texts. From "The Dream of the Rood," which he argues was composed by Cædmon, the dreamer in the poem, and throughout which we hear echoes of the Balder myth,[68] to the OS *Heliand*[69] to Einarr Skúlason's *Geisli*[70] as well as the apocryphal *Gospel of Nicodemus*,[71] we see how ingrained and celebrated Christ's Harrowing of Hell is in the Western tradition lying behind Grundtvig's famous hymn.

The second and final study of a major theme in OE literature coming out of Denmark in the twentieth century is by Andreas Haarder (1934–2014), who was Professor of English Literature at Syddansk University in Odense (1975–88). Haarder is well known in *Beowulf* circles because of his important doctoral dissertation, *Beowulf: The Appeal of a Poem*, which he wrote in English at Aarhus University in 1975, and his and T. A. Shippey's essential *Beowulf: The Critical Heritage* (1998).

---

[65] "dobbelt naturlig for øvrigt for en Munke-Skjald, som havde fundet Ly og Læ, Forstaaelse og Paaskønnelse i Fru Hildes Kloster." Ibid., p. 143.
[66] Ibid., p. 152.
[67] "ind i den stærkes Fæstning, in i Dødens og Djævelens Rige og skildrer, hvordan den anden Adam lægger det øde, udfrier Dødens Fanger og fører dem op med sig--hjem til sin Faders Hus med Folkeskaren! Først da er egentlig Paradis genvundet for Adam og hans Æt. Først da har Kvindens Sæd knust Slangens Hoved. Først do kan Himlens Engle juble over Synderes Frelse." Ibid., p. 166.
[68] Ibid., p. 176.
[69] Ibid., pp. 188–89.
[70] Ibid., p. 193.
[71] Ibid., pp. 197–233.

Haarder's *Det episke liv. Et indblick i oldengelsk heltedigtning* (The Epic Life: A Glimpse into Old English Heroic Poetry, 1979; e-book 2022) consists of a foreword, five chapters, and an afterword and offers a look inside the heroic features of OE poetry as reflections of the same features in the lives of Anglo-Saxons. Where names in OE poems are also known in the Scandinavian tradition, Haarder uses the Scandinavian version – for example, Skjold for Scyld[72] – a strategy that subtly emphasizes the connections between the OE and Scandinavian traditions. Haarder also stresses the connections between the OE tradition and modernity. In the first chapter on existing and lost OE verse, he emphasizes the oral nature of the poetry preserved in four codices[73] and the close contact that poetry has with Germanic prehistory.[74] Lost OE verse, attested to by such things as the *Finnsburg* and *Waldere* fragments[75] and the William of Malmesbury story about Aldhelm's performing OE verse as a professional skald on a bridge over the river Avon to attract passersby to Christ, likewise affirm the orality of the poetry.[76] The bond between the performer and listener gives rise to a "narrative situation" (*fortællesituation*) that occurs frequently outside and inside literature. In *The Canterbury Tales*, *A Thousand and One Nights*, and *The Decameron*, for example, it constitutes part of the fiction itself. In the short stories we are familiar with

> from Steen Steensen Blicher or Thomas Hardy, the narrator is an integral part. In Joseph Conrad's masterpiece "Youth [: A Narrative]" (1902) we find a very clear indication of the narrative situation; it is there first and last and always: the storyteller, Marlow, sits in the midst of representatives from the world left behind and spins his yarn about the hero Marlow.[77]

Similarly, the OE oral poem lives in and is conditioned by the interplay between the skald and everyone around him, from the original AS audience to the present one: "It is not least in this fact that it appeals to us today."[78]

---

[72] *Det episke liv*, p. 7.
[73] Ibid., pp. 9–16.
[74] Ibid., p. 14.
[75] Ibid., pp. 14, 17.
[76] Ibid., p. 17.
[77] "fra Steen Steensen Blicher eller Thomas Hardy, er fortælleren et integreret led. I Joseph Conrads mesterfortælling Ungdom (1902) finder vi en meget tydelig markering af fortællesituationen; den er der først og sidst og hele tiden: historiefortælleren Marlow sidder midt i en kreds af repræsentater fra verden bagved og spinder sin ende om helten Marlow." Ibid., pp. 21–22.
[78] Ibid., p. 22.

The book's second chapter on "The Poetic Tradition" again emphasizes the connection between the skald and audience. The central position of the skald in Anglo-Saxon society is affirmed both outside and inside the poetry. The story of Cædmon in Bede's *Ecclesiastical History* and of Aldhelm in William of Malmesbury are good examples of the former; "Widsith," "Deor," and parts of "The Fates of Men" are good examples of the latter.[79] And the poetry itself – song and music – in "The Fates of Men," lines 165–71) is regarded as relief for the longing and loneliness experienced by every human being.[80] In Anglo-Saxon society, that relief was delivered orally inside the mead hall to a listening audience.[81] How well that oral poetry is conveyed in the written form handed down to us is a matter of debate.[82] Examining the technical features of the verse from the half-line to meter, variation, repetition, and kennings (which link the OE tradition to the Nordic (pp. 27–30) helps move us toward an answer to the question. In the skald's use of variation, repetition, and refrain, we see a clear connection with song and dance, and the variation and repetition principle "is not just a stylistic phenomenon. It is functional. It is integrated into what transpires between poet and audience. In other words, we are on our way from text to skald."[83] Oral-formulaic theory derived from studies of Homer, large sections of the Bible, the *Poetic Edda*, *The Song of Roland*, *The Nibelungenlied*, *Beowulf*, and Yugoslavian song charts that movement.[84] All these works, as Grundtvig pointed out about *The Iliad* in 1832, were heard before they were read. In all of them, the word was and remains "the living word" (*det levende ord*).[85]

The living word that is *Beowulf*, "An Old English Heroic Poem" (*Et old-engelsk heltedigt*), is the subject of the book's third chapter. Haarder relates standard details about the poem's discovery and the scholarly attention it has received since,[86] as well as its importance in the Danish university system for teaching OE in Denmark, an importance arising from the influence of Grundtvig, "whose lifelong enthusiasm for the poem came in a thrilling way to characterize a particularly Danish, popular 'Beowulf' tradition."[87] The poem is used and venerated in the Danish folk high school, for example, for teaching Danish myth for the spiritual edification

---

[79] Ibid., p. 23.
[80] Ibid., p. 24.
[81] Ibid., p. 25.
[82] Ibid., p. 26.
[83] Ibid., p. 33.
[84] Ibid., p. 41.
[85] Ibid., p. 42.
[86] Ibid., pp. 43–44.
[87] "hvis livslange begejstring for digtet på en spændende måde kom til at præge en særlig dansk, folkelig 'Bjovulf'-tradition." Ibid., p. 45.

of its students. The high school stresses Grundtvig's belief that only those words that pass from mouth to mouth in saga and song sustain the life of the people. *Beowulf* does just that.[88] It fulfilled and still fulfills a basic human need for fantasy,[89] and Haarder offers an interpretation of the poem based on the premise that it should be experienced anew in the period in which it is read.[90]

The epic begins with the story of Skjold, familiar to Danes from Grundtvig's 1834 poem "Skjold," and from the 1925 poem "Stæren" (The Starling) by Johannes V. Jensen (1873–1950), the recipient of the 1944 Nobel Prize in Literature. In both poems, and in *Beowulf*, a festive mood and the coming of spring are associated with the arrival and later departure of Skjold.[91] Haarder stresses the importance of the hall, gift giving, the peace weaver, and the skjald or word weaver in Anglo-Saxon society when it is at peace. When it is not, as when the Gendel kin attacks Heorot, those vital social functions cease.[92] They are restored again after Beowulf has slain Grendel and his mother, and the social order remains intact and in harmony inside the hall as he departs.[93] Fifty years later, when Beowulf himself becomes the king ruling inside a great hall, a monster arrives again, this time a dragon spewing fire and death, and suddenly Beowulf's glorious hall burns to ashes. For the third time, and this time as an old man, Beowulf must prove his worth. Sadness and an increasing resignation to the transience of life permeate the last part of the poem,[94] and it is in Beowulf's confrontation with the dragon that the meaning of the battles with monsters becomes clear. If we are not vigilant, we humans can become part of the monster world; we can become wolves. The figures of Unferth and Heremod and Thryth all illustrate the point. A man who kills his brother, as Cain did Abel, is condemned to a life of monstrosity; a king who keeps his gifts to himself is not king in his monstrosity; and a queen who violates the rules of reciprocity is a monstrous parody of a true queen.[95] "The monster is, therefore, not just the threat from without. You bolt your door against it, but it's already there behind you."[96]

We find our meaning in confronting the monstrous; we define our place in an otherwise meaningless world by facing the threat that is the

---

[88] Ibid., pp. 45–46.
[89] Ibid., p. 46.
[90] Ibid., p. 47.
[91] Ibid., pp. 47–48.
[92] Ibid., pp. 49–51.
[93] Ibid., pp. 52–53.
[94] Ibid., pp. 53–54.
[95] Ibid., p. 56.
[96] "Uhyret er altså ikke alene trusselen om angreb udefra. Man bolter sin dør imod det, og så står det der allerede bag ens ryg." Ibid., p. 56.

meaninglessness, the confusion, the chaos. No human being can avoid this condition. You can kill the threat by giving in to a Hitler or Stalin or a rigid ideology, but you dehumanize yourself at the same time. Or you can face what threatens you in the hour of the wolf before dawn when you wake up helplessly alone in a world that has lost all proportion, as Marianne does toward the end of Ingmar Bergman's television series *Scenes from a Marriage* (1973).[97] Hamlet, too, has to take action so that everything could make sense again, and Christ faces the demon of doubt and hesitancy in the Garden of Gethsemane before his crucifixion. *Beowulf*, then, largely concerns the nightmare situation that we all find ourselves in. It is epic, and it is

> a narrative poem in which everyone is involved. Its very first words: "Listen, We have heard –" is the skald's confirmation of this; now we have to hear more … It is also dramatic in the sense that action is what it depends on, and action is what it carries forth. The ship "Judea" in Conrad's *Youth*, which takes the young Marlow towards the promised land, bears the motto: "Do or Die." *Beowulf* is about action, and perhaps the emphasis on the motto to do or die is stronger here than in any other work of human existence.
>
> To act, to win life from the world in confusion, is the same as affirming the community of the hall. Or, if you turn the formula round, it is the community of the hall, which the poem so strongly and unequivocally points to, that gives life meaning; but it must be won from evil, won again and again.
>
> That's just how it is, says the skald.[98]

In the fourth chapter, Haarder deals with the meeting of the native Germanic and Latin Christian traditions in the OE elegies, a meeting graphically illustrated by "The Franks Casket," where one panel depicting the Adoration of the Magi is juxtaposed to another depicting the revenge

---

[97] Ibid., p. 60.
[98] "fortællende digt, som alle er med i. Dets allerførste ord: 'Lyt, Vi har hørt – ' er skjaldens bekræftelse herpå; nu skal vi høre videre… Det er også dramatisk I den forstand, at handling er hvad det hviler på, og handling er hvad det bærer frem. Skibet""Judæ"" i Conrads *Ungdom*, som fører den unge Marlow mod det forjættede land, har som indskrift mottoet: 'Do or Die'. *Beowulf* drejer sig omhandling, og måske er understregningen af mottoet at handle eller dø stærkere her end i noget andet værk om menneskelig eksistens. At handle, at vinde livet fra en verden i forvirring, er det samme som at bekræfte halffællesskabet. Eller, om man vender furmuleringen rundt, det er halffællesskabet, som digtet så stærkt og utvetydigt peger på, der giver livet mening; men det skal vindes fra det onde, vindes igen og igen. Sådan er det, siger skjalden." *Ibid.*, pp. 65–66.

of Weyland, the Germanic smith.[99] It is also seen in the story of Aldhelm on the bridge over the river Avon reciting OE poetry[100] and in Bede's story of the conversion of King Edwin of Northumbria, who – like Blaise Pascal (1623–62) and Thomas Carlyle (1795–1881)[101] – describes life as "a limited field in the limitlessness of eternity."[102] These three scenes lead us to a kind of poetry, the elegy, that differs from the heroic.[103] Elements of the elegiac inhere in *Beowulf*, of course, as in "The Lay of the Last Survivor," but in the OE elegies "Deor," "The Ruin," "The Wanderer," and "The Seafarer," something new transpires as a result of the contact between the native Germanic and Christian traditions.[104] In "Deor," the speaker recollects scenes of defeat and misery from the heroic tradition and observes that his own tragic situation as an exiled poet can resolve itself as well. His despair, then, stops before it truly begins, and he finds consolation in poetry.[105] The other three poems are all anonymous and therefore not bound to a particular situation, and all express the theme of exile.[106] In all three, the hall is absent; it is mere useless rubble in "The Ruin" and a distant memory for the speakers of "The Wanderer" and "The Seafarer,"[107] whose alienation is strikingly expressed through their own words and through descriptions of nature and the sea.[108] Both "The Wanderer" and "The Seafarer" have "The Ruin" incorporated into them, because in both the speaker seeks a lost hall where all the joys of life can be experienced.[109] Both in this regard are traditional Germanic laments, but both differ from that tradition in that the speakers ultimately see the futility of yearning for earthly, transitory things. The wise man understands that "truly no joy for the alienated is found on this earth. One's gaze must be turned elsewhere."[110] This brings us back to the juxtaposed scenes on "The Franks Casket," the meeting of two traditions. In the best OE poetry, as in "The Seafarer" and "The Wanderer," the two unify to create something new, the goal of which is not earthly fame but heavenly consolation.[111]

---

[99] *Ibid.*, pp. 69–70.
[100] *Ibid.*, pp. 70–72.
[101] *Ibid.*, pp. 72–74.
[102] "et afgrænset felt i uendelighedens grænseløshed." *Ibid.*, p. 74.
[103] *Ibid.*, p. 76.
[104] *Ibid.*, p. 77.
[105] *Ibid.*, p. 79.
[106] *Ibid.*, p. 79.
[107] *Ibid.*, pp. 79–80.
[108] *Ibid.*, pp. 81–82.
[109] *Ibid.*, p. 83.
[110] "virkelig ikke findes nogen glæde for den fremmedgjorte på denne jord. Blikket må vendes andetsteds hen." *Ibid.*, p. 86.
[111] *Ibid.*, pp. 92–93.

Haarder returns to the theme of the epic life in his fifth and final chapter on "The Battle of Maldon," a full translation of which he includes in an appendix to the book. The poem differs from *Beowulf* in multiple ways, he observes, including the dates of the poems themselves and the dates of what they depict. But each poem is heroic; each reflects social norms and a view of life remarkably similar to that reflected in the other poem[112] and in Tacitus' *Germania* 900 years before "The Battle of Maldon."[113] "The Battle of Maldon" is about action, obviously, but more than that, it is about the resolve, hardness of thought, and strength of spirit behind that action.[114] It is about the power of resistance, the epic life, and that central theme of the poem helps explain its first line – "was broken" – and its last: "That was not the Godric who fled from the battle." The shield wall was broken, the Anglo-Saxons were defeated at Maldon, but their spirit remained intact except in those like the cowardly Godric.[115] The poem's form and function, like a sword and the hand that wields it, are one.[116]

Det episke liv is a powerful book. Because it explicitly connects OE and ON poetic traditions, anchors the insights of OE poetry to specific modern works of art from *Hamlet* to Bergman's *Scenes from a Marriage*, and ties the central OE and ON epic value of resilience and resistance against the monsters in life – the Grendels, the dragons, the Hitlers and Stalins – it has continuing currency in Denmark. It was understandably reproduced as an e-book in 2022, over four decades after its original publication.

b. Sweden

There is no book-length study of OE literature in Swedish, but Lars Lönnroth (1935–) devotes two chapters to the subject in his *Det germanska spåret: En västerländsk litteraturtradition från Tacitus till Tolkien* (The Germanic Trail: A Western Literary Tradition from Tacitus to Tolkien, 2017). A prominent public intellectual, Lönnroth is Emeritus Professor of Literature at the University of Gothenburg (1982–2000) with previous positions at UC Berkeley (1965–74) and the University of Aalborg (1974–82) as well as a brief appointment as the cultural editor for the newspaper *Svenska Dagbladet* (1991–93). He has translated several Icelandic sagas and the *Poetic Edda* into Swedish and is co-editor of the seven-volume, richly illustrated, encyclopedic history of Swedish literature *Den svenska litteraturen* (1987–90; second edition, 1999).[117]

---

[112] Ibid., p. 97.
[113] Ibid., p. 121.
[114] Ibid., p. 116.
[115] Ibid., pp. 116–18.
[116] Ibid., p. 119.
[117] Jönsson, "Lönnroth." See also Lönnroth's autobiography, *Dörrar till främmande rum*.

Chapter 4 of *Det germanska spåret* offers an overview of OE poetry, beginning with gnomic verse, riddles, and charms, examples of which we also find in ON and OHG, and that were part of oral-traditional literature even if they are preserved in manuscripts produced in monasteries.[118] Of the longer poems, the remarkable "The Dream of the Rood" is reminiscent of some of the riddles in its being a *prosopopoeia* and contains an unusual representation of Christ's suffering "almost as a mystical act of love between the Savior – depicted as a young hero – and the ostensibly dead tree that carries Him into death."[119] The elegies also stand out among OE longer poems and have no real equivalents in other European languages, even though ON does have similar texts where a heroic person, usually a woman, gives voice to her sorrow. The OE genre's strength lies in its concrete, dark descriptions of discordant situations, and the most famous of the elegies are "The Wanderer" and "The Seafarer." Both make use of the *ubi sunt* motif to emphasize the speakers' sense of loss.[120] Both emphasize the speakers' achieving consolation by distancing themselves from the world.[121]

Lönnroth also touches on the OE religious epics, such as *Andreas*, and observes that in them, Christ, the Apostles, and the heroes in both the Old and New Testaments are conceived of as warriors in the same style as Beowulf, Ingeld, and Sigurd Fafnesbane.[122] The heroic characteristics of these narratives lead him finally to discuss short heroic poems such as "Widsith," in which the narrator functions much as Norna-Gest does for Olav Tryggvason's army in the Icelandic sagas – he, too, is said to have lived several hundred years[123] – and "The Battle of Maldon" in preparation for a chapter devoted to *Beowulf*. "The Battle of Maldon," he writes, is a powerful, gripping text about men defying death and fighting a hopeless battle against fate;[124] in it, "belief in destiny, honor of warriors, and Christian piety unite into an indissoluble whole."[125]

In *Beowulf*, the only work in all Germanic literature that can be compared in scope and literary luminosity with classical epics such as *The Aeneid*, we find a similar indissoluble whole. Emerging from an oral-traditional past,

---

[118] *Det germanska spåret*, pp. 34–35.
[119] "nästan som en mystisk kärleksakt mellan frälsaren – skildrad som en ung hjälte – och det endast skenbart döda träd som bär honom in i döden." *Den germanska spåret*, p. 36.
[120] Ibid., pp. 36–37.
[121] Ibid., p. 37.
[122] Ibid., p. 38.
[123] Ibid., pp. 40–41.
[124] Ibid., p. 41.
[125] "Ödestro, krigarära och kristen fromhet förenas till en ouplöslig helhet." Ibid., p. 42.

the poem has come down to us as a monastic brother's free, Christian rendition of it. Grendel is a diabolical creature of the race of Cain, the Danes make sacrifices to the pagan gods and do not know the true God, but Hrothgar and Beowulf are noble heathens who know there is a higher, singular power.[126] Grendel and his mother are reminiscent of the heathen cannibals who attack Christ's apostles in *Andreas*, the OE verse saint's life of St. Andrew. And Beowulf's victory over them is "a divine victory of the damned followers of Satan."[127] The dragon is likewise aligned with demonic forces, this time directed against Beowulf's own kingdom.[128] His and Wiglaf's slaying of the dragon represents the triumph of good over evil, and the poem thus becomes a clear witness to how easily pagan text and Christian worldview could be united.[129]

Like Haarder's treatment of OE literature in *Det episke liv*, Lönnroth's highlights the connections between it and both the ON tradition and modernity, making that literature relevant to a contemporary audience. The theme of the relevance of OE literature is one that grows stronger throughout the history of the Scandinavian engagement in OE prose and, especially, poetry.

4. Individual Texts, Authors, Genres

The remaining scholarly work done in the Scandinavian languages in the twentieth and twenty-first centuries on OE topics spans a variety of subjects and texts, from Ælgifu of Northampton (ca. 900 to after 1036), the first wife of Cnut the Great (ca. 990–1035; r. 1016–35),[130] to "Wulf and Eadwacer,"[131] each receiving attention in just one place.[132] Four other OE works or their subjects, however, have attracted more: "The Dream of the Rood" and "The Battle of Brunanburh" in three places each, "Widsith" in nine, and "The Voyages of Ohthere and Wulfstan," from the OE version of Orosius's *Historia*, in fourteen.

---

[126] Ibid., pp. 43–44.
[127] "en gudomlig seger över Satans fördömda anhang," Ibid., p. 47.
[128] Ibid., p. 48.
[129] Ibid., p. 52.
[130] Torfadóttir, "Í orðastað Alfífu."
[131] Larsen, "Sigrdrífa-Brynhild," p. 67.
[132] See Wadstein, "Ett engelskt fornminne från 700-talet och Englands dåtida kultur" (on the Franks Casket); Brynildsen, "Om tidsregningen i Olav den Helliges Historie" (on *The Anglo-Saxon Chronicle*); Tveitane, "Vá Drottenn kann allar Tungur" (on Ælfric); Björkman, "Några anekdoter om konung Alfred den store i kritisk belysning"; and Sandred, "Domesday Book 1086–1986."

Henry Larsen, as we have seen, deals briefly with "The Dream of the Rood" in his study of Christ's Harrowing of Hell, and in it he hears a strong echo from the Norse myth of Balder, also the son of a god (Odin), also unjustly killed, also mourned by all creation. Along with Frederik Hammerich, he believes that no poet has ever depicted the crucifixion as well as the poet of "The Dream of the Rood" has. The conflict between Christianity and paganism and its resolution – a powerful, warrior-like Christ – first emerges here in an image that the Goths loved.[133]

"The Dream of the Rood" profoundly moved Arthur Olav Sandved (1931–2021) as well. In his first excursion into OE studies, he writes about "The Dream of the Rood"[134] in order to answer Alcuin's famous question to the monks at Lindisfarne, "*Quid Hinieldus cum Christo?*" (What has Ingeld to do with Christ?), and to introduce his fellow Norwegians to some remarkable poetry of unusually high quality.[135] If the converted Anglo-Saxons, he argues, wanted to compose poems about Christian themes, they had only a pre-Christian literary apparatus to do so. A praise poem for Christ had to be based on the same literary techniques used to praise Ingeld – had to be a synthesis of pre-Christian form and Christian content – and Sandved explains those techniques in some detail.[136] "The Dream of the Rood," which he translates into rhythmic, alliterative, Norwegian prose at the end of the article,[137] came to be during the period after the finding of the true cross in Rome in 701, when the *adoratio crucis* (adoration of the Cross) tradition became popular in the Good Friday liturgy of the Catholic Church.[138]

Like Larsen and Sandved, Jan Henrik Schumacher (1947–) is profoundly moved by the poem. Associate Professor of Church History in the Norwegian Lutheran School of Theology (1987–) in Oslo and an ordained minister in the Church of Norway,[139] Schumacher takes particular interest in the spirituality or mentality expressed in "The Dream of the Rood,"[140] one of two visions of the Cross from the English Middle Ages, the other being Julian of Norwich's in her *Revelations of Divine Love*.[141] One striking feature of the poem's Anglo-Saxon spirituality is that Christ never speaks, but the Cross does, and that the Cross, not Christ, is in the heart of the believer. The Cross bleeds, shakes, suffers, is buried and rises again, and

---

[133] *Krist og Satan*, pp. 176–77.
[134] Sandved, "Drømmen om Kristi Kors."
[135] Ibid., p. 209.
[136] Ibid., pp. 203–06.
[137] Ibid., pp. 209–12.
[138] Ibid., pp. 207–08.
[139] Anon., "Jan Henrik Schumacher."
[140] "Drømmen om korset – og angelsaksisk spiritualitet."
[141] Ibid., p. 73.

at the end of the poem, it has even taken on Christ's role as judge of the living and the dead at the Second Coming. Beyond a symbol for Christ, the Cross becomes an embodiment of Him, as it both evangelizes and preaches about the events of Good Friday.[142]

The poem, which seems to have developed into its present form sometime between the first half of the eighth century and the second half of the tenth, retains aspects of the history of Anglo-Saxon spirituality through which it has moved. Christ's being depicted as a powerful Germanic warrior reflects the earliest part of that history, when the traditional image of a mild and merciful Christ would not have been well received.[143] And the poem's fixation on the Cross as an object of veneration fits into a later meditative tradition, as described by Mary Carruthers. The Cross is "a good place (*topos*) of focus for those who wanted a rich supply of associations that could be re-worked in meditation,"[144] associations from, for example, Venantius Fortunatus, the OE *Elene*, Egeria, and Pope Sergius I, where we also find the Cross magnificently adorned.[145] We hear echoes of scripture, such as Luke 23:31, as well, and see in the Cross a transformation from a gallows to "the victory tree" (*sigebeam*)[146] and to a warrior in his lord's Germanic warband.[147] Heroic diction undergoes a transformation as well, from pagan to Christian. Christ is described as *frea* (lord), *dryhten* (lord), *beorn* (warrior), *ricne kyning* (mighty king), *heofona hlaford* (lord of the heavens), and *sigora wealdend* (ruler of victories) as the traditional, pagan lexicon is turned to a Christian purpose.[148]

"The Dream of the Rood" is an important witness to the history of Anglo-Saxon spirituality, not just in its conjoining of native Anglo-Saxon poetic praxis with Christian content, but also in the context of how Good Friday was celebrated in the Anglo-Saxon Church.

> From texts dating from the same time as the Vercelli manuscript, we know that Good Friday was marked ... through worship of the cross that also included a dramatized burial of the cross. The custom itself had a long history that can be traced all the way back to descriptions of the celebration of Holy Week in Jerusalem in the latter half of the fourth century. At the center of this rite was an elaborately designed cross that played the role of Christ.[149]

---

[142] Ibid., p. 75.
[143] Ibid., p. 77.
[144] "et godt sted (topos) å stille seg for den som ønsket et rikt tilfang av assosiasjoner som kunne bearbeides i meditasjonen." Ibid., p. 78.
[145] Ibid., pp. 79–80.
[146] Ibid., p. 81.
[147] Ibid., p. 82.
[148] Ibid., pp. 82–83.
[149] "Fra tekster som stammer fra samme tid som Vercelli-manuskriptet vet vi at

The items touching on "The Battle of Brunanburh" do not actually deal with the poem directly at all. In a 1911 note, the Icelandic minister and historian Jón Jónsson (1849–1920) of Stafafelli[150] seeks to identify the place of the battle (Vínheiðr in the ON *Egilssaga*) with Uinuaed near Leeds rather than with Weondune, where Simeon of Durham locates it.[151] And Per Wieselgren (1900–89), Professor of Swedish Language and Literature at the University of Tartu in Estonia from 1930 to 1941,[152] in two items from 1927 and 1929 discusses the likenesses between the OE poem and chapters 52 to 55 of *Egilssaga* and uses the date of the battle, 937, and Athelstan's victory in it to argue that Erik Bloodaxe could not have reigned in Northumberland before then.[153]

"Widsith" and "The Voyages of Ohthere and Wulfstan," too, have been more the object of historical than literary inquiry. Richard Constant Boer (1863–1929), a Dutch linguist who specialized in ON language and literature,[154] uses "Widsith" in several places in his extensive study of the layered development of the *Hervararsaga* to validate particular readings of the complex saga.[155] Johannes C. H. R. Steenstrup (1844–1935), Professor of History at the University of Copenhagen (1882–1917), takes note of the seventy peoples listed in "Widsith," among whom as a late addition to the text are the Vikings (*mid Lidwicingum ic wæs*, "with the Lidvikings I was"; *ic wæs mid wicingum*, "I was with the Vikings"). There can be no doubt, he states, that by "Vikings" is meant Nordic sea warriors.[156] And Frands Herschend (1948–), Professor Emeritus of Archaeology and Ancient History at Uppsala University,[157] discusses in a 1997 article the relationship among the Finnsburg Fragment, the Finnsburg episode in *Beowulf*, and "Widsith," finding that the first catalogue in "Widsith" is the intermediary text between the fragment and the episode where the poet uses it to specify a cultural setting as well as a time of about 500 CE.[158]

---

langfredagen ble markert … gjennom en korstilbedelse som også omfattet en dramtisert gravlegging av korset. Selve skikken hade an lang historie som lar seg følge helt tilbage til skildringer av feiringen av den stillw uke i Jerusalem i siste halvdel av 300-talet. Sentralt i denne riten stod altså et kunstferdig utformet kors some har spilt rollen som Krist." Ibid., p. 85.

[150] Anon., "Jón Jónsson."
[151] Jónsson, "Uinuaed=vínheiðr."
[152] Anon., "Per Wieselgren."
[153] Wieselgren, *Författarskapet till Eigla*, pp. 78–84, and "Tideräkningsfrågan i norsk niohundratalshistoria," pp. 36, 46–48.
[154] Anon., "Boer, R. C."
[155] "Om Hervararsaga," pp. 39–44, 46 55, 58, 61, 65, and 69.
[156] "Nogle Studier fra Vikingetiden," p. 157.
[157] Anon., "Frands Herschend."
[158] Herschend, "Striden i Finnsborg," pp. 327–28, 332.

Another Danish scholar, Gudmund Schütte (1872–1958), devotes even more attention to "Widsith." A gifted philologist who lectured at the University of Copenhagen 1909–13 and subsequently at the universities of Berlin and Aarhus before becoming financially independent, Schütte was not affiliated with any university after 1915. He instead devoted himself entirely to his research. He had command of several languages, ancient and modern, and published widely in both scholarly and popular venues, such as newspapers and magazines.[159] His doctoral dissertation from 1907 is a remarkable scholarly achievement. The purpose of "Oldsagn om Godtjod: bidrag til etnisk Kildeforsknings metode med særligt henblik på folk-stamsagn" (Ancient Legends of the Gothonic [or Germanic] Nations: A Contribution to Ethnic Source Research Methods with Particular Reference to Folk Legends) is to:

> collect and organize part of the source foundation on which it will be possible in the future to build a description of how our ethnic group from the earliest times perceived itself and its neighbors. It is, in other words, a source study for the history of the ethnological literature of our people.[160]

Schütte scrutinizes a massive amount of material, from Tacitus and Pliny to regnal lists and pedigrees, chronicles, histories, sagas, and other records in multiple languages and traditions. From the OE tradition, he makes use of *Beowulf*, "The Battle of Maldon," *The Anglo-Saxon Chronicle*, "Deor," "The Rune Poem," the OE *Orosius*, "The Battle of Brunanburh," *Elene*, "Durham," *Bede 3*, and "Widsith," which plays a central role in his study to which he appends his translation of the poem.[161]

The work consists of an introduction (pp. 1–12) and five chapters, the first (pp. 13–32) being a literature review of those few scholars who preceded Schütte in the field and the second (pp. 33–51) being an expression of the author's views on points of disagreement among his predecessors, one group of which denies any precise sense of history or geography in ancient texts and one of which affirms it. Chapter 3 (pp. 52–93) focuses on all the factors bearing upon the transmission of texts, including the time and place of composition, but confines itself to individuals or classes of people in its study of tribal or national origins. Chapter 4 (pp. 94–117), which is arguably the most important chapter in the book, deals with the

---

[159] Larsen and Kristensen, "Gudmund Schütte."
[160] "er at samle og tilrette lægge en Del af det Kilde-Grundlag, på hvilket der i Fremtiden vil kunne opbygges en Skildring af, hvordan vor Folkegruppe fra den ældste Tid har opfattet sig selv og sine Naboer. Det er med andre Ord en Kildestudie til vor etnologiske Folkeliteraturs Historie." *Oldsagn om Godtjod*, p. 1.
[161] Ibid., pp. 198–201.

function and structure of catalogue poems and their recurring features. And chapter 5 (pp. 118–97) offers a review of the different classes of ethnological texts such as tribal legends, folk-wandering legends, warfare legends, and other legendary lists.

Chapter 4, however, deserves closer scrutiny, because in it Schütte formulates an important law, the law of initial and terminal stress in the catalogue poems or name lists that appear so frequently in old Germanic literature. The world-renowned folklorist Axel Olrik (1864–1917), to whom Schütte dedicated his dissertation, and who was one of two reviewers of Schütte's book, succinctly formulates the law thus:

> The first member of the list is the one of greatest general importance; the last, the one in which the framers of the tradition have most special interest. This law, here formulated with precision for the first time, especially as regards the importance of terminal-stress, will be recognised by those familiar with mythico-heroic literature as a valuable test in cases which have hitherto perplexed the student. *E.g.* the Widsith list beginning with Attila, the outstanding figure of the migration-period, and closing with the Anglian Offa, the poet's countryman. Indeed, the author does not himself realise how far-reaching and precise in its operation is the law he has formulated; my own investigations induce me to believe that it obtains in the folk literature of many barbaric as well as in that of European peoples, and that "Schütte's law" may prove as efficient in folk-lore analysis as has "Verner's law" in phonetic analysis.[162]

Olrik's prediction proved true, but the law ended up bearing a different name.

In the years after publishing his dissertation, Schütte published two more articles that mention "Widsith." He alludes to the poem twice in his study of "tendentious" poetry or poetry that displays a bias in heroic legend,[163] and he returns to the nature of the catalogue poem in his 1920 study of "Widsith" and the genealogies of Hengest and Angantyr. But first in footnote 1 on p. 2 and later in footnote 1 on pp. 11–12, he expresses his annoyance and frustration over the fact that his "law" has not been recognized as his but instead has become known as the "Epic Laws of Folk Narrative" in England, Germany, and Sweden and attributed to Axel Olrik. This happened because Olrik published an article of that title on the subject in *DS* (1908) that subsequently appeared in Olrik's shorter German version and was also translated into English.[164] Because, Schütte

---

[162] Olrik, review of *Oldsagn om Godtjod* in *Folklore*, p. 353.

[163] "Tendensdigtning," pp. 148 and 156.

[164] I have not yet found the English translation Schütte refers to, but an English translation by Steager of the German version of the article appeared in 1965 as "Epic Laws of Folk Narrative."

asserts, the law is the only part of his work that has gained recognition outside his native Denmark, he "cannot tacitly agree that [it] should be handed over to Olrik as a matter of course."[165] Despite Schütte's protestations, however, Olrik is still considered the formulator of the laws. Niels Ingwersen, for example, begins his article on Olrik for *The Oxford Companion to Fairy Tales*, second edition, by stating that Olrik's "international claim to fame rests mainly on the article 'Episke love i folkedigtningen' ('Epic Laws of Folk Narrative')."[166]

In his article on "Widsith," however, Schütte continues his study of the poem that he started in his dissertation, this time examining a number of items that have "Widsith" as a common starting point: a series of English royal pedigrees, Snorri's lists of sea kings, Bragi's "Ragnarsdrápa," "Hyndluljóð," "Kálfsvísa," "The Battle of Brávalla," *Hervarar saga*, *Örvar-Odds saga*, *Fridleifs saga*, and "Völuspá."[167] These items did not appear individually or independently of each other, which Schütte demonstrates by focusing on the genealogies of Hengest and Angantyr. Hengest appears in "The Finnsburg Fragment" and the Finnsburg episode in *Beowulf* and has commonly been accepted as the Danish figure from Jutland and subsequently Kent after taking a prominent part in what some call "the English Conquest." Comparison of his appearance in "Widsith" with his appearance in Nennius and other texts leaves us with no doubt that the identification of Hengest as a Dane and a Jute is correct.[168] A comparison of "Widsith" with the remaining texts listed above allows us to see five stages of development of the catalogue poem ending with the legend of Angantyr and his brothers in *Hervarar saga* and *Örvar-Odds saga*.[169] Schütte devotes the rest of his paper to the nationality of Angantyr. He asks if the name refers to one person or several and whether or not the Ongenþeow mentioned in "Widsith" is in fact Angantyr.[170] Evidence from Icelandic, Norwegian, and AS sources and a Danish popular ballad confirms that they are the same person.[171] "Just as in the question of the 'Danish' and Jutlandic Hengest, there seems to be no reason whatsoever to reject the present consensus in the saga tradition: the Swedish king Ongenþeow's identification with the berserker Angantyr in Bolm [on the south-west border with Denmark] must henceforth be considered a fact."[172]

---

[165] "kan jeg ikke stiltiende find mig i, at de uden videre foræres til Olrik." "Vidsid og Slægtssagnene," p. 2, note 1.
[166] Ingwersen, "Axel Olrik."
[167] "Vidsid og Slægtssagnene," p. 3.
[168] Ibid., pp. 5–8.
[169] Ibid., pp. 13–23.
[170] Ibid., p. 24.
[171] Ibid., pp. 26–28.
[172] "ligesom i Spørgsmaalet om den 'danske' og den jyske Hengest viser der

The Swede Karl Fritiof Sundén (1868–1945) and the Icelander Stefán Einarsson (1897–1972) are the most recent Scandinavian scholars to turn their attention to "Widsith." Trained in both the Germanic and Romance languages, Sundén was Professor of English Language and Literature at the University of Gothenburg from 1913 to 1935. He displayed an early interest in linguistic and grammatical issues,[173] and he was a great friend of Germany, even showing some sympathy for or understanding of Nazism.[174] He views "Widsith" as the premier example of a catalogue poem, and suggests it has two purposes: to offer three lists containing historical, ethnographic, or heroic material and to showcase the court poet's art and achievement by means of a frame narrative.[175] The poem consists of two main sections: "Widsith A" (lines 1–49) consists of an introduction (lines 1–9) and then Widsith's presenting the first thule or list, this one of princes and the people they ruled. "Widsith B" (lines 50–130) consists of the greatest part of the frame narrative and contains the other two thules, one listing the mainly Germanic tribes Widsith has visited and one listing heroes in Eormanric's army.[176] The poem ends with a reflection on the poet's high calling in the world, for which he earns enduring praise.[177] To lessen the monotony of all three catalogues, famous heroes or stories are introduced at their conclusion and sometimes even before. The frame story serves a similar function and also contains a description of how the court poet worked.[178]

Sundén next talks about three names in the poem, Widsith, Scilling (line 103), and Ealhild (lines 5, 97). This first is a *bahuvrihi* compound (a form of synecdoche) and is fictional. The second is an authentic OE name but probably does not refer to a specific person. And the third probably does refer to a specific person, but there is no agreement on whom she might have been, since there is no reference to her outside of "Widsith."[179] After rehearsing the various arguments for who she might be, Sundén concludes that she was probably a fourth-century Gothic queen of Widsith's own tribe, the Myrgingas. Her name alliterates with Eadgils and Eadwine (her father), and one could surmise "that she was Eadgils' sister and that

---

sig ikke at være nogensomhelst Grund til at vrage den i Sagnoverleveringen foreliggende Samtydning: Sveakongen Ongenþeovs Enhed med Berserken Angantyr i Bolm maa herefter regnes for en Kendsgærning." Ibid., p. 31.

[173] See, e.g., his *Essay I. The predicational categories in English; and Essay II. A category of predicational change in English.*
[174] Tjerneld, "Sundén släkt."
[175] *Den fornengelska dikten Widsið*, p. 4.
[176] Ibid., pp. 6–7.
[177] Ibid., p. 8.
[178] Ibid., pp. 8–9.
[179] Ibid., pp. 9–11.

her presence in the story was perhaps mainly due to his fame."[180] As for the genetic development of the poem, Sundén surveys theories from Karl Müllenhoff (1818–84), Hermann Möller (1850–1923), and Bernhard ten Brink (1841–92), as well as those of Alois Brandl (1855–1940), Raymond W. Chambers (1874–1942), William W. Lawrence (1876–1958), Theodor Siebs (1862–1941), and Richard Jordan (1877–1925), and reaches the conclusion that the frame narrative was originally an independent poem and that the catalogues were added to it.[181] This conclusion is borne out by the work of Eduard Sievers (1850–1932) on OE meter,[182] and Sundén uses Sievers' metrical system in producing his own Swedish translation of "Widsith." It is produced in rhythmic prose, unshackled by alliteration, but faithful to the rhythm of the original poem itself.[183] Sundén rounds out his study of "Widsith" with an examination of the historical and ethnographical material contained in it[184] and then the saga material, concluding that the poem has a more profound meaning than was thought just a decade ago.[185]

Stefán Einarsson, whose article on "Widsith" was examined in the Introduction to this book, published his next article in 1951, fifteen years after his first. In it, he explores a suggestion by Kemp Malone (1889–1971) that the reference in the poem in lines 103 to 108 to Widsith and Scilling jointly singing for their lord is comparable to the Finnish runo-singers' custom of singing alternate lines of a poem to the accompaniment of a harp.[186] Einarsson surveys a range of ON and Finnish material where the phenomenon is recorded and concludes that Malone was most probably correct. Widsith's and Scilling's using the Finnish custom of recital by twos "implies that the practice must have belonged to the Germanic heroic tradition" initially and "might have spread from the Germanic tribes on the Baltic to the Finns as well as west to England."[187] We have no conclusive proof either way.

As we saw in chapter 1, OE studies in Scandinavia began with Andreas Bussæus's appending Christopher Ware's Latin translation of "The Voyages of Ohthere and Wulfstan" from *The Old English Orosius* to his edition of *Landnámabók* in 1733. Interest in that OE text has not diminished over the years, and fourteen publications on it appeared in the twentieth century in Danish, Swedish, Finland Swedish, Norwegian, and Icelandic.

---

[180] "att hon var en syster till Eadgils och att hennes tillvaro i sagan kanske främst berodde på dennes berömmelse." *Ibid.*, p. 13.
[181] *Ibid.*, pp. 13–18.
[182] *Ibid.*, pp. 18–24.
[183] *Ibid.*, p. 24.
[184] *Ibid.*, pp. 30–40.
[185] *Ibid.*, pp. 40–43.
[186] Einarsson, "Alternate Recital by Twos," p. 59.
[187] *Ibid.*, p. 80.

Jón Jónsson of Stafafelli, who speculated on where the battle of Brunanburh took place (see p. 124), for example, recounts Ohthere's voyage to the Beormas in his survey of ancient explorations into the north seas, a survey based on his translation of an 1898 Norwegian article by Alexander Bugge (1870–1929)[188] on the same subject that he emends and expands.[189] Echoing Bugge, Jónsson concludes that "Óttar's journey has great scientific value and from it followed more northern journeys and explorations."[190] Other scholars have tried to locate specific places mentioned in the text, such as "Sciringesheal"[191] and "Sillende,"[192] or outside of it, such as the legendary Viking fortress of Jomsborg,[193] or to demonstrate the likelihood that Hedeby was originally Swedish, not Danish, and modeled after the Viking trading town Birka in Lake Mälaren in Sweden.[194] Two Swedish scholars disagreed on what *The Voyages* tell us about the Vikings' concept of the points of the compass,[195] and a Finland-Swedish scholar examined Henrik Gabriel Porthan's 1800 edition of *The Voyages* in juxtaposition with the 1815 Danish edition by Rasmus Rask.[196]

The winner of the 1922 Nobel Peace Prize, on the other hand, took a distinctly personal view of the Alfredian text. Fridtjof Nansen (1861–1930), polymath and Rector of the University of St. Andrews from 1925 to 1928, obtained a doctorate in zoology from Royal Frederick University in Norway and held a research professorship at the University of Oslo, where he published six volumes of scientific research between 1897 and 1908, when he was appointed Professor of Oceanography. His adventurous expeditions, however, together with his extensive humanitarian work and service as a diplomat, are what made him internationally renowned. He once skied across Norway, for example, from Bergen to Oslo and back, and, with five others, he was the first to traverse the whole of Greenland,

---

[188] Alexander Bugge was the son of the great Norwegian linguist Sophus Bugge (1833–1907) and Professor of History at Royal Frederick University, 1903–12. See Krag, "Alexander Bugge."

[189] "Vore forfædres opdagelsesreiser i polaregnene."

[190] "Ferð Óttars hefir mikið vísindalegt gildi, og af henni leiddi fleiri norðurferðir og landaleitir," "Landaleitir formanna i Norðurhöfum," p. 141. Shetelig recounts Ohthere's voyage in Norwegian in *Det norske folks liv og historie gjennem tidene*. I, pp. 250–54.

[191] Sørensen, *Det gamle Skirinssal* and "Om Skíringssalr?"; Kjær, "Hvad var Skíringssalr?"

[192] Neuhaus, "Sillende=vetus patria=Angel."

[193] Larson, *Jomsborg*.

[194] Lindqvist, "Hedeby och Birka," p. 11.

[195] Ekblom, "Den forntida nordiska orienteringen," and Ellegård, "De gamla nordbornas väderstrecksuppfattning."

[196] Envkist, "Porthans 'Försök at uplysa Konung Ælfreds Geografiska Beskrifning'." Porthan: "Försök." Rask: "Ottars og Ulfstens korte Rejseberetninger."

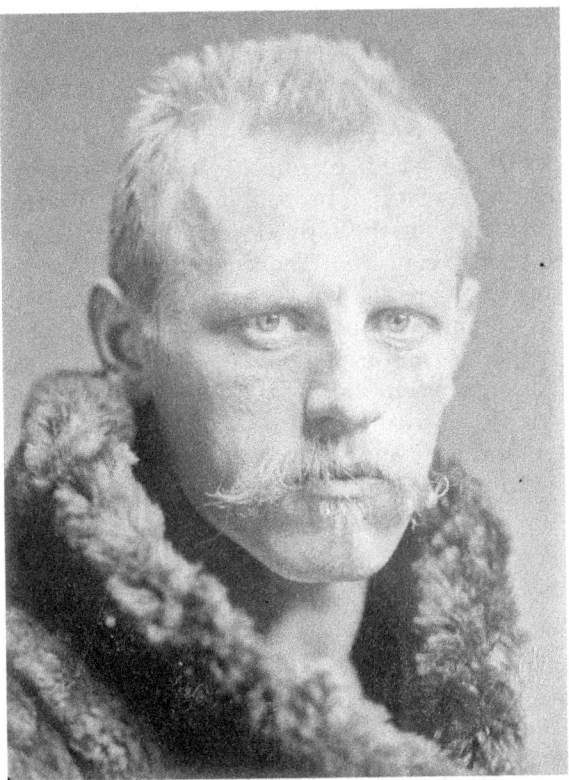

Figure 9. Fridtjof Nansen, 1890.

surviving hunger and exhaustion and temperatures of −45 °C. In 1895, he and one other ventured to the North Pole, getting closer than anyone in history ever had.[197] Understandably, the voyages of Ohthere and Wulfstan would have engaged his interest. In his introduction to *Nord i Taakenheimen. Utforskningen av Jordens nordlige Strók i tidlige Tider* (Copenhagen, 1911), which was translated into English by Arthur G. Chater as *In Northern Mists: Arctic Explorations in Early Times*, he explains why:

> From first to last the history of polar exploration is a single mighty manifestation of the power of the unknown over the mind of man, perhaps greater and more evident here than in any other phase of human life. Nowhere else have we won our way more slowly, nowhere else has every new step cost so much trouble, so many privations and sufferings,

---

[197] Anon., "Fridtjof Nansen."

and certainly nowhere have the resulting discoveries promised fewer material advantages – and nevertheless, new forces have always been found ready to carry the attack farther, to stretch once more the limits of the world.[198]

Nansen surveys the recorded accounts of Northern voyages from Pytheas of Massalia (now Marseilles) in probably 330–325 BCE to the discovery of America by Leif Erikson in the early eleventh century CE. The first half of chapter 5 of his history concerns "The Voyages of Ohthere and Wulfstan."

Nansen contextualizes the voyages by explaining that the frequent Viking raids in the ninth century as well as Charlemagne's wars in the north and Christian mission assignments there meant that contact – peaceful and warlike – between Southern and Northern Europe intensified. The Scandinavian countries became incorporated into the known world and knowledge of their geography became clearer.[199] When King Alfred the Great, therefore, had Orosius' Latin history of the world translated into OE, he augmented those portions concerning the North with newly acquired geographical knowledge.[200] The most important contribution to that knowledge is

> his remarkable account of what the Norwegian Ottar (or 'Ohthere' in the Anglo-Saxon text) told him about his voyage to the North. The brief and straightforward narrative of this sober traveller forms in its clearness and definiteness a refreshing contrast to the vague and confused ideas of earlier times about the unknown northern regions. We see at once that we are entering upon a new period.[201]

Nansen estimates that Ohthere may have undertaken his voyage between 870 and 890 and is only the second northern explorer in history about whom we have firm knowledge. The first was the Greek Pytheas, who seems to have reached the Arctic Circle; Ohthere went farther north along the coast of Norway all the way into the White Sea. He thus became the first known explorer to reach the North Cape, the Polar Sea, and the White Sea.[202] There may have been others, of course, of whom we are not aware. But Ohthere understood that danger lay among the Beormas, and that understanding came from somewhere: "it may be supposed that he knew them by report as a warlike people."[203] Ohthere could communicate with the Beormas, who seem to have spoken a Finno-Ugrian language similar

---

[198] Nansen, *In Northern Mists*, p. 4.
[199] Ibid., p. 168.
[200] Ibid., p. 169.
[201] Ibid., p. 170.
[202] Ibid., p. 172.
[203] Ibid., p. 173.

to Karelian, a point of view shared by *Egilssaga*, where a contemporary of Ohthere's, Thorolf Kveldulfsson, conducts expeditions among the Finns or Lapps of Karelia in about 873 and 874. The "mention of the ravages of the Kirjals [Karelians] agrees with the impression of Ottar's Beormas, who were so warlike that he dared not pass by their country."[204]

Ohthere's mentioning walrus-hunting is striking, says Nansen. It shows that both Norwegians and Finns engaged in it at so early a date and undoubtedly long before; Ohthere may even have given the walrus ivory of which "The Franks Casket" is made to Alfred during his visit with him, although it could have come from some other Norwegian who had brought it to England. Walrus ivory and ropes made of walrus hide were valuable commodities at the time.[205]

Nansen then quotes Ohthere's account of his southern journey and states that it "is remarkable for the same sober lucidity as his narrative of the White Sea expedition; and as, on all the points where comparison is possible, it agrees well with other independent statements, it furnishes strong evidence of his credibility."[206] He concludes with a description of Wulfstan's voyage from Hedeby to Prussia with references along the way to areas belonging to Denmark and Sweden on the port side of the ship and references to "Weonodland" (= Mecklenburg and Pomerania) as far as to the mouth of the Vistula and then to Estonia. "Henceforward we can count these parts of Europe as belonging to the known world."[207]

In 1985, Ove Jørgensen (1908–?), a civil engineer for the city of Odense from 1935 to 1978 and also a skilled amateur cartographer, published *Alfred den Store. Danmarks geografi. En undersøgelse at fire afsnit i Den gamle engelske Orosius* (Alfred the Great: Denmark's Geography: A Study of Four Chapters of the OE *Orosius*). He published two other books in his lifetime, *OTONIVM, Odense 1593* (1981), in which he introduces and comments on Georgius Braunius' (Georg Braun's) 1593 map of Odense,[208] and (with Tore Nyberg) *Sejlruter i Adam af Bremens danske øverden* (Sea Routes in the Danish Archipelago in Adam of Bremen's *Gesta*, 1992). In *Alfred den Store*, he focuses on the portions of the OE *Orosius* that are an important source for the history of the earliest Danish kingdoms,[209] something that had not been done since the period of Romantic Nationalism in Denmark and Rasmus Rask's edition of "The Voyages of Ohthere and Wulfstan" in 1815.[210] After surveying the content of the OE text, its manuscript history,

---

[204] Ibid., p. 175.
[205] Ibid., p. 176.
[206] Ibid., p. 180.
[207] Ibid., pp. 180–81.
[208] Hansen, personal correspondence.
[209] Jørgensen, *Alfred den Store*, p. 1.
[210] Rask, "Ottars og Ulfstens korte Rejseberetninger."

the treatments of *The Voyages* from Hakluyt in the late sixteenth century to 1984, and how the OE *Orosius* was created,[211] Jørgensen spends a good deal of time explaining in great detail Alfred's geographical orientation system with the help of a number of other scholars, chiefly Kemp Malone. Basically, Alfred's north is closer to north-east, and Jørgensen applies that system to several place-names in the section on Germany in the OE *Orosius*.[212] Then he takes up the first mention of Danish territory in the text where King Alfred lists the neighbors of the Old Saxons: "7 be westan eald seaxum is ælfe muþa þære ie 7 frisland, 7 þonan westnorð is þæt lond þe mon ongle hæt 7 sillende 7 sumne dæl dene, 7 be norþan him is afdrede ..."[213] (to the west of the Old Saxons is the mouth of the river Elbe and Frisia, and then northwest is that land one calls Anglia and Sillende and a certain portion of [the land of] the Danes, and to the north of it is the Abodriti ...). The last part of the description is somewhat ambiguous, and Jørgensen surveys the scholarly opinions on how it should be interpreted: 1) Anglia, Sillende, and the portion of Danish land can all be objects of the verb *hæt*; 2) Anglia and Sillende are objects with the portion of Danish land being in apposition to them; 3) Anglia is the object with Sillende and the portion of Danish land in apposition; or 4) all three are subjects, which would require emending the accusative *sumne* to the nominative *sum*.[214] Reference to other geographical descriptions, especially of Frisia and Anglia, helps Jørgensen conclude that the fourth possibility listed above is the correct one. Anglia is therefore the region between the North Sea and the Baltic from which the Angles emigrated; Sillende is the trade route from Hedeby to the west; and the area north of the river Eider during Alfred's time was part of Danish territory.[215]

King Alfred offers his second description of Denmark after finishing describing Eastern Europe as far north as the Riphaean Mountains, and he mentions the South Danes, the North Danes, and Bornholm: "Since Denmark is an island kingdom, its 'neighbors' or borders in several instances become the surrounding seas."[216] The terms "South Danes" and "North Danes" that King Alfred introduces here are not used in either Ohthere's or Wulfstan's accounts of their voyages and, Jørgensen claims, are not known from other sources (but see *Beowulf*, where North, South, East, and West Danes are all mentioned). Jørgensen devotes the rest of

---

[211] Jørgensen, *Alfred den Store*, pp. 2–8.
[212] Ibid., pp. 9–56.
[213] Ibid., p. 57.
[214] Ibid., pp. 58–61.
[215] Ibid., p. 75.
[216] "Da Danmark er et ørige bliver 'naboerne' eller grænserne i flere tilfælde til de omgivende have." Ibid., p. 76.

his chapter to determining what was meant by South Danes and North Danes.[217] Alfred's observations about what lay to the north, south, east, and west of those regions as well as scholarly commentary on the text and place-name evidence helps Jørgensen locate the South Danes in south and the North Danes in north Jylland (Jutland), with the boundary between the two regions marked differently in Alfred's time than in ours. An archaeological boundary line from the late Roman Iron Age seems to be at work in the former and a boundary line resulting from a political decision made in 1115 in the latter.[218]

The third description of Denmark in the OE *Orosius* occurs in Ohthere's account of his second voyage, this time to Sciringesheal in Vestfold on the western side of the Oslo fjord in southern Norway and then on to Hedeby, the Viking market town probably founded by Swedes on the model of Birka and eventually taken over by Danes. Ohthere says that it "stent betuh winedum 7 seaxum 7 angle 7 hyrð in on dene"[219] (it lies between the Wends and the Saxons and the Angels and belongs to the Danes). It was near the end of the Jutland peninsula. Jørgensen discusses the problems raised by the description of Sciringesheal and the Oslo fjord (including the absence of the word "fjord" in OE)[220] before turning to Hedeby, which was a five-day sail south or south-east from Sciringesheal.[221] Scholars do not agree on what route Ohthere took to Hedeby. It could have been through the Sound separating Denmark and Sweden, the Great Belt strait between the islands of Zealand and Funen, or the Little Belt strait between Funen and the Jutland peninsula. The distance regardless of route is about 650 kilometers,[222] and the landmarks and locations Ohthere enumerates along the way are unspecific enough to support arguments for all three routes.[223]

The fourth and final description of Denmark in the OE *Orosius* comes immediately after the third in the abruptly appearing account of Wulfstan of his voyage from Hedeby to Truso: "The town of Truso (on Lake Druzno) was situated on the Gulf of Danziger at the present-day Elbing."[224] During the seven-day trip, Wulfstan passed the land of the Wends on the starboard side of the ship "7 on bæcbord him wæs langaland 7 læland 7

---

[217] Ibid., p. 76.
[218] Ibid., p. 81.
[219] Ibid., p. 103.
[220] Ibid., p. 102.
[221] Ibid., p. 103.
[222] Ibid., p. 107.
[223] Ibid., pp. 108–12.
[224] "Byen Truso (ved søen Druzno) lå ved Danzigerbugten ved det nuv ærende Elbing." Ibid., p. 114.

falster 7 sconeg 7 þas land eall hyrað to dene mearcan"²²⁵ (and to port was Langland, Lolland, Falster, and Skåne island, and all that land belongs to Denmark). After that came Bornholm, which had its own king, and then territory belonging to the Swedes, namely Blekinge, Möre, Öland, and Gotland. Jørgensen comments on all of these place-names and their histories, noting, for example, that the land of the Wends encompasses "the entire country along the Baltic Sea coast from *limes saxoniae* (at the Gulf of Kiel) to the Gulf of Danziger."²²⁶ He also suggests with other scholars that Wulfstan – of whom we know nothing – may have been a Dane from Hedeby, who perhaps met the Norwegian Ohthere there.²²⁷

A common perception of "The Voyages of Ohthere and Wulfstan" has been, observes Jørgensen, that the two travelers were merchants and that what they describe are simply two major Viking trade routes. This may be true, but in their emphasis on boundaries and geography and place-names and peoples, their interest seems also to be political, and that may have been more important to King Alfred than anything else.²²⁸ Jørgensen concludes that the two narratives were included in the OE *Orosius* first because of Ottar's description of his homeland and initial voyage and second because of Wulfstan's record of the customs of the Osti people. "The conditions in these remote parts of Europe have to be assumed to have been unknown at that time in King Alfred's court,"²²⁹ or at least relatively so. Jørgensen also concludes that, besides the kingdom of Bornholm and the Swedish Blekinge, all of medieval Denmark had already been unified in the ninth century.²³⁰ "The Voyages of Ohthere and Wulfstan" lends credence to that conclusion.

"Widsith" and "The Voyages of Ohthere and Wulfstan" thus dominate the scholarly interest in Scandinavia in individual OE texts because of the works' clear relevance to the Nordic countries. When Scandinavians turn their hands to translating OE literature, however, those two texts no longer take such prominence, as we shall see in chapter 7. Before we get there, though, we must examine how *Beowulf* is treated from a scholarly point of view and from the point of view of translators in the North.

---

[225] Ibid., p. 113.
[226] "hele landet langs Østersøens kyst fra limes saxoniae (ved Kielerbugten) til Danzigerbugten." Ibid., p. 114.
[227] Ibid., pp. 121–23.
[228] Ibid., pp. 123–25.
[229] "Forholdene i disse fjerne egne af Europa må antages hidtil at have vaeret ukendte ved kong Alfred s hof." Ibid., p. 128.
[230] Ibid., p. 129.

PART 3

THE CONTINUING INTEREST: *BEOWULF* AND TRANSLATIONS OF *BEOWULF* AND OTHER OLD ENGLISH LITERATURE, 1733 TO 2022

5

Scandinavian Approaches to *Beowulf*

The Scandinavians first approached *Beowulf* and other Old English (OE) literature through Romantic Nationalism, as we saw in chapter 1, and with greater complexity with Grundtvig and his vision of Denmark's place, and his own, in world history in chapter 2. Grímur Jónsson Thorkelin (1752–1829), the first editor of the poem who introduced it to the world, was primarily motivated by nationalism when he ventured to England to find as many Danish and Norwegian manuscripts as possible and happened upon the poem in the late 1780s – although there is some credible evidence that he knew about it beforehand[1] – and was the first to do so. He was born and raised in Iceland and continued his education in Denmark, where he earned degrees from the University of Copenhagen in philosophy (1774) and law (1776), produced a number of editions and translations of Old Norse (ON) texts, and became secretary to the Arnamagnaean Commission in 1777, assistant keeper in the Royal Privy Archives in 1780, and "professor extraordinarius" in 1783, which virtually assured him an eventual chair in philosophy at the university.[2] The six years he spent in the libraries of England, Scotland, and Ireland assured him a place in the history of *Beowulf* studies.

After "happening" upon *Beowulf*, Thorkelin commissioned a transcription of the poem in 1787 and then produced another himself between 1789 and 1791, the year he was appointed keeper of the Royal Privy Archives upon the death of his predecessor. Those transcripts have enabled subsequent editors of *Beowulf* to reconstruct much of a manuscript that was disintegrating, having been damaged by fire in 1731, and have thus been highly praised as essential documents in the history of the study of the poem.[3] Kevin Kiernan has thoroughly analyzed those transcripts and included them in his indispensable *Electronic Beowulf* project along with numerous other documents, including his essay on Thorkelin's discovery of the *Beowulf* manuscript.[4] Thorkelin's first edition and Latin translation of *Beowulf*, however, were universally excoriated. Grundtvig led the charge against Thorkelin's sloppy work; John Josias Conybeare followed

---

[1] Fjalldal, "To Fall by Ambition," p. 323.
[2] Wolf, "Thorkelin and Rask," pp. 114–15.
[3] Bjork, "Thorkelin's Preface," pp. 291–92.
[4] Kiernan, *The Electonic Beowulf*.

suit, listing hundreds of mistakes in both the edition and translation; and John M. Kemble, the second editor of the poem in 1833, mercilessly drove the final nail into the coffin: "not five lines of Thorkelin's edition can be found in succession, in which some gross fault either in the transcript or the translation, does not betray the editor's utter ignorance of the Anglo-Saxon language."[5] "[S]uch," as Jorge Luis Borges observed, "is the singular story of Thorkelin and his ill-fated passion."[6]

After the ignominious publication of Thorkelin's edition and the numerous condemnatory reactions to it, interest in the poem burgeoned in multiple cultures, first among the learned and then the unlearned and in a wide range of media.[7] In Scandinavia among the learned, interest tended to settle into three sometimes overlapping categories: cultural and historical; literary interpretations; and translations. Translations will be dealt with in the next chapter.

Denmark: Cultural and Historical

Over thirty articles and sections of books have been produced in Danish about some aspect of *Beowulf* studies, including textual criticism, since the discussion about Thorkelin and his edition subsided in the early nineteenth century (see Appendix A, section II.A). Some seven books and substantial articles have also appeared, beginning with a long contribution by Gísli Brynjúlfsson "the younger" (1827–88), whose father drowned two months before he was born. Gísli was an Icelandic writer whose amorous disappointments "turned him into an ardent love poet and left him in a state of mind vacillating between Byronic despondency ('Faraldur' [his poem 'The Plague']) and Viking-like activism."[8] In his diary, *Dagbók í Höfn* (Diary in Copenhagen), which was not published until 1952, he proclaims, "In general I dislike mankind."[9] Besides being a misanthrope, a Romantic, and a political activist, Gísli was also a philologist and eventual lecturer in Icelandic history and literature at the University of Copenhagen (1874–88) who wrote several monographs on skaldic poetry,[10] and contributed ON translations of two OE texts for George Stephens' 1853 *Tvende Old-Engelske*

---

[5] Bjork, "Thorkelin's Preface," p. 291. See Haarder, *Beowulf*, for a discussion of reviews of Thorkelin's edition, and Hall, "The First Two Editions of *Beowulf*," for a reassessment of it.
[6] Borges, "Thorkelin y el *Beowulf*," p. 469.
[7] See Bjork, "Reception History of *Beowulf*."
[8] Einarsson, *A History of Icelandic Literature*, p. 242.
[9] Quoted in Óskarsson, "From Reformation to Englighenment," p. 280.
[10] Anon., "Brynjulfsson."

Digte (see chapter 1)[11] and an important and substantial paper in Danish on OE and ON that includes a discussion of *Beowulf*. George Stephens and his interest in the Skando-Saxon origin of English make their appearance in Gísli's article, which was published around the same time as Stephens' *Tvende Old-Engelske Digte*. Clearly, the two men had been talking. Gísli had also read Stephens' article in the April and May 1852 issues of *The Gentleman's Magazine* on the relationship of OE to the Scandinavian languages, and he translated a large portion of it for inclusion in his article. Stephens spiritedly defends the idea that OE is not a West Germanic language but rather a South Scandinavian one;[12] Gísli substantiates Stephens' view by examining *Beowulf* in its light.[13] Comparison of the poem with the ON *fornaldarsögur* confirms for Gísli that the legendary material in it is Scandinavian, not German,[14] and the ties between the English and the Scandinavians that he alluded to in the first sentence of his article become further affirmed. "It has to be truly gratifying for all Northerners," he exclaims, "to see how the English, the more they become absorbed in the study of their own antiquity, the more clearly they start becoming conscious of their kinship with the Scandinavian peoples and as a result turn their gaze to the North as one of the principal sources from which the ever-growing greatness of their mighty country must chiefly be derived."[15]

About thirty years after the publication of Gísli's article, Frederik Vilhelm Valdemar Rønning (1851–1929), whom we first met in chapter 1, received his Ph.D. for his dissertation, *Beovulfs-Kvadet: en literær-historisk undersøgelse* (The Lay of Beowulf: A Literary-Historical Study, 1883). He was an N. F. S. Grundtvig devotee and produced numerous publications about him and his work, the most significant of which for our purposes were three articles in 1885 on Grundtvig's three trips to England[16] and a richly detailed biography in four large volumes published between 1907 and 1914: *N. F. S. Grundtvig: et bidrag til skildring af dansk åndsliv i det 19. århundrede* (N. F. S. Grundtvig: A Contribution to the Description

---

[11] On his translations from OE, see Ísaksson, "Þýðingar," parts 1 and 2.
[12] For a more recent version of this idea (2014) applied to Middle English on syntactic grounds, see Emonds and Faarlund, *English: The Language of the Vikings*.
[13] For the academic and military background for Gísli's article, see Shippey and Haarder, *Beowulf*, pp. 44–47. For a translation of the part of Gísli's paper dealing with *Beowulf*, see pp. 291–96.
[14] Shippey and Haarder, *Beowulf*, p. 291.
[15] "Det maa i Sandhed være glædeligt for alle Nordboer at see, hvorledes Englænderne, jo mere de fordybe sig i Studiet af deres egen Oldtid, ogsaa desto tydeligere begynde at blive sig Slægtskabet med de skandinaviske Folkeslag bevidste, og som en Følge deraf vende Blikket imod Norden, som en af de Hovedkilder, hvorfra deres mægtige Lands stedse voxende Storhed fornemmelig maa udledes." Brúnjulsson, "Oldengelsk og Oldnorsk," p. 81.
[16] Rønning, "Grundtvig og den oldengelske literatur."

of Danish Intellectual Life in the Nineteenth Century). The influence Grundtvig exerted over Rønning is manifest in his *Beovulfs-Kvadet*, in which he first assesses the applicability of *Liedertheorie* (ballad theory) to *Beowulf* as articulated by the German philologist Karl Müllenhoff (1818–84).[17] Point by point, Rønning scrutinizes and refutes Müllenhoff's assertion that the poem is the work of six poets, as evidenced by numerous contradictions in the narrative structure of the poem (pp. 11–30)[18] and by a plethora of inconsistencies in tone and style in it (pp. 31–87). Rønning concludes that the Müllenhoffian *Liedertheorie* cannot be right and that *Beowulf*

> did not arise from a mechanical assemblage of independent elements that one can take apart and put back together again at will, but it is a real reworking and revision of the underlying material, the folk songs about Beowulf's life and exploits handed down from paganism through oral tradition ... [what] we have here [is] a true unity, a whole, a poetic work of art, and, as far as we know, the first in the Gothic-Germanic world.[19]

Having dispensed with *Liedertheorie*, Rønning then takes up the problem of the *Beowulf* poet and the poem's place of origin (pp. 88–107). An examination of the Northumbrian dialect features shining through the West Saxon dialect of the poem as well as the Christian elements that have been introduced into the poem lead Rønning to conclude that the author of *Beowulf* must have lived in Northern England, most probably in a monastery. The poem originated in southern Sweden and was transported during the Migration Period to Northern England, where it was revised into an epic whole by a Northumbrian poet, probably sometime in the eighth century.[20] Finally, Rønning concludes his study with a lengthy discussion of the poetic character of *Beowulf* (pp. 108–75). This is the most Grundtvigian chapter in the book, especially in Rønning's examination of the poem's "poetic style." Poetry is a "spiritual power" (*en ånds-kraft*) measurable by the effect it has on the human mind, which depends on

---

[17] On "The victory and development of *Liedertheorie*," see Shippey and Haarder, *Beowulf*, pp. 47–54.

[18] For a translation of pp. 24–30, see ibid., pp. 410–15, and for a statement on the importance of Rønning's book, see ibid., pp. 58–59.

[19] "Beovulfsdigtet ikke opstået ved en mekanisk sammenstykning af selvstændige enkeltheder, som man kan tage fra hinanden og sætte sammen igen efter behag, men det er en virkelig bearbejdelse og sammenarbejdelse af det til grund liggende stof, de fra hedenskabet, gennem den mundtlige tradition, overleverede folke-kvad om Beovulfs live og bedrifter ... vi har her en virkelig sammenarbejdelse, et hele, et konstdigt, og det, så vidt vi véd, det første i den gotisk-germanske verden." *Beovulfs-Kvadet*, p. 87.

[20] Ibid., p. 107.

two factors: the soul of poetry, or the richness and deepness of poetry, and the technical means by which poetry becomes revelatory. If the poetry is meant to evoke a mood or feeling or something else invisible, then its means are musical; if it is meant to portray an external object, then its means must emphasize the plastic.[21] This discussion is reminiscent of Grundtvig's concerning earthly, historical, and luminous poetry and the power of the living word. For Rønning, the wholeness and unity of *Beowulf* is realized through the poet's command of the poem's language, through his word choice and his exchanging old, worn-out, colorless words for other words that have newer and fresher colors and imagistic power.[22] If a poet wanted to describe the profusion of a giant's beard, he could use a simile: the giant's beard was like a forest. Or, instead of a simile, he could use a metaphor and call his beard a "cheek-forest." By so doing, the image and the object merge.[23] *Beowulf* contains multiple examples of such refined and specific diction as applied to weapons (pp. 143–45), warriors, chieftains, and kings (pp. 145–49), battle (pp. 149–51), ships and sea (pp. 151–53), death and blood and wounds (pp. 153–56), to name some of the most conspicuous terms of interest. The poem is also characterized by two other features that contribute to its wholeness and unity: technical features of OE poetry such as descriptions of nature (pp. 161–68) and meter and verse form (pp. 168–73). All of these aesthetic effects ensure that the poet's story glides along "like a broad, epic stream, winding steadily forward wherever its path may best fall; here are no waterfalls, no roar and froth; calm and still it glides along until it reaches its goal and winds itself around the foot of Beowulf's burial mound towering high by the seashore."[24]

A scholar whom we met in the previous chapter, Axel Olrik, made significant observations about *Beowulf* in a book in which the poem plays a vital role. Olrik (1864–1917) is one of the most important medievalists of the late nineteenth and early twentieth centuries and has had several biographical essays written about him. A student of Svend Grundtvig (1824–83), the son of N. F. S. Grundtvig, and a Romantic nationalist and patriot, Olrik is considered "the founder of folkloristics in Denmark and of the geographic-historical (or 'Finnish') school of folkloristics."[25] He published over 200 books and articles and helped found several scholarly

---

[21] Ibid., p. 129.
[22] Ibid., p. 131.
[23] Ibid., p. 141.
[24] "som en bred, episk strøm, der slynger sig jævnt fremad, hvor dens vej bedst kan falke; her er ingen fossefald, ingen brusen og syden; rolig og stille glider den afsted, til den når sit mål, og slynger sig om foden på Beovulfs gravhøj, knesende højt ved havets bred." Ibid., p. 173.
[25] Hemmingsen, "Axel Olrik," p. 267.

entities such as the "Danish Folklore Archives" (p. 269) and co-founded the journal *DS*, in which he published many articles. His major publication, which was projected to encompass seven volumes, is *Danmarks Heltedigtning* (Denmark's Heroic Poetry), an exhaustive examination of the whole history of heroic legend pertaining to Denmark. He managed to produce just two volumes, the first in 1903 on *Rolf Krake og den ældre Skjoldungrække* (Rolf Kraki and the Elder Scyldings, translated into English and revised in collaboration with the author by Lee M. Hollander as *The Heroic Legends of Denmark* in 1919) and the second in 1910 on *Starkad den gamle og den yngre Skjoldungrække* (Starkad the Old and the Younger Scyldings). It is in the first volume that he makes frequent mention of *Beowulf* and touches on other OE texts as well, such as "The Battle of Maldon," "The Finnsburg Fragment," and "Widsith," which he alludes to sixteen times in the English translation. *Beowulf* and "Widsith" contain "our earliest information concerning the Danish kings of the oldest times,"[26] and Olrik devotes his first chapter to exploring *Beowulf* in particular. Shippey and Haarder have translated the most important part of that chapter concerning future strife in Heorot, Wealhtheow's speech (lines 1159–91), and the presence of Unferth, which underscores the hints at the catastrophe to come for the Danes.[27] Olrik observes that the role that Unferth plays as troublemaker

> corresponds completely to a list of the oldest Gothic and Scandinavian hero-legends, where we find in the king's court the evil counsellor who incites strife: Bikke or Sifka with Jarmunrik [i.e., *Völsunga saga*], Blind the Malicious among the race of Sigar [*Helgakviða Hundingsbana II*], Gissur Grytingaliði with the Gothic king Angantyr [*Hlöðskviða*].[28]

It should be noted that the Danish edition of the book was reviewed in several journals, and the augmented English version was reviewed in several more. The author of one of the latter reviews was Gudmund Schütte, who wrote a lengthy and laudatory essay[29] that – together with his publishing a series of articles in Olrik's *DS* – indicates that the indignity he felt that he had suffered at Olrik's hands in 1907 or so had been forgiven if not forgotten. This was fortunate because Olrik did not live long. He died a broken man at the age of fifty-two after the death of his wife, Margarete, with whom he spent the happiest years of his life when he had "not yet learned what sorrow is."[30] He left behind many

---

[26] Olrik, *Heroic Legends of Denmark*, p. 12.
[27] Shippey and Haarder, *Beowulf*, pp. 497–99. Cp. Olrik, *The Heroic Legends of Denmark*, pp. 49–65.
[28] Shippey and Haarder, *Beowulf*, p. 498.
[29] In *SS* 6 (1920–21), 210–21.
[30] Hemmingsen, "Axel Olrik," p. 269.

incomplete projects, one being his *Nogle Grundsætninger for Sagnforskning* (Some Principles for Oral Narrative Research) that his successor Hans Ellekilde assembled from Olrik's papers dealing with the nine epic laws (later, rules)[31] of oral narrative and published in 1921. That book was translated into English by Kirsten Wolf and Jody Jensen and published in 1992. One of the laws enumerated in it is the law or rule of twins, which states that "[w]hen two characters appear in the same role, they are both depicted as being weaker than a single character." Thus, only together do Hrothgar's sons Hrethric and Hrothmund in *Beowulf* have the power of a single strong character such as Beowulf.[32] This law, then, along with Hrethric's being known as "the stingy with rings" in the ON tradition,[33] when a king should be liberal with them, perhaps gives Wealhtheow's seeming anxiety about Hrethric's becoming king more weight.

Christian Ludwig Kier (1839–1934) was an attorney and prominent community official in Aarhus after fighting in the eight-month Dano-Prussian or Second Slesvig–Holstein War of 1864 when Denmark lost Slesvig and Holstein to Prussia and Austria.[34] He was, for example, a Superior Court Prosecutor in Aarhus beginning in 1869, Director of the Jydsk Handels- og Landbrugsbank 1874–76, Member of the Aarhus City Council 1876–87 and 1891–99, and Chairman of the Danish Market Association 1894–1900. He was also a legal historian and made several contributions to the field including a book asserting a close connection between Nordic and Lombard law.[35] His 1915 *Beowulf: Et Bidrag til Nordens Oldhistorie* (Beowulf: A Contribution to the Legendary History of the North) so impressed a reviewer of the book for its originality that he declared that it "by all means deserves, through a translation into German or English, to be made available to a broader audience."[36]

Kier's purpose in writing his book is to try to specify where the tribes mentioned in *Beowulf* originated, because scholars do not agree on the issue. Some believe the Angles came from southern Jutland, some from southern Germany where the *lex Angliorum & Werinorum* prevailed. Some believe that the Geats, on the other hand, came from Jutland or Gotland or Bornholm or Öland or Västergötland.[37] Kier's study basically argues for Danish provenance for all of them, even the Geats, because the Goths (from

---

[31] Ibid., p. 276.
[32] Olrik, *Principles for Oral Narrative Research*, p. 51.
[33] Shippey and Haarder, *Beowulf*, p. 64.
[34] Nordstrom, *Scandinavia since 1500*, p. 211.
[35] Dahl, "Kier, Christian Ludvig."
[36] "verdient unbedingt, durch eine übersetzung ins Deutsche oder Englische weiteren kreisen zugänglich gemacht zu werden." Björkman review of Kier, p. 245.
[37] Kier, *Beowulf*, p. 2.

Västergötland) and Swedes were never at war, but the Jutes and Swedes have always been.[38] In equating the Geats with the Jutes, Kier is in agreement with, among others, Heinrich Leo in 1839, Frederik Schaldemose in 1847, and Pontus Fahlbeck in 1884.[39] The poem is about old Denmark: in the first part, a hero from Jutland (Beowulf) sails to Sælland to help the Danish king, Hrothgar, battle Grendel and his mother. In the second part, having returned to Jutland, Beowulf fights the dragon and dies. Kier notes (in agreement with Rønning) that the poem was composed in Mercia or Northumbria, and the Angles who settled there mainly came from the Jutland peninsula.[40] The mythic elements aside, the poem is replete with names that substantiate Kier's view. He devotes a chapter each to the Danes, the Geats, the Angles, the Geatish and Danish royal genealogies, and then to Frode (OE Froda), Halfdan (OE Healfdene), and Ongentheow. The chapters on Froda and Ongentheow are the most striking in the book.

Froda appears once in *Beowulf* at line 2025b of the Ingeld or Heathobard episode, and Kier claims that the Danes under his brother Healfdene, who appears first in line 57a as the son of Beow, killed him (line 2050) and that he is the one who had to be avenged.[41] He is Ingeld's father, the Heathobard lord, and therefore has been widely considered a Heathobard as well. The situation is more complicated than it seems, however, and does not necessitate that conclusion. Saxo tells us that Froda subjugated the Saxons and made it all the way to Hannover; his son Ingeld's connection with the Heathobards was thus naturally established.[42] Froda, however, remained king of the Danes, and there was good peace under his rule. Then his brother Healfdene came home and Froda was killed, where and by whose hand is unknown, although Sven Aggesen in the late twelfth century identified Healfdene as the culprit.[43] "Ingeld then seeks refuge with the Heathobards, from where he returns again and again to his homeland, Denmark. The above result is confirmed by all the best Nordic sources."[44] Froda thus is a Dane, not a Heathobard, but Ingeld is still considered one. The ramifications of these facts, which Kier does not mention because his focus is historical, is that the theme of the destructive

---

[38] Ibid., pp. 46ff.
[39] Ibid., p. 31.
[40] Ibid., p. 12.
[41] Ibid., p. 98.
[42] Ibid., p. 99.
[43] Ibid., p. 100. For the relevant passage from Aggesen, see Fulk et al., *Klaeber's Beowulf*, p. 302.
[44] "Ingeld søger da Ly ned hos Headobarderne, hvorfra han atter gentagne Gange hjemsøger sit Fædreland, Daneriget. Ovenstaaende Resultat bekræftes ved alle de bedste nordiske Kilder." Ibid., p. 100.

power of the blood feud in *Beowulf* arises as early as line 57a with the introduction of Healfdene, his brother's slayer.

The focus on blood vengeance and its consequences continues throughout *Beowulf* and is seen again in the poem's second half in the renewed strife between the Swedes and the Geats beginning at line 2472. Ongentheow, the king of the Swedes slain by Hygelac of the Geats, is first mentioned in line 1968a. The question Kier tries to answer concerning these warring factions is where they came from. The Geats lived in Jutland, as he has already demonstrated. But what about the Swedes? Most mentioned in *Beowulf*, as affirmed by Swedish sources such as Thjódólf of Hvinir's *Ynglingatal* and *Ynglingasaga*, came from Uppland, Sweden. But Ongentheow stands apart from them as not being mentioned in those Swedish sources except in their "speak[ing] against attributing Ongentheow's realm to Uppland."[45] Kier reminds us that the *Beowulf* poet descended from the Angles of southern Jutland, that the poem originated in England, and that the legends that formed the basis of the poem migrated to Mercia and Northumbria from the Jutland peninsula. The audience for the poem would therefore perhaps be expected to recognize place-names from the homeland from long ago but not necessarily from Swedish Uppland. And there are numerous specific place-names in lines 2922–99 of the poem, such as Ravenswood in line 2925b, which is also referred to as Hrefnes Holt in line 2935a. A Northumbrian or Mercian audience descended from Angles of the Jutland peninsula would be unlikely to recognize that name unless it came from Denmark, where *Ravenholt* is a very common place-name even today.[46] On this and other evidence, then, Kier identifies Ongentheow with Angeltheow of the Mercian genealogy from *The Parker Chronicle*[47] and Ongen in the *Historia Brittonum*.[48] He further locates the battle of Ravenswood in or around Schleswig and fleshes out that identification in the next chapter on "Kampen omkring Hedeby" (the battle near Hedeby).[49]

One ancient Danish place-name that does not appear in *Beowulf* is nevertheless important to it: Lejre. Tom Christensen, Emeritus Archaeologist at Roskilde Museum in Denmark, published the results of the excavations that he directed in the 1980s at the home of the legendary kings of Denmark in his book *Lejre: syn og sagn* (Lejre: Fact and Fable, 1991). That book, with an additional chapter on a new round of excavations up to 2005 that includes the discovery of a previously unknown hall complex from the sixth century at the farm called Fredshøj on the outskirts of Lejre,

---

[45] "tale begge imod ogsaa at henføre Ongentheows Rige til Upland." Ibid., p. 126.
[46] Ibid., pp. 129–30.
[47] See Fulk, *Kaleber's Beowulf*, p. 292.
[48] Kier, *Beowulf*, p. 130.
[49] Ibid., pp. 137–44.

was translated into English by Faith Ingwersen as *Lejre: Fact and Fable* for John D. Niles's *Beowulf and Lejre* (2007). The remnants of the long house found at Fredshøj indicate that the building was originally 45 to 47 meters long and seven meters wide and "therefore must be classed among the very largest buildings known from the sixth century in Denmark. With its stout posts, as evidenced by the holes they left, and its situation on top of this prominence [høj] with a broad view across the surrounding landscape, this building was large, high, and broad-gabled," comparable in splendor to Hrothgar's hall in *Beowulf*:

> It came into his mind that he would order his people to build a great hall, a mead hall bigger than the children of men had ever heard of ... In due time – quickly, as it seemed to people – it was completely finished, the most magnificent of halls; he named it "Heorot."[50]

Denmark: Literary Interpretations

Of the five Nordic countries, only Denmark has produced any extended literary interpretations of *Beowulf*. N. F. S. Grundtvig began those interpretations in 1815. In his "Et Par Ord om det nys udkomne angelsaxsiske Digt" (A Few Words about the Recently Published Anglo-Saxon Poem),[51] Grundtvig primarily responds to a review of Thorkelin's first edition of the poem. Dependent as the review was on that faulty edition for its description of the poem's content, it too was faulty. By correcting both Thorkelin and reviewer, Grundtvig produced "the first, mostly accurate published account of the poem's plot and characters and one of the first deliberations over the poem's artistic value. These achievements establish Grundtvig's article as a milestone in *Beowulf* scholarship"[52] and are undoubtedly part of the impetus for Kemp Malone's having characterized Grundtvig as "[t]he first and greatest of *Beowulf* scholars."[53] As we saw in the Introduction to this book, Grundtvig says of *Beowulf*, for example, that "in its plan and execution one traces genuine artistry ... It is a beautiful, tastefully ordered and ornamented whole ... "[54] He would move away from such an absolute evaluation of the poem as he grew more familiar with it,[55] but he maintained his ability to combine his scholarly acumen with his aesthetic sensibility.

---

[50] Christensen, *Lejre*, pp. 121–22.
[51] Translated into English by Mark Bradshaw Busbee as "A Few Words."
[52] Ibid., p. 7.
[53] Malone, "Grundtvig as *Beowulf* Critic," p. 129.
[54] Busbee, "A Few Words," p. 29, cols. 1027–28.
[55] Haarder, *Beowulf*, p. 26.

Two years later, Grundtvig published his most important literary interpretation of *Beowulf*, "Om Bjovulfs Drape" (Concerning the Heroic Praise Poem of Beowulf). In this essay, represented in Shippey and Haarder's *Beowulf* by the summation Grundtvig offers on pp. 271–88 of the original, Grundtvig the scholar identifies Hygelac (Hilac) as Chochilaicus (Chohilac), whom Gregory of Tours claims was killed somewhere in the Netherlands in 512, and thus makes "the most important discovery ever made in the study of *Beowulf*."[56]

> The gain from this small piece of information is considerable for we learn not only that Higelac is a historical person and his Frankish expedition a real event, but we also know in what period the other historical figures and events must belong if they are rightly placed in the poem, and we shall now be pleased to realise that as far as we are able to judge at this stage everything fits together as well as could be expected in any ancient legend. For if Hrodulf is Rolf, he might be expected to reign at the very time when Higelac was killed, seeing that Hrodgar must be supposed to have died before then) [sic], and as we know a son of Ottar (Adils) is thought to have reigned simultaneously with Rolf in Lejre. Now, counting back about fifty years, as we see the poet doing, we get to the middle of the fifth century as the time when the old Hal[v]dan must have died, and it agrees perfectly with this that Hengest, who went to Britain in 449, is mentioned as a hero at the time of Halvdan.[57]

Grundtvig had hinted at this identification in 1815[58] and here fully develops it. In a note, he explains that his sources for making the connection were two books by the historian P. F. Suhm.[59] Pointing to Grundtvig's reliance on secondary sources in 2005, Arne Søby Christensen (1945–), Emeritus Professor of History at the University of Copenhagen, examined the three primary sources on which Suhm based his analysis and found that all three are unreliable. He concluded, therefore, "that Grundtvig's identification of Hygelac with Chlochilaichus is no longer tenable, and as a consequence the events related in *Beowulf* can no longer be placed within a chronology of the sixth century. *Beowulf* remains what it always has been: a poem from the past, not a history of the past."[60] Christensen's conclusion has not been widely accepted.

Grundtvig the scholar's insights have withstood the text of time, and so have Grundtvig the poet's. In the same 1817 article, he reassesses the art of *Beowulf* and finds it less perfect than he originally thought. It lacks taste or

---

[56] Chambers, *Beowulf: An Introduction*, p. 4, note 1.
[57] Shippey and Haarder, *Beowulf*, p. 150.
[58] Busbee, "A Few Words," p. 31.
[59] Shippey and Haarder, *Beowulf*, p. 152.
[60] Christensen, "Beowulf, Hygelac og Chlochilaichus," p. 79.

decorum;[61] the episodes are tastelessly inserted;[62] the poem mixes history and folktale producing a lack of internal unity; and the poem consists of two parts producing a lack of external unity.[63] Nevertheless, in his introduction to his translation of *Beowulf* in 1820, Grundtvig states that the poem bodies forth the hostile relationship between truth and falsehood "partly in history, and partly in nature" and that "the stories correspond to this as shadow pictures, in that Grendel functions as the evil spirit of time, the dragon as the evil spirit of nature."[64] In addition, the poem's style has much to recommend it:

> ... the language is ingenuous, without the German circumstantiality, and without becoming dark through brevity as so often in the Eddic lays; it is flowery without teeming, like later Icelandic verse, with far-fetched comparisons. Add to this the decency of the poem, its frequent fervour, and its basic religious note, and one will have to grant that it is in every way an excellent monument of the past.[65]

Haarder cautioned in 1975 that in Grundtvig's symbolic reading "we are not anywhere near the holistic interpretation advanced by Tolkien, because Grundtvig makes a point of distinguishing between on the one hand *Beowulf*, the work of art, and on the other, the poem in which the totality receives a deeper significance" that is mythical.[66] Tolkien's famous lecture, therefore, is not "Grundtvig brought up to date," as Kemp Malone described it.[67] Work on Tolkien's drafts of "*Beowulf*: The Monsters and the Critics," however, suggests that Grundtvig and Tolkien are much closer in their views of the poem than Haarder believed.[68] Those drafts make clear that Tolkien knew of Grundtvig's work on the poem and benefited from it in various ways. Busbee summarizes how "through a process of indirect inheritance and direct engagement, Tolkien gathered the most promising seeds of Grundtvig's thinking on *Beowulf* and nurtured them into full blossom. His lecture is both an extension of Grundtvig's thinking – Grundtvig updated – and a product of his own mind."[69]

Grundtvig was brought up to date before Tolkien as well. Ludvig Schrøder (1836–1908) was his disciple and published a biography about

---

[61] Haarder, *Beowulf*, p. 62.
[62] Ibid., p. 66.
[63] Ibid., p. 73.
[64] Ibid., p. 75, note 38.
[65] Ibid., p. 85, note 64.
[66] Ibid., pp. 75–76.
[67] Malone, "Grundtvig as *Beowulf* Critic," p. 129.
[68] Drout, Beowulf and the Critics.
[69] Busbee, "Grundtvig and Tolkien," p. 28.

Figure 10. Ludvig Schrøder, 1894.

him as the father of the Danish folk high school in 1900.[70] He was also a prolific author on other subjects, an influential teacher and administrator, and an imposing man who seemed "brusque and choleric" (*brysk og kolerisk*) especially because of his "powerful head that sat so close to his broad shoulders and was surrounded by an abundance of jet-black hair that hid his neck entirely and, as it were, made his bust more immovable."[71] For twenty-four years, he was co-editor of three periodicals, *Nordisk Maanedsskrift* (1871–83), *Historisk Maanedsskrift* (1883–88), and *Danskeren* (1888–94), and from 1864 to 1906 he was headmaster of Askov, a folk high school that he built into the largest such institution in the Nordic region.[72] It was in that capacity that he turned his attention to *Beowulf* in his 1875

---

[70] *N. F. S. Grundtvig: Den nordiska folkhögskolans fader: En levnadsskildring* (N. F. S. Grundtvig: Father of the Nordic High School: A Description of a Life).

[71] "'det kraftfulde hoved der sad så tæt på de brede skuldre og var omgivet af den kulsorte hårfylde som helt skjulte hans hals og ligesom gjorde hans buste mere ubevægelig'." Rosenblad, "Ludvig Schrøder."

[72] Ibid.

study *Om Bjovulfs-Drapen: Efter en række foredrag på folkehöjskolen i Askov* (The Heroic Poem of Beowulf: From a Series of Lectures at the Folk High School in Askov). This contribution to our understanding of the poem has gone relatively unnoticed.[73] Chambers alludes to Schrøder in a footnote;[74] Andreas Haarder alludes in a footnote to Chambers' footnote;[75] Stanley B. Greenfield and Fred C. Robinson in their bibliography list him with a cryptic allusion to Chambers' note;[76] Roberta Frank alludes to Schrøder's explicating certain scenes in *Beowulf* as "foretelling the fall of the house of the Scyldings, the poem's ominous backdrop";[77] and Brad Busbee briefly refers to Schrøder's work in the context of discussing Grundtvig's 1820 translation of *Beowulf* as a work for young readers.[78] All but the last deal with Schrøder's treatment of the Unferth–Hrothgar relationship. The Danish family feud, including the introduction of the treacherous Unferth into the Danish royal household, Chambers claims, was first fully described by Schrøder;[79] Shippey and Haarder agree. Schrøder "was the first modern reader to lay stress on the scene in Heorot in which Unferth is juxtaposed with Hrothgar and Hrothulf, and Wealhtheow addresses her husband, a scene whose implications have formed the basis for almost all twentieth-century criticism."[80] Schrøder regards *Beowulf* as a work of art comparable to *The Iliad* and *The Odyssey*, as did Grundtvig before him.[81] Despite his dependence on Grundtvig, however, his reading is more elaborate and detailed and convincing than that of his great predecessor, whom scholars such as Malone,[82] George Clark,[83] and S. A. J. Bradley[84] have said anticipated Tolkien's symbolic interpretation of the poem from 1936. Had critics been aware of Schrøder, in fact, 1875 instead of 1936 might have become the traditional turning point in the history of *Beowulf* criticism and subsequent scholarship might have become a footnote to Schrøder.

---

[73] The following discussion of Schrøder's book is a slightly revised version of my discussion of it in "Nineteenth-Century Scandinavia," pp. 123–25.
[74] Chambers, *Introduction*, p. 30.
[75] Haarder, *Beowulf*, p. 97, note 18.
[76] GR, item 2715.
[77] Frank, *The Etiquette of Early Northern Verse*, pp. 143–44.
[78] Busbee, "'A Little Shared Homer'," pp. 34–35.
[79] Chambers, *Introduction*, pp. 30–31. In this regard, see Olrik, *The Heroic Legends of Denmark*, p. 49, note, who was the first to acknowledge the importance of Schrøder's discovery.
[80] Shippey and Haarder, *Beowulf*, p. 372. See also Hall, "England, Denmark, America," p. 446.
[81] Schrøder, *Bjovulfs-drapen*, p. 48.
[82] Malone, "Grundtvig as *Beowulf* Critic," p. 135.
[83] George Clark, *Beowulf* (Boston, 1990), p. 11.
[84] Bradley, "First New-European Literature," p. 57.

Schrøder's interpretation is fairly comprehensive. "It is certain," Schrøder writes, "that there is a connection between the completion of Heorot and the coming of the troll."[85] He reviews secular and Christian history and finds that the building of such magnificent edifices usually coincides with the decline of a society: the Egyptian pyramids are an example, as are the heathen temples in Athens and Solomon's temple, which Solomon built in Jerusalem when the glory of Israel was past. The Church of Hagia Sophia was erected in Constantinople as the power of the Greek Church waned and the great monument waited for the Turks "like another Grendel to swallow it."[86] And when Leo X built St. Peter's in Rome, he sold indulgences to help subsidize it, and that was one of the great causes for the Luther's Reformation.[87] Heorot is a similar edifice, and Grendel's descending on it has unmistakable meaning.

Grendel – and this idea actually comes from Grundtvig[88] – symbolizes sloth or lethargy, which represents the decline of society and which casts sleeping spells over those who inhabit the great hall. Grendel has deprived the Danes not only of Heorot and greatness, but also of the giant sword with its inscription about the flood and the previous owner's name. That sword represents great deeds past, a symbol of honor captured by sloth;[89] Beowulf can return it to Hrothgar, and tries to, but the blade itself melts in Grendel's blood. This, says Schrøder, means that a time of remarkable achievement will not return to the Danes as a permanent fruit of Beowulf's great deed.[90]

The dragon's role in the poem parallels that of Grendel, and his treasure hoard has symbolic value paralleling that of the giant sword.

> If the troll broods over the sword, so the dragon broods over the gold. But if the sword is for the Nordic warrior race the natural reflection of their illustrious feats, the gold is the expression in imagery for happiness and joy which can flower under the protection of peace. As the troll Grendel casts sleep on the Danes, the dragon Starkheart casts fire on the Goths. If there is a connection between the sword's being stolen and sleep's ruling, there is also a connection between the gold's being the dragon's booty and fire's ruling. The fire may signify evil strife; we still talk, after all, about anger flaring up, about the fire of battle, and about

---

[85] "Det kan ikke fejle at der er en sammenhæng imellem Hjorteborgens fuldendelse og troldens komme." Schrøder, *Bjovulfs-drapen*, p. 50.
[86] "Som en anden Grændel for at sluge den." Ibid., p. 51.
[87] Ibid., p. 51.
[88] Haarder, *Beowulf*, pp. 82–83.
[89] Schrøder, *Bjovulfs-drapen*, p. 38.
[90] Ibid., p. 41.

the flame of discord. It is anger and dissension that destroys peace and drives away joy, just as it is sloth that brings achievements to an end.[91]

Schrøder's reading is holistic, Tolkienesque, and frequently compelling, although also occasionally quaint and fanciful. And it exemplifies Scandinavian Anglo-Saxonism, although it seems not to concern itself with nationalism. It emerged, after all, in the context of Grundtvig's educational program in the folk high schools that he founded in Denmark, and *Beowulf* was being used by Schrøder as the nationalistic reader Grundtvig had hoped it would be. Schrøder concludes his book by affirming its Grundtvigian purpose. Although Grundtvig's goal of inspiring Scandinavians to embrace *Beowulf* was still far from being realized, Schrøder sought it, too, and hoped that "my talk and my writing will contribute a little to that purpose."[92]

The final literary interpretation of *Beowulf* from Denmark also marks the chronological end of this history of OE studies in Scandinavia, 2023. Written in Danish, Keld Zeruneith's *Beowulf: The Tragedy of a Hero: A Reading* (*Beowulf. En helts tragedie. En læsning*) was first published in the English translation of Paul Russell Garrett. The book consists of five sections that outline the incremental, cumulative argument that Zeruneith constructs based on discussions of the poem, the poet, the hall, Beowulf's life story, and Beowulf's legacy. The first two sections concern 1) the poem's manuscript history as well as aesthetic features deriving from the oral tradition such as ring structure, and 2) the poet, whom Zeruneith considers one of the poem's two main characters (the other being Beowulf) and "the work's structuring and compositional consciousness."[93] That consciousness is cognizant of the pagan past depicted in the poem, reflected through the prism of the poet's Christian present, and also "taps into the central characters' psychological reality."[94] The next three sections focus on 3) the hall, 4) Beowulf's life story, and 5) Beowulf's legacy. The

---

[91] "Når trolden ruger over *sværdet*, så ruger dragen over *guldet*. Men er sværdet for Nordens kæmpefolk det naturlige billede på de lysende *bedrifter*, så er guldet på billedsproget udtrykket for *lykken* og *glæden*, der kun blomstrer i fredens skjöd. Når trolden Grændel spyer *søvn* på de danske, da spyer dragen Stærkhjort *ild* på Gotherne. Er der sammenhæng imellem dette, at sværdet er røvet, og det, at søvnen råder, så er der tilvisse også sammenhæng imellem det, at guldet er dragens bytte, og det, at ilden råder. Ilden må betyde den onde kiv; vi taler jo også endnu om, at vreden blusser op, om kampens ild og om tvedragts-luen. Det er vreden og splidagtigheden, som forstyrrer freden og fordriver glæden, som det er sløvheden, der bringer bedrifterne til at ophører." Ibid., p. 43.
[92] "Skulde min tale og min skrift derom gjærne bidrage lidet til." Ibid., p. 94.
[93] Zeruneith, *Beowulf: The Tragedy*, p. 61.
[94] Ibid., p. 75.

hall is the arena in which most of the poem takes place and symbolizes the totality of the heroic life. Zeruneith articulates the social norms, such as the importance of the king as ring-giver,[95] the importance of custom,[96] and the importance of women, particularly those of high rank as "peace-weavers,"[97] as he sketches the Scandinavian background of the story, such as its probably taking place in Lejre[98] and the presence of the earliest Danish kings and their parallels in the ON tradition (for example, Skjöldr/Scyld, Hrólfr Kraki/Hrothulf).[99] He also discusses "the oscillating semantics" and thematic ramifications of the word *wlenco* (daring or pride) in the poem.[100] All of the first three richly detailed sections of the book are a prolegomenon to Zeruneith's intricate, nuanced interpretation of Beowulf, the tragic hero.

Beowulf's life story is largely an internal one. "Even though psychological insight did not exist in a modern sense in the literature of the time, it is still possible to find something universally psychological in the history of Beowulf's development."[101] It is also possible to find in Beowulf's story some archetypical patterns. Although details in the poem are sparse, Beowulf seems to have had a traumatic childhood. His nameless mother seems to have died early,[102] and his maternal uncle Hæthcyn accidentally kills his maternal uncle Herebeald, which leaves his maternal grandfather Hrethel in extreme grief. His grandfather takes him into his home at age seven, and Beowulf's father, Ecgtheow, then disappears from his life.[103] He has now lost both parents. Hrethel's warriors do not think much of Beowulf and humiliate him on the mead bench for his indolence ("*hean wæs længe*," [his humiliation was long], line 2183b), but Hrethel treats him well. Hygelac's taking over Hrethel's role with Beowulf after Hrethel's death prolongs the "loving care he receives from his maternal family,"[104] which contributes to his inhibition as a child. When he reaches young manhood and hears of Grendel's depredations in Denmark, he defies Hygelac and sails to Heorot, thus beginning (along with his fighting sea monsters in his youth) a maturation process.[105] His rejection of the mother (or maternal family) is transformed into the fight with the Terrible

---

[95] Ibid., p. 126.
[96] Ibid., p. 131.
[97] Ibid., pp. 162–73.
[98] Ibid., pp. 138–42.
[99] Ibid., pp. 142–46.
[100] Ibid., pp. 174–80. See also p. 126.
[101] Ibid., p. 192.
[102] Ibid., p. 197.
[103] Ibid., pp. 197–98.
[104] Ibid., p. 201.
[105] Ibid., p. 205.

Mother (or Grendel's mother), who tries to destroy the rebel[106] but fails and is herself killed. Aeschylus' *Oresteia* provides proof for the necessity of matricide in the individuation process,[107] and Hrothgar, whose prideful building of Heorot brought God's punishment down on the Danes,[108] is the patriarchal figure meant to be Beowulf's spiritual father who warns him of the dangers of arrogance, the dangers of *wlenco*.[109] The second part of the poem is a test of whether Beowulf heeded that warning. He did not.[110]

> We are left with the impression of a degenerate hero, a king lacking a queen and heir leaving his country to its ruin. From this perspective, *Beowulf* is an obituary for the heroic protagonist, whose way of life in its superindividual meaning reflects heroism's strength and weakness, since is locked in a reactionary pattern of egoism without any transformative ability or even aims beyond increasing one's reputation. This approach to life, in its reticence, forgoes the possibility of maturing as an individual and ultimately shuns humanity as a whole by following the trails of blood vengeance.[111]

A great strength of Zeruneith's study is its contextualizing *Beowulf* within three literary traditions, one a primary source and the other two, secondary: OE with references to a wide range of texts such as "The Wife's Lament," the Guthlac poems, "The Voyages of Ohthere and Wulstan," and Bede; ON with references to a number of Eddic poems, Icelandic sagas, Snorri Sturluson, and Saxo Grammaticus; and classical with references to authors such as Aeschylus, Euripides, and Eumenides and texts such as the *Odyssey*. Zeruneith also refers to works by Tacitus, Boethius, St. Augustine, and Erich Neumann to help deepen our understanding of his compelling new reading of the poem.

Sweden: Cultural and Historical

Numerous historians and five archaeologists in Sweden have produced over ninety items in Swedish, most of them articles, on the cultural and historical aspects of *Beowulf*. The first of these, a historical piece, appeared in 1884 and the most recent, an archaeological one, in 2018.

---

[106] Ibid., p. 207.
[107] Ibid., pp. 209–12.
[108] Ibid., p. 229.
[109] Ibid., pp. 232–33.
[110] Ibid., pp. 237–56.
[111] Ibid., pp. 275–76.

Scandinavian Approaches to Beowulf

Pontus Fahlbeck (1850–1923), schooled in Latin, philosophy, history, the Nordic languages, and physics, was – among many other things – Professor of History and Political Science at the University of Lund, 1909–15, and a member of parliament, 1903–11. He "had a fine appearance and in his conduct was elegant and engaging," and "[t]he study of antiquity – 'a protected place,' F[ahlbeck]'s 'time out' – and pondering the riddle of the world, life and death, constituted for him two refuges from the troubles of the day."[112] During a couple of those time outs, Fahlbeck produced an important, two-part contribution to the study of *Beowulf*.[113] "Beovulfskvädet såsom källa för nordisk fornhistoria" (The Beowulf Poem as a Source for Nordic Legendary History, 1894) begins with a substantial, detailed summary of *Beowulf* and a lament over the fact that, while the Danes have two, the English four, and the Germans just as many translations of the poem, there is none in Swedish.[114] That would not be remedied until 1889. He then discusses the royal genealogy of the Geats,[115] Beowulf's history,[116] the royal genealogies of the Swedes and the Danes,[117] and that of the Swedish people[118] before reaching the main subject of his paper, the identification of the Geats.[119] He then discusses the Danish people[120] and finishes his study by considering the poem's composition[121] and reaching the conclusion that "*Beowulf* must, despite its saga-like character, be regarded as a very dependable source for the oldest history of the North."[122]

Fahlbeck, the foremost proponent of what has been called "The Jute Theory," identifies the Geats of *Beowulf* with the Jutes of the Jutland peninsula. While he was not the first to do so (Heinrich Leo was in 1839), his study has "raised the Geat question from the realm of conjecture to that of scholarly debate and still [in 1925] makes the weightiest contribution in favor of the Jute theory."[123] He looks first at several passages

---

[112] "hade ett fint utseende och var i sitt uppträdande elegant och förbindlig," "Studiet av antiken – 'en fridlyst plats', F:s 'pax i leken' – och grubbel över 'världsgåtan', över liv och död, utgjorde för honom två tillflykter undan dagens bekymmer." Carlsson, "Pontus E. A. Fahlbeck."
[113] "Beovulfskvädet såsom källa för nordisk fornhistoria," 1884 and 1913.
[114] Ibid. p. 2. The summary covers pp. 4–21.
[115] Ibid., pp. 21–23.
[116] Ibid., p. 23.
[117] Ibid., pp. 24–26.
[118] Ibid., pp. 26, 60–69.
[119] Ibid., pp. 26–57.
[120] Ibid., pp. 57–64.
[121] Ibid., pp. 69–88.
[122] "Beovulfsqvädet måste, trots dess sagolika karakter i det stora hela, betraktas såsom en mycket tillförlitlig källa för Nordens äldsta historia." Ibid., p. 84.
[123] "lyfte upp geaterfrågan från gissningarnas område till den vetenskapliga

in the poem that problematize the Geats' originating from Västergötland or Östergötland, as most scholars think they did: 1) lines 1921b–24 tell us that Hygelac's court lies close to the sea and lines 3131a–36 that the dragon's lair does as well [29–31][124]; 2) lines 2333–35 describe the dragon's destruction of the land of the Geats, *ealond utan* (on an island out there), an epithet that does not fit Västergötland or Östergötland[125]; and 3) lines 2380a, 2394a, 2473a, and 2477a relate that the wars between the Swedes and the Geats took place across the sea or wide water, a description that does not apply to Västergötland or Östergötland.[126] Where, then, did the Geats come from, if not from Västergötland or Östergötland? The problematic passages are no longer problematic if the Geats came from an area that fits those descriptions; that place would be the Jutland peninsula, separated from southern Sweden by the Kattegat strait connecting the North Sea with the Baltic.[127] Other details in the poem, such as the Geats' being referred to as the "Weather Geats" or "Wind Geats," strengthen the identification of the Geats with the Jutes. Jutland is well known as a windy landscape.[128] Fahlbeck acknowledges the linguistic difficulty with equating the Geats with the Jutes but does not think it is insuperable given the Anglo-Saxons' use of two terms for Jutes, *Geatas* and *Jotas*.[129] In his follow-up article thirty years later, Fahlbeck lays even more stress on the OE terms characterizing the wars between the Geats and Swedes as occurring across the sea and stands by his original conclusion that the sea would have to be the Kattegat or the Baltic.[130]

A nationalist, Knut Stjerna (1874–1909), on the other hand, would locate the Geats on the Swedish island of Öland in the Baltic. Stjerna had a tragically short but successful life as a journalist and influential and controversial archaeologist. He was deeply influenced when he studied literature at the University of Lund by his teacher Henrik Schück and later by the archaeologist Oscar Montelius (1843–1921), from whom he was eventually estranged. Stjerna was appointed Lecturer in Scandinavian and Comparative Archaeology in 1907 at the University of Uppsala, where two of his students were Birger Nerman and Sune Lindqvist. He was famous for his immense energy, but in 1908 his heart began to fail, and in 1909 he collapsed at the Kafé Solidar in Uppsala while waiting for

---

diskussionens och alltjämt utgör det mest vägande inlägget till jutteteoriens förmån." Nerman, *Det svenska rikets uppkomst*, p. 109.
[124] "Beovulfskvädet såsom källa för nordisk fornhistoria," pp. 29–31.
[125] Ibid., pp. 31–32.
[126] Ibid., pp. 32–35.
[127] Ibid., p. 40.
[128] Ibid., p. 41.
[129] Ibid., p. 52.
[130] "Beovulfskvädet såsom källa för nordisk fornhistoria," 1913.

dinner and died instantly from cardiac arrest.[131] In his brief life of thirty-five years, however, he succeeded in raising the status of archaeology (and teaching) at the university, producing a series of articles on *Beowulf* that has added substantially to our understanding of the poem,[132] and earning for himself "a brilliant reputation in his own country as a scholar of unusual industry and thoroughness and of active imagination."[133] That reputation spread beyond his homeland as well because of his consequential work on *Beowulf*.

Stjerna's eight articles were posthumously translated into English by John R. Clark Hall and published as *Essays on Questions Connected with the Old English Poem of Beowulf* in 1912. In the first of these, "Helmets and Swords in *Beowulf*," Stjerna ties the frequent references to both items in the poem to archaeological finds in Scandinavia and elsewhere that help date the events described. The adjective *heaðosteap* (towering in battle) in lines 1245a and 2153a, for example, would appropriately describe helmets from before the middle of the seventh century but not after it.[134] Similarly, the *hringmæl* (ringed sword) in lines 1521b and 1564b belongs to a large group of swords discovered in Sweden, Denmark, Norway, England, Germany, and Italy from the period 550 to 650 CE but not before or after that period.[135] Stjerna gives further support for the sixth- to early seventh-century dating of the events in *Beowulf*, and therefore of when the poem's original lays were created in the next essay, "Archæological notes on *Beowulf*." The mention in the poem of a *hafoc* (hawk, falcon) in line 2263b, for instance, reflects an early Swedish custom, as shown by the remains of a gyrfalcon having been found in the third Vendel grave from the seventh century in Sweden.[136]

The next two essays focus more on historical than on archaeological matters. In "Vendel and the Vendel Crow," Stjerna disputes the suggestion made by Sophus Bugge (1833–1907) that the Vendel mentioned in *Beowulf*, line 348 ("Wulfgar maþelode; þæt wæs Wendla leod," Wulfgar spoke; that was a man of the Vendels), is Vendill in North Jutland; Stjerna argues it is instead Vendel in Uppland, Sweden. Grave finds in Uppland, which are more plentiful there than in all other Swedish regions combined, confirm its centrality during the period 500 to 700 CE. The *fæsten* (line 2950b, stronghold) that Ongentheow (the Vendel Crow) retreats to during the Geatish-Swedish wars is undoubtedly located in Uppland.[137] It should

---

[131] Nordström, "Knut Stjerna," p. 119.
[132] Ibid., pp. 120–28.
[133] J. R. Clark Hall, "Introduction," to Stjerna, *Essays on Questions*, p. xvii.
[134] Stjerna, *Esssays on Questions*, p. 18.
[135] Ibid., pp. 26–27.
[136] Ibid., p. 36.
[137] Ibid., p. 54.

be noted that in this article, Stjerna was the first to observe that the name "Wulfgar" alliterates with "Wendla," "Wægmund," "Weohstan," and "Wiglaf," all part of the same family branch, "probably on the female side, of the Swedish line of the Scylfings (v. 2602)" from Vendel.[138] In his article "Swedes and Geats during the Migration Period," Stjerna advances the theory that the Geats in *Beowulf* came from Östergötland, Västergötland, and had their center of power on Öland.[139] (See Curt Weibull's rebuttal of this theory, below, as well as Clark Hall's.[140])

The last three articles by Stjerna concerning *Beowulf* return to archaeology. "Scyld's Funeral Obsequies" focuses on burial practices around the world, from the Bronze Age to the sixth and seventh centuries, in order to contextualize the description of Scyld's burial in the poem. The burial fits in the first of three stages of burial customs seen in Europe, Australia, India, and elsewhere, in which the dead man is laid out in a boat and pushed out from shore.[141] The second stage is the custom of burying both man and ship or hanging them in a tree;[142] and the third stage is when the living provide no means of transport to the other world.[143] Since stage one burial cannot be confirmed on archaeological grounds, Stjerna turns to literary sources such as the description of Balder's cremation in *Gylfaginning*, chapter 49.[144] He concludes that the description of Scyld's burial in *Beowulf* accurately reflects a stage one burial custom "which was actually in vogue in the North" around 400 CE.[145] He concludes as well that the inconsistent description of "The Dragon's Hoard in *Beowulf*" results from the poem's depending on successive versions of the descriptions that reflect hoarding customs at various periods. In the earliest period, all treasure items were interred; in the latest, only select items were.[146] Stjerna also examines each item belonging to the dragon's hoard and connects each with actual archaeological finds.

The final article, "Fasta fornlämningar i *Beowulf*" (Fast Remains in *Beowulf*), has been divided into two in the English translation. In the first, "The Double Burial in *Beowulf*," Stjerna uses three graves from the fourth century in which two men were interred to elucidate how the foster-brother obligations in the fourth and fifth centuries informed the cremation practices in *Beowulf*, line 1117a, for example, where Hildeburh's

---

[138] Ibid., p. 56.
[139] Ibid., pp. 74ff.
[140] Ibid., pp. xxiv–xxv.
[141] Ibid., p. 106.
[142] Ibid., p. 108.
[143] Ibid., p. 109.
[144] Ibid., p. 112.
[145] Ibid., p. 127.
[146] Ibid., pp. 154–55.

two sons are placed on the funeral pyre together.[147] The poem therefore offers a literary example of the custom of burying (or cremating) brothers and foster brothers together.[148] In "Beowulf's Funeral Obsequies," Stjerna explores to what extent the description of Beowulf's funeral is corroborated by archaeological evidence. After reviewing evidence we have for burial practices in Scandinavia for the period in question, the fifth century, Stjerna points to the royal burial mound in Gamla Uppsala known as "Odinshög" (Odin's Mound)[149] from around the year 500 CE as being analogous to "Beowulf's Mound" in the poem. He then compares the literary description with the archaeological one and concludes that there is "a complete identity between the funeral customs in use by the Swedes at the burial of their king, and those which the Geats followed in honour of Beowulf."[150]

Henrik Schück (1855–1947), who so profoundly influenced Knut Stjerna, was a literary historian and Professor of Aesthetics, Literature, and Art History at the University of Lund (1890–98) and then at the University of Uppsala (1898–1920). He was Rector Magnificus there (1905–18), a member of the Swedish Academy (1913–47), a member of the Nobel Committee (1920–36), and Chair of the Nobel Foundation (1918–29), among many other distinctions. His broad academic interests included early Swedish literature, Shakespeare and other Elizabethan authors, world literature, and *Beowulf*.[151] Of his five publications touching or focusing on the poem, two have particular importance. *Folknamnet Geatas i den fornengelska dikten Beowulf* (The Tribal Name Geats in the Old English Poem *Beowulf*) takes up the issue of the provenance of the Geats and, *contra* Fahlbeck, argues that they did not come from Jutland but from the south-west coast of Sweden near the Göta river.[152] Schück reviews Fahlbeck's argument point by point in reaching this conclusion.[153] For example, Fahlbeck would have Beowulf and Breca begin their swimming contest on Jutland and end up on Fyen or King Finn's land in Friesland. Fahlbeck does not explain how Fyen could be referred to as Finna land (line 580b) or how Finna (genitive plural) land could mean Finn's (genitive singular) land. There is a logical, geographical problem here as well. If the swimmers begin on Jutland opposite Fyen, swim for five nights and then are separated and driven to opposite shores equidistant from the point of separation, one would reach the Gulf of Kristiana and the other Fyen again or Frisia on the other

---

[147] Ibid., pp. 189–93.
[148] Ibid., p. 196.
[149] Ibid., pp. 221–34.
[150] Ibid., pp. 235–37.
[151] "John Henrik Emil Schück."
[152] Schück, *Folknamnet Geatas*, pp. 22–27.
[153] Ibid., pp. 16–22.

side of Jutland. A far better solution that fits the narrative much more fully is to identify Finna land with Finneidhi or Finnheden in Småland, Sweden. The competitors start from Kungsbacka fjord in Halland in south-western Sweden and are later separated by stormy weather, "after which one – if we use the modern geographical names – steps ashore approximately at Fredriksstad [in Norway], the other at Laholm [in southern Halland, Sweden]."[154]

Schück's *Studier i Beowulfsagan* (Studies in the Beowulf Saga) explores not the poem of *Beowulf*, but the Nordic stories that lie behind it from the Migration Period. The relationship between the poem and the Nordic tales it exploits is exactly analogous to that between the Norwegian/Icelandic tales of Sigurd Fafnesbane and the continental stories first developed on the Rhine before migrating north. In the case of *Beowulf*, the Angles and Saxons first learned the relevant stories on the mainland and then brought them to England, where the OE poem was written first in the Northumbrian or Mercian dialect and then translated into West Saxon during the first part of the eighth century.[155] Distinguishing the poem of *Beowulf* from the story of Beowulf is crucial.[156] The poem is a unified whole; the stories are not. Basically, there are two or three of them: the fight with Grendel, the fight with Grendel's mother (or taken together as one story), and the fight with the dragon. The protagonist of the first story (perhaps two stories) is a brave warrior in one locale (Denmark) and time period; the protagonist for the third is an old king in another locale (Götaland in Sweden) and time period. Discovering where, when, and how those stories first arose and then how they were united with each other and then moved to England is Schück's goal in this essay.[157]

Behind the first story of Grendel and his mother lies the primitive tendency to try to explain the unexplainable dark and incomprehensible forces in the world through folktale, saga, and myth. The manifestations of those dark forces can be confronted and defeated by a powerful human.[158] We see this story in *Grettissaga*, for example (pp. 8–9), and in various folktales from Lorraine, Flanders, Brittany, Italy, Portugal, Spain, and Switzerland. The motif is also seen in the first story in *Beowulf* and is firmly tied to Danish legendary history and the only place it could take place: Denmark.[159]

---

[154] "hvarefter den ene – om vi insätta de moderna geografiska namnen – stiger i land ungefär vid Fredriksstad, den andre vid Laholm." Ibid., pp. 28–29.
[155] Schück, *Studier*, p. 3.
[156] Ibid., p. 5.
[157] Ibid., pp. 6–7.
[158] Ibid., p. 7.
[159] Ibid., p. 10.

The second story about the dragon also has ancient roots, this time in the primitive belief seen among many peoples in death as a devouring beast.[160] In the Norse tradition, the motif lives in several forms: the wolf Fenrir, the dog Garm, the serpent Niðhögg, and the Midgard Serpent. The beast can be killed by an intervening hero or god, or it can kill the intervening hero or god and then itself be killed by a younger hero avenging the older. Such is the case in *Beowulf*.[161] The dragon story is firmly tied to Geatish legendary history, and the intervening hero was probably the national hero.[162] The two (or three) stories were probably originally independent of each other, each with its own hero with his own name, and first became joined in England with the three heroes turned into one with one name.[163] Schück reasons that Beowulf's life's work parallels Scyld's in significant ways, "and when Beo in the genealogies is now made Scyld's son, it is therefore probable that the hero in *this* adventure [the fight with Grendel] bore the name Beo."[164] The hero in the fight with Grendel's mother was the unnamed son of Ecgtheow, and the hero of the dragon story bore a different name such as Wulf. That would alliterate with the tribal name Wægmunding that includes him, Wiglaf, Weohstan, and Wihstan.[165] From those three heroes, then, arose the unified hero Beowulf, son of Ecgtheow, in the OE poem.[166] Schück speculates that the stories from Denmark and Götaland met in Frisia en route to England and were then revised into a unified whole.[167] The unifier was probably an English missionary sent to Frisia beginning in 678 CE with St. Wilfrid of York,[168] who spent time there listening to tales told by merchants and others passing through Frisia. He was probably himself a poet with a fondness for tales; he assembled what he heard into a single narrative about a single hero and wrote that narrative in Northumbrian or Mercian; and that narrative was translated into West Saxon after its arrival in England.[169]

Curt Weibull (1886–1991) was Professor of History at the University of Gothenburg from 1927 to 1953 and Rector from 1946 to 1956. It was in the latter capacity that he aided Norwegian students fleeing to Sweden during the Nazi occupation of Norway during WWII. The University of

---

[160] Ibid., p. 11.
[161] Ibid., pp. 12–13.
[162] Ibid., p. 14.
[163] Ibid., pp. 22–23.
[164] "och då nu Beo i genealogierna göres till Scylds son, är det därför antagligt, att hjälten i *detta* äfventyr burit namnet Beo." Ibid., p. 24.
[165] Ibid., p. 25.
[166] Ibid., p. 26.
[167] Ibid., p. 40.
[168] Ibid., p. 43.
[169] Ibid., pp. 44–50.

Oslo recognized him for this important work by giving him an Honorary Doctorate in 1946. His scholarly work is grounded in source criticism, which he developed with his brother Lauritz Weibull.[170] In his *Om det svenska och det danska rikets uppkomst* (On the Rise of the Swedish and Danish Kingdom, 1921), his sources are many and come from the Greeks, from the Romans, and from OE works, especially *Beowulf*, which earlier scholars had used to argue for a prehistoric origin of the Swedish kingdom. Weibull, on the other hand, uses *Beowulf* to promote his thesis that the origin of the Swedish and Danish kingdom lies not during the reigns of the kings buried in the massive burial mounds in Uppsala or around 500 or 600 CE,[171] as was commonly assumed, but during the Viking period. The most prominent and influential scholar arguing for an early date was Knut Stjerna, who used both *Beowulf* and archaeological discoveries to substantiate his dating.[172]

But, Weibull asks, is Stjerna's view defensible? Its foundations are ultimately 1) that the Geats of *Beowulf* are the east Götar of Sweden and 2) that the great wealth and dominance of Uppland from the sixth century onward is explained by the Swedes' rule spreading south over richer but less populated areas of the country – for example, Östgötland.[173] The conclusion of *Beowulf*, therefore, where the conquest of the Geats by the Swedes is predicted after the death of Beowulf, in essence predicts the birth of a unified Swedish nation. Weibull dismisses the first, essential, premise by pointing out that the east Götar have never been a seafaring people and thus do not fit the narrative of the poem well at all. He reinforces the point by referring to the work of Pontus Fahlbeck, who asserts, along with the OE translation of Bede's *Ecclesiastical History*, that the Geats of *Beowulf* are the Jutes of Jutland or Geataland.[174] The battles that the poem describes are not between Swedes and Götar but between Swedes and Jutes; and they seem to have emerged from the competition for booty and power on the major pathways between the countries of the Baltic Sea Basin and Western Europe.[175] The results of the battles did not produce a unified Sweden or Denmark. That phenomenon did not occur until the Viking period.

Carl Wilhelm von Sydow (1878–1952), one of whose mentors was Axel Olrik, was a leading, pioneering folklorist in Sweden and Professor of Nordic and Comparative Folkloristics at the University of Lund, 1938 to

---

[170] Wasberg, "Curt Weibull."
[171] Weibull, *Om det svenska och det danska rikets uppkomst*, p. 301.
[172] See Stjerna, *Esssays on Questions*.
[173] Weibull, *Om det svenska och det danska rikets uppkomst*, p. 308.
[174] Weibull, *Om det svenska och det danska rikets uppkomst*, pp. 310–11. See Pontus Fahlbeck, "Beovulfskvädet såsom källa för nordisk fornhistoria," p. 26.
[175] Weibull, *Om det svenska och danska rikets uppkomst*, pp. 324–25.

1947. From his youth, he was deeply interested in botany and zoology;[176] he studied at the Askov folk high school in Denmark and there became interested in folklore; and his son, who looked very much like him, was the internationally famous star of film, stage, and television Max von Sydow (1929–2020).[177] One of his specialties was the Celtic influence on Germanic literature and folklore, the initial manifestation of which for *Beowulf* studies is his article on Thor's journey to Utgard in Snorri Sturluson's *Gylfaginning*. He argues that the earliest example or the motif of the glove so massive that Thor and Loki mistake it for a house is first found in Beowulf's retelling of his fight with Grendel, who had a huge glove hanging at his waist into which he wanted to put Beowulf (line 2085b).[178]

In his other articles touching on *Beowulf*, von Sydow focuses on the mythic and folktale dimensions of the poem. He denies the mythic underpinnings of Scyld Scefing,[179] for example, maintains the association of the name Grendel with folk belief in a water troll in southern England reflected in eight OE place-names,[180] affirms the close connection between Beowulf and Böthvar Bjarki,[181] and situates the treasure-guarding dragon in *Beowulf* in a long, widespread tradition across Europe and Asia.[182] Finally, he examines mythic interpretations of the poem such as Müllenhoff's construal of Beowulf as a semi-divine being whose function it is to protect humans from nature. In his youthful contest with Breca, Beowulf swims against the polar stream and defeats the cold and wildness and storm of the winter sea, represented by Breca; in his mature fights with Grendel and Grendel's mother, who likewise represent the destructive power of the sea and the sea's depths respectively, he emerges victorious; and in his battle with the dragon in his old age, he again beats back the forces of storm and sea but dies in the process.[183] Other scholars either agree or disagree with Müllenhoff. Von Sydow lays out the bases for all the various points of view, offers arguments against them and their methodologies, and ends his discussion with his own interpretation of the poem and its mythic elements. It is brief. The story of Beowulf's fight with the Grendel kin is borrowed from Ireland, where it belongs to the Gaelic Finn cycle of narratives. Grendel is a giant recognizable from Indo-European folk-

---

[176] This interest is shown in his article "Geografi," in which von Sydow points out that the natural descriptions in *Beowulf* reflect the author's homeland in Northumbria, especially in Derbyshire.
[177] Bringéus, "Carl Vilhelm von Sydow."
[178] von Sydow, "Tors färd," p. 156.
[179] von Sydow, "Scyld Scefing."
[180] von Sydow, "Grendel."
[181] von Sydow, "Beowulf och Bjarke."
[182] von Sydow, "Draken som skattevaktare," pp. 107, 114–15.
[183] von Sydow, "Mytforskiningen," pp. 99–100.

tales and does not have symbolic import; he lives with his mother out in the sea, where the Gaelic hero must pursue them. The AS poet was not familiar with the idea of a sea giant and therefore associated him with the AS water troll, Grendel, whose name is linked to eight watery places in southern England.[184] Similarly, the dragon in *Beowulf* is not to be interpreted symbolically. It belongs to folktale, not myth, and is a combination of stories of an attacking dragon and one that guards treasure.[185]

In the introduction to his unpublished memoirs, Birger Nerman (1888–1971) declares that "from a psychological point of view," he is "completely uninteresting."[186] From many other points of view, however, he is an intriguing figure in the history of OE studies in Scandinavia. Along with his twin brother Einar (1888–1983) and his older brother Ture (1886–1969), he would become a major player in Swedish cultural life. Einar became a renowned artist whose "Sun Stick match boy" still graces every box of Solstickan (Sun Stick) matches sold in Sweden;[187] Ture became a socialist journalist, author, poet, and politician; and Birger became an esteemed academic and human rights activist for the Baltic states who, by combining literary history, philology, and archaeology in his research, created his own subject area at the University of Uppsala and finished his career as Director of the National Historical Museum in Stockholm, 1938–69.[188] His first book is a collection of his poetry, *Pan och Eros* (1912), and his most important contribution to *Beowulf* studies is his *Det svenska rikets uppkomst* (The Swedish Kingdom's Origin, 1925), which he condensed for an English-speaking audience as "The Foundation of the Swedish Kingdom" (16 April 1924) and revised for a popular Swedish audience as *Sveriges rikes uppkomst* (Origin of the Kingdom of Sweden, 1941).

Nerman considers archaeology, literary records (ON sagas, Procopius, Jordanes, and Cassiodorus), and *Beowulf* as the three most significant sources for the early history of Sweden. Taken separately, they are subject to dispute; taken together when they reinforce each other, they have compelling power. Knut Stjerna's mainly archaeological argument for the foundation of the Swedish kingdom has the Svear of what is now middle Sweden or Svealand moving south to conquer areas in southern Sweden or Götaland and establishing the Swedish realm sometime in the middle of the sixth century.[189] Literary material supports this interpretation. In *Beowulf*, written ca. 700 CE, the *sweon* are the Svear, the *geatas* are the

---

[184] See von Sydow, "Grendel."
[185] von Sydow, "Mytforskningen," pp. 133–34.
[186] "ur psykoligisk synpunkt fullständigt ointressant." Nordström, "Birger Nerman," p. 214.
[187] Anon., "Einar Nerman."
[188] Nordström, "Birger Nerman," p. 207.
[189] Nerman, "Foundation," pp. 113–14.

Västgötar, and the *wylfingas* are the Östgötar. The *wylfingas* are known as *Ylfingar* in northern sources such as the *Sögubrot af fornkonungum i Dana ok Svía veldi* (Fragments of the History of Ancient Kings in Denmark and Sweden).[190] The poem mentions the frequent conflicts between the *sweon* and the *geatas* and twice foretells the downfall of the latter in lines 2886b–90a ("Every man of this tribe shall wander without right to a country") and in line 3019b (Geatish women "shall tread foreign soil"). Of the man making this prophesy, the poet says in lines 3029b–30a that "not very falsely did he speak of fate and words." The downfall of the Västgöta realm, then, and the triumph of the Svear must have occurred between 550 and 575 CE, during the reign of the Swedish king Adils.[191] Wulfstan's account of his voyage from the OE *Orosius* substantiates Nerman's claim. After passing lands belonging to Denmark and the Burgundians (Bornholm), Wulfstan passes Blekinge, Möre, Öland, and Gotland on the port side of his ship. These lands, states Wulfstan, belong to the Svear. Thus, writes Nerman, we see "that at that time, during the second half of the ninth century, the origin of the Swedish kingdom is completed."[192]

Sune Lindqvist (1887–1976) worked in the National Historical Museum in Stockholm for eighteen years before becoming Professor of Scandinavian and Comparative Archaeology at the University of Uppsala, a position he held from 1927 to 1953. He was one of the most influential Swedish archaeologists of the twentieth century.[193] During WWII, rumors of his being a Nazi sympathizer made their way through Uppsala, but he was actually working undercover as an anti-Nazi operative to report any possible Nazi infiltration at the university. Although he even gave refuge to Jews and anti-Nazi protesters in his own home, he refrained from debunking the myth for his whole life to protect those refugees and to keep that mission secret.[194] He and Birger Nerman combined, as their teacher Knut Stjerna had before them, written and archaeological material in their research.[195] He mentions, for instance, the appearance of Ohthere (Ottar) in *Beowulf* to help contextualize his discussion of the archaeological finds in Ottar's burial mound in Vendel;[196] he uses the descriptions of funeral pyres and burials in *Beowulf*, *Ynglingasaga*, and *Ynglingatal* to help us understand the burial mounds in Old Uppsala;[197] he compares

---

[190] Ibid., pp. 119–20.
[191] Ibid., p. 121.
[192] "att vid denna tid, under andra hälften av 800-talet, det svenska rikets uppkomst är fullbordad." *Det svenska rikets uppkomst*, p. 263.
[193] Gräslund, "Sune Lindqvist," pp. 189–90.
[194] Ibid., p. 194.
[195] Ibid., p. 192.
[196] Lindqvist, "Ottarshögen," pp. 127–29.
[197] Lindqvist, "Ynglingaättens gravskick," pp. 119–36.

the architectural description of Heorot in *Beowulf* to that of Scandinavian stave churches and to the reliquary in that style found in Eriksberg's church in Västergötland;[198] and he uses *Beowulf* as a gloss on the Sutton Hoo ship burial in East Anglia and vice versa.[199]

In his magnum opus, *Uppsala Högar och Ottarshögen* (Uppsala Mounds and Ottar's Mound, 1936), Lindqvist uses archaeological data from the Swedish burial mounds to elucidate the cremations and burials of Hnæf and Beowulf in *Beowulf*. The final compositor of the poem, living as he did a couple centuries after the events depicted in the poem and being as he was a Christian, sometimes misunderstood details of the original cremation ceremonies and burials. Hnæf's cremation in lines 1107–24 contain two troublesome lines. The first is *Guðrinc astah* (the warrior rose up, line 1118b), which has been typically interpreted to mean that a warrior, Hnæf or Hildeburh's son, was placed on the funeral pyre; *Guðrinc* has also been emended as in *Klaeber's Beowulf* (2008) to *Guðrec* (battle smoke) so that the smoke from the cremation would rise to the heavens. Lindqvist, however, interprets the line as reflecting a tradition going back to Roman times in which the inheritor of the throne vacated by the man about to be cremated stood up to kindle the fire. Others would then join him, lighting the fire on all sides. The second line is *hlynode hlawe* (line 1120a), conventionally taken to mean "the mound roared," which does not make good sense. If we take *hlawe* to mean not mound, but pyre, as it does in Snorri's description of Frey's burial, it makes perfect sense. The excavations of the mounds in Uppsala clarify how the pyres were built; they were hollow in construction, which would cause them to roar as the wind and fire swirled within them.[200] Similarly, in Beowulf's cremation scene, Lindqvist would emend *windblond gelæg* (the agitation of winds subsided, line 3146b) to *windblonde gelic* (like the whirlwind) and *bronda lafe* (remainder of brands = ashes, line 3160b) to *bronda hlawe* (the hollow pile of brands).[201] Years later, in 1958, Lindqvist would bring these observations and many others about the underlying texts in *Beowulf* to bear in his translation and commentary on the poem, *Beowulf Dissectus*.[202]

Carl Otto Fast or Svionum (1885–1969) was a mining engineer in Stockholm and an amateur historian who published books and articles on or relating to *Beowulf* between 1929 and 1950. He was associated with Samfundet Manhem (The Manhem Society), which had pro-Nazi leanings, and consciously or unconsciously published some of his rejected work in

---

[198] Lindqvist, "Hednatemplet i Uppsala," pp. 110–12.
[199] Lindqvist, "Sutton Hoo och *Beowulf*."
[200] Lindqvist, *Uppsala högar*, p. 252.
[201] Ibid., p. 256.
[202] For the English summary of the above argument, see Ibid., pp. 347–48.

openly Nazi journals.²⁰³ Nevertheless, his work is considered important enough in Sweden to have been reprinted in 1984.²⁰⁴ He has been called the father of the "Västergötland School" that considers the area south and west of lake Vänern in Sweden to be the landscape for old Germanic poetry including *Beowulf*.²⁰⁵ Fast's interests are insistently historical, and he seeks to prove that the Geats definitely came from Västergötland in Sweden, not Jutland in Denmark, as some of his predecessors (such as the Swede Pontus Fahlbeck and the Dane Christian Kier) had tried to prove. In striving for his goal, he offers us a unique way of looking at, for example, the prologue to *Beowulf*.

The Scyld episode, Fast claims, is relevant to the rest of the poem because it offers us the glorious genealogy of the Swedes, not the Danes.²⁰⁶ Scyld is Swedish, not Danish, and the proof of that depends on our looking mainly at two things: the genealogy itself; and *hronrad* (whale road) in line 10 of the poem (cf. *Hrones Næs* in lines 2805, 3136). The first part of the argument is relatively simple. The flow of the genealogy follows the flow of expanding power south from Bohuslän in Sweden through Halland in Sweden and Skåne in Sweden to Sjælland in Denmark. Scyld was a king near the Göta river near Göteborg in Sweden; Beow expanded his inherited influence south through Skåne in Sweden; Halfdan continued the expansion south through Sjælland; Hrothgar solidified the power in Sjælland. Danes in the ancient sense (when all Scandinavians were known generically as Danes) were not born in Denmark but were rather Swedes who settled there.

The other part of the argument is more complex. A secondary reason, says Fast, that scholars have mistaken the Swedes in the prologue for Danes is that they have misinterpreted the word *hronrad* to be a kenning for "ocean." But whales go in many different directions, so why is *hronrad* in the singular? If Scyld was indeed a king near the Göta river, as Fast claims, and if much of the poem takes place near that river or north of it in Vänern (the largest Swedish lake), the river itself might be the single "whale road." The highest hill on the west side of the Göta river was originally called *Wal-klätten* (whale cliff) and is about 135 meters high and quite visible from the Kattegat Sea between north Denmark and south Sweden even though it lies about 20 miles inland. It apparently gave its name to at least parts of the region. Some estates still bore the name "whale" through the nineteenth century, and the point of land where Beowulf

---

²⁰³ Råsled, *Landet Vädermark*, p. 13.
²⁰⁴ *Beowulf, germanernas äldsta epos*; *Västgöta-Dal*; *Götaland*; *Svenska rikets ursprung*; *Vänerbygdens sägner*.
²⁰⁵ Janson, *Till frågan*, p. 13.
²⁰⁶ *Beowulf, germanernas äldsta epos*, pp. 15ff.

was buried – *Hrones Næs* (Whale Headland, perhaps?)[207] – seems likewise tied to that dominant piece of landscape. Read through Fast's eyes, the prologue to *Beowulf* becomes more thoroughly attached to the poem and more thoroughly Swedish than it ever has before.

Read through the eyes of a professional archaeologist, the whole of *Beowulf* can be seen to have distinctly Swedish roots. Bo Gräslund (1934–) is Emeritus Professor of Archaeology at the University of Uppsala, where he was employed from 1974 to 1999. Prior to that, he was a research assistant, curator, and head of department at the National Historical Museum in Stockholm, 1964–72, and during his tenure at Uppsala, among other things, he served as vice dean for the historical-philosophical section 1987–90, then as dean in 1989; he was also editor of the journal *Tor* 1972 to 1983 and 1998 and editor-in-chief from 1985 to 1998 as well as editor of the journal *Fornvännen* 1966–72 and editor-in-chief 1987–96. He was also Chair of the board for the "Societas Archaeologica Upsaliensis" from 1998 to 2005 and remains a member of that board.[208] In 2018, he published the important *Beowulfkvädet: Den nordiska bakgrunden* (translated into English by Martin Naylor as *The Nordic Beowulf*, 2022), which locates Beowulf and the Geats on the island of Gotland, a considerable distance from the Swedish mainland in the Gulf of Bothnia, and not in Västergötland or Östergötland or on Öland or on the Jutland peninsula in Denmark.

The suggestion that the Geats come from Gotland was first made by Grundtvig in 1820[209] and 1861[210] and then independently of Grundtvig and in much more detail by Gad Rausing in 1985[211] and Tore Gannholm in 1992.[212] Focusing mostly on the description of Beowulf's journey to Denmark, Rausing (1922–2000), a wealthy industrialist and respected archaeologist with a Ph.D. from Lund,[213] investigated the provenance of the Geats. At the beginning of *Beowulf*, the hero and his men set sail across open seas until "oþeres dogores" (line 219b, on the second day) they "land gesawon, // brim-clifu blican, / beorgas steape, // side sæ-næssas" (saw land, the shining sea-cliffs, the steep hills, the vast headlands, lines 221b–23a). Most take the description as largely poetic license, Denmark being almost entirely flat. But Rausing takes the lines literally and reasons backwards from them and from the archaeological fact that the richest burial sites for late Iron Age Denmark are concentrated in south-east

---

[207] See also Johansson, *Beowulfsagans Hrones-Næsse* and *Beowulfsagans historiska fragment*, pp. 76–79, for further reflections of a layman on *Beowulf*.
[208] Gräslund, "Bo Gräslund."
[209] Grundtvig, *Bjowulfs Drape*, p. lvii.
[210] Grundtvig, *Beowulfes Beorh*, pp. xliii and lvi.
[211] "*Beowulf, Ynglingatal* and the *Ynglinga saga*."
[212] Gannholm, *Beowulf*.
[213] Ambrosiani, "In Memoriam."

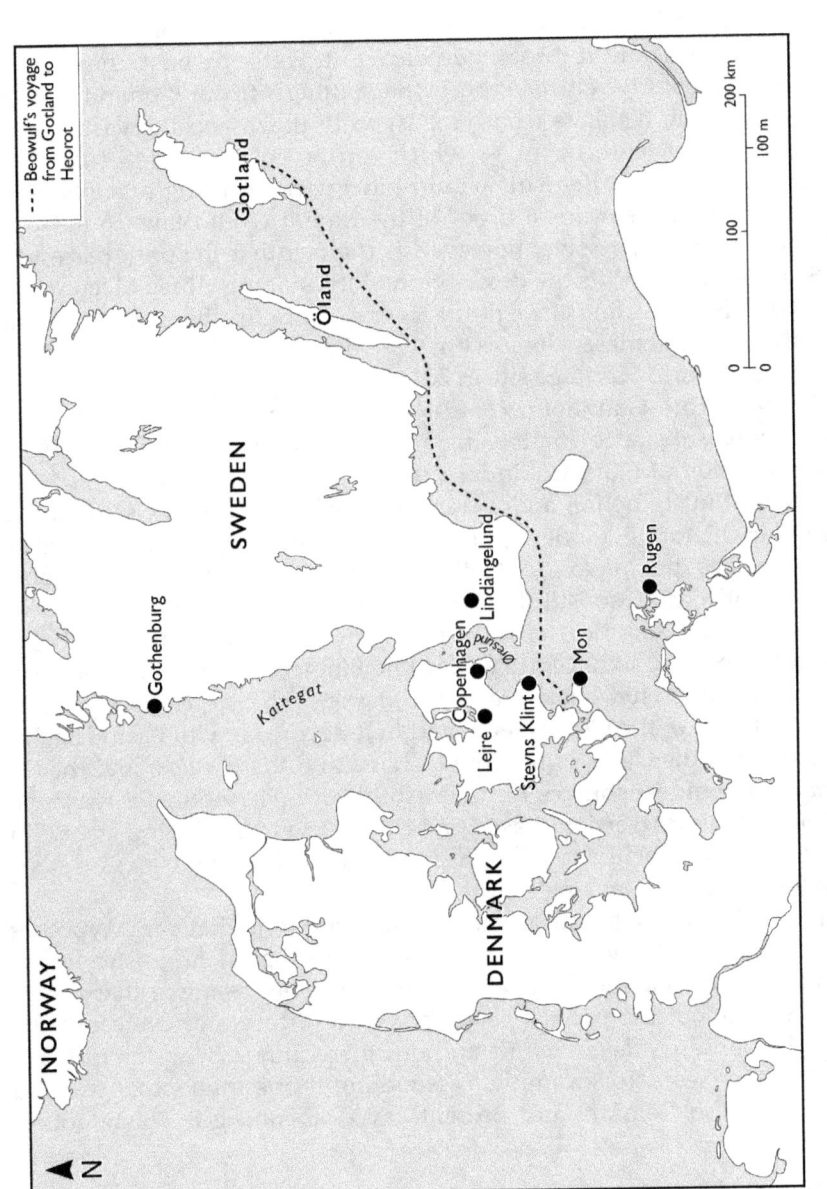

Map 1. Beowulf's route from Gotland, Sweden, to Stevns Klint, Denmark.

Zealand, south of modern-day Copenhagen, with Stevns at their center. The Stevns area is probably, he thinks, where Heorot was located, not in Lejre, which is to the west of modern-day Copenhagen. He reasons further that if Beowulf sails the open sea, that sea would have to be east of Zealand, and if it took two days to traverse by boat, the origin of the journey could well have been the southern tip of Gotland at Cape Hoburgen. The distance from Hoburgen to Stevns on the east coast of Zealand is 229 nautical miles, which can be covered in 48 hours in a sailboat of the kind Beowulf would have used. Rausing actually sailed the route, giving empirical proof of the time it would take to make the journey. More impressive, however, is the fact that the only place in all of Scandinavia that fits the description of the shining cliffs of Denmark in *Beowulf* is Stevns Klint (the Cliff of Stevns), a bright, shining, white-chalk cliff that is 15 kilometers long, 41 meters high, and so dramatic that it was declared a World Heritage site in 2014.[214]

In 1992, Tore Gannholm (1940–), an amateur historian of the Baltic, gave more substance to Rausing's hypothesis. He reprinted a lightly edited version of Björn Collinder's translation of *Beowulf* together with a substantial introduction and a translation of *Guta saga*, the Old Gutnish legendary history of Gotland, probably from the early thirteenth century. The changes he makes to Collinder's text are minimal and consist almost entirely of substituting *gutar* for *gautar* (Gotlanders for Geats) and *vädursmän* for *vädersmarksborna* (men of the ram – the symbol for Gotland since the sixth century – for inhabitants of Weder land or Geats). Gannholm titles his book *Beowulf. Gutarnas nationalepos* (Beowulf: The National Epic of the Gotlanders), and in it he argues with Grundtvig and Rausing that the Geats came from Gotland and that *Beowulf* and the *Guta saga* are the oldest sources for Gutnish history. He mounts a reasonable defense of these assertions based on historical sources ranging from Pliny, Procopius, and Tacitus to runic inscriptions and Gotlandic picture stones, and, of course, on Rausing's work.[215]

In his book, Gräslund advances the Grundtvig–Rausing hypothesis considerably with even more abundant archaeological, linguistic, literary, and historical evidence.[216] That evidence may clarify much that remains enigmatic about the poem's geography and history and even lexicography. The phrase *ealand utan* (island out there, line 2334a) describing the land of the Geats, for example, is troubling if one thinks that the Geats lived near the Göta älv and present-day Gothenburg in Västergötland,

---

[214] Rausing, "*Beowuf, Ynglingatal* and the *Ynglinga saga*," pp. 174–77.
[215] Gannholm, *Beowulf: Gutarnas nationalepos*, pp. 25–29.
[216] The following discussion is based primarily on my review of Gräslund's book in the original Swedish. See Bjork, *Review of Bo Gräslund*. References to his book are to the English translation.

because Västergötland is not an island. Gotland, however, is. It lies far out in the Baltic Sea from the east coast of the Swedish mainland and is therefore aptly described as *ealand utan*.[217] The epithet *weder* (always translated as "weather") likewise would make more sense if Beowulf came from Gotland and the word was a mis-transcription of *weðer* ("wether" or "ram"). From at least the late Middle Ages until the present day, the ram has been the official symbol of Gotland, and "Wether-Geats" or "Ram-Geats" nicely differentiates the Geats (or Gutes) on Gotland from the Geats of Väster- and Östergötland.[218]

The topography of south-east Gotland seems to fit the OE description of Beowulf's home as well. For instance, Hygelac's hall is described in the poem as being *sæwealle neah* (near the sea wall, line 1924b), a phrase that has puzzled many a translator. The Littorina Ridge just inside Bandlund Bay on Gotland, however, is about four meters high, dominates the landscape and could easily be designated a "sea wall."[219] The archaeology of the area confirms that the OE may refer to precisely this area, because near that sea wall at Känne in Burs lies a remarkable number of foundations for structures of various size including a 67x11-meter main building, the largest on Gotland from the period and larger than any in Sweden and Denmark.[220] Stavgard, as it is referred to locally, must have been the abode of a powerful king such as Hygelac. Sailing from that south-east point on Gotland to Heorot in Denmark would take about two days, as the poem affirms. Beowulf's ship arrived "ymb antid oþres dogore" (after a normal amount of time on the next day, line 219b).[221]

The point of arrival, Gräslund (and Rausing before him) argues, was not Lejre in north-west Zealand, as is commonly thought, however, but Stevns Klint in the south-east. Topography and archaeology once again reinforce the possibility. "Shining white cliffs" is a good description of Stevns Klint, and the path "paved with stones" (*stanfah,* line 320a,) could very well be one of the paved paths of the Stevns area, which boasts the highest number of such paths in all of Scandinavia, including the unique and impressive stone path at Broskov south-west of Stevns.[222] The area has a number of rich grave finds, which suggests that the peerless path originally led to something very important such as a royal site, which could have been Heorot.[223]

---

[217] Gräslund, *The Nordic Beowulf*, pp. 46–48.
[218] Ibid., pp. 48–50.
[219] Ibid., pp. 109–11.
[220] Ibid., pp. 111–13.
[221] Ibid., pp. 121–23.
[222] Ibid., pp. 124–28.
[223] Ibid., p. 130.

Gräslund offers much, much more to concretize an idea that Grundtvig intuited and to which Rausing gave evidentiary support. Through meticulous argument interwoven with an impressive assemblage of data, archaeological and otherwise, which is inadequately adumbrated here, Gräslund offers possible answers to the questions of the provenance of the Geats, the location of Heorot, and many more, such as the significance of Sutton Hoo and the meaning of the Grendel kin and dragon in the sixth century when the events of the poem, coinciding with cataclysmic events in northern Europe, took place. "That a profound crisis shook Scandinavian society to its foundations, demographically, socially, economically, and culturally – of that there can be no doubt."[224] Readers will undoubtedly find a secondary thesis that Gräslund promotes in his study of *Beowulf* less compelling than the first and will more likely meet it with skepticism, just as Thorkelin's analogous thesis was met 200 years before Gräslund's. Thorkelin regarded *Beowulf* as a Danish poem in an OE dialect (*Poëma Danicum dialect Anglo-Saxonica*); Gräslund regards *Beowulf* as an eastern Scandinavian poem "given an Old English linguistic form."[225] Nationalism still lives in serious scholarship on the poem. Gräslund incorporates his many findings into his 2022 revision of Rudolf Wickberg's revised translation of *Beowulf* from 1914, and we will consider that translation in the next chapter.

Iceland, Norway, Finland: Cultural, Historical, and Manuscript Studies

The contributions to OE studies in the remaining Nordic countries are few: three from Iceland, three from Norway, and one from Finland. The Icelandic minister and historian Jón Jónsson (1849–1920) of Stafafelli, whom we have met before, published two articles in *AfNF*, the first on Liserus, the one-eyed old man mentioned in book 1 of Saxo's *Gesta Danorum*, and the connection between the name Beowulf and the god Beow and the similar connection between the name Bjarki and the god Biar.[226] Jónsson observes that it is not unlikely that Beowulf (Bjólfr) actually existed as a chieftain of the Jutes in the sixth century and later got mixed up with the god-like hero Beo or Beaw, which is the equivalent of Biar. That version of the tale was then taken to England in the seventh to eighth centuries.[227] The second article concerns the lineage of Harald Wartooth, the semi-legendary king of Denmark who died in the battle of Brávalla;

---

[224] Ibid., p. 191.
[225] Ibid., p. 108.
[226] Jónsson, "Liserus – Béow," pp. 258–61.
[227] Ibid., p. 260.

in this, Jónsson mentions *Beowulf* and "Widsith" as casting some light on Hrólfr Kraki and his contemporaries. Finally from Iceland is Bjarni Guðnason (1928–2023), who was Professor of Icelandic Literary History from 1963 to 1998 at the University of Iceland[228] and published his doctoral dissertation, *Um Skjöldungasögu* (Concerning the Saga of the Skjoldungs) in 1963. In it, he mentions *Beowulf* six times in his exploration of evidence for a saga now lost but referenced by Snorri Sturluson around 1220 in his *Ynglingasaga*, the saga of the Skjoldungs.[229]

In Norway, just two authors of whom I am aware have written about *Beowulf*, Niels Christian Brøgger (1914–66) and Tor H. Strand (no dates). Brøgger was a novelist, essayist, journalist, and critic trained in the history of literature at the University of Oslo and in London. He was a member of the resistance during the Nazi occupation of Norway during WWII and was imprisoned in a concentration camp for a period of about six months. He wrote crime novels under the pseudonym Johnny W. Lambeth such as *Mordet i Nationaltheatret* (Murder in the National Theater, 1952) and published a number of books, three of which were on mythology: one on classical, one on Celtic, and one on Nordic myth.[230] His encyclopedic *Nordens demring. Nordiske myter og sagn* (The Dawn of the North: Nordic Myths and Legends) from 1949 retells the myths and legends concerning the creation of the universe,[231] the Norse gods,[232] the dwarves and giants,[233] Thor's various adventures,[234] Balder's death,[235] and other important aspects of Norse myth including Ragnarok,[236] before talking about heroic poetry[237] and then the various Scandinavian dynasties beginning with the Skjoldung.[238] Bjovulf, whom Brøgger classes among the kings and warriors who undoubtedly lived,[239] and among the good friends of Rolf Krake,[240] is discussed in the context of the Skjoldung dynasty in Lejre, and the poem itself is always in the background because of all the Skjoldung names that it contains. It moves into the foreground in Brøgger's discussion of Roar's

---

[228] Anon., "Bjarni Guðnason."
[229] Guðnason, *Um Skjödungasögu*, pp. 3, 61, 80, 165, 175, and 221.
[230] Anon., "Niels Christian Brøgger."
[231] Brøgger, *Nordens demring*, pp. 35–39.
[232] Ibid., pp. 40–95.
[233] Ibid., pp. 105–12.
[234] Ibid., pp. 119–44.
[235] Ibid., pp. 145–51.
[236] Ibid., pp. 177–83.
[237] Ibid., pp. 184–88.
[238] Ibid., pp. 189–235.
[239] Ibid., p. 184.
[240] Ibid., p. 245.

building of the great hall Hjort and then his recapitulation of the poem blended with details from Danish history.[241]

Tor H. Strand, an author who identifies himself as an engineer but for whom I can find no other biographical information, wrote two newspaper articles about *Beowulf* in 1953[242] and 1958[243] and a chapter in a book for a general audience, ages fifteen and up, in 1956. In the articles, he asserts that *Beowulf* comes from Norway in the region of Telemark; all the names in it can be traced back to Norwegian roots, he claims, and some are still in use today. Ecglaf, for example, whom scholars have assumed was a patronymic attached to Unferth in the poem, is actually a woman's name that descends into Norwegian as Egglæf. He made this argument about names in his book, *Norrønafolket* (The Norwegians), which gives glimpses into the history, culture, religion, geology, biology, archaeology, ethnography, and legends of the Norwegian people from the Stone Age to 2956 CE, in a fictional future. In that year, a professor of what used to be called ethnography gave a lecture at a place of learning once called the University of Oslo on the subject of what used to be called Norway.[244] Chapter 46 of the book deals with Beowulf (Bjå-Ulv) and Heorot, which the Danes maintain was in Roskilde but Strand argues was in Norway in Vestfold, built on the highest part of what is now called Brårudåsen (Brårud hill) behind the village of Horten. Geography and archaeology substantiate Strand's claim, as do two other facts: Beowulf's name still exists as "Biuff" in Telemark and Setesdal, Norway, and Heorot's architecture was of the Norwegian stave church type, as asserted by the Swedish art historian Gerda Boethius (1890–1961) in her 1931 book *Hallar, tempel och stavkyrkor* (Halls, Temples and Stave Churches).[245] Strand himself was Norwegian and so had a slight national bias. As R. W. Chambers remarked about a scholar from Jutland arguing for the Geats originating from Jutland, "No amount of learning will eradicate patriotism."[246]

And in Finland, a lecturer who has specialized in text and book production at the University of Turku in the Department of English since 2018, Mari-Liisa Varila (1984–),[247] published the single Finnish contribution to the study of *Beowulf* in the Nordic region. Her "Beowulf seurueineen. Nowell Codexin mysteeri" (Beowulf and his Troup: The Mystery of the Nowell Codex) in *Papyruksesta PDF: ään. Tutkielmia kirjan historiasta* (From Papyrus to PDF: Essays on the History of the Book) appeared in 2008. The

---

[241] Ibid., pp. 210–35.
[242] "Heltediktet *Beowulf*."
[243] "Bøheringen Beowulfs Kongesaga i Nytt lys."
[244] Strand, *Norrønafolket*, pp. 165–80.
[245] Ibid., pp. 158–61.
[246] Chambers, *Beowulf: An Introduction*, p. 7.
[247] Varila, "Biography."

article focuses on Beowulf in its manuscript context, first reviewing some of the existing research and debate on the topic to about 2007, and then

> trying to provide an overview for Finnish readers. I deal with issues such as the rationale of the contents of the Nowell Codex, the dating of the manuscript(s), and the potential audience(s) of the collection. I introduce the contents of Cotton Vitellius A.xv before focusing on the Nowell Codex and its contents in more detail. I briefly talk about the debate regarding the dating and production context of Beowulf and the potential sources for the story. I also discuss the other texts in the manuscript and the suggestions that have been made regarding the theme of the compilation.[248]

Preceding Varila's work on *Beowulf* in Finland are the efforts of four scholars to translate the poem into Finnish beginning in 1927, as we will shortly see.

---

[248] Varila, personal email received 25 May 2023.

6
Scandinavian Translations of *Beowulf*

The *Beowulf* diaspora in Scandinavia does not end with the many and continuing scholarly investigations of the poem that started in the early nineteenth century. That diaspora is limited in scope, because the audience for those scholarly investigations is itself mainly scholarly. With the publication of the first Danish translation of the poem in 1820, however, and then the Swedish in 1899, Norwegian in 1921, Icelandic in 1983, and Finnish in 1999 (partial translation in 1927), the poem became accessible for the first time to the general public in the North and, with that, to poets, illustrators, city planners, artists, and other creative individuals working in all media. For example, in 1899, Valdemar Rørdan (1872–1946), the Danish nationalist poet, novelist, playwright, and Nazi sympathizer, published his epic poem *Bjovulv: Et digt*, which "doesn't have much to do with the OE [Old English] poem";[1] in 1954, the Swedish artist Per Engström (1895–1992) contributed his distinctive linoleum cuts to Björn Collinder's Swedish translation of the poem; in 1956, the map of Djursholm outside Stockholm included "Grendel" as one of its street names;[2] in the 1980s, the Gotlandic/Swedish artist Erik Olsson (1919–2006) depicted Beowulf's sea voyage from southern Gotland to Stevns Klint in Denmark in an oil painting housed in Gotlands Museum, Visby;[3] and in 1983, Alfreð Flóki (1938–87), a controversial and provocative Icelandic artist and illustrator, added his stunning drawings to the only Icelandic translation of *Beowulf* ever produced. He was influenced by the Expressionists Paul Klee, Wilheim Heinrich Otto Dix, and Helmut Görsz, and was drawn to the irrational.[4] For him, "man is born corrupt, without hope of redemption, and should simply accept his wickedness with a modicum of dignity. That way, life will not disappoint."[5]

The following list indicates the Scandinavian languages (and neo-Latin by Thorkelin) that *Beowulf* has been translated into and the dates for the publication of those translations. Seventeen are for adults and nine

---

[1] Möller-Christensen, "Valdemar Rørdan." "ikke har meget at gøre med det oldengelske kvad." Haarder, *Sangen om Bjovulf*, p. 15.
[2] Mjöberg, *Drömmen om sagatiden*, vol. 2, pp. 9–10.
[3] Sanda 82, "Beowulf."
[4] Ingólfsson, *Furðuverörld Alfreðs Flóka*, p. 6.
[5] Ibid., p. 7.

explicitly for children; twelve are by Danes, seven by Swedes, three by Norwegians, two by Finns, and one each by an Icelander and a Sámi; and they range in date from 1815 to 2022. The interest that *Beowulf* enjoys in the Nordic countries is strikingly consistent.

1815 Danish Neo-Latin
1820 Danish; 2nd ed. 1865
1847 Danish
1889 Swedish; 2nd ed. 1914
1902 Swedish prose summary to line 2206; translation lines 2207–3182
1910 Danish
1914 Danish – Part I for children; 2nd ed. 1952
1921 Norwegian (Nynorsk)
1954 Swedish; 2nd ed. 1955
1958 Swedish (excerpts)
1976 Norwegian (Riksmål)
1983 Danish
1983 Icelandic
1984 Danish; repr. 2001
1999 Finnish
1999 Finnish
1999 Norwegian – for children (Riksmål)
2000 Swedish – for children from Robert Nye's *Beowulf: A New Telling*; 2nd ed. 2007
2002 Danish – for young adults
2003 Danish – for children; 2nd ed. 2005
2004 Danish and Persian – Part I for children
2011 Swedish – for children from Rob Lloyd Jones's *Beowulf* 2009
2012 Danish – Part I for children
2018 Danish
2019 Saami – for children from Rob Lloyd Jones
2022 Swedish revision of 1889 translation, 2nd ed.

Danish Translations

The first two translations on this list were briefly considered already, Thorkelin's in chapter 5 and Grundtvig's in chapter 2. Thorkelin's Latin translation was roundly condemned at the time and has rarely been referred to by translators since. Grundtvig's "Danishing" of the poem, however, his "dynamic equivalence"[6] rendition in which he tried to recreate in his contemporary audience the same response to the poem that

---

[6] Gutt, *Translation and Relevance*, p. 67.

the original audience had, has been subsequently referred to despite its being initially met with astonishment or indifference. The next translator of *Beowulf*, Frederik Schaldemose (1783–1853), expresses sympathy for one of his predecessors and disdain for the other. A prolific author and an even more prolific translator, Schaldemose began his publishing career with two collections of poetry in 1815 and 1819 followed by a steady stream of books, including translations of Sir Walter Scott, Alexandre Dumas, Cervantes, Henrik Steffens, Reinecke Vos, Apuleius, and *Beowulf*. Mainly because of his translations, he became one of the most widely read Danish authors of his generation.[7] Of Thorkelin's error-ridden edition, he compassionately observes that it was only Thorkelin's "burning zeal for our Nordic antiquity"[8] that had moved him to take on a task for which he was not fit. He soon suffered the consequences of his actions. A young student (Grundtvig), who has distinguished himself even into his own old age by his pedestrian coarseness in numerous literary feuds, "heaped dirt on the old man without taking into consideration the many sacrifices he had made in bringing the old book to light."[9] Schaldemose has no doubt that "that now old literary gamecock"[10] would want to dip his hand into the gutter and besmirch him, too. "Let him!" he says, abruptly ending his short foreword to his translation. Grundtvig ignored the challenge completely.[11]

The translation itself is printed in columns parallel with John Mitchell Kemble's 1835 edition of *Beowulf*, which Schaldemose leaves virtually unchanged except for expanding abbreviations such as a crossed thorn for *þæt*. He does not reprint Kemble's glossary or list of names, replacing those with remarks on the geographical, historical, and mythic dimensions of the poem that come essentially from the introduction to Ettmüller's 1840 German translation of the poem and Leo's 1839 edition of it.[12] He agrees, therefore, that Heorot lay somewhere near Lejre and that the Geats came from Jutland;[13] and he credits Leo with the identification of Clochilaichus with Hygelac instead of Grundtvig, whom he does not mention.[14] He does mention Thorkelin just one more time when he points out Thorkelin's

---

[7] Rubow, "Fr. Schaldemose."
[8] "hans brændende Iver for vort Nordens Oldtid." Schaldemose, *Beo-Wulf*, p. ii.
[9] "overøste den gamle Mand med Snavs, uden at tage Hensyn til de mange Opoffrelser, som han havde gjort for at bringe den gamle Bog for Lyset." Ibid.
[10] "denne nu gamle literaire Kamphane." Ibid.
[11] Pedersen, "Indledning til 'Bjovulfs Drape'," 7.2.
[12] Munch, Review of Schaldemose, p. 133.
[13] Schaldemose, *Beo-Wulf*, p. 152.
[14] Ibid., p. 157.

error in misconstruing the accusative plural *Hugas* (Franks) in line 2914a of the poem for the accusative singular name of a Frankish prince, Hugo.[15]

Schaldemose does not talk about his translation method, but his rendering of *Beowulf* is basically an alliterative one in iambic trimeter. It is lyrical and enjoyable to read, as one would expect from such an accomplished poet as he. Here is his description of Grendel's first approach to Heorot, lines 115–25. Note the six-syllable lines:

Saa gik han at speide	So he went scouting
I Huset det hoie	in the high building
hvorledes Hring-Daner,	how the Ring-Danes
naar Laget var endt, sig	when the company had finished
leire" i Hallen;	had encamped themselves in the hall;
der inde da fandt han	in there he found
Ædlingers Skare	a crowd of nobles
sove efter Sviren	sleeping after the carousing
med Sorger ukjendt,	with unknown sorrows,
de Menneskets Plager	the plagues of man
og med Ulykker.	and with misfortunes.
Grim og glubende	Hideous and ravenous
den Grumme var rede,	the ferocious one was ready,
med graadig Gridskhed	with gluttonous greed
greb han de Sovende,	he seized the sleepers,
tredive Thegner,	thirty thanes,
saa tog han Veien,	so he took the road,
glad ved sit Bytte,	glad with his booty,
tilbage til Hjemmet	back to his home
med de Slagnes Kroppe	with the bodies of the slain
at soge sin Bolig.[16]	to seek his dwelling.

Schaldemose's translation was first published in 1847 and was welcomed in a review in 1848 as a great improvement for Scandinavians over Kemble's edition.[17] The second edition of Schaldemose's book, very little changed from the first except for the addition of *Anden Udgave* (second edition) on the title page, appeared in 1851. The book was considered of such cultural value that it was reprinted in 2022. It also appeared in a Chinese edition in 2010.

---

[15] Ibid., p. 158.
[16] Ibid., p. 6, lines 229–50.
[17] Munch, review of Schaldemose.

Fifty-nine years later, the next translation of *Beowulf* appeared in Denmark. Schaldemose's Danish had aged by then, and the mistakes in the text that he inherited from Kemble as well as his own misreadings of the OE remained, so Adolf Hansen (1850–1908), whom we met in chapter 5, was determined to produce a new translation.[18] Hansen was a literary historian, tutor, schoolteacher, and, beginning in 1894, lecturer at the University of Copenhagen. He published books on Addison, Pope, Swift, Gay, and Arbuthnot and translated a large amount of English poetry into Danish, from Shakespeare's sonnets to poems by Shelley, Tennyson, Arnold, and Swinburne. He was known for his knowledge and intelligence and for his faithfulness to the original texts he translated.[19] He had nearly finished his translation of *Beowulf* when he fell gravely ill. Shortly before his death, he asked his brother Oskar to fill in the remaining lacunae in the translation and to add an introduction and a list of names to the book. Oskar consulted Axel Olrik about completing the project and was directed to Viggo J. von Holstein Rathlou, who took on the task.[20] He filled the gaps, wrote an introduction, but did not compile a list of names, instead adding his own translation of "The Fight at Finnsburg."

Finishing Hansen's work was not easy. Von Holstein Rathlou lists dozens and dozens of emendations that had to be made to the text, which had been written in ink with alternative translations of words written above them in pencil with a question mark beside them.[21] In making his own decision about what the words meant, von Holstein Rathlou found that dictionaries did not help and the numerous translations of the poem from Müllenhoff's German translation to Clark Hall's English one were not useful, either. So he turned to the only *Beowulf* scholar he knew who was both a great linguist and a great poet, N. F. S. Grundtvig, and used his translation of the poem as the mediator among disputing parties.

Here are the opening lines of Hansen's translation:

> Om spyd-daners færd i fortids dage,
> om dåd og bedrift, af drotterne øvet,
> om ædlingers sejrsry sagn har vi hørt!
> Ofte Skjold Skéfing drev skarevis fjendernes
> myldrende flokke fra mjødsalens bænke
> og slog dem med jammer. Som hjælpeløst barn
> blev først han fundet, men fanged så lykke
> og voksed i hæder o gry under himlen,

---

[18] Hansen, *Bjovulf* (2019), p. 11.
[19] Haislund, "Adolf Hansen."
[20] Hansen, *Bjovulf* (2019), p. 7.
[21] Ibid., p. 14. The manuscript of Hansen's translation is held in the Royal Danish Library where it is catalogued as "Ny kgl. sml. Folio, 1597." Ibid., p. 15.

så alle de folk, der fjernt over hval-vejen
rundt om leved, lyde ham måtte
og skat ham give: godt var hans styre!

Of the Spear-Danes dealings in days of yore,
of deed and feat performed by the lords,
of the nobles' fame of victory have we heard!
Oft Scyld Scefing drove crowds of enemies
swarming bands from meadhall benches
and struck them with misery. As a helpless
child first was he found but had good luck
and grew in honor and glory under the sky
so all people who far over the whale-road
lived round about had to obey him
and give him treasure; good was his rule!

One could object to the omission of the formal, introductory "Hwæt!" (Behold! or Listen!) from the first line and the emphasis on rule rather than ruler in the last ("þæt wæs god cyning!" [that was a good king]), but Hansen here and throughout the translation abides by his goal of replicating the original meter of the poem without slavishly adhering to it.[22]

Thora Constantin-Hansen (1867–1954) took up the *Beowulf* mantle four years after Hansen (they were not related), but this time explicitly for children and for only the first part of the poem, the Denmark part. She was born into a loving home as part of the Grundtvigian congregation at Vartov in central Copenhagen, where Grundtvig had been the minister from 1839 until his death in 1872 and where a famous statue of him kneeling still stands in the courtyard. In the summer of her sixteenth year, she went to Askov folk high school and subsequently worked as a tutor there, but later, tragedy struck the family. Her father developed dementia, a brother drowned, a sister went insane, and she was left to fend for herself. She did so by becoming a teacher for disabled children, later following the teaching principles of Montessori. She wrote many articles for education journals, translated books on teaching and on Montessori, and wrote children's books and biographies as well as her memoir, *Et Skolelive i Strid og Fred* (A School Life in Strife and Peace) in 1935. "Thora Constantin-Hansen was a pioneer and in many ways a forerunner of the pedagogical innovations of the decades 1910–30."[23]

Constantin-Hansen's background, principles, and experience seem to have led her to paraphrase the first part of *Beowulf* for children, as her foreword to the first edition of her book makes clear. She praises Grundtvig

---

[22] Hansen, "Ett Brudstykke," p. 468.
[23] "Thora Constantin-Hansen var pioner og på mange måder forløber for de pædagogiske nyskabelser i årtierne 1910–30." Hilden, "Thora Constantin-Hansen."

for being the first to take the poem seriously and translate it in its entirety. And she says that it had been his wish that the poem (in Danish) would be found in every house, would become a book for all children, would become for all the Nordic countries what the *Iliad* and the *Odyssey* were for the Greeks. Her book, hopes Constantin-Hansen, would "give Danish children the desire, when they get older, to read Grundtvig's translation of *Beowulf* in beautiful and amusing Danish verse."[24] They could later move on to Hansen's translation in a verse form that replicates the OE as closely as possible and then Axel Olrik's discussion of the poem in his *The Heroic Legends of Denmark*. Her preparatory rendition of the poem begins thus:

> Vi har hørt meget fortælle om Danernes Færd i gamle Dage, om Kongernes Stordaad og Heltenes Sejre. En af de bedste Fortællinger er dog den om Kong Skjold, ham der blev fundet som et hjælpeløst Barn, men havde Lykken med sig og steg saaledes i Magt og Hæder, at alle moboende Folk derovre paa den anden Side af Havet maatte adlyde ham og give ham Skat. Han styrede sit Rige godt. (9)

> We have heard many stories about the dealings of the Danes in olden days, about kings' great deeds and heroes' victories. Yet one of the best stories is the one about King Skjold, he who was found as a helpless child but had luck with him and so rose in power and honor so that all the neighboring people over there on the other side of the sea had to obey him and give him treasure. He ruled his kingdom well.

The captivating simplicity of this paraphrase would surely attract young readers. The fascinating, whimsical illustrations accompanying the paraphrase would surely keep them reading. They are by Niels Skovgaard (1858–1938), a famous artist, sculptor, and book illustrator who created the statue of a kneeling Grundtvig at Vartov mentioned above and who was the brother of Joakim Skovgaard, the equally famous artist who painted "Christ in the Realm of the Dead" in response to Grundtvig's hymn 243 on the Harrowing of Hell that was discussed in chapter 2 (see p. 65, figure 6). Niels was famous, too, for his humorous sketches of trolls and other mythical creatures.[25]

Another seventy-three years passed after Hansen's book before the next translator took on the task of rendering *Beowulf* into Danish. Barry Wilmont (1936–), a renowned Canadian-born Danish artist and book illustrator and member of the Royal Danish Academy of Fine Arts whose work

---

[24] "give danske Børn Lyst til, naar de bliver ældre, at læse Grundtvigs Gengivelse af Beowulfsdrapen i smukke og morsomme danske Vers." Constantin-Hansen, "Forord" to *Bjovulf*.
[25] Schultz, "Niels Skovgaard."

is exhibited in galleries worldwide,[26] both updated Hansen's translation of the poem and accompanied the translation with close to fifty lithographs. In the foreword to the book, Ebbe Kløvedal Reich (1940–2005), a popular Danish author and political activist, reflects on the time gap between Hansen's book and Wilmont's. Hansen's, he says,

> became the next generation's access to one of the oldest sources for what happened in Denmark in the old, old days. Adolf Hansen lasted for most of a century. It was a good piece of work. But lately he had started to creak and gather dust ... And that, in brief, is the history of this book's origin.[27]

Not a scholar of *Beowulf* but a painter and great admirer of the poem, Wilmont thought that the time was right to dust off Hansen and make his translation readable again for a contemporary audience; ample illustrations would give visual currency to the text as well. The publication was celebrated in a public event in Copenhagen on 19 October 1983 titled "Barry hilse Beowulf" (Barry Greets Beowulf), with music by Leif Johansson's orchestra and comments by Ebbe Kløvedal Reich.[28] Here are the opening lines of Hansen's translation again with Wilmont's updated version below them. As you will see, there are quite a few changes:

> Om spyd-daners færd i fortids dage,
> om dåd og bedrift, af drotterne øvet,
> om ædlingers sejrsry sagn har vi hørt!
> Ofte Skjold Skéfing drev skarevis fjendernes
> myldrende flokke fra mjødsalens bænke
> og slog dem med jammer. Som hjælpeløst barn
> blev først han fundet, men fanged så lykke
> og voksed i hæder o gry under himlen,
> så alle de folk, der fjernt over hval-vejen
> rundt om leved, lyde ham måtte
> og skat ham give: godt var hans styre!
>
> Om spyddaners våbenfærd i svundne dage,
> om dåd og bedrifter udøvet af drotter,
> og om slægters sejre har vi hørt mange sagn.
> Ofte Skjold Skéfing drevet i skarevis

---

[26] See his website at https://www.wilmont.dk.
[27] "blev de næste slægtsleds adgang til en af de allerældste kilder til, hvad der gik for sig i Danmark i gamle, gamle dage. Adol Hansen holdt i det meste af et århundrede. Det var et godt stykke arbeide. Men i den sidste tid var han begyndt at knirke og samle støv ... Og det er i korte træk denne bogs tillblivelseshistorie." Wilmont, *Bjowulf*, p. 3 of "Forord."
[28] Wilmont, personal email correspondence.

fjenders myldrende flokke, bort fra salens bænke,
og slået dem med frygt. Som forældreløs barn
blev han fundet, og senere skulle han få
bade hæder og jarlers hyldest,
så folkeslag, fjernt overe havet,
måtte lyde, lovprise og hædre ham,
Samt yde store skatter, thi godt var hans styre.

A year after Wilmont's book appeared, Andreas Haarder, whose work was discussed in chapter 5, published his translation of *Beowulf*. He had been working on the translation since 1980, he says in his foreword, and he had a personal reason for doing so. A scholar a long time ago had postulated that Beowulf's burial mound stood on the headland in Haarder's home district in Denmark, Rønshoved, and the poem and the place had been linked for him ever since. (Zeruneith makes a similar remark in his 2023 book.)[29] Haarder also had professional reasons for translating *Beowulf*. Such a poem transcends boundaries of time and place, is what Grundtvig called "the living word," and the time was ripe for a new Danish translation of it.[30] The *Beowulf* tradition in Denmark is unique in all the world; there the poem is directly connected to the people because of Grundtvig's translations of many parts of it into songs for the folk high schools and that anyone, regardless of background, can sing. In Denmark, without any knowledge of the poem whatsoever, one can sing about Beowulf's fight with Grendel or Hrothgar's being liberated from monstrous violence.[31]

There are four Danish translations of the poem, too, and Haarder comments briefly on them all. He considers Grundtvig's 1820 translation "a feat of power, delivered by a remarkable personality who insisted as a pioneer researcher on having contact with scholars and as an intermediary, on addressing a wide readership."[32] He deems Schaldemose's 1847 translation to be derivative, absolutely unoriginal and unlearned, but still with some limited value to readers until 1910, when Hansen's translation appeared.[33] He lauds that translation as possessing a combination of fidelity to the original text and a "sense of wording, sound, and verse rhythm that makes the whole thing ring."[34] Constantin-Hansen's transla-

---

[29] Haarder, *Sangen om Bjovulf*, p. 7.
[30] Ibid., p. 11.
[31] Ibid., p. 13.
[32] "en kraftpræstation, leveret af en mærkværdig personlighed, der insisterede på som pionerforsker at have kontakt med de lærde og som formidler at henvende sig til en bred læserskare." Ibid., p. 15.
[33] Ibid., p. 17.
[34] "sans for ordføring, lydvirkning og versrytme, der får det hele til at klinge." Ibid., p. 17.

tion, however, is troublesome, mainly because it contains only part of the text, but Haarder praises Skovgaard's masterful illustrations, several of which are timeless.[35] Finally, Haarder is least generous with Wilmont's translation, which he finds problematic as a whole, "obviously because of an inadequate knowledge of the OE as well as the Danish language."[36]

Where to go after Hansen, Haarder asks? The answer is to turn back to the original text, and he gives lines 320–31a, describing the paved path to Heorot, as an example of how he intends to do so. The use of half-lines bound by alliteration and two stressed and a variable number of unstressed syllables characterize these lines and the rest of the poem; Haarder reproduces those features in his translation to a great degree.[37] The lines in question read:

> Vejen var stenlagt, stein førte dem,
> krigere i klynge. Kampbrynjen skinnede,
> fast, håndknyttet; funklende ringjern
> sang i kamptøjet på samme tid,
> som de kom duvende dådklædt til hallen.
> De søtrætte satte de side skjolde,
> den benhårde skjoldrand mod bygningens mur;
> så tog de plads på bænken – brynjerne klirrede,
> krigsmændens kampudstyr; deres kastespyd stod,
> de seljendes våben og værktøj stod samlet,
> gråspidset asketræ; gruppen var jernstærk,
> våbenudsmykket.[38]

> The road was paved, stone guided them,
> warriors in a group. Battle byrnies shone,
> first, linked by hand; sparkling ring iron
> sang in war gear at the same time
> that they came dressed in deeds to the hall.
> The sea-weary ones put their broad shields,
> the bone-hard shield bosses, against the building's wall;
> then they took their places on the bench – their byrnies
> clanged, the warriors' battle gear; their spears stood,
> the weapons of the sailors and tools stood gathered,
> grey-tipped ash-trees; the group was iron strong,
> adorned with weapons.

---

[35] Ibid., p. 15.
[36] "øjensynlig på grund af et utilstrækkeligt kendskab til såvel det oldengelske som det danske sprog." Ibid., p. 19.
[37] Ibid., p. 20.
[38] Ibid., p. 21.

Haarder observes that translation is a balancing act between fidelity to the original text and to the norms of the target language into which the text is being translated.[39] Even if one does not know Danish or OE, reading his translation and the OE original together and out loud drives home his achievement:

> Stræt wæs stanfah, stig wisode
> Gumum ætgædere. Guðbyrne scan ...
>
> Vejen var stenlagt, stien førte dem,
> krigere i klynge. Kampbrynjen skinnede ...

Where OE names in the text have their counterparts in ON, Haarder uses the ON form as well as the conventional Scandinavian name for Beowulf since Grundtvig, "Bjovulf." To make his translation even more useful to readers, Haarder supplies summaries of each of the forty-three fitts or songs of the poem, and Viggo Kragh-Hansen supplies numerous line drawings to illustrate the narrative as it proceeds. Haarder's translation was reprinted in 2001.

Following Haarder's translation of *Beowulf* come five retellings of the poem for children seven years and older from 1986 to 2012. Children are not a scholarly audience or an educated general one, but are extremely important, nonetheless. One of the many uses of enchantment, to borrow Bruno Bettelheim's title for his famous book, is to engender interest in such things as the early Middle Ages or *Beowulf* that may lead to greater appreciation in adulthood. We do not know how well these books succeeded in producing serious readers or scholars of *Beowulf* in Denmark, but the books themselves clearly have the power to entertain and delight. The first of these is by the Danish author Ole Pedersen (1939–), whose *Nordiske guder og sagnhelte* (Nordic Gods and Legendary Heroes, 1986) includes the story of Beowulf's fight with the Grendel kin among stories about gods and heroes from Thor to Sigurd and Brynild.[40] Two more are by Lars-Henrik Olsen (1946–), a children's author and zoologist who has written several books about wildlife but is best known for a trilogy of novels about a boy's encounter with the Norse gods.[41] Norse heroes interest Olsen as well. Among a plethora of them, such as Weyland the smith, Rolf Krake, Sigurd, Gudrun, Svanhild, and Sigrid in his *Nordiske heltesagn* (Nordic Heroic Tales, 2003), Olsen places Scyld Scefing and Beowulf. Scyld is second in the book after Weyland, and Beowulf comes

---

[39] Ibid., p. 23.
[40] Pedersen, *Nordiske guder*, pp. 110–17.
[41] Weinreich, "Lars-Henrik Olsen."

three heroes later just after King Frode the First. Olsen's welcoming Beowulf into this host of legendary figures is significant because Beowulf thus becomes unmistakably Scandinavian, not English, to an audience of young adult readers who will quickly become adults. Olsen's first book on Beowulf, *Bjovulf: Et sagn fra Danmarks oldtid* (Beowulf: A Story from Denmark's Legendary History, 2002), prepared the way for the welcoming of Beowulf. Here are the opening two paragraphs of Olsen's retelling of the tale in his *Nordiske heltesagn*:

> En af Skjoldungerne hed Roar. Han drog udenlands på store hærtogter, vandt guld, hæder og ære og blev berømt som sine forfædre. Folk flokkedes om ham, og hans hird blev stor og mægti. Landet voksede i ry og rigdom.
>
> Kong Roar fandt da på, at der ved Lejre skulle bygges en stor og flot hal, større end nogen anden, hvor folk kunne more sig, spise og drikke. I denne pægtige hal ville han sidde på en tronstol for enden of højbordet. Taget skulle glimte af guld. Der skulle være stengulv, og hallen skulle være så smuk og imponerende, at det ville tag pusten fra selv de fornemmeste mænd, der kom på besøg.[42]
>
> One of the Scyldings was called Roar. He went abroad on great expeditions, won gold, honor and glory and became famous like his forefathers. People flocked to him, and his army became great and mighty. The country grew in reputation and wealth.
>
> King Roar then decided that there at Lejre a big and elegant hall should be built, bigger than any other, where people could enjoy themselves, eat and drink. In this stately hall, he would sit on a throne at the end of the high table. The roof would glitter with gold. There would be a stone floor, and the hall would be so beautiful and impressive that it would take the breath away from even the most distinguished men who came on a visit.

Because of the complex cultural work it tries to do, the Danish rendering of Henriette Barkow's *Beowulf: An Anglo-Saxon Epic* (2003) is the most intriguing translation mentioned in this book. Barkow, a children's author, editor, and "Story Re-Teller" at Mantra Lingua Ltd. in London, retold *Beowulf* for young children, and that retelling was then translated into several languages to accommodate the migration of peoples and their children across the world today. In multi-lingual elementary school classrooms, *Beowulf* can be read or heard in Barkow's English adaptation and

---

[42] Olsen, *Nordiske heltesagn*, p. 49.

in parallel translations of it into Albanian, Arabic, Bengali, Cantonese, Farsi, German, Gujarati, Portuguese, Punjabi, Somali, Mexican Spanish, Spanish, Turkish, and Urdu. In Denmark, *Beowulf og hvordan han bekæmpede Grendel – et angelsaksisk epos* (Beowulf and How He Fought Grendel – An Anglo-Saxon Epic, 2004) can be read or heard in a Danish translation by Jakob Kjær and a Persian translation by Sajida Fawz and with captivating illustrations by Alan Down. Mantra Lingua Ltd.'s mission is a laudable one: to enhance home language acquisition as well as acquisition of the host country's language "in bilingual versions of bestsellers, such as *The Hungry Caterpillar, Brown Bear* ... We publish books with high quality illustrations and production standards so that our books sit proudly in any mainstream bookshelf. We cover a wide range of genres and ages, and our family of 'Story Re-tellers' ensure that home languages are child friendly and not mechanically translated."[43] The power of translation to cross multiple boundaries – geographic, linguistic, and cultural – is made manifest daily in the work of this remarkable publisher.

The most recent retelling of *Beowulf* in Danish is by John Rydahl (1959), a textbook author who spent a lot of time on storytelling, myths, and legends when he was a primary school teacher.[44] His book for children aged ten to thirteen, *Bjovulf: Den gamle dragedræber* (Beowulf: The Old Dragon Slayer), was published in 2012. Gitte Skov supplied the amusing and sometimes gruesome illustrations. When Grendel first attacks Heorot in the poem, for example, the text reads:

> Grendel tog først den ene og så den anden af kong Roars sovende krigere og kvaste dem mellem tænderne, så blodet sprøjtede ud over gulv og vægge i den store hal.[45]

> Grendel took first one then another of king Hrothgar's sleeping warriors and squashed them between his teeth so that blood spurted out across the floor and walls in the big hall.

One can imagine kids recoiling gleefully from this grizzly description and the seemingly twenty-feet-tall Grendel troll on the same page grinning out at them with mouth agape, rows and rows of spiked teeth like a shark's thrusting up and down, and with the impaled head of a horn-helmeted Dane on one tooth and half the body of another Dane dangling from Grendel's right hand. Grendel is fearsome, beastly, grotesque; the children are enchanted.

---

[43] See Mantra Lingua's website at https://uk.mantralingua.com/content/about-us.
[44] Rydahl, email communication to Bjork.
[45] Rydahl, *Bjovulf*, p. 17.

Figure 11. "Uhyret Grendel" by Gitte Skov, 2012.

Enchantment grips us beyond childhood as well. Keld Zeruneith, whose work was discussed in chapters 4 and 5, remembers his first encounter with ancient Greek texts in Danish translation in his youth:

> The first books I bought with my own money, earned by weeding beets, were Otto Gelsted's translations of *The Iliad* and *The Odyssey*. They were so inspiring that they later led me to Homer in the original language. So now that I have occupied myself with *Beowulf* for several years, I have felt motivated in all humility to follow in Gelsted's footsteps and create a new version of the major work of Anglo-Saxon poetry.[46]

---

[46] "De første bøger, jeg købte for penge, jeg selv havde tjent ved at luge roer, var Otto Gelsteds oversættelser af Iliaden og Odysseen. De var så inspirerende, at det siden førte mig til Homer på originalsproget. Så da jeg nu har beskæftiget mig med Beowulf i adskillige år, har jeg følt mig motiveret til i al beskedenhed at gå i Gelsteds fodspor og lave en gendigtning af angelsaksisk digtnings hovedværk." Zeruneith, *Beowulf*, p. 126.

Zeruneith is the most recent Dane to translate that major work, and his *Beowulf: En gendigtning med efterskrift og noter* (Beowulf: A New Version with an Afterword and Notes, 2018) differs from all its predecessors: it is in prose, just as Gelsted's translations of Homer are. The first editions of those translations are from 1954 (*Odysseen*) and 1955 (*Illiaden*), and by 2001 they had reached their nineteenth edition. By 2022, both were available as audiobooks. Gelsted's translations are so dominant and well respected that they were even translated into other languages such as Swedish. Aspiring to Gelsted's level is therefore a lofty goal. It is comparable to aspiring to the level of E. Talbot Donaldson (1910–87), whose prose translation of *Beowulf* from 1966 dominated the field and was read by thousands of students in *The Norton Anthology of English Literature* until it was replaced in the seventh edition in 2000 by Seamus Heaney's verse translation. As well as being inspired by Gelsted to translate into prose, Zeruneith had two other inspirations: his students, who had trouble understanding Haarder's verse translation of the poem, and Goethe, who greatly preferred prose translations of foreign texts over verse ones.[47]

The initial reception of Zeruneith's translation was quite positive. One reviewer, for example, praised it as "a magnificent gift" (*en prægtig gave*), perfect in style and solemn and noble in tone. It "flows so easily and effortlessly along that reading and reciting it become the purest pleasure. It has in a noble way succeeded in retaining the poem's heroic diction without adding anything to convey the dramatic tale."[48] Here's a sampling:

> Hør her! Vi har før fået fortalt, hvordan spyddanskeres konger i tidligere tid høstede stort ry ved tapperhed. Sådan vandt Skjold Skefing et væld af mjødbænke fra sine fjender i mange lande; han indgød alle skræk og rædsel tilbage fra dengang, hvor han [var] blevet fundet, alene og hjælpeløs. Men han fandt trøst, for under himlen voksede han sig stor og blomstrede i ære; enhver, der var i hans nærhed, ja, selv hinsides havet, hvalers våde vej, måtte adlyde og betale skat til ham. Han var en god konge!"[49]

> Listen here! We have been told before how the kings of the Spear Danes in earlier times gained great fame for bravery. So Skjold Skefing won an abundance of mead benches from his enemies in many lands; he brought back all the terror and fear from the time when he had been found, alone and helpless. But he found comfort,

---

[47] Zeruneith, email communication with Bjork, 2 August 2023.
[48] "flyder den så let og ubesværet af sted, at læsning og oplæsning bliver den reneste lyst. Det er på fornemste vis lykkedes at holde kvadets heroiske ordvalg uden at sætte noget til, hvad angår det at formidle den dramatiske historie." Skyum-Nielsen, "Nyoversættelsen af 'Beowulf'."
[49] Zeruneith, *Beowulf*, p. 4.

for under heaven he grew great and flourished in glory; everyone who was in his presence, yes, even beyond the sea, the wet whale-road, had to obey him and pay him tribute. He was a good king!

Zeruneith uses ON equivalents of AS names when possible, just as Haarder does, except for Beowulf, and he has added features to his text that make it even more enriching and accessible. He includes full annotations and a detailed afterword, of course, and has also inserted useful cross references in the summaries of each of the fitts or songs. These are especially welcome in the second, often confusing, part of the poem. For fitt or song 40, for example, the summary reads, "The messenger awaits the hours of the wolf: the Franks and Frisians will attack in revenge for Hygelac's attack (mentioned in songs 18, 33, and 35). The old Swedish king Ongentheow kills King Hæthcyn and is attacked by Hygelac (mentioned in song 35)." [50]

Swedish Translations

Gustaf Wilhelm Gumælius (1789–1877), author, minister, and politician,[51] in his 1817 review of Thorkelin's first edition of *Beowulf*, tried his hand at translating a few passages of the poem into Swedish and was the first to do so. He composed in the ON *fornyrðislag* meter, which resembles that of OE, and writes this about the experience: "The metre of the whole work is quite like Norse. Pure Fornydislag, most of it regular. The reviewer has tried to reconstruct them in the attempts at translation given above, but the difficulties were so great that only partial success could be achieved."[52]

Rudolf Mauritz Wickberg (1851–1940) was much more successful. He earned his Ph.D. at the University of Lund in 1877, briefly served as a reader there in comparative Germanic linguistics, and then became a lecturer in French and English at the state secondary grammar school in Västervik, teaching from 1883 to 1917. According to the 1921 edition of the encyclopedia *Nordisk Familjebok* (Nordic Family Book), his major achievement was translating *Beowulf* into Swedish and therefore having "incorporated that unparalleled poetic work into Swedish literature."[53]

---

[50] "Sendebuddet venter ulvetider: Frankere og frisere vil angibe som hævn for Hygelaks angreb (omtalt i 18., 33. og 35. sang). Den gamle svenskekonge Ongenteov dræber kong Hætkyn og angribes af Hygelak (omtalt i 35. sang)." Zeruneith, *Beowulf*, p. 115.
[51] Amenius, "Gustaf Wilhelm Gumælius."
[52] Shippey and Haarder, *Beowulf*, p. 142.
[53] "införlifvat detta enastående diktverk med svenska litteraturen." Anon., "Rudolf Mauritz Wickberg."

The translation was originally attached to the annual report on the Västervik school for 1888–89 as a mere appendix. Twenty-five years later in 1914, *Beowulf: En fornengelsk hjältedikt* (Beowulf: An OE Heroic Poem) was issued in a second edition with an updated introduction as volume five in "Askerbergs populär-vetenskapliga bibliotek" (Askerberg's Popular Scholarly Library). That series was intended for an educated, but not professional, audience and would approach that audience in a way "that, through lucidity, clarity and precision, makes reading a pleasure and a revitalization."[54] The introduction gives an overview of the poem,[55] its historical and legendary background,[56] its prehistory, age, and manuscript,[57] and its language, style, and meter.[58] Wickberg also supplies a glossary of names, all of which are in the original OE, and breaks the poem into four parts instead of forty-three fitts or songs: the fight with Grendel,[59] the fight with Grendel's mother,[60] Beowulf's return,[61] and the fight with the dragon.[62] Over 100 years later in 2022, Bo Gräslund would give Wickberg's translation and introduction currency yet again. See the discussion below.

Erik Björkman (1872–1919) trained in Nordic philology, German, and English, and held professorships at Lund, Göteborg, and Uppsala, where he was appointed Professor of English Language in 1911. He published much of his work in German and English, his thesis on *Scandinavian Loan-Words in Middle English* (1900–02) and treatises on *Nordische personennamen in England in alt- und frühmittel-englischer zeit* (1910) and *Zur englischen namenkunde* (1912) being good examples. His major work in *Beowulf* studies is *Studien über die Eigennamen im Beowulf*, published posthumously in 1920.[63] Among the several items in Swedish that he published during his lifetime is his translation of the last part of the poem, the fight with the dragon, in 1902. Wickberg mentions this translation in his 1914 introduction to his translation,[64] and Sune Lindqvist would later come to prefer it to Wickberg's as more accurate.[65]

"Beowulf, Fornengelsk Dikt" (*Beowulf*, OE Poem) was published in Henrik Schück's *Världslitteraturen i urval och öfversättning* (Selected World

---

[54] "som genom åskådlighet, klarhet och precision gör läsandet till ett nöje och en vederkvickelse." Wickberg, *Beowulf*, 2nd ed., inside front cover.
[55] Ibid., pp. 5–6.
[56] Ibid., pp. 7–10.
[57] Ibid., pp. 10–13.
[58] Ibid., pp. 13–15.
[59] Ibid., pp. 16–55.
[60] Ibid., pp. 56–76.
[61] Ibid., pp. 77–86.
[62] Ibid., pp. 87–118.
[63] Ekwall, "Erik Björkman."
[64] Wickberg, *Beowulf*, 2nd ed., p. 13.
[65] See, e.g., Lindqvist's "Sutton Hoo and *Beowulf*."

Literature in Translation) in 1902. Björkman offers an extremely detailed and accurate prose summary of lines 1–2207,[66] which is followed by a brief essay on *Beowulf* by Schück, anticipating his more fully developed 1909 argument in *Studier i Beowulfsagan*.[67] Björkman's "prosaic," line-by-line translation of lines 2207–17, 2232–310, and 2313–3182 with footnotes to the translation mostly by Schück follows Schück's essay.[68] Lines 2207 through 2217 of Björkman's translation are below, followed by the OE text. I have given literal English translations of both under each of the first few lines to emphasize how close Björkman's translation is to the original OE:

> Så kom det vida konungariket
> *So the broad kingdom came*
> I Beowulfs händer; väl han det styrde
> *into Beowulf's hands; well he ruled it*
> I femtio vintrar – en grånad konung var han,
> *for fifty years – a hoary king he was*
> En åldrig odalherre – tills en drake begynte
> *an old landlord – until a dragon began*
> I nätternas mörker visa sitt välde.
> *in the darkness of the nights to show its power.*

> syððan Beowulfe brade rice
> *Afterward the broad kingdom*
> on hand gehwearf; he geheold tela
> *passed into Beowulf's hands; he ruled well*
> fiftig wintra – wæs ða frod cyning,
> *fifty years – he was then a wise old king,*
> eald eþelweard – oð ðæt an ongan
> *an old land guardian – until a dragon began*
> Deorcum nihtum draca ricsian.
> *in the dark nights to hold sway.*

The rest of the passage and my translation of it read:

> På högan hed han vaktade sin skatt
> Sin branta klippborg; en stig gick där nedan,
> Okänd för människor. Där trängde en gång
> En främling in. Begärligt grep han tag i
> Den hedniska skatten.[69]

---

[66] Björkman, *Beowulf*, pp. 463–70.
[67] Ibid., pp. 471–74.
[68] Ibid., pp. 475–501.
[69] Ibid., p. 475.

On the mound, he guarded his treasure
his steep rock fortress; a path went down there,
unknown to humans. There one time a
stranger forced himself in. He eagerly grabbed
hold of the heathen treasure.

Björn Collinder (1894–1983), who published the most widely read and popular Swedish translation of *Beowulf* in 1954, renders the same lines this way:

så kom sedan det stora riket
i Beowulfs hand. Han hävdade det väl
i femtio vintrar – han var en vis king,
den åldrige drotten – tills en drake kom
för att öva sin makt i mörka nätter.
I vindsvepte viste vaktar han sin skatt
på en stupbrant bergshöjd. En stig ledde dit,
som var okänd för alla – men en gång tog sig
en man dit in och roffade åt sig
ur hednaskatten en herrlig bägare

so then the great kingdom came
into Beowulf's hands. He ruled it well
for fifty winters – he was a wise king,
the aged chieftain – until a dragon came
to exercize power in the dark nights.
In windswept wisdom, he guards his treasure
on a steep sloping mountain summit. A path led
there that was unknown to all – but one time
a man found his way there and grabbed for
himself from the heathen hoard a glorious cup.

The alliteration is there, the regular rhythm of the original, and the translation carries one away on its beauty and force, much as Seamus Heaney's translation carries its readers away. It was called "a monumental work" by one reviewer in the Swedish newspaper *Svenska Dagbladet* and a "momentous cultural achievement" by another in *Stockholms Tidningen*.[70] In their scholarly review of the book, A. S. C. Ross and E. G. Stanley concur, writing, "It must surely be an unusual event for a great specialist in one Philology to translate into the verse of his native language the most famous work of quite another Philology. This is, however, what Professor Collinder has done – and done excellently."[71]

---

[70] Knut Hagberg and Bertil Molde respectively. Quoted on the dust jacket on the 1955 issue of the book.
[71] Ross and Stanley, Review of Collinder, p. 110.

Figure 12. Björn Collinder, 1957.

Collinder was Professor of Finno-Ugric Philology at the University of Uppsala, 1933 to 1961, and he was a formidable force in the field. His *Fenno-Ugric Vocabulary* (1955), *Survey of the Uralic Languages* (1957), and *Comparative Grammar of the Uralic Languages* (1960), for example, have become classics in Finno-Ugric studies. He also translated important works by authors such as Euripides, Sophocles, and Shakespeare, and his translation of *The Kalevala*, like his translation of *Beowulf*, "is considered pithy and brilliant," especially in its fourth edition published in 1970. He was a fellow of learned societies in Finland, Norway, Denmark, Austria, and Hungary, and in his later years he stood out "as a giant of education who combined profound Swedishness with extensive knowledge of world cultures."[72]

---

[72] "betraktas som kärnfull och snillrik." "en bildningens jätte som förenade ursvenskheten med omfattande kunskaper om världskulturerna." Tarkiainen, "Collinder."

Sune Lindqvist, the distinguished archaeologist discussed in chapter 5, published the extremely complicated and detailed *Beowulf Dissectus. Snitt ur fornkvädet jämte svensk tydning* (Beowulf Dissected: Excerpts from the Ancient Poem and a Swedish Interpretation) in 1958. He had planned to work with his colleague Björn Collinder in developing the translation for the book, but the freedom Collinder had to take in his translation to make the alliterative verse function in Swedish rendered that translation too loose for Lindqvist's purposes. He consequently did his own.[73] His main goal is relatively simple: to excise from the surrounding superfluous tissue of Christian interpolation and digression the original text of the poem and arrange it chronologically so that modern readers (especially modern Swedish readers) could better appreciate it. It could thus take its rightful place as Sweden's national epic. Denmark has its Saxo Grammaticus, after all (Grundtvig would say that it has its *Beowulf*), and Norway and Iceland their Snorri Sturluson, so why should Sverige not have its comparable monument?[74] Lundqvist supplies a complex diagram of what the original text and subsequent additions look like on pp. 123–25.

Lindqvist felt that since the main characters of the central narrative of *Beowulf* are Geatas, and Geatas are generally accepted as the *Götar* of Västgötaland in mainland Sweden, the basic material of that narrative has to derive from Swedish, especially *götisk*, tradition.[75] If we accept that premise, then we can also accept the implied premise that the language of the original narrative was East ON or OldSwed. That probability in turn can directly affect the way we interpret the language of the narrative, even in its present incarnation in OE. Thus, although Lindqvist had always read *Beowulf* as an archaeologist, fixing on funerary customs and material culture, in this book he delves largely into the archaeology of the word, what has become known since the 1990s as "textual archaeology."[76] As T. S. Eliot remarks in "Whispers of Immortality" about the Elizabethan dramatist John Webster, Lindqvist "saw the skull beneath the skin,"[77] the underlying original text beneath subsequent textual layers.

Supplementing the glosses and commentaries of major editions of the poem such as Klaeber and Clark Hall/Wrenn with reference to dictionaries of old Swedish laws, medieval Swedish, and Swedish etymology,[78] Lindqvist tackles some hard words. Take just two examples: *aldorleas* (lines 1587a, 3003a) and *garsecg* (49a, 515a, 537b). *Aldorleas* appears three times

---

[73] Lindqvist, *Beowulf Dissectus*, p. 6.
[74] Ibid., p. 5.
[75] Ibid., p. 8.
[76] Herschend, "Striden i Finnsborg."
[77] Eliot, *Complete Poems*, p. 52.
[78] Lindqvist, *Beowulf Dissectus*, p. 9.

in *Beowulf*, where it means "lordless" once and has been taken to mean "lifeless" or "dead" the other two times. In lines 1586–87a in the cave in Grendel's mere, however, the poet has Beowulf encountering "guðwerigne Grendel licgan, aldorleasne" (battle-weary Grendel lying lifeless). Lindqvist thinks that, here especially, a better meaning for the adjective than traditional OE glossaries provide is found in OSwed, where the comparable word (*alster* related to *ala* related to *aldor*) as a substantive does mean "lifetime, life, or age" but metaphorically also means "offspring," because offspring are what make us live on. The great weight in ancient Scandinavia that was put on a man's having a son who could avenge his death and take over his position and responsibilities is well known,[79] writes Lindqvist, and the appropriateness of "battle-weary Grendel lying sonless" is manifest. The adjective "sonless," in fact, could have been originally used in the two other places where it appears as well and seems especially appropriate when applied to Beowulf in line 3003a. The Swedes are predicted to attack the Geats once they hear that "our lord is sonless, he who once held the hoard and kingdom against all enemies."

Garsecg (lines 49a, 515a, 537b), which is almost universally interpreted to mean "ocean," likewise appears three times in the poem and presents an equally interesting problem. Two of those instances occur in the Breca episode, which Lindqvist regards as an interpolation and therefore much later than the original narrative. The first instance of the word, on the other hand, does occur in that original narrative. It concerns Scyld Scefing, whom the Danes "geafon on garsecg." Lindqvist believes there are two possibilities for interpreting this line in its original Scandinavian context, both having to do with Odin. First, *garsecg* or "spear man" could simply be an epithet for Odin, not Neptune, the god of the spear. So the Danes gave Scyld Scefing to Odin or the realm of the dead. Or, second, the word could originally have been the OSwed word *Geirs-oddr* (spear point) and refer to the broader analogous story of Sigurðr Hringr in *Skjoldunga saga*.[80] In the saga, the aged Swedish king, gravely wounded in battle, climbs onto his own burial ship and stabs himself (or is stabbed) to death to begin his journey to Odin's realm. Scyld Scefing could also have begun his journey to the afterworld at the point of the spear, a perfectly natural, according to Lindqvist, way to meet your end in the Nordic tradition. And so, digging down to the ur-lexicon in this manner, scalping away superfluous digressive and Christian tissue from the skull, Lindqvist moves *Beowulf* closer to the heart of Iron Age Sweden.

The Swedes have taken the young audience for *Beowulf* seriously, just as the Danes and Norwegians have, and produced two appropriate trans-

---

[79] Ibid., p. 105.
[80] Ibid., pp. 121–22.

lations of retellings of the poem. The first is of the version for children aged twelve to fifteen by Robert Nye (1939–2016), the best-selling British novelist and poet,[81] who published his retelling of the whole of *Beowulf* in 1968. He writes in his afterword to the book that he offers an interpretation, not a translation. Myths have great meaning for children, he continues, and he has tried to make his retelling of this one live for children and young adults of future generations.[82] Birgitta Gahrton (1935–), a renowned translator of children's books and Margaret Atwood's works, has in turn tried to make it live for future generations of Swedes. Here is her version of the scene in which Hrothgar decides to build Heorot:

> En dag bestämde sig Hrodgar för att bygga en stor festhall för en del av allt krigsbyte som han hade vunnit. "Jag har drömt om en festhall", sade han till sina undersåtar, "och i drömmen såg jag i denna hall en festsal som var större än alla andra salar sedan tidernas begynnelse. Golvet glänste och taket var av guld. Det fanns elfenben överallt och en tron där en kung kunde sitta. Precis en sådan sal tänker jag bygga. Skalder ska sjunga där – om segrar och nederlag och om min farfarsfar, Skyld Skefing, som var så stark. Och mina egna modiga krigsmän ska äta och dricka där. Jag ska kalla hallen för Heorot.[83]

> One day, Hrodgar decided to build a great ceremonial hall with part of all the spoils of war that he had won. "I have dreamed of a ceremonial hall," he said to his subjects, "and in the dream I saw in this hall a banquet room that was greater than all others since the beginning of time. The floor shone and the ceiling was made of gold. There was ivory everywhere and a throne where a king could sit. I'm thinking of building just such a room. Scalds will sing there – about victories and defeats and about my great-grandfather, Scyld Scefing, who was so strong. And my own brave warriors will eat and drink there. I will call the hall Heorot.

The book was published in 2000 with a second edition following in 2007.

Rob Lloyd Jones (1977–), an award-winning British children's author, likewise retold the whole of *Beowulf* for children but even younger ones than those that Robert Nye chose as his audience. Lloyd Jones retells the whole Beowulf story for readers around age seven. Those readers benefit from a simple text embedded in engaging illustrations. Victor Tavares, a children's book illustrator who believes that "Beauty seduces! It creates

---

[81] Worley, "Robert Nye."
[82] Nye, *Beowulf*, p. 109.
[83] Ibid., p. 15.

affection links between readers and books,"[84] has provided rich, provocative, exceedingly bright illustrations on almost every page of this retelling. Grendel's mother, for example, appears as a giant octopus with a talon at the end of each arm and with huge, devouring fangs. Birgit Lönn, a widely published author and translator of children's books, transforms the text into modern Swedish. Here is the start of her chapter 1 about Heorot:

> För länge, länge sedan var Danmark ett land i skräck. Hemska monster strövade över de dimmiga mossarna. Om nätterna skrek de och skränade, ylade och brölade.
>
> Kung i Danmark var en krigsherre som hette Hrodgar. Han vägrade att låta sig skrämmas. Han byggde en jättestor byggnad åt sig själv, högste uppe på ett brant berg och vid utkanten av en stor mosse.
>
> Den uppfördes av det finaste virke och pryddes med elfenben, silver och glittrande guld. Kungen kallade den Heorot.[85]

> Long, long ago, Denmark was a land in terror. Horrible monsters roamed the misty bogs. At night, they screamed and hooted, howled and bellowed.
>
> The king in Denmark was a warlord called Hrothgar. He refused to let himself be scared. He built a huge building for himself, highest up on a steep mountain and at the edge of a big bog.
>
> It was built of the finest wood and adorned with ivory, silver and glittering gold. The king called it Heorot.

In 2022, Bo Gräslund put his archaeological work that we learned about in the previous chapter to work in a revised version of Rudolf Wickberg's translation of *Beowulf*. The first change comes in the book's title. Wickberg's is *Beowulf: En fornengelsk hjältedikt* (*Beowulf*: An OE Heroic Poem); Gräslund's is *Beowulf: En nordisk berättelse från 500-talet* (*Beowulf*: A Nordic Tale from the Sixth Century), which obviously moves the provenance of the poem back from England to Scandinavia, where Gräslund argues the poem originated.[86] He has modernized Wickberg's Swedish in regard to word choice, verb forms, and syntax, and he has changed the OE forms of names in Wickberg to the ON forms except for Beowulf. In revising Wickberg's text, Gräslund has been sensitive to poetic concerns but has always prioritized factual correctness. Most importantly, "Wickberg's

---

[84] Anon., "Victor Tavares."
[85] Jones and Lönn, *Beowulf*, pp. 5–6.
[86] Gräslund and Wickberg, *Beowulf*, p. 7.

text has also been updated in accordance with the conclusions of my above-mentioned work [*Beowulfkvädet: Den nordiska bakgrunden*, 2018], as well as with modern archaeological, historical, philological, and religious-historical research in general." It includes an interpretation of the monsters in the poem, not as fiction, but as reflections of the Nordic reality of extreme famine during the period when the events in the poem take place.[87] Here is a sample of Wickberg's translation followed by Gräslund's updating of it. I have italicized the changes in Gräslund's version. The scene is Beowulf's departure from Geatland in lines 207–16:

>   Själv femtonde
> Gick han till havsträdet. Den sjökunnige man
> Ledde kämparne till landets gräns.
> Tiden förrann, farkosten låg på vågorna
> Vid bergets fot. Rustade stego
> Kämparne uppå stäven: havets strömmar
> Böljade mot sanden. Männen buro
> I skeppets sköte glänsande smycken,
> Ståtliga rustningar, sköto sedan ut
> På önskad färd det timrade skeppet.[88]

> Själv femtonde *man*
> gick han till *fartyget*, den *sjövane* mannen
> ledde kämparna till *stranden*.
> *Snart var det tid att ge sig av. Båten* låg *i vattnet*
> *nedanför Burgen. Väl* rustade steg
> *männen ombord över* stäven. Havets
> *böljor slog* mot sanden. I skeppets sköte
> *lade de* glänsande smycken *och*
> *praktfulla* rustningar, sköt sedan ut
> *för den avsedda färden.*[89]

>   Himself the fifteenth
> he went to the sea-wood. The sea-savvy man
> led the warriors to the land's edge.
> Time passed, the boat lay on the waves
> at the mountain's foot. Armed stepped
> the warriors onto the stern: the sea currents
> billowed against the sand. The men carried

---

[87] "Wickbergs text har vidare uppdaterats in enlighet med slutsatserna i mitt ovan nämnda arbete, liksom med modern arkeologisk, historisk, filologisk och religionshistorisk forskning i övrigt." Ibid., pp. 8–9.
[88] Wickberg, *Beowulf*, p. 22.
[89] Gräslund and Wickberg, *Beowulf*, pp. 25–26.

> to the bosom of the ship shining ornaments,
> stately armaments; then shoved out
> on the desired journey the timbered ship.
>
> Himself the fifteenth man
> he went to the ship, the sea-accustomed man
> led the warriors to the shore.
> Soon it was time to leave. The boat lay in
> the water below Burgen. Well armored
> stepped aboard over the stern. The sea's
> waves struck the sand. In the ship's bosom
> the laid the shining ornaments and
> splendid armaments, then shoved out
> on the intended journey.

On his changing *vid bergets fot* (at the mountain's foot) to *nedanför Burgen* (below Burgen) five lines into the text, Gräslund notes that the OE word *beorge* can refer to Burgen, "the majestic part of the Littorin embankment above Bandlund cove's northern sandy beach on southeast Gotland."[90]

Gräslund concludes his volume with a useful synopsis of the major findings from his book *Beowulfkvädet* as well as maps and pictures of relevant archaeological sites.[91] He also gives his answer to the question of whether *Beowulf* is an OE or Nordic poem:

> As transmitted orally in OE, covered with Christian polish, and preserved in writing in OE on a manuscript in England, *Beowulf* can be called OE literature in a formal sense. But if one bears in mind that the epic was originally created during the Iron Age by proto-Nordic poets in the proto-Nordic language, deals exclusively with a pagan North, not touching England with a single syllable, then *Beowulf* appears in substance to be a Nordic work of poetry in OE dress.[92]

---

[90] "det mäktiga partiet av Littorinavallen ovanför Bandlundvikens norra sandstrand på sydöstra Gotland." Ibid., p. 26, note 3.

[91] Ibid., pp. 152–92.

[92] "Som muntligt traderad på fornengelska, belagd med kristen polityr och som skriftligt bevarad på fornengelska på ett manuskript i England, kan Beowulf i formell mening kallas för fornengelsk litteratur. Men tar man fasta på att eposet ursprungligen skapades under järnåldern av urnordiska diktare på urnordiskt tungomål, uteslutande handlar om ett hedniskt Norden och inte med en enda stavelse berör England, så framstår Beowulf i allt väsentligt som ett nordiskt diktverk i fornengelsk klädnad." Ibid., p. 191.

Norwegian Translations

Norwegian comes in two varieties, one deriving from the union of Norway and Denmark, which lasted from the late fourteenth century until 1814, as briefly discussed in chapter 1, and the other from Romantic Nationalism after 1814 and the desire for a pure Norwegian tongue that would reflect Norway's independence and nationhood. *Riksmål* or *Bokmål*, or Dano-Norwegian, comes from the first part of Norway's history, and Nynorsk or New Norwegian (known initially as *landsmål* because of its connection with the dialects of rural Norway) comes from the second. The latter was created in 1853 by Ivar Aasen (1813–96), a dialectologist without any formal training who studied contemporary Norwegian, chiefly western, dialects and their relationship to ON. The results of his work *Det norske folkesprog grammatik* (Grammar of the Norwegian Dialects, 1848; revised 1864) and *Ordbog over det norske folkesprog* (Dictionary of the Norwegian Dialects, 1850; revised 1873) quickly advanced the idea of a national language going back to its roots, and in 1885, Nynorsk achieved co-official status with Dano-Norwegian.[93] *Beowulf* has been translated into both.

First came the Nynorsk version. Henrik Rytter (1877–1950) published his *Beowulf og striden um Finnsborg frå angelsaksisk* (Beowulf and the Fight at Finnsburg from the Anglo-Saxon) in 1929. Rytter was a poet, playwright, and translator and is considered one of the most important writers of Nynorsk literature published between the world wars. It is primarily his poetry, however, that has earned him a place in the history of Norwegian literature, although he thought of his translation work as equally important. His versions of Shakespeare's plays (1932–33) and Dante's *Divine Comedy* (revised edition with Sigmund Skard, 1965) are still highly regarded. As a poet, Rytter was known as one of the first Norwegian modernists, mixing high and low styles and employing various traditional poetic forms, such as the ottava rima and sonnet, and free verse.[94]

Rytter's Nynorsk translation of *Beowulf*, begun in 1907, completed in 1921, and published in 1929, is in alliterative verse with a foreword, notes, and a brief bibliography. Rytter has taken pains to follow the poem line by line and further explains his methodology in his foreword: he found it most appropriate to give the translation as old a sense as he dared without presenting too many difficulties. He accordingly used a number of archaic words, mostly those for weapons, weapon usage, treasure, chieftains, and other terms relating to life in the poem. He also relieved the tedium of repetition in the poem by supplying synonyms where the original text does not, and he was not afraid to retain the inversions, insertions, and

[93] Hoel, "Aasen."
[94] Spaans, "Henrik Rytter."

other aspects of the original. "On the whole, what was important to me, I thought, was to reproduce the old poem itself, with all its idiosyncracies, so to speak, to reflect the Anglo-Saxon form in the Norwegian language. A difficult task! – An impossible task!"[95]

As he sometimes uses archaic words, this necessitates the use of glosses, which he supplies, and the care he takes to make his translation faithful to the original extends to the scholarly reading he did in preparing it. He consulted the Heyne, Holthausen, and Sedgefield editions as his source texts, and he benefited from the advice of scholars such as Axel Olrik, to whose memory he dedicates his book. Here is Rytter's masterful rendition of Beowulf's troop's approach to Heorot:

> Stigen var steinlagd, styrde rettleides
> hermannshopen. Harde, handfletta
> brynjer briste, brystringar skire.
> Det song i slagham då fram mot salen
> stridsklædde dei steig etter vegen.
> Sjøtrøytte sette skjoldar breide,
> *vigfaste verjer, mot veggen til huset,
> sette seg på setet. Då singla brynjer,
> våpna til *vigmenn. Valspjot ihop,
> oddgråe askeskaft, over deim stod,
> stridsham åt sjømenn.[96] (26)

> The path was paved, rightly steered
> the warrior troop. Hard, hand-braided
> byrnies shone, bright breast-rings.
> It sang in war gear when toward the hall
> battle-clad they strode along the road.
> Sea-weary ones set the broad shields,
> bosses firm in war, against the building's wall,
> sat down on the seat. Then byrnies rang,
> warriors' weapons. Slaughter spears together,
> grey from above ash-shafts, stood over them,
> war equipment for the sea men.

Rytter adds notes on the words above marked with my asterisks. Of *vigfaste*, he explains that the OE adjective *regnhearde* in the original means

---

[95] "I det heile galdt det for meg, tykte eg, å attergjeve sjølve det gamle kvædet, med alle sine sermerke, so å segje spegle den angelsaksiske form av i norsk mål. Eit vanskeleg arbeid! – Eit umogleg arbeid!" Rytter, *Beowulf*, pp. 13–14.
[96] Ibid., p. 26.

"rain-hard" or "having been made hard in showers of arrows" or "firm in war."[97] Of *vigmenn*, he notes that *vig* means *strid* or "war."[98]

Close to fifty years after Rytter's verse translation, a prose *Riksmål* translation of *Beowulf* appeared by Jan W. Dietrichson (1927–2019), a philologist and Professor of Literature at the University of Oslo, 1993–97. Educated at Cornell, Harvard, and the University of Oslo, Dietrichson published his dissertation, *The Image of Money in the American Novel of the Gilded Age*, in 1969.[99] He followed that with several books, including translations of important medieval texts, such as Tondal's visions in 1984, *Sir Gawain and the Green Knight* in 1988, *Troilus and Creseyde* in 2010, and Christine de Pizan in 2013. His *Beowulf-kvadet* (The Poem of *Beowulf*, 1976) begins with a foreword and introduction in which he first outlines his translation strategy. In contradistinction to Rytter, who writes in Nynorsk, translates into verse, and embraces archaic words, syntactic complexity, inversions, and other peculiarities of the original OE, Dietrichson eschews them all. His translation, in *Riksmål*, is in prose. Where Rytter saw the impossibility of a verse translation of *Beowulf* and attempted one anyway, Dietrichson saw the impossibility and chose another path. He chose a middle way between an archaic verse translation and a mundane prose one in everyday Norwegian.[100] Rytter, for example, translated lines 1501–07 about Grendel's mother dragging Beowulf into her lair as follows. I have italicized words that would be the most problematic for readers:

> Ho treiv imot og tok kring kjempa
> *kufst* med *klombrom*; kunde ikkje skade
> *kvate* kroppen; kring han var brynja;
> *slaghamen* ikkje ho slite kunde
> med fule fingrar, fletta ringbrynja.
> *Brimulva* bar då, til botnen komen,
> ringfyrsten radt til *ræheimen* sin.[101]

> She reached out and seized the warrior
> *kufst* with *klombrom*; she could not harm
> the *kvate* body; around him was the byrnie;
> she could not tear the *slagham*
> with ugly fingers, penetrate the chain mail.
> *Brimulva* bore when she came to the bottom
> the ring prince right to her *ræheimen*.

---

[97] Ibid., p. 142.
[98] Ibid., p. 138.
[99] Anon., "Jan Waldemar Dietrichson."
[100] Dietrichson, *Beowulf-kvadet*, pp. 7–9.
[101] Ibid., p. 9.

Dietrichson's version contains no stumbling blocks:

> Hun strakte ut armen og grep fatt i kjempen med fæle klør. Likevel kunne hun ikke skade kroppen hans, for ringbrynjen vernet den. Hun kunne ikke trenge igjennom den jernsmidde skjorten med de avskelige fingrene sine. Da sjøulven hade kommet ned till bunnen, bar hun ringfyrsten til hulen sin ... [102]

> She stretched out her arm and grabbed the warrior with her hideous claws. But she could not harm his body because the chain mail protected it. She could not penetrate the iron-forged shirt with her repulsive fingers. When the sea wolf had reached the bottom, she bore the ring prince to her cave ...

Dietrichson makes his translation even more accessible to modern Norwegians by writing a detailed, contextualizing introduction, which he urges his audience to read before the translation, and explanatory notes where appropriate.[103] Despite its manifest virtues, however, the book attracted a smaller audience than expected. In a personal communication, Dietrichson wrote, "The book did not attract much attention when it appeared on the Norwegian market, but from time to time I happen to meet people who – surprisingly enough! – have read it and thank me for it."[104] The gratitude is warranted.

A third Norwegian version of *Beowulf* appeared in 1999, when Tor Åge Bringsværd (1939–) published his *Beowulf: han som ville bli husket* (Beowulf: He Who Wanted to Be Remembered) with illustrations by Arne Samuelsen (1950–), a well-known artist and book illustrator. Bringsværd is an award-winning author of science and fantasy fiction and children's books as well as a dramatist and translator.[105] His *Riksmål* prose retelling for young adults is a carefully researched and executed production, as reflected in his afterword to the book, which contains information about the poem, its manuscript and background as well as helpful notes to the text and a list of works, with commentary, that Bringsværd consulted to write the book. He benefited from the Dietrichsen, Rytter, and Collinder translations of the poem, for example, and used George Jack's edition of *Beowulf* as his base text.[106] In telling Beowulf's story, Bringsværd straightens out its chronology so that we meet Beowulf first as a child. We meet his mother and father then, too:

---

[102] Ibid., p. 66.
[103] Ibid., p. 11.
[104] Dietrichson, personal letter to Bjork.
[105] Sjöberg, "Bringsværd."
[106] Bringsværd, *Beowulf*, pp. 76–77.

Beowulfs mor var kongesdatter, og hans far het Ecgtheow.
Ecgtheow var en stor kriger, men ofte slo han først og tenkte etterpå.
I en krangel drepte han en høvding fra den andre siden av Østersjøen. For å unngå hevn måtte han rømme landet. Da var sønnen bare noen få vintre gamel – og de skulle aldri se hverandre igjen.
Gutten Beowulf ligner ikke mye på sin far. Der Ecgtheow var brå og hissig, var Beowulf mild og vennlig. Nesten altfor treg! sa folk. Hva i all verden skal det til for å gjøre ham sint? Er han bare lat og doven, eller mangler han rett og slett mot?
Da Beowulf var syv vintre gammel, døde moren, og han blev sendt til sin morfar, kong Hrethel. Her vokste han opp – og blev behandlet som en av kongens egne sønner.
Ingen ventet seg noe særlig av ham. Han var bare en gutt av god familie – som kanskje hade det bedre enn hann fortjente.[107]

Beowulf's mother was the daughter of a king, and his father was called Ecgtheow.
Ecgtheow was a great warrior, but he often hit first and thought afterward.
In a dispute, he killed a chieftain from the other side of the Baltic. To avoid revenge, he had to flee the country. His son was only a few winters old then – and they would never see each other again.
The boy Beowulf doesn't resemble his father much. Where Ecgtheow was abrupt and angry, Beowulf was gentle and friendly. "Almost too easy going!" people said. What on earth would it take to make him mad? Is he just slothful and lazy, or does he simply lack courage?
When Beowulf was seven winters old, his mother died, and he was sent to King Hrethel, his grandfather on his mother's side. Here he grew up – and was treated just like one of the king's own sons.
No one expected anything special from him. He was just a boy from a good family – who maybe had it better than he deserved.

Bringsværd's book is an oversized one, which gives Arne Samuelson's numerous powerful images even more power.

Finnish Translations

Finland has produced two translations of *Beowulf*, the first begun by the engineer and naval captain Johan Rudolf Dillström (1885–1928) and completed by the Finnish translator and editor Matti Järvinen. Dillström published his alliterative verse rendition of lines 1–1472 and 2961–81 in 1927 in

---

[107] Bringsværd, *Beowulf*, p. 8.

Figure 13. Johan Rudolf Dillström, 1920s.

Laivastolehti (Navy Magazine), a publication of the Finnish Navy Officers' Association, and Järvinen finished Dillström's work and published it in book form in 1999 more or less simultaneously with the publication of the second Finnish translation. In their introduction to that publication, Osmo Pekonen (1960–2022) and Clive Tolley comment on Dillström's 1927 work, unaware that it had been finished. Because I do not know Finnish, Clive Tolley kindly sent me the English version of the introduction, which I quote here:

A full translation of *Beowulf* has not previously been published in Finnish. However, in the 1920's a sea-captain by the name of Dillström published about half the poem in successive issues of the *Laivastolehti*; the considerable concentration in the poem upon the sea and water was obviously a point of attraction for a maritime man. Dillström's efforts mark a considerable achievement; not only has he translated on the whole fairly accurately, but he is also conversant with much of contemporary scholarship. Unfortunately he did not have sufficient discrimination always to distinguish the plausible from the hare-brained, and his background notes, while noble in intent, are perilous to venture upon. In particular his forced attempts to link aspects of the poem with Finland represent a sort of desperate historicizing nationalism now relegated to the dustbin in all respectable scholarly circles.[108]

Pekonen, a mathematician, historian of science, author, and translator,[109] and Tolley, a lecturer in the Department of Folkloristics at the University of Turku,[110] make just two connections between Finland and *Beowulf*. They note in the opening paragraph of the introduction that the poem contains the first reference in English literature to Finland in line 580b, *Finna land* (land of Finns), the Finns being the occupants of far distant and mysterious Lappland. They try to preserve the mystery of the OE name by translating it as *Turjanmaa*, the Lapps of the modern Russian Terskij Bereg region called *Terfinnas* in Ohthere's account of his northern voyage in the ninth century.[111] They also connect *Beowulf* and Finland through the mythic figure of Beow in line 18a, who corresponds to the Finnish agricultural deity Pekko, "a name which is probably borrowed from the ancient Germanic word for 'barley' from which Beow also derives."[112]

The source text for *Beowulf. Suomennos, johdanto ja selitykset* (*Beowulf*: Translation, Introduction, and Annotations, 1999) is George Jack's 1994 edition of the poem supplemented by others, most notably Klaeber's and Wrenn's; the translators also consulted Björn Collinder's Swedish translation of the poem.[113] Because their translation was to be the first in the Finnish language, they felt it necessary to be as faithful to the original as possible, "except where this would result in something unreadable in Finnish." For instance, they translate lines 157–58 (rendered cumbersomely in literal English as "none of the wise men there had any need to hope for a more splendid recompense at the hands of the murderer")

---

[108] Tolley, "Introduction," p. 28.
[109] Anon., "Professori Osmo Pekonen."
[110] See his website at http://www.clivetolley.co.uk/About.html.
[111] Tolley, "Introduction," p. 1.
[112] Ibid., p. 12.
[113] Ibid., p. 27.

as *mielevänkään miehen oli turha toivoa saavansa sakkoja surmaajan kädestä* ("it was useless even for a willing man to hope to receive *wergild* from the hand of the slayer").[114] They also exploit the richness of Finnish in order to reproduce the poetic power of the original, occasionally using the vocabulary of prominent Finnish poets to do so and sometimes paralleling the poetic force of the original instead of giving a literal rendering.[115] As for the style of the translation, they decided that a verse translation is preferable to a prose one. They based their translation on the style of the original without strictly adhering to all its rules. Alliteration, for example, is not ubiquitous, and stress patterns differ from those of the OE mainly because the distinction possible between stressed and unstressed syllables in OE does not exist in Finnish.[116] Here is a brief example of the finished product with the OE original preceding it. Grendel's approach to Heorot is described, beginning in lines 702b–709.

    Com on wanre niht
scriðan sceadugenga.   Sceotend swæfon,
þa þæt hornreced   healdan scoldon,
ealle buton anum.   þæt wæs yldum cuþ
þæt hie ne moste   þa metod nolde,
se scynscaþa   under sceadu bregdan;
ac he wæccende   wraþum on andan
bad bolgenmod   beadwa geþinges.

    Kolkosta yöstä
vaappui hahmo   hämärässä häilyen.
Avaran salin   vartijat nukkuivat,
kaikki paitsi yksi.   Ihmiset tiesivät,
ettei häijy hätyyttäjä   saattaisi heitä
Luojan sallimatta   varjoihin raastaa.
Yksi vain valvoi   raivoa rinnassaan,
kiivaana odotti   kamppailun päätöstä.[117]

    The walker in shadows came
gliding in the dark night. The warriors slept,
those that were to hold that gabled house,
all but one. That was known to men
that the demonic foe, when God did not want it,
could not draw them into the shadows;

---

[114] Ibid., p. 27.
[115] Ibid., p. 27.
[116] Ibid., p. 28.
[117] Tolley, "From Anglo-Saxon England to Modern Finland," p. 10.

but he, keeping watch with fierce indignation,
awaited, swollen with rage, the outcome of the battle.

Icelandic Translation

The lone Icelandic translation of *Beowulf* was done by Halldóra B. Björnsson (1907–68), a poet, novelist, activist, and telephone operator who was one of the founders of the "Icelandic Women's Culture and Peace Association" (*Menningar- og friðarsamtaka íslenskra kvenna*) and served on the board of the "Writers' Association of Iceland" (*Rithöfundafélags Íslands*). Her first book, *Ljóð* (Poems), was published in 1949. She published her novel *Eitt er það land* (There is a Land), focused on her rural childhood, in 1955, *Trumban og lútan* (The Drum and the Lute), a collection of Greenlandic and African poems in translation, in 1959, and completed a draft of her greatest work, her translation of *Beowulf*, in 1968 just before she died.[118] A collection of essays and two other volumes of poetry were published posthumously, as was her translation of *Beowulf*.[119] Björnsson knew medieval Icelandic literature well and even wrote some medieval Icelandic *ríma* (ballad) poems, a tradition that extends into the modern period.[120] Her translation of *Beowulf* benefited from that knowledge and experience, as it did from the closeness of modern Icelandic and OE, a closeness that we first witnessed in the early Middle Ages, as seen in the Introduction to this book. OE and ON seem to have been mutually intelligible. Björnsson puts the connection to good use. She used Klaeber as her source text, and did not consult any other translations to do her work. "Her translation gives the Icelandic reader a clear sense of the tone of the original, its intonation and range of meaning; it is as if the long-lost sound of the harp is reborn in her performance."[121] She left three copies of her work, each mostly complete but with different changes and notes by Björnsson herself but also by others, Stefán Einarsson among them.[122] Pétur Knútsson Ridgewell collated and edited the three versions and published the translation with his foreword as *Bjólfskviða* (The Lay of Bjólfur) in 1983.

---

[118] Anon., "Halldóra B. Björnsson."
[119] Knútsson, "Intimacy," p. 189.
[120] Ibid., p. 189.
[121] "Þýðing hennar gefur íslenskum lesanda glögga mynd af máli frumtextans, hljómfalli þess og merkingasviði, það er eins og löngu hljónaður hörpusláttur kvikni aftur á ölbekkjum í meðförum hennar." Björnsson, *Bjólfskviða*, "Formáli," p. 7.
[122] Ibid., p. 8.

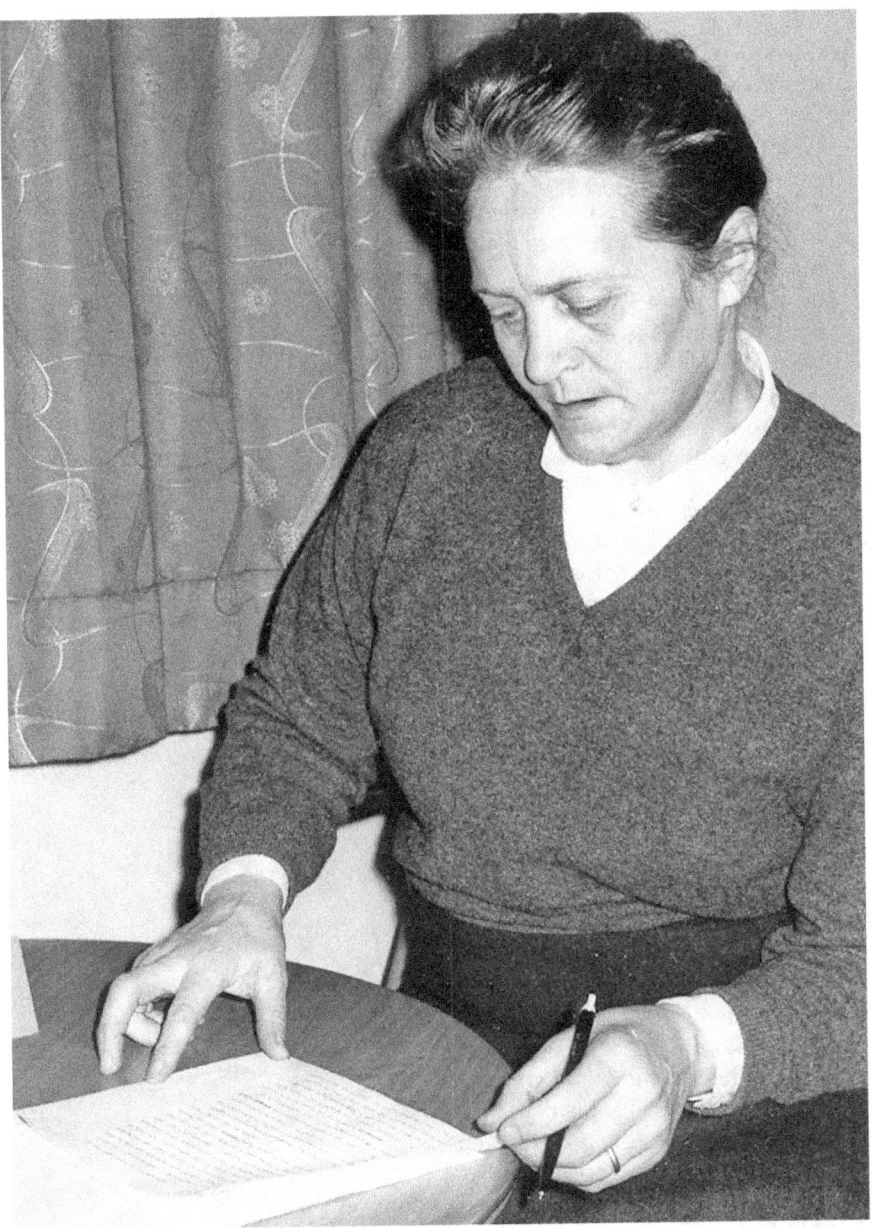

Figure 14. Halldóra B. Björnsson, ca. 1963–65.

To give readers a feel for Björnsson's considerable accomplishment, here are the opening lines again of *Beowulf*, this time juxtaposed to the Icelandic translation of them:

Hwæt! We Gardena   in geardagum,
þeodcyninga,   þrym gefrunon,
hu ða æþelingas   ellen fremedon.
    Oft Scyld Scefing   sceaþena þreatum,
monegum mægþum,   meodosetla ofteah,
egsode eorlas.   Syððan ærest wearð
feasceaft funden,   he þæs frofre gebad,
weox under wolcnum,   weorðmyndum þah,
oðþæt him æghwylc   þara ymbsittendra
ofer hronrade   hyran scolde,
gomban gyldan.   þæt wæs god cyning.[123]

Heyrðum vér í árdaga   herfrægð Dana
þjóðalofðunga   lofstír spurðum
hversu öðlingar   örlög drýgðu!
    Oft Skjöldar Skefingur   skæður féndum
bægði mörgum   frá bekki mjaðar,
hann sem áður var   allslaus fundinn
ægði herskáum   sér til hugarléttis.
Óx hróður hans   und himinskautum
uns einn og sérhver   umhverfis sátu
handan hvalvega   hlýða urðu
gjöld guldu.   Það var góður konungur!

My English translation of Björnsson's Icelandic reads:

We have heard in days gone by the military fame of the Danes,
have tracked the praises of the people kings,
    how the nobles performed their fate!
        Often forceful Skjöld Skefing drove many enemies
from the mead benches,
he who before was found completely destitute
terrified warriors for his peace mind.
His fame grew to the high heavens
until each and everyone around sat
beyond the whale-road, became obedient,
paid tribute. That was a good king!

The last half-line in source and target languages are clearly related: *þæt* / *það* / **that** / *wæs* / *var* / **was** / *god* / *góður* / **good** / *cyning* / *konungur* / **king**.

[123] Ibid., p. 9.

The rest of the OE passage's relationship to the Icelandic is more vexed and requires more effort on the part of the reader to work out. But it can be done. One half-line, however, seems largely unrelated to its Icelandic version: *ellen fremedon* (performed acts of courage) is rendered *örlög drýgðu* (performed their fate). Pétur Knútsson (not the editor of the poem) points out, however, that Björnsson's phrase occurs in *Völundarkviða*, stanza 3, line 10, and the same formula occurs in *Judgment Day 1*, line 29: *orleg dreogan* (accomplish deeds of war). That formula in turn shows up as *ellen dreogan* (accomplish deeds of valor) in *Riddle 58*, line 1, *ellen dugan* (achieve deeds of valor) in *Andreas*, line 460, and *Genesis*, line 1288, and finally as *ellen fremman* (execute deeds of valor) in *Beowulf*, line 3.[124] Such connections between OE and modern Icelandic appear frequently in Björnsson's translation. It therefore "not only insists on the inexorable presence of the original text, but also opens up a complex intertextual environment with threads of connection in both the Old English and Old Icelandic corpora ... it is as if her text moves freely through the established landscapes of Old English poetic formulae without her knowledge."[125]

Saami Translation

Johan Sandberg McGuinne (1987–) took the unique step of making the story of Beowulf available in Saami, a group of the languages within the Uralic language branch spoken by the Saami people of the northern parts of Norway, Sweden, Finland, and the Kola Peninsula in Russia. It is an endangered group of languages, and South Saami, the target language for McGuinne, is the most endangered of all according to the Indigenous Peoples' Secretariat, with just around 500 people still speaking it in Sweden and Norway.[126] McGuinne, who is both South Saami and Scottish and active in the Saami revitalization movement, chose Rob Lloyd Jones's retelling of *Beowulf* to translate in consultation with the South Saami elders because "we felt that we lacked adventure stories aimed at a younger audience, and the Beowulf myth is both exciting and, as retold by Rob Lloyd Jones, appropriate for a younger audience." The book, complete with Victor Travares' illustrations, was published in Norway in 2019 but was not as simple as one might assume to translate into Saami. McGuinne had to find old, "now often forgotten words, for specific things in the story," one of which is the dragon. "There is an old word, ie. *fuemtie*, that could be used, but seeing as fire, and the ability to

---

[124] Knútsson, "Intimacy," p. 194.
[125] Ibid., p. 193.
[126] See https://www.arcticpeoples.com/sagstallamin-the-saami-languages.

fly and attack the villagers from above is essential to the understanding of this dragon, we opted to create a [new] name, ie. *dålle-såaja*, which could be roughly translated as the Winged One of Fire."[127] Here is the opening of McGuinne's translation:

> Dejpeli, Danmarhke akte isveligs, miehtjies dajve lij. Dubpene ïskeres våårenjassh dohk-diekie vaanterdin. Jïjjege, askedibesne, almetjh meehtin våårenjasside goltelidh mah ujkierdin jïh krïtnin, streadjoejin jïh meerin.
>
> Daaroen gånka lij dåarohke man nomme Hrothgar. Idtji gånka dejstie våårenjassijste bïllh. Jïjtsasse alvas stoerre båarkenem tseegki, gaejsien nelnie goelpenen lïhke. Dovres moerijste båarkenem tseegki, jïh dam dovne sïlpine, gulline jïh måersjie-baeniejgujmie rïesi. Gånka båarkenem Heorot gåhtjoeji.[128]

> A long, long time ago, Denmark was a land in terror. Horrible monsters roamed the misty bogs. At night, they screamed and hooted, howled and bellowed.
>
> The king in Denmark was a warlord called Hrothgar. He refused to let himself be scared. He built a huge building for himself, highest up on a steep mountain and at the edge of a big bog. It was built of the finest wood and adorned with ivory, silver and glittering gold. The king called it Heorot.

McGuinne heads the Saami Writers' Union of Sweden (Bágo) and is Head of Department of Saami Studies and English at Finnbacken Secondary School in Lyksele Council / Lïksjuon Kommuvdna in Lappland, northern Sweden. The Laponian or Arctic Circle region was named a World Heritage site in 1996 by UNESCO.[129]

---

[127] McGuinne, personal email communication to Bjork.
[128] Jones and McGuinne, *Beowulf*, pp. 5–6.
[129] See https://whc.unesco.org/en/list/774/.

7

Scandinavian Translations of Old English Literature other than *Beowulf*

The urge to translate Old English (OE) literature in Scandinavia has extended well beyond *Beowulf* into lesser-known poetry as well as into OE prose. As it has done so, the motives for translation have extended beyond Scandinavia as well. *Beowulf*, after all, has clear and immutable connections to the region, especially Denmark and Sweden. But the rest of OE literature, except for a few items such as "The Voyages of Ohthere and Wulfstan," "Widsith," "Deor," and "The Finnsburg Fragment," does not. The list below of the Scandinavian translations of OE literature produced up to 2017 contains a striking number of religious texts and lyric poems. Spiritual interests, coupled with an attraction to the beauty of the texts, thus seem to motivate many Scandinavian translators of OE; aesthetic interests seem primarily to motivate others. Author of such powerful books as *Deliver Us from Love* (1973; English translation 1976); *Crème Fraîche* (1974); and *The Jade Cat* (1997; English translation 2009), jazz singer,[1] member of the Danish Academy, and the most recent Scandinavian translator of OE poetry, Suzanne Brøgger (1944–) articulates the latter motivation well:

> The reason why I took to these ancient poems was that they in all their simplicity seemed so modern. Especially the vibrant ambiguity of having to endure the contradictions of the old and the new world. Something those of us who are old enough can relate to. And the feeling of being lost in between. Being lost and forsaken, the existential drama of the Wanderer and the Seafarer was my start. But also the misery in the intimate sphere interested me, thus I took to The Husband's Message and The Wife's Lament. Even Deor, the poet who is no longer in favour because times are a-changing, is moving.[2]

Brøgger is the first to translate "Deor" and "The Husband's Message" into Danish. See the final item in the list below:

1733 Neo-Latin: "Voyages of Ohthere and Wulfstan"
1772 Danish Neo-Latin: "Voyages of Ohthere and Wulfstan"
1800 Swedish: "Voyages of Ohthere and Wulfstan"

---

[1] E.g., *Sløret – To suiter*.
[2] Brøgger, Personal email correspondence with Bjork.

Figure 15. Suzanne Brøgger, 2022.

1815 Danish: "Voyages of Ohthere and Wulfstan"
1817 Danish: "The Battle of Brunanburh"
1820 Danish: "The Finnsburg Fragment"
1828 Danish Neo-Latin: "Deor" (partial)
1836–37 Danish: *The Advent Lyrics* 1, 7, 8; *Christ and Satan* (partial); *Christ II* (partial)
1840 Danish: *The Phoenix*
1846 Danish: "De falsis diis"
1847 Danish: "The Finnsburg Fragment," "Widsith"
1853 Danish: "Letter of Christ to Abgarus" from Ælfric's *Lives of the Saints* XXIV, versified homily for third Sunday in Lent ca. 1853 Icelandic: "Battle of Brunanburh"
1857 Swedish: "Gloria Patri," "Pater Noster," "Credo in Deum Patrem Omnipotentem," "Precationes A," "Precationes B"
1858 Swedish: *Judith*; partial rev. 1872
1864 Danish: Bede's *Historia Ecclesiastica*, "Bede's Death Song"
1866 Swedish: "Cædmon's Hymn"

1873 Danish: "The Dream of the Rood" (partial), "The Grave," "Cædmon's Hymn," "The Ruthwell Cross," passages from *Genesis A, Genesis B, Exodus, Daniel, Christ and Satan, Judith, Christ I, Andreas, Guthlac B, The Phoenix*, "Soul and Body II," and "Meters of Boethius"
1882 Danish: "The Battle of Brunanburh," "The Battle of Maldon," "The Five Buroughs"
1885 Danish: *Judith*
Late nineteenth-century Icelandic: "The Battle of Brunanburh"
1900 Swedish: Runic inscription on the Franks Casket
1903 Danish: *Christ and Satan*, "The Dream of the Rood," "Cædmon's Hymn," inscription on "The Ruthwell Cross," *Genesis A* (partial), *Genesis B* (partial)
1907 Danish: "Widsith"
1910 Norwegian: "The Battle of Brunanburh"
1929 Swedish: "Widsith"
1936 Danish: *Anglo-Saxon Chronicle* (partial)
1936 Icelandic: "Widsith"
1941 Swedish: "The Battle of Maldon" (partial)
1962 Swedish: "Deor," "The Seafarer"
1979 Danish: "Riddle 27," "The Battle of Maldon," selections from "The Fates of Men," "Maxims I," "The Ruin," "The Wanderer," "The Seafarer"
1981 Norwegian: "The Dream of the Rood"
1983 Danish: *Genesis A* (partial), *Genesis B, Christ and Satan* (partial), *Christ II*
1983 Danish: "The Finnsburg Fragment"
1983 Danish: "Voyages of Ohthere and Wulfstan"
1983 Swedish: "Voyage of Wulfstan"
1987 Norwegian: "Cædmon's Hymn," "Bede's Death Song," "The Ruin," "The Wanderer," "The Seafarer," "The Dream of the Rood," "The Battle of Brunanburh," *Genesis B, Judith*, "The Battle of Maldon"
1991 Danish: "The Battle of Maldon," extracts from Byrthferth of Ramsey's *Life of St. Oswald, The Anglo-Saxon Chronicle*, Æthelred's agreement with the Vikings (994), Æthelred's confirmation of bishop Æscwig to the seat at Risborough, Ælfgar's will, Æthelflæd's will, Ælfflæd's will, Æthelric of Bocking's will, Æthelred's confirmation of Æthelric's will; obituary notice from New Minster, Winchester; obituary notice from Ely; extracts from John of Worcester's *Chronicon ex chronicis*, Henry of Huntingdon's *Historia Anglorum*, the Ely Book, *Chronicon Abbatiæ Rameseiensis, Symoneonis Monachi Opera Omnia*
1991 Danish: paraphrase of "Æcerbot," trans of "Wulf and Eadwacer" and part of "The Finnsburg Fragment," Bede's story of Cædmon
1991 Swedish: "The Battle of Maldon," "The Ruin," "The Wanderer," "The Seafarer," "Deor," "The Wife's Lament," "The Husband's Message," "Wulf and Eadwacer"

1996 Danish: *The Advent Lyrics,* "The Dream of the Rood," "Cædmon's Hymn," "Pater Noster"
1997 Swedish: "The Finnsburg Fragment"
2004 Finnish: "Widsith"
2005 Finnish: "Waldere"
2017 Danish: "Cædmon's Hymn," "The Wanderer," "The Seafarer," "Deor," "The Wife's Lament," "The Husband's Message," "The Ruin"

The great breadth of this list testifies to the deep interest in the Nordic countries in what Grundtvig called "the first new-European literature," the body of OE work that heralded the rise of post-pagan European literature as a whole. That interest was initially focused on history and geography but by 1828 had expanded to historical elegy with the first partial translation of "Deor" and then branched out further in 1836 to Christian poetic and prose texts including OE homilies and Bede's *Ecclesiastical History*.

In chapter 1, the first two translations on the above list were mentioned. Bussæus in 1733 published the OE "The Voyages of Ohthere and Wulfstan" as an appendix to his edition of the Old Norse (ON) *Íslendingabók*, the first complete edition of that text, and included what is probably Christopher Ware's 1678 Latin translation from John Spelman's *The Life of Ælfred the Great*.[3] In 1773 in volume two of his *Scriptores rerum Danicarum*, Langebek likewise included the OE text of the "Voyages" and offered an introduction to the text, Ware's Latin translation of it in parallel columns, and extensive, detailed notes to the text. The first sentence of Ware's translation reads:

> Ohtherus dixit domino suo Ælfredo Regi se omnium Nordmannorum locis maxime Septentrionalibus habitare, in illa regione, quæ ad aqvilonem oceano occidentali terminatur.[4]

> Ohthere said to his lord King Alfred that he lived in the northern most location of all the Northmen, in that region that borders on the western ocean called Aquilon.

Thus, in the international language of scholarship, OE literature officially entered Scandinavia and Scandinavian scholarship, first attached to an ON text and then grouped among many other documents in other languages having to do with things Danish. The initial historical OE text of interest would be revisited and translated three more times, once in Swedish in 1800 and twice in Danish, in 1815 and nearly 150 years later in 1983, and Wulfstan's voyage alone would be translated by itself in 1983 as

---
[3] Adams, *Old English Scholarship*, pp. 77–78.
[4] Langebek, *Periplus*, p. 108.

well. The voyages together would be thoroughly scrutinized many more times than that, as we saw in previous chapters.

The early Swedish and early Danish editions and translations were compared in 1953 by Nils Erik Enkvist (1925–2009), who for a long time was Finland's most internationally recognized linguist specializing in stylistics and text linguistics but also known as a phonetician and literary scholar. He was an effective administrator as well, serving as Rector (1966–69) and Chancellor (1991) of Åbo Akademi in the city of Turku (Åbo in Swedish). It is the only exclusively Swedish-language university in Finland. One of Envkist's predecessors as Rector there was Henrik Gabriel Porthan (1739–1804), Professor of Eloquence (1777–1804), librarian, and historian who is known as the father of Finnish history because of his groundbreaking work.[5] Enkvist looks at a relatively neglected piece by Porthan, his edition and translation of "The Voyages of Ohthere and Wulfstan,"[6] and finds that it is superior in many respects to its predecessors, the best edition of the text before Rask's in 1815.[7] In some cases, it is even better than Rask's.[8] Porthan's "encyclopædic knowledge, good sense and independent judgment" inform his entire edition and translation.[9]

The next two translations of "The Voyages" came over 150 years later in 1983. Niels Lund provides a translation of both sea voyages in parallel OE and Danish columns, appropriately published in a book issued by the Viking Ship Hall in Roskilde. *Ottar og Wulfstan. To rejsebeskrivelser fra vikingatiden* (Ohthere and Wulfstan: Two Travel Narratives from the Viking Period) surrounds "The Voyages" with commentary by Lund and essays by Ole Crumlin-Pedersen on Ohthere's and Wulfstan's ships, sails, routes; Peter H. Sawyer on Ohthere and trade during the Viking period; and Christine E. Fell on the language of "The Voyages." Fell translated the book into English as *Two Voyagers at the Court of King Alfred* (1984). Karl Inge Sandred (1925–2008), famous for his work on English place-names,[10] published his translation in 1983 as well, but only of Wulfstan's voyage. The book that includes his work deals with Goths, including Gotlanders, and Vikings in the Baltic, where Wulfstan's voyage takes place.[11]

After translations of "The Voyages of Ohthere and Wulfstan" come translations of "The Battle of Brunanburh," with Grundtvig taking the lead with his 1817 study and translation of the poem discussed in the

---

[5] Tarkiainen, "Porthan."
[6] Porthan, "Försök."
[7] Rask, "Ottars og Ulfstens korte Reiseberetninger."
[8] Enkvist, "Porthans 'Försök," p. 120.
[9] Ibid., p. 121.
[10] Coates, "Karl Inge Sandred," p. 163.
[11] Sandred, "Wulfstans resa."

Introduction to this book. Two Icelanders, two Danes, and a Norwegian were next to do so. Gísli Brynjúlfsson, who contributed translations to Stephens' *Tvende Old-Engelske Digte* (Two OE Poems, 1853) produced one, perhaps in the 1850s, but it was not published until 2007.[12] And Benedikt Gröndal Sveinbjarnarson (1826–1907) produced a partial one in the late nineteenth century that was not published until 2003.[13] Gröndal studied natural history, poetry, and philosophy extensively and received a master's degree in ON philology in 1864. After serving as a teacher at the Latin School in Reykjavík from 1874 to 1883, he divided the rest of his life "between drinking, study of nature, drawing, and writing."[14] He was an influential poet and renowned humorist in both prose and verse,[15] and he saw the clear affinity between West Germanic poetry and ON. In a parallel column to Langebek's edition of "The Battle of Brunanburh," he wrote his own Icelandic translation but only made it to line 68 or line 34 in a modern edition.[16]

The next translation of the poem, however, was completed and published. Johannes C. H. R. Steenstrup (1844–1935), Professor of History at the University of Copenhagen (1882–1917), specialized in medieval law and social relations and was influenced by the German school of legal history with its emphasis on nationalism. He was a prolific author, and his works on Danish place-names and legal history are considered groundbreaking. One of his major works is the four-volume history of the Norsemen titled *Normannerne* (The Norsemen, 1876–82), the last volume of which on the Danelaw earned him a doctorate.[17] In chapter 3 of the third volume, on the Nordic colonies in England from 901 to 954, Steenstrup introduces the translation of "The Battle of Brunanburh" by stating that the poem takes the place of a prose account of the battle in the AS Chronicle, and he offers "a translation that sticks fairly well to the words of the original."[18] Despite this ambiguous statement, we assume nonetheless that the translation is his. The two remaining translations of "The Battle of Brunanburh" are in verse by the Norwegian Alexander Bugge in his 1910 *Norges Historie fremstillet for det norske Folk* (Norway's History for the Norwegian People)[19] and in prose by the Dane Torsten Dahl (1897–1968), Professor of English

---

[12] Ísaksson, "Þýðingar Gísla Brynjúlfssonar ur fornensku," pp. 95–96.
[13] Tómasson, "Iarlar árhvatir," pp. 181–83.
[14] Einarsson, *A History of Icelandic Literature*, p. 240.
[15] Ibid., p. 241.
[16] Tómasson, "Iarlar árhvatir," p. 181.
[17] Tiemroth, "Johannes Steenstrup."
[18] "en Oversættelse, der holder sig temmelig nær til Originalens Ord." Steenstrup, *Normannerne*, vol. 3, p. 76.
[19] Bugge, *Norges Historie*, I, 2, pp. 177–78.

Philology at the University of Aarhus from 1934 to 1967,[20] in his 1936 *Den oldengelske Krønike i Udvalg* (Selections from the AS Chronicle)[21] focusing on the Viking period.

Interest in translating "Brunanburh" in Scandinavia was followed by interest in translating "The Finnsburg Fragment," another historical-heroic text, and once again Grundtvig was the first to render it in his native tongue. In his introduction to his 1820 translation of *Beowulf*, he includes the entire fragment in parallel columns with his literal, not poetic, translation of the poem and prefaces the poem by stating that the events it depicts took place under King Halvdan. The questions that readers must ask, however, are "where Finn was king, how the heroes were slain, how Hengest got away, and what relationship Hildeborg, Hoke's daughter, the weeping woman at the heroes' funeral pyre, had with the chieftains mentioned in the legend?"[22] We have no sources for the story to answer these questions. Here are the first few lines of the fragment from Grundtvig's introduction, with my translation below them. The full text is readily available online at grundtvigsværker.dk:

..............nas...Hleoþrode þa	Saa tog da til Orde
Hearo-geong cyning	Kongen hin unge:
Ne þis ne dagaþ eastan	Ei dages det i Øster
Ne her draca ne fleogeþ	Ei flyver Dragen her,
Ne her þisse healle	Ei heller paa Hallen
Hornas ne byrnaþ	Hornene brænde
Ac her forþ-beraþ	Men .....[23]

So took he then to words,
the young king:
Day does not dawn in the east
the dragon does not fly here
nor on the hall
the gables burn
but

---

[20] Sørensen, "Torsten Dahl."
[21] Dahl, *Den oldengelske Krønike i Udvalg*, pp. 34–36.
[22] "hvor Finn var Konge, hvorledes Heltene blev svegne, hvorledes Hengestundkom, og i hvad Forhold Hildeborg Hokes Daatter, den høibaarne Græde-Kvinde ved Helte-Baalet, stod til de Høvdinger, Sagnet omtaler?" Grundtvig, *Bjowulfs Drape*, p. XL.
[23] Ibid., pp. xl–xli.

The next three translators of *Beowulf* all offer translations of "The Finnsburg Fragment" as well. Schaldemose provides a parallel OE/Danish translation of the text, which he characterizes as "very obscure" (*meget dunkelt*), on pp. 161–64 of his *Beo-Wulf*. In his discussion of the historical background of *Beowulf*, he uses the fragment to help explicate the Finnsburg episode in the epic. On the other hand, Hansen includes the fragment as a separate text with its own section at the end of his translation of *Beowulf* rather than including it in a historical discussion. Apart from that minor distinction, Hansen offers not only the translation of the text (based on Grundtvig's 1820 and 1861 editions, Trautmann's 1904 and Holthausen's 1905 editions, and Grundtvig's 1865, Clark Hall's 1901, and Gering's 1906 translations) but his own additions to the fragment to make it more understandable. Those additions at the 1) beginning, 2) middle, and 3) end of the OE poem Hansen marks as his own, and they read as follows:

1)
Da fred blev fastsat mellem friser og daner,
fik Hildeburg, Hoke's datter, til husbond
friserkongen Finn, Folkvaldes søn.--
Hendes bror, Hnæf, heltekongen,
gæsted engang den grumme Finn.
Hørt jeg har, at Hengest ham fulgte
samt Eaha og Sigfred, Oddlaf og Gudlaf.
De helte fik hus i det høje Finsborg.

Men Finn, den falske, friserne samled;
i midnattens mulm i mængde de drog,
med Gunnar og Geirulf, deres gæster at svige.[24]

2)
Finn og friserne stormed nu Finsborg;
han bød sine kæmper gå kraftigt frem.[25]

3)
Da segned i striden sønnen af Hildeburg,
så dræbtes drotten, den dristige Hnæf.
Men Hengest, den hårde helt, sig værged,
samt Oddlaf og Gudlaf, så ingen dem skaded.
I dynger lå danske hos dræbte friser.---
Finn bød da fred, og fastsat blev den.

---

[24] Hansen, *Bjovulf* (2019), p. 120.
[25] Ibid., p. 121.

Ed blev aflagt om evig troskab.
På bål nu de brændte de blodige helte.[26]

1)
When peace was made between the Frisians and
Danes, Hildeburg, Hoke's daughter, took as
husband Finn, the son of Folkvald.–
her brother, Hnæf, the hero-king,
the fierce Finn visited once.
I've heard that Hengest followed him
as well as Eaha and Sigfred, Oddlaf, and Gudlaf.
The heroes got lodging in the high Finsborg.
But Finn, the false, gathered the Frisians;
in the dead of night, they came in droves,
with Gunnar and Geirulf, to deceive their guests.

2)
Finn and the Frisians now stormed Finsborg;
he ordered his warriors to go strongly forward.

3)
Then the son of Hildeburg fell in battle,
and so the lord, the bold Hnæf, was killed.
But Hengest, the hard hero, defended himself
as did Oddlaf and Gudlaf so no one was
wounded. Danes lay in piles with slain Frisians–
Finn then offered peace, and it was
settled. Oaths were sworn of eternal loyalty.
On the pyre now they burned the bloodied heroes.

Barry Wilmont, too, includes a translation of "The Finnsburg Fragment" in his 1983 translation of *Beowulf*. He bases it on the English translations by Clark Hall and David Wright and the Danish translation by Oskar Hansen.

In his 1997 article "Striden i Finnsborg" (The Fight at Finnsburg), Frands Herschend (1948–), Professor Emeritus of Archaeology and Ancient History at the University of Uppsala, juxtaposes translations of both "The Finnsburg Fragment" and the Finnsburg episode in *Beowulf* and explores the differences and similarities between the two in an effort to ascertain which came first and how the two versions of the story relate to archaeological and historical evidence. He finds that the fragment preceded the episode, which is probably based on another section of the poem of which the fragment is a part, because of its emphasis on the royal struggle for

---

[26] Ibid., p. 122.

power. The episode focuses instead on the retainers in the battle, and that represents a later stage in the development of aristocratic power. The battle undoubtedly took place during the move of the Danes southward to rule over the Jutes "somewhere between the migration of the Jutes to Kent and the construction of the first Danevirke ramparts"[27] – that is, in the late Iron Age in the fifth to seventh centuries. The hall discovered at Dankirke that was violently destroyed during this period is a plausible site for the battle.[28]

Given the interest in OE battle poems in Scandinavia, one would expect "The Battle of Maldon" to be the next in line for translation there. It is not; "Deor" is. The Icelander Finnur Magnússon or Finn Magnusen in Danish (1781–1847), a Danish civil servant and antiquarian,[29] included three stanzas from the poem in his *Priscae Veterum Borealium Mythologiae Lexicon* (Lexicon of Ancient Nordic Myths) in 1828, stanzas of prime Northern interest concerning Weland and Beadohild, with Deor himself ending up in a footnote. Here you have a taste of Magnusen's translation, the first two lines about Weland and the refrain, first in the original OE and then in Magnusen's Latin:

Veland him bevurman vræces cunnaðe,
anhydig eorl eorfaða dreag ...
ðæs ofereode ðisses swa mæg.

Velandus sibi animum inflammari
Exilio (sive injuria) sensit.
Pervicax dux
Difficultatem pertulit ...
hoc ille superavit
Haec etiam tu (superare) potes.[30]

Weland knew persecution among the snakes,
the single-minded man endured troubles.
That passed; so will this.

Weland felt his soul to be
on fire in exile (without revenge).
The unyielding leader
endured difficulty ...
He surmounted that;
you can likewise (surmount) this.

---

[27] Herschend, "Striden," p. 332.
[28] Ibid.
[29] Posselt, "Finnur Magnússon."
[30] Magnusen, *Lexicon*, p. 583.

The distinguished and popular Swedish runologist at the University of Stockholm (1955–66), National Antiquarian (1966–72), and editor of several volumes of *Sveriges runinskrifter* (Sweden's Runic Inscriptions),[31] Sven B. F. Jansson (1906–87), produced the next translation of "Deor" and this time the whole poem in alliterative verse. He translated the first lines about Weland and the refrain in this way:

Welund, de välsmidda	Welund, the master of
vapnens mästare,	well-smithied weapons,
länge fick pröva	long had to test
landsflyktens våda ...	the danger of exile ...
Glömd är den sorgen,	Forgotten is that sorrow,
så också min plåga	so too my torment
skall glömmas.[32]	shall be forgotten.

The poet Gunnar D. Hansson's Swedish version of the same lines from his *Slaget vid Maldon och sju elegier* (The Battle of Maldon and Seven Elegies, 1991) is somewhat different:

Völund kände   vandrandets vedermöda,
länge prövade   de välsmidda
vapnens jarl   landsflyktens plåga ...
Förbi är den våndan;
förbi snart min ... [33]

Weland felt the hardship of the wandering,
for a long time the earl of the well-smithied
weapons tested the torment of exile ...
Past is that agony;
past soon will be mine.

Hansson (1945–), poet, novelist, translator of OE and ON poetry, Emeritus Professor from the Department of Literature, History of Ideas and Religion at the University of Gothenburg, and winner of the Translation Prize of the Swedish Academy in 2010, assembled the collection of OE poems in translation to right the balance of OE literature available to a Swedish audience. The poems represent high points, besides *Beowulf*, of literary achievement in the AS period.[34]

---

[31] Anon., "Sven B. F. Jansson."
[32] Jansson, "Deor," p. 17.
[33] Hansson, *Slaget vid Maldon*, p. 83.
[34] Ibid., p. 7.

In Denmark, they are so regarded as well, and the poet Suzanne Brøgger's 2017 version in Danish of the same lines from "Deor" is different still:

Weland (*him be wurman*) kendte hjemløsheds plage.

Den ubændige kriger tålte mange trænglser,

med sorg og savn som følgesvende
i eksilets vinterkulde ...
Men alt går over; også det![35]

Weland (*him be Wurman*) felt the torment of homelessness.

The indomitable warrior endured many hardships,

with sorrow and want as companions
in the winter cold of exile ...
But all things pass; that as well!

While Magnusen translates the enigmatic phrase *him be wurman* in the first line literally as the equally enigmatic "among the snakes," both Jansson and Hansson interpret it to mean "among well-smithied weapons," which were probably damascened. Brøgger leaves the phrase untranslated and enigmatic and mysterious.

"Deor" captured the imaginations of the Scandinavians relatively early, and "Widsith" did as well. We now have translations of the poem in Danish, Swedish, Icelandic, and Finnish. The first in Danish is by Schaldemose from 1847 in his *Beo-Wulf og scopes Widsið*, and he publishes his translation in a column parallel with the OE original text.[36] The next translation, also in Danish, is by Gudmund Schütte in an appendix to his *Oldsagn om Godtjod* from 1907. He says of Schaldemose's translation that it is "not especially accurate"[37] and so offers his own alliterative verse translation, which he keys to his ethnographical study of the Germanic peoples.[38] Then, in 1929, the Swede Karl F. Sundén (1868–1945) published his study of the poem (examined in chapter 4) together with a rhythmic prose translation of it from Holthausen's 1905–06 edition of *Beowulf*. His translation, unfettered by alliteration, begins:

Widsiþ talade, sin ordskatt upplät,
han som besökt de flesta av stammar,

---

[35] Brøgger, *OE Translations*, p. 99.
[36] Schaldemose, *Beo-Wulf*, pp. 176–82.
[37] "ikke særlig nøjagtig." Schütte, *Oldsagn om Godtjod*, p. 197.
[38] Ibid., pp. 198–201.

av folk på jorden: ofta han i salen
tog mot värdefull dyrgrip.³⁹

Widsith spoke, his wordhoard unlocked,
he who visited most of the tribes,
of the people on earth: often in the hall he
received valuable things of great worth.

In 1936, the Icelander Stefán Einarsson likewise included a translation of "Widsith" in his study of the poem that we examined in chapter 4, and his is in alliterative verse. The opening lines read,

Viðförull mælti – varp fram orðum –
sá er flest fólklönd um farið hafði,
vitjað lýða lengst: en að launum þegið
munfagrar meiðmar.⁴⁰

Viðförull spoke – he threw out words –
he who had passed through most people's lands,
visited people longest; and in reward received
very beautiful gifts.

Note that *meiðmar* (gifts), cognate with OE *maðm*, is only used in poetry.⁴¹

The most recent translation to emerge from the Nordic countries did so from Finland in 2004. Osmo Pekonen and Clive Tolley, who published their Finnish translation of *Beowulf* in 1999, contributed their alliterative Finnish translation of the poem as *Widsith: Anglosaksinen muinaisruno* (Widsith: An Ancient AS Poem) and, with Jonathan Himes, offered in 2005 the only translation of the OE poem "Waldere" to come out of the Nordic countries in any language.⁴² They chose to translate "Widsith" into Finnish because it, like *Beowulf*, mentions Finns and because some readers of their translation *Beowulf* might "like to pursue somewhat further the heroic background to Old English verse."⁴³ Here is what the opening of "Widsith" looks like in Finnish:

Widsith virkkoi,   sana-arkkunsa avasi;
eniten hän oli nähnyt   heimoja ja kansoja
kautta maanpiirin,   armaita aarteita
saleissa saanut.⁴⁴

---

³⁹ Sundén, *Den fornengelska dikten*, p. 25.
⁴⁰ Einarsson, "Wídsíð = Víðförull," p. 185.
⁴¹ Cleasby, Vigfusson, and Craigie, *An Icelandic-English Dictionary*, p. 422.
⁴² Himes, Pekonen, and Tolley, *Waldere: Anglosaksinen muinaisruno*.
⁴³ Tolley, English version of his "Introduction", p. 1.
⁴⁴ Pekonen and Tolley, *Widsith*, p. 14.

> Widsith spoke, opened his word chest;
> he had seen the most tribes and peoples
> across the globe, gracious treasures
> received in the halls.

After "Deor" and "Widsith," the OE texts that translators in Scandinavia focus on become less obvious because most of them do not concern national or even regional interests. Again, Grundtvig was the first to broaden the perspective on OE literature beyond texts of national relevance, beginning in 1836 with his Danish renditions of *The Advent Lyrics* 1, 7, 8, *Christ and Satan* (partial), and *Christ II* (partial), and then of *The Phoenix* in 1840. It was close to twenty years later that other scholars began following suit. The titles of their works reveal that broadened, non-national interest just as the titles of the earliest works on OE literature dealt with in chapter 1 reflect the influence of Romantic Nationalism. Stephens' simple *Tvende Old-Engelske Digte* (Two OE Poems, 1853), Nilsson's *Några fornengelska andeliga quäden på grundspråket* (Some OE Spiritual Poems in the Original Language, 1857), and Hammerich's *De episk-kristelige Oldquad hos de gothiske Folk* (Christian Narrative Poetry among the Gothic People, 1873) are good nineteenth-century examples. Good twentieth-century examples are Larsen's *Krist og Satan* (Christ and Satan, 1903), Noack's *Helvedstorm og himmelfart: stykker af oldengelsk kristen digtning* (Hellish Storm and Heavenly Journey: Samplings of OE Christian Poetry, 1983), *Menneskevordelse og korsdød: stykker af oldengelsk kristen digtning* (Human Beings and Death on the Cross: Samplings of OE Christian Poetry, 1996), and Borgehammar's *Från tid och evighet: Predikningar från 200-tal till 1500-tal* (From Time to Eternity: Sermons from the Third to Sixteenth Centuries, 1992), which contains sermons from Origenes to Laurentius Petri and Borgehammar's translation of Ælfric's "In dedicatione ecclesiae" from *The Catholic Homilies*.[45] Nevertheless, the first OE religious prose text to have attracted attention in Scandinavia is Ælfric's *De falsis diis*, a homily on the false gods of the Romans and Scandinavians with both religious and regional interests. The title of the translation reflects that reality: "Fragment af en allitereret angelsaxisk Homili, hvori nævnes nogle af Nordens hedenske Guddome" (Fragment of an Alliterative AS Homily in which Some of the Nordic Heathen Deities are Mentioned). The text, in which only Thor, Odin, and Frigg appear, is printed in parallel columns with a literal translation by the Norwegian C. R. Unger (1817–97), Professor of Germanic and Romance Philology at the University of Christiana from 1862 to 1897.[46] Ælfric's homily was not translated again into a Scandinavian language.

---

[45] Borgenhammar, *Från tid till evighet*, pp. 191–200, commentary pp. 200–02.
[46] Halvorsen, "C R Unger."

Between the publication of Stephens' book and Hammerich's comes the translation of another important AS text, certainly through the encouragement and guidance of Grundtvig.[47] Christian Malta Kragballe (1824–97), a vicar, well-published author, and hymn writer, translated the Latin version of Bede's *Ecclesiastical History* into Danish. His *Anglerfolkets Kirkehistorie af Beda den Æværdige* (Church History of the Angle People by the Venerable Bede) was published in 1864, and Kragballe offers a decidedly Grundtvigian reason for his translation in his preface. Bede's history, he states, "gives the Christian congregation information about how our Lord Jesus Christ's Christmas message in the days of Gregory the Great came to our AS brethren in Britain towards the end of the sixth century and what fruits it bore among them" thereafter.[48]

Further information for the Danish congregation on how the word of God reached England comes through the OE paraphrases of scripture, and the OE poem *Judith* is the first to attract attention in Scandinavia. We looked at the first of these translations – the first in any language – in the Introduction to this book. Lars Gabrielle Nilsson produced it a year after publishing *Några fornengelska andeliga quäden på grundspråket* (Some OE Spiritual Poems in the Original Language) in 1857. That collection includes facing-page translations of "Gloria Patri," "Pater Noster," "Credo in Deum Patrem Omnipotentem," "Precationes A," and "Precationes B." Nilsson's OE reader from 1871[49] includes Matthew, chapter 2; Mark, chapter 5; Luke, chapter 2; John, chapter 15; and a passage from *Judith*. Nilsson was clearly a gifted and productive linguist who had decidedly spiritual interests as well, who focused much more on the City of God than on the nations of Sweden or Denmark.

The next complete translation of *Judith* is by Frederik Rønning in 1885 in his essay on OE poetry. That article contains a brief survey of OE poetry[50] followed by an assessment of its poetic characteristics[51] and then a translation of *Judith*.[52] In terms of content, OE literature shows – as does ON literature – a relentless struggle of good versus evil, as in *Beowulf*,[53] and a sense of fair play, as in *Beowulf*, where the hero decides not to use

---

[47] Bradley, "Grundtvig, Bede," p. 115.
[48] "giver den christne Menighed Oplysning om, hvorledes vor Herres Jesu Christi Julebud i Gregor den Stores Dage kom til vore angelsachsiske Frænder i Brittanien mod Slutningen af det sjette Aarhundrede, og hvad Frugter det bar hos dem." Kragballe, *Anglerfolkets Kirkehistorie*, p. iii.
[49] Nilsson, *Anglosaxsk läsebok*.
[50] Rønning, "Den oldengelske digtning," pp. 1–7.
[51] Ibid., pp. 7–19.
[52] Ibid., pp. 19–36.
[53] Ibid., p. 7.

weapons if his opponent does not.[54] In terms of form, Rönning points out three major features, the second two of which differentiate OE poetry from ON. Although they share the four-stress line bound together by alliteration,[55] there is logical unity in a line of ON but not in OE,[56] and OE uses more qualifiers than ON does.[57] He also points out the use of kennings and the transference of poetic techniques and social terms from heathen to Christian poetry, terms such as those for chieftain or lord to God. His analysis of the aesthetic features of OE poetry serves as an introduction to his translation of *Judith*, a poetic fragment that Rønning feels embodies the melding of the heathen and the Christian very well. Here is his rendition of the same passage that I gave you from Nilsson in the introduction to this book:

>   Den lokkede slog da
> med det *skinnende* sværd   den afskylige røver
> med de hadske tanker,   så hun halvt gennemskar
> hans *vældige* hals,   så uden vid han lå
> drukken og *døende*;   var ej død dog helt,
> ej livet henledet.   Med *lyst* da slog
> én gang endnu   den ædle mø
> den hedenske hund,   så hans hoved rulled
> *med gjald* på gulvet.

> The one with curly hair struck then
> with the *shining* sword the detestable thief
> with the savage thoughts, so she cut half through
> his *powerful* neck, so he lay there witless,
> drunken and *dying*; he wasn't completely dead yet,
> his life not spent. With *pleasure* then struck
> one more time, the noble women,
> the heathen dog so his head rolled
> *resoundingly* on the floor.

Rönning carefully maintains alliteration here and does so without compromising much at all. I have italicized those few instances where the demands of alliteration forced him to deviate slightly from the original text. The adjective "powerful" attached to the about-to-be severed neck and the adverb "resoundingly" in the last line are the only qualifiers clearly not in the OE.

---

[54] Ibid., p. 8.
[55] Ibid., p. 9.
[56] Ibid., pp. 10–11.
[57] Ibid., p. 12.

The most recent translation of *Judith* is by Artur Sandved in his *Vers fra vest* in 1987. He offers his prose translation as an example of the Cædmonian revolution,[58] a revolution that produced additional scriptural paraphrases and Scandinavian translations of some of them, ending with Sandved's prose translation of *Genesis B*[59] but beginning with Hammerich's 1873 alliterative Danish verse translations of *Genesis A*, *Genesis B*, *Exodus*, and *Daniel*. No other Scandinavian translations exist of the latter two poems. Then comes Larsen's 1903 translations of large sections of *Genesis A* and *Genesis B* to the birth of Cain and Abel in his *Krist og Satan*[60] and Bent Noack's 1983 alliterative verse translations of *Genesis A*, lines 1–91, pp. 5–11, and *Genesis B*, pp. 12–67, in his *Helvedstorm og himmelfart: stykker af oldengelsk kristen digtning* (Hellish Storm and Heavenly Journey: Samplings of Old English Christian Poetry).[61] Noack's intended audience for these translations is the general public, not academics, and so his accessible translations allow the reader to get a good sense of the original.[62] Take this sampling from his translation of *Genesis B*:

> Hun talte til Adam, "Min husbond og herre!
> Denne frugt er så sød og liflig at smage;
> Den lyse gesandt er Guds gode engel;
> på hans dragt kan jeg se, han er sendt af vore herre,
> som bor i det høje.[63]
>
> She spoke to Adam, "My husband and lord!
> this fruit is so sweet and delicious to taste;
> The bright messenger is God's good angel;
> by his dress can I see, he's sent by our Lord,
> who dwells on high.

Noack (1915–2004) was Professor of New Testament Exegesis at the University of Copenhagen (1955–77), Rector for the Priest College at Løgumkloster (1977–85), and the author of many publications on theological subjects. He translated several of the Old Testament pseudoepigraphical books and participated in the new Danish translation of the Bible authorized in 1992.[64]

"The Battle of Maldon" is, at last, next in line for translation. In 1882, Steenstrup in volume three of his *Normannerne* incorporates a retelling

---

[58] Sandved, *Vers fra vest*, p. 93.
[59] Ibid., pp. 77–91.
[60] Larsen, *Krist og Satan*, pp. 102–34.
[61] See also his *Menneskevordelse og korsdød*.
[62] Noack, *Helvedstorm*, p. 103.
[63] Ibid., p. 48.
[64] Harding and Hyldahl, "Bent Noack."

of the poem on pp. 229–37. In the chapter titled "Gudmund, Justin, Olaf Tryggvessøn og Svend Tveskjæg paa Hærtog i England (991–995)" (Gudmund, Justin, Olaf Tryggvessøn and Svend Tevskjæg on Military Campaign in England [991–995]), the retelling begins thus:

> After three years of silence, new guests came to England. The leaders were Gudmund, the son of Stegitan, Justin and Olaf Tryggvessøn, the future Norwegian king. With 390 ships, they came to Staines on the Thames and ravaged around there, then moving on to Sandwich on the Kentish coast and then towards the North. They reached Ipswich at Onvell (in Suffolk), which was plundered, and then sailed south to Essex and up the narrow Blackwater bay or, as it was then called, Panta. The Ealdorman of the East Angles then was the brave and highly esteemed Brihtnoth, who would not let the country fall undefended to their violence, but roused a courageous defence. With his house troops and the warriors he could gather, he moved against the Vikings. These had taken position at Maldon. This town sits on a hill, and at its foot runs an arm of the Panta estuary, over which there is a bridge, while another arm runs for some distance in a northern direction. The Vikings seem to have situated themselves in the space between the two rivers, while Brihtnoth came from the north and had both streams between himself and the town.[65]

Ninety-seven years passed after Steenstrup's translation before the next one appeared. Andreas Haarder in his 1979 *Det episke liv* offers a free-verse translation of the poem in an appendix to his book about the heroic life.[66] "The Battle of Maldon" provides probably the clearest expression we have of the essential values of that life distilled into a

---

[65] "Efter tre Aars Tavshed kom der nye Gjæster til England. Anførerne vare Gudmund, Stegitans Søn, Justin og Olaf Tryggvessøn, den senere norske Konge. Med 390 Skibe kom de til Staines ved Themsen og hærgede deromkring, senere droge de til Sandvich paa Kentkysten og derefter mod Nord. De ankom til Ipswich ved Onvell (i Suffolk), som plyndredes, og derpaa sejlede de Syd paa til Essex og op ad den smalle Blackwaterbugt eller, som den da hed, Panta. Øst- angels Ealdorman var dengang den tapre og højt ansete Brihtnoth, der ikke vilde lade Landet uværnet falde i deres Vold, men opildnede til et modigt Forsvar. Med sine Hustropper og de Krigere, han i øvrigt kunde samle, drog han mod Vikingerne. Disse havde taget Stade ved Maldon. Denne By ligger paa en Høj, og ved dens Fod løber en Arm af Havvigen Panta, hvorover der er en Bro, medens en anden Arm gaar i nogen Afstand i nordlig Retning. Vikingerne synes at have staaet i Rummet mellem de to Floder, medens Brihtnoth kom Nord fra og havde begge Strømme mellem sig og Byen." Steenstrup, *Normannerne*, vol. 3, pp. 228–29.

[66] Haarder, *Det episke liv*, pp. 131–39.

relatively short poem. Artur Sandved's *riksmål* prose translation of the poem follows shortly after Haarder's in 1987,[67] and then come two more, Hansson's Swedish verse translation in 1991[68] and, also in 1991, Lund's Danish translation along with several other documents pertaining to Sven Tveskæg's and Olav Tryggvesson's excursions into England in the 990s.[69] These are extracts from Byrthferth of Ramsey's *Life of St. Oswald, The Anglo-Saxon Chronicle,* Æthelred's agreement with the Vikings (994), Æthelred's confirmation of bishop Æscwig to the seat at Risborough, Ælfgar's will, Æthelflæd's will, Ælfflæd's will, Æthelric of Bocking's will, Æthelred's confirmation of Æthelric's will; an obituary notice from New Minster, Winchester; an obituary notice from Ely; and extracts from John of Worcester's *Chronicon ex chronicis,* Henry of Huntingdon's *Historia Anglorum,* the Ely Book, *Chronicon Abbatiæ Rameseiensis,* and *Symoneonis Monachi Opera Omnia.*

Interest in what are commonly accepted as the nine OE elegies began in 1828 with Magnusen's Latin translation of part of "Deor," but was slow in developing thereafter. It took over 100 years, in fact, for the poems that concern psychological and spiritual experience more than biographical or regional or national truths to capture the Scandinavian imagination. All but two of the elegies ("The Rhyming Poem" and "Resignation"), however, have now been translated in full into one or more of the Scandinavian languages. Sven B. F. Jansson was the first to translate any of them. His Swedish translation of "The Seafarer" from about 1955 begins:

Låt mig för mig själv	Let me for myself
besjunga vad jag upplevt,	sing what I have gone through,
skildra mina färder:	describe my journeys;
hur under svunna dagar	how during days long past
många bitter	many bitter
möda jag prövade.[70]	hardships I experienced.

Jansson's translation was reprinted in 1962 in an anthology of medieval world literature.[71]

Andreas Haarder is the next in 1979 to translate "The Seafarer," but only selections from it as well as brief selections from "The Ruin" and

---

[67] Sandved, *Vers fra vest,* pp. 109–16.
[68] Hansson, *Slaget vid Maldon,* pp. 13–29.
[69] Lund, *Sangen om Slaget ved Maldon.*
[70] Jansson, "Sjöfararen," p. 19.
[71] In Hildeman ed., *Medeltidens litteratur,* pp. 19–22.

"The Wanderer" to illustrate the basic content and purpose of the OE elegy.[72] Artur Sandved, on the other hand, offers the next full translation of "The Seafarer" and the first full translations into a Scandinavian language of "The Ruin" and "The Wanderer" in 1987. Here are the first few lines of the two latter poems in Sandved's translation:

> Storlsagne disse byggverk av sten,
> men nu lagt i grus av den mektige skjebne;
> byens bygninger ligger i ruiner,
> kjempers byggverk brytes ned og smuldrer bort.[73]

> 'Ofte får den ensomme vandringsmannen
> oppleve Herrens nåde og barmhjertighet,
> selv om han i lang tid har måttet ro sin båt,
> tung i sinn, over iskoldt hav,
> traske møysommelig utlendighets stier.
> Menneskets lodd ligger fast!'[74]

> Magnificent these edifices of stone,
> but now reduced to rubble by mighty fate;
> the town's buildings lie in ruins,
> warriors' edifices break down and crumble away.

> Often the lonely wanderer gets
> to experience the Lord's grace and mercy,
> although for a long time he has had to row
> his boat, heavy in heart, over the ice-cold
> sea, laboriously tread the paths of exile.
> Mankind's fate is fixed!

In Gunnar Hansson's 1991 collection of OE poems in Swedish translation, he includes full versions of "The Seafarer," "The Wanderer," and "The Ruin" as well as the first translations into a Scandinavian language of three more elegies: "The Wife's Lament," "The Husband's Message," and "Wulf and Eadwacer." Here are the first few lines of "The Husband's Message," which Hansson translates from the unemended original OE text:

> Bara för dig skall jag nu berätta
> om ... av trä ...
> när jag var ung blev mig ...

---

[72] Haarder, *Det episke liv*, pp. 80–90.
[73] Sandved, "Ruinen" in *Vers fra vest*, p. 41.
[74] Sandved, "Vandringsmannen" in *Vers fra vest*, p. 47.

och jag kom till män i ett annat land ...
och saltströmmarna ...[75]

Just for you shall I tell
about ... of tree ...
when I was young, became me ...
and I came to men in another land ...
and the salt currents ...

And finally, in 2017, Suzanne Brøgger offers the first translations into Danish of "Deor" and "The Husband's Message" along with her renditions of "The Seafarer," "The Wanderer," and "The Ruin."[76] For example, she translates the first few lines of the emended text of "The Husband's Message" thus:

Til dig, frue, alene vil jeg fortælle,
at jeg som ung groeded mellem træer;
mangen et budskab blev skrevet på mig,
sendt fra fremmended lande på skibe,
ført af salten strømme.[77]

To you alone, lady, will I relate
that I as a youth grew among trees;
many a message was written on me,
sent from foreign lands on ships,
borne by the salt currents.

And so ends this chapter, but not quite. Its end is not in its beginning but in the beginning of the previous chapter on the Scandinavian translations of *Beowulf*: the scholarly examination of OE literature that allows the production of scholarly editions of texts opens the way for vernacular translations of those texts. In turn, those vernacular translations open OE literature to a non-scholarly audience and an array of imaginative uses of OE literature. Two Scandinavian novelists, one Swedish, the other Danish, have incorporated OE texts into the narratives of one of their novels and thus have exposed hundreds of lay readers to OE poetry and prose both in their own languages and in the languages into which their novels have been translated.

Frans G. Bengtsson (1894–1954), poet, essayist, biographer, and translator of such texts as *The Song of Roland*, Milton's *Paradise Lost*, and Henry David Thoreau's *Walden*, is most famous in Sweden for two works: his

---

[75] Hansson, *Slaget vid Maldon*, p. 89.
[76] In Zeruneith, *De siste tider*, pp. 318–32.
[77] Ibid., p. 330.

prize-winning two-volume biography of King Charles XII of Sweden published in 1935 and 1936 and his only novel, the two-volume *Röde Orm*, published in 1941 and 1945. Volume one was translated into English in 1943 as *Red Orm* and the whole novel in 1954 as *The Long Ships: A Saga of the Viking Age*. In 1964, *The Long Ships*, a movie loosely based on the novel and starring Richard Widmark and Sidney Poitier, made its debut,[78] and in Sweden, the novel became the seventh best-selling book of the entire twentieth century.[79] Its legacy lives on worldwide in Bluetooth technology, the inventor of which took the name from King Harald Bluetooth in Bengtsson's novel.[80]

The novel takes place over a thirty-year period from about 980 to 1010 and concerns the adventures of Orm Tostessons whom Vikings capture as a boy and take with them on their exciting journeys throughout the Mediterranean. As a man, Orm becomes known as Röde Orm (Red Serpent) because of his red beard. He distinguishes himself in battle in the Mediterranean, is captured in Muslim Spain, made a galley slave and then bodyguard for al-Mansur, the Abbasid Caliph, and eventually gains his freedom. One of his adventures is a Yule-time visit to the court of Harald Bluetooth in Jelling, Denmark, and another is a springtime visit to England where he has decided to raid a place called Maldon.

In the novel's first volume, section two ("I kung Ethelreds rike" [In King Æthelred's Kingdom]), chapter 1 ("Om den strid som stod vid Maeldun och vad därav kom" [Of the battle in Maldon and what came of it]), Bengtsson retells and contextualizes and embellishes the OE poem "The Battle of Maldon" in this way:

> Soon after Easter of that year, which was the fifth year after King Ethelred's coming-of-age, the beacons were lit along the Kentish coasts. Men gazed pale-faced into the morning mists, and turned and ran to hide what they could and drive their cattle into the forest and take themselves into hiding with them, and word was sent to King Ethelred and his Jarls as fast as horse could ride that the biggest fleet that had been sighted for many years was rowing along his coasts, and that the heathens had already begun to wade ashore ...
>
> King Ethelred and his Archbishop, whose name was Sigerik, promptly offered up longer prayers than ever; and when they heard that the heathens, after sacking a few villages, had put out to sea again, they had rich gifts distributed among those priests who had prayed most assiduously, believing themselves to be rid at last of these unwelcome

---

[78] Anon., "The Long Ships."
[79] Arvidsson and Malmquist, *Frans G. Bengtsson*, pp. 9–12.
[80] Kardach, "Tech History."

visitors. No sooner had this been done than the Vikings rowed in to a town called Maldon, at the mouth of the river Panta, pitched camp on an island in the middle of the estuary, and prepared to assault the town.

The Jarl of the East Saxons was called Byrhtnoth. He had a great name in his country, and was bigger than other men and very proud and fearless. He assembled a powerful army and marched against them, to see whether blows might prove more effectual than prayers against the invaders. On reaching Maldon, he marched past the town towards the Vikings' camp until only the arm of the river separated the two forces. But now it was difficult for him to attack the Vikings, and equally difficult for them to attack him. The tide came in, filling the river arm to the level of the banks. It was no broader than a spear's-throw, so that the armies were able to hail one another, but it did not appear as though they would be able to come to close grips. So they stood facing each other in merry spring weather.

A herald of Thorkel the Tall's army, a man skilled in speech, stepped forward to the river's edge, raised his shield, and cried across the water: "The seamen of the north, who fear no man, bid me address you thus. Give us silver and gold, and we will give you peace. You are richer than we, and it will be better for you to buy peace with tribute than to meet men of our mettle with spear and sword. If you have wealth enough, it will not be necessary for us to kill each other. Then, when you have bought your freedom, and freedom for your families and your houses and all that you possess, we shall be your friends and will return to our ships with your freeing money, and will sail away from this place, and will remain faithful to our word." [lines 29–41]

But Byrhtnoth himself stepped forward and, brandishing his spear, roared back: "Hearken well, sea-rover, to our reply! Here is all the tribute you will get from us: pointed spears and keen-edged swords! It would ill become such a Jarl as I, Byrhtnoth, Byrhthelm's son, whose name is without spot, not to defend my country and the land of my King. This matter shall be settled by point and blade, and hard indeed must you hew before you find aught else in this land." [lines 45–61]

They stood facing each other until the tide turned and began again to run towards the sea. Then the herald of the Vikings cried across the river: "Now we have stood idle long enough. Come over to us, and we will let you have our soil as battle-ground; or, if you prefer it, choose a place on your bank and we will come over to you."

Jarl Byrhtnoth was unwilling to wade across the river, for the water was cold and he feared lest it might make his men's limbs stiff and their clothing heavy. At the same time, he was eager to join battle before his men should begin to feel tired and hungry. So he cried back: "I will give you ground here, and do not delay but come now to fight us. And God alone knows which of us will hold the field." [ll. 93–95]

And these are the words of Byrhthnoth's bard, who was present at this battle and escaped with his life:

The sea-men's army feared not the flood.
Blood-wolves waded west through Panta.
Clear through the current's crystal water
Bore they their linden-shields to the strand [lines 96–99]

Byrhtnoth's men stood awaiting them like a hedge of shields. He had ordered them first to cast their spears, and then to advance with their swords and drive the heathens back into the river. But the Vikings formed into battle-order along the bank as they emerged from the water, each ship's crew keeping together, and, straightway, raised their battle-cries and charged, with the captain of each ship running at the head of his crew. A swarm of spears flew towards them, bringing many of them to the ground, whence they did not rise; but they continued to advance relentlessly until they found themselves shield to shield with the Englishmen. Then there was fierce hewing, and loud alarums; and the Vikings' right and left wings were halted and hard pressed. But Thorkel the Tall and the two captains nearest to him – Orm was one, and the other was Fare-Wide Svensson, a famous chieftain from Själland, whom King Harald had proclaimed outlaw throughout the Danish kingdom, and who had fought with Styrbjörn at the battle on Fyris Plain before Uppsala – assaulted Byrhtnoth's own phalanx and broke it. Thorkel cried to his men to fell the tall man in the silver helmet, for then the day would be theirs. Straightway the fighting became fiercest in this part of the field, and there was little elbow-room for men of small stature. Fare-Wide hewed his way forward, slew Byrhtnoth's stand-bearer, and aimed a blow at Byrhtnoth, wounding him; but he fell himself in the same instant, with a spear through his beard. Many of the chieftains on both sides were killed; and Orm slipped on a fallen shield which was greasy with blood, and tumb[l]ed headlong over the body of a man he had just slain. As he fell, he received a blow on the back of his neck from a club, but at once those of his men who were closest to him threw their shields over his body to cover him and protect his back.

When he regained his senses, and was able, with Rapp's assistance, to get to his feet again, the battle had moved away from that part of the field, and the Vikings had gained the upper hand. Byrhtnoth had fallen, and many of his men had fled, but others had formed themselves into a tight ring and, although surrounded, were still resisting valiantly. Thorkel shouted to them over the noise of the battle that he would spare their lives if they cast down their arms; but the cry came back from their midst: "The fewer we be, the fiercer we shall hew, and the shrewder shall be our aim and our courage crueller." [lines 311–12]

They fought on until they all lay dead upon the ground, together with many of their foemen, about their chieftain's corpse. The Vikings marvelled at the valour of these Englishmen, praising the dead; nevertheless, this battle at Maldon, fought three weeks before Whitsun in the year 991, was a grievous setback for King Ethelred, and a disaster for his realm. For now, far and wide about them, the land lay helpless before the fury of the invaders from the north.[81]

Röde Orm, or *The Long Ships*, the fast-paced, mesmerizing, witty, and parodic tale of the Viking called Red Serpent, has been translated into well over twenty languages. Bengtsson's retelling of "The Battle of Maldon" has been translated along with it.

Vibeke Vasbo (1944–) is a poet, novelist, LGBTQ activist, and onetime assistant nurse and crane operator whose first book builds on the latter experience. *Al den løgn om kvinders svaghed* (All the Lies about the Weakness of Women, 1976) tells the story of a female crane operator working in a man's world in Oslo. Her collection of poems, *Måske har jeg haft en anelse* (I May Have Had a Clue, 1980), recounts her own story of ending her relationships with men in favor of women. And her best-selling two-volume, meticulously researched and executed novel, *Hildas sang: Historisk roman fra 600-årenes England* (Hilda's Song: A Historical Novel from Seventh-Century England, 1991) chronicles the life of Abbess Hilda (ca. 614–80), the founder of the famous monastery at Whitby and one of the most remarkable women in AS England living in one of the most remarkable periods of AS history. The book has been received exceedingly well and, according to the author, has been read by many different people who like it for completely different reasons. A thirteen-year-old, for example, consumed it in four days, declaring it "dødspændende" (absolutely thrilling).[82] It appeared in Norwegian translation in 1994 and in English as *The Song of Hild* in 2018. Vasbo's depiction of Hilda's early years makes for "wonderful reading, filled with graphic details of a woman's loves and passions in a stormy world of religious conflict, regal war, and scheming revenge."[83] And her seamless interweaving of her fictionalized account of the Abbess with Bede's sparse historical account in Hilda's later years is masterful. In volume two of the novel, Vasbo also skillfully weaves some OE texts – a few lines of "Metrical charm 1," part of "The Finnsburg

---

[81] Bengtsson, *The Long Ships*, pp. 195–98.
[82] Vasbo personal correspondence with Bjork.
[83] Isaacson, review of *Hildas sang*, p. 727.

Figure 16. Vibeke Vasbo, 2018.

Fragment," and "Wulf and Eadwacer" – into her narrative. Here is how she uses the charm:

> They had soon seeded the cleared land, but the rain failed to fall. While the monastery people, led by Begu, walked up and down blessing their soil with holy water, the neighbours stood at the boundary line to make sure not a drop of the stuff fell on their land: none of that filth on our fields, they said, and their corn was already growing well. After eleven days of relentless wind from the east, the corn had blown away and the monastics had to re-seed their land. By now it was the middle of the month of three milkings, and the rain started to fall, non-stop. At night, the water dripped on them in the temporary huts they had erected – during the day, too. Some days the rain fell steadfastly yet hushed, other days it lashed down. The air turned abnormally cold.
>
> All they could do was pray and walk the fields again – this time to pray for the rain to stop. The neighbours stood in the deluge uttering ungodly jeers in an attempt to drown out the monastics' singing:
>
> *Erce, Erce, mother of the earth,*
> *the almighty Lord everlasting grant you*
> *fields that sprout and grow,*

invigorate fertility.
Hallelujah, amen.

By the time the rain stopped, most of the corn had rotted away. They would now have to sow the seed they would otherwise have eaten throughout the summer. The corn was re-sown on the first day of the first mild month.

Nor did they have much luck with the livestock. One of the milking cows died suddenly, with no sign of any cause – it was simply lying dead in its shed one morning.

They decided to slaughter the goat, mostly to get away from its evil eyes; having eaten it, they all fell ill. Begu and Hild dragged themselves around handing out medicine to the others. It was a stomach upset, and the chicken-slave, as she was called, also had an abscess under her left buttock – big as a chicken's egg, said Begu, who attended to it, and Hild lost all appetite for eggs.[84]

The Song of Hild compares favorably with Sigrid Undset's internationally renowned epic *Kristin Lavransdatter*. In it, Lanae Isacsson writes in her review,"Vibeke Vasbo has produced an admirable, serious, and conscientious blend of historical record and creative fiction about an era filled with human passion, conflict on all fronts, and final religious commitment."[85] Vasbo's inclusion of OE literature within her narrative lends it authenticity and piques the interest in the field in readers of both the original Danish and the English translation. It also testifies to the continuing appeal for present-day Scandinavian writers.

---

[84] Vasbo, *The Song of Hild*, pp. 432–33.
[85] Isaacson, review of *Hildas sang*, p. 728.

Conclusion: "A Truly Splendid Ruin"

Nationalism, aesthetics, spirituality – these have been the chief motivations for Old English (OE) studies in Scandinavia, initially embodied in the work of one man, N. F. S. Grundtvig, but eventually embracing the whole history of the field. Grundtvig's interests definitely exerted great influence on his contemporaries and successors. Without him, for example, Hammerich would not have written about the Old Germanic Christian epic, Kragballe would not have translated Bede's *Ecclesiastical History*, Joakim Skovgaard would not have painted his picture of Christ's descent into hell,[1] Denmark would not be the only country on earth where laypersons are in frequent touch with OE poetry because of Grundtvig's hymns and songs, and OE studies in Scandinavia would not have been so abundant. There is a great deal of it published in English and German – the other part of the picture that is not painted in this book – but its manifestation in the languages of the region is remarkable for its vigor and breadth as well as its relative obscurity. Should readers stumble on Scandinavian contributions to OE scholarship now, a comment by R. W. Chambers in 1921 could well typify their response. Looking back on Frederik Rönning's 1883 *Beovulfs-kvadet: En literær-historisk undersøgelse* (The Heroic Poem of Beowulf: A Literary-Historical Study), Chambers pointed out that it contained a view of *Beowulf* that was fifty years old but only then had come to be generally accepted.[2]

The relative neglect of Scandinavian scholarship is, of course, understandable because of the language barrier for many readers and because the nationalistic bias in OE studies has shifted decidedly away from Scandinavia (and Germany) to England and North America. To be sure, the Danes were present at the birth of OE studies – they even induced labor – but they were immediately driven from the room. Today we pay some homage to the prominent names (Thorkelin, Grundtvig, Rask), due in large part to several scholars who have recognized the importance of the Scandinavian involvement in OE studies. We would have less of *Beowulf* without Thorkelin's transcriptions, as Kevin Kiernan has shown,[3] and we would have seen the poem only much later had it not been for Thorkelin and Grundtvig. And our knowledge of OE grammar and that

---

[1] Noack, "Den oldengelske digtning og Grundtvig," p. 155.
[2] *Beowulf: An Introduction*, p. 400.
[3] *The Thorkelin Transcriptions of Beowulf* (Copenhagen, 1986).

Conclusion: "A Truly Splendid Ruin"

of antiquarians such as Thorpe and Kemble would have progressed much more slowly had it not been for Rask, as Hans Aarsleff has demonstrated.[4] But we have been unaware of, much less paid homage to, many other Scandinavian names. Once ejected from the delivery room of OE studies, however, the Scandinavians developed their own brand of the discipline in a different direction and at a different pace from that of the ungrateful English. In particular, they achieved an early aesthetic appreciation for OE poetry that scholars still have not discovered, despite occasional inroads into the field of the Scandinavian engagement in OE studies by a handful of them (see Appendix A.II). This book, I hope, has helped to rectify the situation. As we become increasingly aware of the political and ideological dimensions of scholarship in any age, we also come to see that the birth of a discipline in one culture is not synonymous with its birth in another. Studying that phenomenon is vital. It serves as a corrective to mistaken notions about progress – or stasis – in a field, and it helps us better understand why we find ourselves where we do. Lars Lönnroth describes the present scene in OE studies very well:

> Slutligen har modernismens genombrott medfört att diktens funktion i samhället har förändrats. Den nationalistiska retoriken och hyllandet av förfädernas ära har fått träda tillbaka för mer individualistiska, existentiella och formmässiga egenskaper. I dag är det inte längre mandom, mod och morske män eller förkristna asagudar som i första hand förtjänar att lyftas fram i den germanska dikten utan andra kvaliteter: dramatiken, de djärva metaforerna, de gåtfulla visionära myterna, de lakoniska formuleringarna om livets hårda villkor i dödens skugga.[5]

> Finally, the breakthrough of modernism has led to poetry's function in society changing. The nationalist rhetoric and tribute to the honor of our forefathers has given way to more individualistic, existential, and formal characteristics. Today, it is no longer manhood, bravery, and dark men or pre-Christian Æsir gods that primarily deserve highlighting in Germanic poetry, but other qualities: the drama, the bold metaphors, the enigmatic visionary myths, the laconic formulations about life's harsh conditions in the shadow of death.

The qualities Scandinavians seek now in OE literature – that we all seek in that truly splendid ruin – are transnational, existential, spiritual, and human.

---

[4] *The Study of Language in England*, pp. 182–85.
[5] Lönnroth, *Det germanska spåret*, p. 6.

Works Cited

Primary Works

Balslev, Thora, ed. *N.F.S. Grundtvig: Christenhedens Syvstjerne* (1860). Copenhagen, 1955.

Blake, Norman F., ed. *The Phoenix*. Rev. ed. Exeter, 1990.

Bussæus, Andreas. *Periplus Otheri, Halgolando-Norvegi, ut et Wulfstani, Angli, secundum narrationes eorundem de suis, unius in ultimam plagam Septentrionalem; utriusqve autem in mari Balthico Navigationibus, jussu Aelfredi Magni, anglorum regis, seculô à nativitate Christi nonô factis; ab ibso rege Anglo-Saxonicâ lingvâ descriptus, demum à collegii magnae aulae universitatis oxoniensis alumnis, Latinè versus &, unà cum Joh. Spelmanni vita Aelfredi Magni, è veteri codice manuscripto bibliothecae Gottonianae editus; jam verè, ob antiqvitatem & septentrionalis tum temporis statûs cognitionem.* Copenhagen, 1733.

Calder, Daniel G., Robert E. Bjork, Patrick K. Ford, and Daniel F. Melia, trans. *Sources and Analogues of Old English Poetry: II: The Major Germanic and Celtic Texts in Translation*. Cambridge and Totowa, NJ, 1983.

Damon, S. Foster, and Robert Silliman Hillyer, trans. Selected and annotated by Oluf Friis. *A Book of Danish Verse*. New York, 1922.

Ekblom, Richard. "Den forntida nordiska orienteringen och Wulfstans resa till Truso." *Fornvännen* 33 (1938), 49–68.

Eliot, T. S. *The Complete Poems and Plays of T. S. Eliot*. London, 1969.

Ellegård, Alvar. "De gamla nordbornas väderstrecksuppfattning." *Lychnos* (1954–55), 1–20.

Finnegan, Robert Emmett, ed. *Christ and Satan: A Critical Edition*. Waterloo, 1977.

Fulk, R. D., Robert E. Bjork, and John D. Niles, eds. *Klaeber's Beowulf and the Fight at Finnsburg*. 4th ed. Toronto and Buffalo, 2008.

Grundtvig, N. F. S. (Grundtvig's collected published works are available online at http://www.grundtvigsværker.dk/ and are arranged both alphabetically and chronologically).

—. *Beowulfes Beorh eller Bjovulfs-Drapen, det Old-Angelske heltedigt paa grundt-sproget*. Copenhagen, 1861.

—. *Bibliotecha Anglo-Saxonica. Prospectus and Proposals of a subscription for the publication of the most valuable Anglo-Saxon Manuscripts illustrative of the early poetry and literature of our Language, most of which have never yet been printed*. London, 1830.

—. *Bjovulvs-Drapen, et Høinordisk Heltedigt, fra Anguls-Tungen fordansket.* Copenhagen, 1865.

—. "Bjovulfs Drape eller det Oldnordiske Heltedigt." *Brage og Idun* 4 (1841), 481–538.

—. *Bjowulfs Drape. Et Gothisk Helte-Digt fra forrige Aar-tusinde af Angelsaxisk paa Danske Rim.* Copenhagen, 1820.

—. "Bruneborg-Slaget og et Riim i den Anledning." *Dannevirke* 2 (1817), 79–87.

—. "Et Par Ord om det nys udkomne angelsaxsiske Digt." *Nyeste Skilderie af Kjøbenhavn* (1815), nos. 60, 63, 64, 65, and 66. Go to http://www.grundtvigsværker.dk/. Translated into English by Mark Bradshaw Busbee in *GS* 66.1 (2015), 7–36.

—. *Nordens Mytologi eller Udsigt over Eddalæren for dannede Mænd der ei selv ere Mytologer.* Copenhagen, 1808. 2nd ed. 1832.

—. "Om Bjovulfs Drape eller det af Hr. Etatsraad Thorkelin 1815 udgivne angelsachsiske Digt." *Dannevirke* 2 (1817), 207–89.

—. *Phenix-Fuglen: Et Angelsachsisk Kvad.* Copenhagen, 1840. GV edition 2018 by Vibeke A. Pedersen. http://www.grundtvigsværker.dk/tekstvisning/16841/0#{%220%22:0,%22v0%22:0,%22k%22:0}

—. "Phønix-Gaarden," 1836. GV edition 2018 by Vibeke A. Pedersen. http://www.grundtvigsværker.dk/tekstvisning/18405/0#{%220%22:0,%22v0%22:0,%22k%22:0}

—. *Sang-Værk til den danske Kirke.* Copenhagen, 1836–37.

Grundtvig, Svend, ed. *N. F. S. Grundtvigs Poetiske Skrifter.* Vols. 1–7. Copenhagen, 1880–89.

—, and Georg Christensen, eds. *N. F. S. Grundtvigs Poetiske Skrifter.* Vol. 8. Copenhagen, 1929.

Haugen, Einar, ed. *First Grammatical Treatise: The Earliest Germanic Phonology.* 2nd ed. London, 1972.

Holder, A., ed. *Beowulf.* 2nd ed. Frieburg im Br., 1899.

Kemble, John Mitchell, and Jakob Grimm. *A Correspondence, 1832–1852: Unpublished Letters of Kemble and Translated Answers of Grimm.* Ed. Raymond A. Wiley. Leiden, 1971.

Kiernan, Kevin. *The Electronic Beowulf.* 4th ed. Lexington and London, 2015. https://ebeowulf.uky.edu

—. *The Thorkelin Transcripts of Beowulf.* Anglistica 25. Copenhagen, 1986.

Kragballe, Chr. M. *Anglerfolkets Kirkehistorie af Beda den Æværdige.* Copenhagen, 1864.

Krapp, George Philip, and Elliott van Kirk Dobbie, eds. *The Exeter Book.* Anglo-Saxon Poetic Records 3. New York, 1936.

Langebek, Jacob. *Scriptores rerum Danicarum medii ævi.* 6 volumes. Copenhagen, 1772–86.

Leo, Heinrich. *Bëówulf, dasz älteste deutsche, in angelsächsischer Mundart erhaltene, Heldengedicht.* Halle, 1839.

Muir, Bernard J. ed. *The Exeter Anthology of Old English Poetry*. 2 vols. Exeter, 1994.
Nansen, Fridtjof. *Nord i Taakenheimen. Utforskningen av Jordens nordlige Strók i tidlige Tider*. Copenhagen, 1911. Translated into English by Arthur G. Chater as *In Northern Mists: Arctic Explorations in Early Times*. 2 vols. New York, 1911.
Nutzhorn, H., ed. *Melodierne til Sangbog udgivet af Foreningen for højskoler og landbrugsskoler*. Nyborg, 1904.
—, and L. Schrøder, eds. *Historiske sange*. Copenhagen, 1872.
Nyerup, Rasmus, and K. L. Rahbek, eds. *Udvalgte Danske Viser fra Middelalderen* 5. Copenhagen, 1814.
O'Donnell, Daniel Paul, ed. *Cædmon's Hymn: A Multimedia Study, Archive and Edition*. Cambridge, 2005.
Rask, Rasmus. "Ottars og Ulfstens korte Rejseberetninger med dansk Overesættelse, kritiske Anmerkninger og andre Oplysninger." *Det Skandinaviske Litteraturselskabs Skrifter* 11 (1815), 1–132.
Stephens, George. *Tvende Old-Engelske Digte med Oversættelser og Tillæg*. Copenhagen, 1853.
The Oxford Annotated Bible. Edited by Herbert G. May and Bruce M. Metzger. Oxford, 1962.
Thorkelin, Grímur Jónsson. *De Danorum rebus gestis secul. III et IV. Poëma Danicum dialecto Anglo-Saxonica*. Copenhagen 1815.
Wülcker, Richard Paul, ed. *Bibliothek der Angelsächsischen Poesie*. 2nd ed. Kassel, 1898.

Secondary Works

Adams, Eleanor N. *Old English Scholarship in England from 1566–1800*. New Haven, CT, 1917.
Allchin, Arthur M. *N. F. S. Grundtvig: An Introduction to his Life and Work*. Aarhus, 1997.
—, D. Jasper, J. H. Schjørring, and K. Stevenson, eds. *Heritage and Prophecy: Grundtvig and the English-Speaking World*. Aarhus, 1993.
Ambrosiani, Björn. "In Memoriam: Gad Rausing död." *Fornvännen* 95 (2000).
Amenius, Ragnar. "Gustaf Wilhelm Gumælius." *SBL*. https://sok.riksarkivet.se/sbl/artikel/13296. Accessed 15 July 2023.
Anonymous. "Bjarni Guðnason." https://www.althingi.is/altext/cv/is/?nfaerslunr=67. Accessed 20 May 2023.
—. "Boer, R. C. (Richard Constant) 1863–1929. https://worldcat.org/identities/lccn-no93036725/. Accessed 5 February 2023.
—. "Brynjulfsson, 2. Gisle B d y." *Nordisk familjebok*, 2nd ed (1905). http://runeberg.org/nfbd/0215.html. Accessed 23 April 2023.

—. "Einar Nerman." https://www.lexikonettamanda.se/show.php?aid=18559. Accessed 27 June 2023.

—. "Frands Herschend." https://www.katalog.uu.se/profile?id=N96-2615. Accessed 18 February 2023.

—. "Fridtjof Nansen – Biographical." https://www.nobelprize.org/prizes/peace/1922/nansen/biographical/. Accessed 16 March 2023.

—. "Hansson, Gunnar D." *Baltic Sea Library*. http://www.balticsealibrary.info/authors/swedish/item/863-hansson-gunnar-d.html. Accessed 15 August 2023.

—. "Jan Henrik Schumacher." https://spartacus.no/forfattere/jan-henrik-schumacher. Accessed 26 January 2023.

—. "Jan Waldemar Dietrichson." *Norsk Telegrambyrå*. 26 April 2002.

—. "Johan Henrik Emil Schück." http://runeberg.org/nfcd/0687.html. *Nordisk familjebok*, 2nd ed (1916). Accessed 10 June 2023.

—. "Jón Jónsson." https://www.althingi.is/altext/cv/is/?nfaerslunr=317. Accessed 20 December 2022.

—. "Keld Zeruneith." https://www.gyldendal.dk/forfattere/keld-zeruneith-f7143. Accessed 20 December 2022.

—. "Niels Christian Ursin Brøgger." *Store norske leksikon (2005–2007)*. https://snl.no/Niels_Christian_Ursin_Brøgger. Accessed 20 July 2023.

—. "Per Wieselgren." http://runeberg.org/vemardet/1957/1077.html. Accessed 20 December 2022.

—. "Professori Osmo Pekonen on kuollut." https://yle.fi/a/3-12657751. Accessed 13 July 2023.

—. "Sven B. F. Jansson." *Nationalencyklopedin*. Accessed 15 August 2023.

—. "The Long Ships." *International Movie Database* (IMDb). https://www.imdb.com/title/tt0057259/?ref_=fn_tt_tt_1. Accessed 29 July 2023.

—. "Vibeke Vasbo." *The History of Nordic Women's Literature*. https://nordicwomensliterature.net/writers/vasbo-vibeke/. Accessed 29 July 2023.

—. "Victor Tavares." https://childrensillustrators.com/VictorTavares/about. Accessed 13 July 2023.

Auerbach, Erich. "Figura." English translation by Ralph Mannheim. In *Scenes from the Drama of European Literature: Six Essays*. New York, 1959. Pp. 11–76.

Baatz, Christine. *Beowulf in Deutschland Zur literarischen und wissenschaftlichen Rezeption altenglischer Literatur in Deutschland am Beispiel des Beowulf*. University of Tübingen Dissertation, 2014.

Barnekow, Christian, and N. F. S. Grundtvig. *Sange fra Nordens Sagnhistorie af N.F.S. Grundtvig*. 2 parts. Copenhagen, 1873.

Bech, Claus. "Jacob Langebek." *DBL*. 3rd ed. 1979–84. https://biografiskleksikon.lex.dk/Jacob_Langebek. Accessed 19 June 2020.

Bengtsson, Frans G. *Karl XII:s levnad*. 2 vols. Stockholm, 1935–36.

—. *Röde orm.* 2 vols. Stockholm, 1941 and 1945. English translation of vol. 1 by June Barrows Mussey as *Red Orm.* New York, 1943. English translation of both vols by Michael Meyer as *The Long Ships: A Saga of the Viking Age.* New York, 1954.

—, trans. Milton, *Det förlorade paradiset.* Stockholm, 1926.

—, trans. *Rolandssången.* In *Världslitteraturen 9:1 Medeltidsdiktning.* Stockholm, 1929. Pp. 15–86.

—, trans. Thoreau, *Skogsliv vid Walden.* Stockholm, 1924.

Bexell, Oloph. "Jesper Swedberg." *SBL.* https://sok.riksarkivet.se/sbl/artikel/34820. Accessed 30 June 2020.

Bjork, Robert E. "Grímur Jónsson Thorkelin's Preface to the First Edition of *Beowulf,* 1815." *SS* 68.3 (1996), 291–320.

—. "N. F. S. Grundtvig's 1840 Edition of the Old English *Phoenix:* A Vision of a Vision of Paradise." In Katherine O'Brien O'Keeffe and Mark Amodio, eds. *Anglo-Saxon Studies in the New Millennium: Essays in Memory of Edward B. Irving, Jr.,* Toronto and Buffalo, 2003. Pp. 217–39.

—. "Nineteenth-Century Scandinavia and the Birth of Anglo-Saxon Studies." In Allen J. Frantzen and John D. Niles, eds. *Anglo-Saxonism and the Construction of Social Identity.* Gainesville, FL, 1997. Pp. 111–32.

—. *Old English Shorter Poems.* Volume II. *Wisdom and Lyric.* Dumbarton Oaks Medieval Library, vol. 32. Cambridge, MA, 2014.

—. "On N. F. S. Grundtvig's Becoming an Old English *Scop, Leoðwyrhta, Woðbora,* Poet." *GS* (2020–21), 25–51.

—. Review of Bo Gräslund. *Beowulfkvädet: Den nordiska bakgrunden. SS* 92.2 (2020), 247–49.

—. "Scandinavian Relations." In Phillip Pulsiano and Elaine Treharne, eds. *A Companion to Anglo-Saxon Literature.* Oxford, 2001. Pp. 388–99.

—. "The Reception History of *Beowulf." SELIM: Journal of the Spanish Society for Medieval English Language and Literature* 25 (2020), 1–19.

Björkman, Erik. "*Beowulf,* Fornengelsk Dikt." *Världslitteraturen i urval och öfversättning,* ed. Henrik Schück. Stockholm, 1902. Pp. 463–501.

—. "Några anekdoter om konung Alfred den store i kritisk belysning." *Finsk Tidskrift* 69 (1910), 332–48.

—. *Nordische personennamen in England in alt- und frühmittel-englischer zeit.* Halle, 1910.

—. Review of Kier, *Beowulf: Et bidrag til Nordens Oldhistorie. Beibl* 27 (1916), 244–46.

—. *Scandinavian Loan-Words in Middle English.* Halle, 1900–02.

—. *Studien über die Eigennamen im Beowulf.* Halle, 1920.

—. *Zur englischen namenkunde.* Halle, 1912.

Bjørn, Claus, and Povl Engelstoft. "Erik Kroman." *DBL.* 3rd ed., 1979–84. https://biografiskleksikon.lex.dk/Erik_Kroman. Accessed 21 June 2022.

Björnsson, Halldóra. *Bjólfskviða*, ed. Pétur Knúttson Ridgewell. Illustrated by Alfreð Flóki. Reykjavík, 1983.
Blanck, Anton. *Den nordiska renässansen i 1700-talets litteratur: En undersöknikng av den "götiska" poesins allmänna och inhemska förutsättningar.* Stockholm, 1911.
Boer, R. C. "Om Hervararsaga." *Aarbøger for nordisk Oldkyndighed og Historie* 3 (1911), 1–80.
Borgehammar, Stephan, ed. *Från tid och evighet: Predikningar från 200-tal till 1500-tal*. Skellefteå, 1992.
Borges, Jorge Luis. "Thorkelin y el *Beowulf* / Thorkelin and *Beowulf*. Introduction and translation by Joe Stadolink. *PMLA* 132.2 (2017), 462–70.
Borum, Poul. *Danish Literature: A Short Critical Survey*. Copenhagen, 1979.
—. *Digteren Grundtvig*. Copenhagen, 1983.
Bosworth, John. *The Elements of Anglo-Saxon Grammar*. London, 1823.
Bradley, S. A. J. "'A Truly Proud Ruin': Grundtvig and the Anglo-Saxon Legacy." In A. M. Allchin et al., eds. *Grundtvig in International Perspective: Studies in the Creativity of Interaction*. Aarhus, 2000. Pp. 147–62.
—. "'Det er hvad jeg kalder at oversætte Digte': Grundtvig as Translator." *GS* 51.1 (2000), 36–59.
—. "Grundtvig, Bede and the Testimony of Antiquity." *GS* 57.1 (2006), 110–31.
—. "Grundtvig's *I Kveld*: Reflections of an Anglo-Saxonist." *GS* 67.1 (2016), 142–81. https://doi.org/10.7146/grs.v67i1.96652.
—. *N. F. S. Grundtvig's Transcriptions of the Exeter Book: Grundtvig Archive Fascicle 316, nrs 1–8 in the Royal Library Copenhagen*. Copenhagen, 1998.
—. "'Stridige Stykker snild jeg forbandt': Grundtvig's Creative Synthesis of Anglo-Saxon Sources." *GS* 47.1 (1996), 97–127.
—. "'The First New-European Literature': N. F. S. Grundtvig's Reception of Anglo-Saxon Literature." In A. M. Allchin et al., eds. *Heritage and Prophecy: Grundtvig and the English-Speaking World*. Aarhus, 1993. Pp. 45–72.
—, N. A. Helm, and J. H. Schjørring, eds. *Grundvig in International Perspective: Studies in the Creativity of Interaction*. Aarhus, 2000.
Branch, Michael. "Finnish Oral Poetry, *Kalevala*, and *Kanteletar*." In George C. Schoolfield, ed. *A History of Finland's Literature*. Histories of Scandinavian Literature, vol. 4. Lincoln and London, 1998. Pp. 3–33.
Bringéus, Nils-Arvid. "Carl Wilhelm von Sydow (1887–1952). In Mats Hellspong and Fredrik Skott, eds. *Svenska etnologer och folklorister*. Acta Academiae Regiae Gustavi Adolphi 109. Uppsala, 2010. Pp. 79–85.
Bringsværd, Tor Åge. *Beowulf: han som ville bli husket*. Illustrated by Arne Samuelsen. Oslo, 1999.
Broadbridge, Edward, trans. and ed. *Living Wellsprings: The Hymns, Songs, and Poems of N. F. S. Grundtvig*. Aarhus, 2015.

—, and Niels Lyhne Jensen, trans. and eds. *A Grundtvig Anthology: Selections from the Writings of N. F. S. Grundtvig*. Cambridge and Viby, 1984.

Brøgger, Niels Christian. *Mordet i Nationaltheatret*. Oslo, 1952.

—. *Nordens demring: Nordiske myter og sagn*. Foreword by A. W. Brøgger. Illustrated by Knut Yran. Oslo, 1949.

Brøgger, Suzanne. *Crème Fraîche*. Copenhagen, 1974.

—. *Fri os fra kærligheden*. 1973; Translated into English as *Deliver Us from Love*. New York, 1976.

—. OE Translations. In Keld Zeruneith. *De siste tider: hedenskap heroism kristendom: en angelsaksisk overgangshistorie*. Copenhagen, 2017. Pp. 317–32.

—. *Sløret – To suiter*. 13 songs. Copenhagen, 2008.

—. *Jadekatten*. 1997; Translated into English as *The Jade Cat*. New York, 2009.

Brynildsen, R. K. "Om tidsregningen i Olav den Helliges Historie." *Avhandlinger fra Universitetets Historiske Seminar* Utgit av Halvdan Koht 2.2 (Kristiania, 1916), 37–120, especially chapter 7.

Bugge, Alexander. "Vore forfædres opdagelsesreiser i polaregnene." *Kungsjaa* 11 (1898), 497–509.

Busbee, Mark Bradshaw. "A Few Words about the Recently Published Anglo-Saxon Poem, the First Edition of *Beowulf*." *GS* 66.1 (2015), 7–36.

—. "'A Little Shared Home for England and the North': The First *Beowulf* for Young Readers." In Bruce Gilchrist and Britt Mize, eds. *Beowulf as Children's Literature*. Toronto, Buffalo, London, 2021. Pp. 20–55.

—. "Grundtvig and Tolkien on *Beowulf*: A Comparative Analysis." *GS* 61.1 (2010), 12–30.

Cable, Thomas. *The Meter and Melody of Beowulf*. Urbana, 1974.

Carlsson, Sten. "Pontus E. A. Fahlbeck." *SBL*. https://sok.riksarkivet.se/sbl/Presentation.aspx?id=15618. Accessed 6 June 2023.

Chambers, R. W. *Beowulf: An Introduction to the Study of the Poem with a Discussion of the Stories of Offa and Finn*. With a supplement by C. L. Wrenn. 3rd ed. Cambridge, 1959; repr. 1963.

—. "Modern Study of the Poetry of the Exeter Book." In R. W. Chambers, Max Förster, and Robin Fowler, eds. *The Exeter Book of Old English Poetry*. London, 1933. Pp. 33–43.

Christensen, Arne Søby. "Beowulf, Hygelac og Chlochilaichus: Om beretnings-kronologien i *Beowulf*." *Historisk Tidsskrift* 105.1 (2005), 40–79.

Cleasby, Richard, and Gudbrand Vigfusson. *An Icelandic-English Dictionary*. 2nd ed. by Sir William A. Craigie. Oxford, 1957.

Clunies Ross, Margaret, and Lars Lönnroth. "The Norse Muse: Report from an International Research Project." *Alvíssmál* 9 (1999), 3–28.

Coates, Richard. "Karl Inge Sandred (1925–2008)" *Nomina* 32 (2009), 163–65.

Colbert, David W. "The Medieval Ballad." In Sven H. Rossel, ed. *A History of Danish Literature*. Histories of Scandinavian Literature, vol. 1. Lincoln and London, 1992. Pp. 46–70.

Collinder, Björn. *Comparative Grammar of the Uralic Languages*. Stockholm, 1960.

—, trans. *Beowulf översatt i originalets versmått*. Stockholm, 1954.

—. *Fenno-Ugric Vocabulary*. Stockholm, 1955.

—, trans. *Kalevala*. Stockholm, 1950.

—. *Survey of the Uralic Languages*. Stockholm, 1957.

Conybeare, J. J. "Account of an Anglo-Saxon Paraphrase of the Phoenix Attributed to Lactantius." *Archæologia* 17 (1814), 193-97. Reprinted in *Illustrations of Anglo-Saxon Poetry*, ed. W. D. Conybeare, 1826; repr. New York, 1964. Pp. 24–28.

Cooley, Franklin. "Grundtvig's First Translation from *Beowulf*." *SS* 16 (1941), 234–38.

Cross, F. L., and E. A. Livingstone, eds. *The Oxford Dictionary of the Christian Church*. 3rd ed. Oxford, 1998.

Dahl, Frantz. "Kier, Christian Ludvig, 1839–1934." *DBL*. 2nd ed., 1932–44, vol. 12. pp. 411–12. https://www.rosekamp.dk/DBL_All/DBL_12_text.pdf. Accessed 8 May 2023.

Dehn-Nielsen. "George Stephens." *DBL*. 3rd ed., 1979–84. https://biografiskleksikon.lex.dk/George_Stephens. Accessed 2 June 2021.

Derry, T. K. *A History of Scandinavia: Norway, Sweden, Denmark, Finland, and Iceland*. Minneapolis and London, 1979.

Dietrichson, Jan W., trans. *Beowulf-kvadet*. Oslo, 1976.

—, trans. *Boken om damenes*. Oslo, 2013.

—, trans. *Sir Gawain og den grønne ridder*. Oslo, 1984.

—. *The Image of Money in the American Novel of the Gilded Age*. Oslo, 1969.

—, trans. *Troilus og Criseyde*. Oslo, 2010.

—, trans. *Tundals visjon*. Oslo, 1988.

Dillström, R. "Beowulf," *Laivastolehti* 2 (1927), 35–40, 73–78, 137–44, 176–80, 201–04, 243–46, 284–89, 316–21, 349–56.

—. *Beowulf*. Completed by Matti Järvinen. Helsinki, 1999.

Drout, Michael. *Beowulf and the Critics by J. R. R. Tolkien*. Tempe, 2002.

Earle, John. "An Ancient Saxon Poem of a City in Ruins Supposed to be Bath." *Proceedings of the Bath Natural History and Antiquarian Field Club* 2 (1870–73), 259–70.

Einarsson, Stefán. *A History of Icelandic Literature*. Baltimore, 1957.

—. *Icelandic: Grammar, Texts, Glossary*. Baltimore, 1945.

—. "Víxlkveðandi í Widsíþ (?), Sturlungu og á Finnlandi." *Skírnir* 125 (1951), 109–30. Translated into English as "Alternate Recital by Twos in Wídsíth (?), *Sturlunga* and *Kalevala*." *Arv* 7 (1951), 59–83.

—. "Wídsíð = Víðförull." *Skírnir* 110 (1936), 164–90.

Ekwall, Eilert. "Erik Björkman." *SBL*. https://sok.riksarkivet.se/sbl/Presentation.aspx?id=18300. Accessed 18 July 2023.

Elsness, Johan. "Minnetale over professor Arthur Olav Sandved." *Året 2021 i Det Norske Videnskaps-Akademi* (forthcoming).

Emonds, Joseph Embley, and Jan Terje Faarlund. *English: The Language of the Vikings*. Olomouc, 2014.

Enefalk, Hanna. *En patriotisk drömvärld: Musik, nationalism och genus under den långa 1800-talet*. Acta Universitatis Upsaliensis Studia Historica Upsaliensia 234. Uppsala, 2008.

Engberg, Hanne. "Ludvig Christian Müller." *DBL*. 3rd ed., 1979–84. https://biografiskleksikon.lex.dk/Ludvig_Christian_Müller. Accessed 1 June 2021.

Envkist, Nils E. "Porthans 'Forsök at uplysa Konung Ælfreds Geografiska Beskrifning åfver den Europeiska Norden' [Ohtheriana vii]." *Årskrift utgiven av Åbo Akademie* 38–41 (1953–57), 103–22.

Enoksen, Lars Magnar. *Runor: historia, tydning, tolkning*. Falun, 1998.

Eriksson, Karin. "George Stephens." In Gunilla Byrman, ed. *En värld för sig själv: Nya studier i medeltida ballader*. Växjö, 2008. Pp. 29–72.

Fahlbeck, Pontus. "Beovulfskvädet såsom källa för nordisk fornhistoria." *ATfS* 8.2 (1884), 1–88.

—. *Beovulfskvädet såsom källa för nordisk fornhistoria*. N. F. Kungl. Vitterhets Historie och Antikvitets Akademiens Handlingar, 13, no. 3 (1913) = 33, no. 2 (1924). Pp. 17.

Fast, Carl Otto [as Svionum]. *Beowulf, germanernas äldsta epos*. Stockholm, 1929.

—. *Götaland, den forngermanska diktningens landskap*. Göteborg, 1933; repr. 1984.

—. *Svenska rikets ursprung*. Göteborg, 1944; repr. 1984.

—. *Vänerbygdens sägner*. Stockholm, 1950.

—. *Västgöta-Dal. Daner och Anglo-sachsare*. Stockholm, 1930.

Fjalldal, Magnús. "To Fall by Ambition – Grímur Thorkelín and his *Beowulf* Edition." *Neophilologus* 92 (2008), 321–32.

Flood, Alison. "UNESCO Lists Exeter Book among World's Principal Cultural Artefacts." 22 June 2016. https://www.theguardian.com/books/2016/jun/22/unesco-lists-exeter-book-among-worlds-principal-cultural-artefacts. Accessed 17 July 2021.

Frank, Roberta. "A Taste for Knottiness: Skaldic Art at Cnut's Court." *ASE* 47 (2020), 197–217.

—. "Old Norse Memorial Eulogies and the Date of *Beowulf*." *The Early Middle Ages, Acta* 6 (1979), 1–19.

—. *The Etiquette of Early Northern Verse*. Notre Dame, 2022.

Fulk, R. D. *A Comparative Grammar of the Early Germanic Languages*. Amsterdam and Philadelphia, 2018.

Gammeltoft, Peder, and Jakob Holck. "Gemsten and Other Old English Pearls: A Survey of Early Old English Loanwords in Scandinavian." *NOWELE* 50/51 (2007), 131–61.

Gannholm, Tore. *Beowulf. Gutarnas nationalepos samt Gutasagan.* Visby, 1992.

Gerven, Tim van, 2018. "Oehlenschläger, Adam Gottlob," *ERNIE.* Joep Leerssen, ed. (electronic version; Amsterdam: Study Platform on Interlocking Nationalisms, https://ernie.uva.nl/), article version 1.1.2.1/a, last changed 10 August 2018, consulted 15 May 2020.

Gilchrist, Bruce, and Britt Mize, eds. *Beowulf as Children's Literature.* Toronto, Buffalo, London, 2021.

Glob, P. V. *Denmark: An Archaeological History from the Stone Age to the Vikings*, trans. Joan Bulman. Ithaca, 1971.

Gorst, E. K. C. "Latin Sources of the Old English *Phoenix.*" *N&Q* 53.2 (2006), 136–42. https://doi-org.ezproxy1.lib.asu.edu/10.1093/notesj/gjl002.

Gram, Hans. "Prøve af Danske Ord og Talemaader, af det Engel-Saxiske Sprog forklarede." *Det Københavnske Selskabs Skrifter* 5 (1751), 127–208.

Grant, Tom. "Beow in Scandinavia." *ASE* 48 (2022), 105–20.

Greenfield, Stanley B., and Fred C. Robinson. *A Bibliography of Publications on Old English Literature to the End of 1972.* Toronto and Buffalo, 1980.

Grell, Helge. *England og Grundtvig.* Aarhus, 1992.

Gräslund, Bo. "Bo Gräslund." https://www.arkeologi.uu.se/personal/presentationer/Bo_Graslund/. Accessed 4 June 2023.

—. *The Nordic Beowulf.* Trans. by Martin Naylor. Leeds, 2020. (Translation of *Beowulfkvädet: Den nordiska bakgrunden.* Acta Academiae Regiae Gustavi Adolphi 149, OPIA 64. Uppsala, 2018.

Grønbech, Vilhelm. *The Culture of the Teutons.* Translated by William Worster. London, 1931.

—. *Vor Folkeæt i Oldtiden.* 4 vols. Copenhagen, 1909–12.

Grønvik, Ottar. "Ordet norr. víkingr m. – et tidlig lån fra anglo-frisisk område?" *AfNF* 119 (2004), 5–15.

Grundtvig, Stener, ed. *N. F. S. Grundtvigs Breve til hans Hustru under Englandsreiserne 1829–1831.* Copenhagen, 1920.

Guðnason, Bjarni. *Um Skjöldungasögu.* Reykjavík, 1963.

Gurteen, S. Humphreys. *The Epic of the Fall of Man: A Comparative Study of Cædmon, Dante and Milton.* 1896; repr. New York, 1964.

Gutt, Ernst-August. *Translation and Relevance: Cognition and Context.* Oxford, 1991.

Haarder, Andreas. *Beowulf: The Appeal of a Poem.* Viborg, 1975.

—. *Det episke liv. Et indblick i oldengelsk heltedigtning.* Copenhagen, 1979; e-book 2022.

—. *Sangen om Bjovulf i dansk gengivelse.* Illustrated by Viggo Kragh-Hansen. Copenhagen, 1984; repr. 2001 with a foreword by Thomas A. Shippey.

Hall, J. R. "Anglo-Saxon Studies in the Nineteenth Century: England, Denmark, America." In Phillip Pulsiano and Elaine Treharne, eds. *A Companion to Anglo-Saxon Literature*. Oxford, 2001. Pp. 434–54.

—. "The First Two Editions of *Beowulf*: Thorkelin's (1815) and Kemble's (1833)." In D. K. Scragg and Paul E. Szarmach, eds. *Editing Old English Texts: Proceedings of the 1990 Manchester Conference*. Cambridge, 1994. Pp. 239–50.

Hall, John A., Ove Korsgaard, and Ove K. Pedersen, eds. *Building the Nation: N. F. S. Grundtvig and Danish National Identity*. Montreal and Kingston, 2015.

Halvorsen, Eyvind Fjeld. "C R Unger." *Norsk biografisk lexikon*. https://web.archive.org/web/20150609153826/https://nbl.snl.no/C_R_Unger. Accessed 5 August 2023.

Hammerich, Frederik. *De episke-kristelige oldkvad hos de gotiske folk*. Copenhagen, 1873.

—. "Erindring" in Steen Johansen and Henning Høirup, eds. *Grundtvigs Erindringer og Erindinger om Grundtvig*. Copenhagen, 1948. Pp. 262–66.

Hansen, Adolf, trans. *Bjovulf*. Copenhagen, 1910. Rev. ed. *Bjovulf og Kampen i Finsborg*, ed. Carsten Lyngdrup Madsen. Copenhagen, 2019.

—. *Engelsk Litteraturhistorie*. Copenhagen, 1929.

—. "Oldengelsk Litteratur." In *Illustreret Verdens-Litteraturhistorie*, vol 3. Copenhagen, 1901. Pp. 5–19.

—. *Oversatte engelske Digte (Shelley, Tennyson, Arnold, Swinburne)*. Copenhagen, 1884.

Hansson, Gunnar D., trans. *Slaget vid Maldon och sju elegier*. Uddevalla, 1991.

Harding, Merete, and Niels Hyldahl. "Bent Noack." *DBL* 3rd ed., 1979–84. https://biografiskleksikon.lex.dk/Bent_Noack. Accessed 16 August 2023.

Haß, Ulrike. "The Germanic Languages other than English from c. 1700." In John Considine, ed. *The Cambridge World History of Lexicography*. Cambridge, 2019. Pp. 460–83.

Haugen, Einar, ed. *First Grammatical Treatise: The Earliest Germanic Phonology*. 2nd ed. London, 1972.

—. *The Scandinavian Languages: An Introduction to Their History*. Cambridge, MA, 1976.

Hemmingsen, Lars. "Axel Olrik (1864–1617)." In Helen Damico, ed. *Medieval Scholarship: Biographical Essays on the Formation of a Discipline*. Volume 2: Literature and Philology. New York, 1998. Pp. 267–81.

Herschend, Frands. "Striden i Finnsborg." *Tor* 29 (1997), 295–333.

Hickes, George. *Institutiones grammaticæ Anglo-Saxonicæ et Moeso-Gothicæ.* Oxoniæ, 1689.
Hilden, Adda. "Thora Constantin-Hansen." *Dansk Kvindebiografisk Leksikon.* https://kvindebiografiskleksikon.lex.dk/Thora_Constantin-Hansen. Accessed 5 July 2023.
Himes, Jonathan, Osmo Pekonen, and Clive Tolley, trans. *Waldere: Anglosaksinen muinaisruno.* Jyväskylä, 2005.
Holm, Anders. *Historie og efterklang. En studie i N. F. S. Grundtvigs tidsskrift Danne-Virke.* Odense, 2001.
—. *The Essential N. F. S. Grundtvig.* Aarhus, 2019.
—. "The Luther of Denmark." *I. A. H. Bulletin* 45 (2017), 10–23.
Hoel, Oddmund L. "Aasen, Ivar." *ERNIE.* https://ernie.uva.nl/viewer.p/21/56/object/131-158347. Accessed 18 July 2023.
Howitt, William and Howitt, Mary. *The Literature and Romance of Northern Europe.* London, 1852.
Hvidtfeldt, Arild. "Vilh. Grønbech." *DBL.* 3rd ed., 1979–84. https://biografiskleksikon.lex.dk/Vilh._Grønbech. Accessed 11 April 2024.
Hødnebø, Finn. "Hvem var de første vikinger?" *Maal og Minne* (1987), 1–16.
Ingólfsson, Aðalsteinn. *Furðuveröld Alfreðs Flóka / The Singular World of Alfred Flóki.* Reykjavík, 1986.
Ingwersen, Niels. "Axel Olrik (1864–1917)." In Jack Zipes, ed. *The Oxford Companion to Fairy Tales.* 2nd ed. Online. Oxford, 2005. https://www.oxfordreference.com/search?q=Axel+Olrik&searchBtn=Search&isQuickSearch=true. Accessed 19 February 2023.
Ireland, Colin A. *The Gaelic Background of Old English Poetry before Bede.* Berlin, Boston, 2022. https://doi.org/10.1515/9781501513879
Isaacson, Lanae Hjortsvang. Review of Vasbo, *Hildas sang. World Literature Today,* 66.4 (1992), 727–28.
Ísaksson, Sigurjón Páll. "Þýðingar Gísla Brynjúlfssonar ur fornensku." *Gripla* 18 (2007), 95–96.
Janson, Henrik. *Till frågan om Svearikets vagga.* Gällstad, 1999.
Jansson, Sven B. F. "Deors klagan" (Deor) and "Sjöfararen" (The Seafarer). In Karl-Ivar Hildeman, ed. *Medeltidens litteratur: Episk diktning m.m.,* vol. 4 of *Litteraturens klassiker,* ed. Lennart Breitholtz. Stockholm, 1962; repr. 1996, 2000. Pp. 17–22.
Johannesson, Kurt. *The Renaissance of the Goths in Sixteenth-Century Sweden.* Trans. and ed. James Larson. Berkeley and Los Angeles, 1991.
Johansen, Steen, and Henning Høirup, eds. *Grundtvigs Erindringer og Erindringer om Grundtvig.* Copenhagen, 1948.
Johansson, Gust. *Beowulfsagans historiska fragment.* Göteborg, 1964.
—. *Beowulfsagans Hrones-Næsse: Lekmannafunderingar angående det Gamla Götland.* Göteborg, 1947.
Jones, Rob Lloyd. *Beowulf.* Illustrated by Victor Tavares. London, 2009.

—. *Beowulf*. Illustrated by Victor Tavares. Sámi translation by Johan Sandberg McGuinne as *Beowulf: dïhte staalehke alma*. Trøndelag, 2019.

—. *Beowulf*. Illustrated by Victor Tavares. Swedish translation by Birgit Lönn. Stockholm, 2011.

Jónsson, Jón. "Landaleitir formanna í Norðurhöfum." *Tímarit hins íslenzka bókmenntafélags* 23 (1902), 138–57.

—. "Liserus – Beów." *AfNF* 15 (1899), 255–61.

—. "Uinuaed=vínheiðr." *AfNF* 27 (1911), 94–95.

—. "Um Erík blóðöx." *Tímarit hins íslenzka bókmenntafélags* 16 (1895), 176–203.

—. "Ætt Haralds hilditannar." *AfNF* 31 (1915), 26–46.

Jönsson, Lena. "Lönnroth, Lars." http://runeberg.org/vemardet/2001/0760.html. Accessed 7 January 2023.

Jørgensen, Jesper Düring, and Carl S. Petersen. "R. Nyerup." *DBL*. 3rd ed., 1979–84. https://biografiskleksikon.lex.dk/R._Nyerup. Accessed 24 June 2020.

Jørgensen, Lea Grosen. "Reconstructing the Past and the Poet: Grundtvig and the Anglo-Saxon Phoenix," *GS* 69 (2018), 17–35.

Jørgensen, Ove. *Alfred den Store. Danmarks geografi. En undersøgelse at fire afsnit i Den gamle engelske Orosius*. Odense, 1985.

—. *OTONIVM, Odense 1593*. Odense, 1981.

—. *Sejlruter i Adam af Bremens danske øverden*. Odense, 1992.

Kardach, Jim. "Tech History: How Bluetooth Got Its Name." *EE Times* 5 February 2008. Accessed 29 July 2023. https://www.eetimes.com/tech-history-how-bluetooth-got-its-name/.

Kelly, L. G. *The True Interpreter: A History of Translation Theory and Practice in the West*. Oxford, 1979.

Kemble, John Mitchell. *Anglo-Saxon Runes*. 1840; repr. Middlesex, 1991.

Kiernan, Kevin S. *Beowulf and the Beowulf Manuscript*. Ann Arbor, 1981. Reprinted 1997 with a foreword by Katherine O'Brien O'Keeffe.

Kjersgaard, Erik. "Vilh. la Cour." *DBL*. 3rd ed., 1979–84. https://biografiskleksikon.lex.dk/Vilh._la_Cour. Accessed 22 June 2022.

Kjær, A. "Hvad var Skíringssalr?" *Norsk historisk Tidsskrift*. 4th ser., 5 (1909), 267–83.

Knudsen, Johannes, ed. and trans. *Selected Writings: N. F. S. Grundtvig*. Philadelphia, 1976.

Knútsson, Petúr. "The Intimacy of *Bjólfskviða*." In Jana K. Schulman and Paul E. Szarmach, eds. *Beowulf at Kalamazoo: Essays on Translation and Perfomance*. Kalamazoo, 2014. Pp. 186–206.

Kock, Ernst. *Fornjermansk forskning. LUÅ*, n.s. 1, 18, no. 1 (1922), [iv], 43.

—. "Interpretations and Emendations of Early English Texts: III." *Anglia* 27 (1904), 218–37.

—. "Interpretations and Emendations of Early English Texts: IV." *Anglia* 42 (1918), 99–124.

—. "Interpretations and Emendations of Early English Texts: V." *Anglia* 43 (1919), 298–312.

—. "Interpretations and Emendations of Early English Texts: VI." *Anglia* 44 (1920), 97–114.

—. "Interpretations and Emendations of Early English Texts: VII." *Anglia* 44 (1920), 245–60.

—. "Interpretations and Emendations of Early English Texts: VIII." *Anglia* 45 (1921), 105–31.

—. "Interpretations and Emendations of Early English Texts: IX." *Anglia* 46 (1922), 63–96.

—. "Interpretations and Emendations of Early English Texts: XI." *Anglia* 47 (1923), 264–73.

—. "Jubilee Jaunts and Jottings: 250 Contributions to the Interpretation and Prosody of Old West Teutonic Alliterative Poetry." *LUÅ* n.s. 1, 14, no. 26 (1918), 1–82.

—. "Notationes Norroenæ: Anteckningar till Edda och Skaldediktning." *LUÅ* n.s. 1, 19, no. 2 (1923), 1–107.

—. "Plain Points and Puzzles, 60 Notes on OE Poetry." *LUÅ* n.s. 1, 17, no. 7 (1922), [iv], 26.

Krag, Claus. "Alexander Bugge." *Norsk biografisk leksikon*. https://nbl.snl.no/Alexander_Bugge. Accessed 2 April 2023.

Kroman, Erik. *Det Danske Rige i den ældre Vikingetid*. Copenhagen, 1976.

La Cour, Vilhelm. *Det danske Folks Historie*. Copenhagen, 1927.

—. "Lejrestudier." *DS* 17 (1920), 49–67.

—. "Lejrestudier: Mindesmærkerne." *DS* 18 (1921), 147–66.

—. "Lejrestudier: Navnet." *DS* 21 (1924), 13–22.

—. "Skjoldungefejden." *DS* 23 (1926), 147–56.

Lane, Barbara Miller. *National Romanticism and Modern Architecture in Germany and the Scandinavian Countries*. Cambridge, 2000.

Larsen, Helge, and Marius Kristensen. "Gudmund Schütte." *DBL*. 3rd ed., 1979–84. https://biografiskleksikon.lex.dk/Gudmund_Schütte. Accessed 5 Feburary 2023.

Larsen, Henning. "Sigrdrífa-Brynhild." *SSN* 4 (1917), 65–73.

Larsen, Henry. *Krist og Satan: nogle Blade af gammel kristelig Digtning særlig hos Angelsakserne (Cædmon)*. Copenhagen, 1903.

Larson, James. "The Reformation and Sweden's Century as a Great Power: 1523–1718." In Lars G. Warme, ed. *A History of Swedish Literature*. Histories of Scandinavian Literature, vol. 3. Lincoln and London, 1996. Pp. 58–101.

Larson, Sofus. *Jomsborg, dens Beliggenhed og Historie*. Copenhagen, 1932.

Lawson, Max. "N. F. S. Grundtvig, 1783–1872." *Performance Magazine*. https://www.performancemagazine.org/thinkers-on-education/

grundtvig-n-f-s-1783-1872/. Accessed 20 May 2022. Article was originally published in *Prospects: The Quarterly Review of Comparative Dducation* 23, no. 3/4 (1993), 613–23.

Lawson, M. K. *Cnut: The Danes in England in the Early Eleventh Century.* London, 1993.

Leersen, Joep. *National Thought in Europe: A Cultural History.* Amsterdam, 2006.

Liberman, Anatoly, ed. *Studies in Germanic Philology.* Hamburg, 1986.

Lindhardt, P. G. "Frederik Hammerich – teolog." *DBL.* 3rd ed., 1979–84. https://biografiskleksikon.lex.dk/Frederik_Hammerich_-_teolog. Accessed 29 June 2020.

Lindqvist, Sune. "Hednatemplet i Uppsala." *Fornvännen* 18 (1923), 83–118.

—. "Ottarshögen i Vendel." *Fornvännen* 12 (1917), 127–43.

—. "Sutton Hoo och *Beowulf*." *Fornvännen* 43 (1948), 94–110.

—. *Uppsala Högar och Ottarshögen.* Stockholm, 1936.

—. "Ynglingaättens gravskick." *Fornvännen* 16 (1921), 83–194.

Livingston, Michael, ed. *The Battle of Brunanburh: A Casebook.* Exeter, 2011.

Lund, Niels. *De danske vikinger i England: Røvere og bønder.* Copenhagen, 1967.

—. *De hærger og de brænder: Danmark og England i Vikingetiden*, 2nd ed. Copenhagen, 1997.

—. trans. *Ottar og Wulfstan. To rejsebeskrivelser fra vikingatiden.* With commentary by Lund, essays by Ole Crumlin-Pedersen, Peter H. Sawyer, Christine E. Fell. Roskilde, 1983. Translated into English by Christine E. Fell as *Two Voyagers at the Court of King Alfred.* York, 1984.

—, trans. *Sangen om Slaget ved Maldon og andra Kilder til Sven Sveskægs og Olav Tryggvessons Kampe i England i 990erne.* Copenhagen, 1991.

Lönn, Birgit. See Jones, Rob Lloyd.

Lönnroth, Lars. *Det germanska spåret. En västerländsk litteraturtradition från Tacitus till Tolkien.* Stockholm, 2017.

—. *Dörrar till främmande rum: Minnesfragment.* Stockholm, 2009.

—, and Sven Delblanc, eds. *Den Svenska Litteraturen.* Vol. 2: *Upplysning och romantik.* Stockholm, 1988.

Madsen, Lone Brink, Jens Grøn, and Ditte Krøgholt, eds. *Folkehøjskolens sangbog.* 17 ed. Copenhagen, 1997.

Magnusen, Finn. *Priscae Veterum Borealium Mythologiae Lexicon.* Copenhagen, 1828.

Malone, Kemp. "Grundtvig as *Beowulf* Critic." *RES* 66 (1941), 129–38.

McGuinne, Johann Sandberg. See Jones, Rob Lloyd.

McGuire, Brian Patrick. *Min amerikanske Barndom.* Copenhagen, 2016.

McKinnell, John. "The Context of *Völundarkviða*." *Saga-Book of the Viking Society* 23 (1990), 1–27.

Meier, F. J. "Bussæus, Andreas." *DBL*. 1st ed. 1887–1906. http://runeberg.org/dbl/3/0269.html. Accessed 20 June 2020.

Miller, D. Gary. *External Influences on English: From Its Beginnings to the Renaissance*. Oxford, 2012.

Mitchell, Stephen A. "The Middle Ages." In Lars G. Warme, ed. *A History of Swedish Literature*. Histories of Scandinavian Literature, vol. 3. Lincoln and London, 1996. Pp. 1–57.

Mjöberg, Jöran. *Drömmen om sagatiden*. Vol. 1: *Återblick på den nordiska romantiken från 1700+talets mitt till nygöticismen (omkr. 1865)*. Vol. 2: *De senaste hundra åren: idealbildning och avidealisering*. Stockholm, 1967, 1968.

—. "Romanticism and Revival." In David M. Wilson, ed. *The Northern World: The History and Heritage of Northern Europe, AD 400–1100*. New York, 1980. Pp. 207–38.

Möller-Christensen, Ivy York. "Valdemar Rørdan." *Den Store Danske*. Revised 23 April 2023. https://denstoredanske.lex.dk/Valdemar_Rørdam. Accessed 14 May 2023.

Morley, Henry. *A First Sketch of English Literature*. London, 1873.

Munch, P. A. Review of Schaldemose, *Beo-Wulf og Scopes Widsið*. *Norsk Tidsskrft for Videnskab og Litteratur* 2 (1848), 133–38.

Naess, Harald S. "Holberg and the Age of Enlightenment." In Harald S. Naess, ed. *A History of Norwegian Literature*. Histories of Scandinavian Literature, vol. 2. Lincoln, London, 1993. Pp. 53–81.

—. "Norwegian Literature 1800-1860." In Harald S. Naess, ed. *A History of Norwegian Literature*. Histories of Scandinavian Literature, vol. 2. Lincoln, London, 1993. Pp. 82–106.

Nedergaard, Paul. *Personalhistoriske, sognhistoriske og statistiske Bidrag til en dansk Præste og Sognhistorie (Kirkelig Geografi) 1849–1949*. Roskilde Stift, vol. 2. Copenhagen, 1954.

Nerman, Birger. *Det svenska rikets uppkomst*. Stockholm, 1925.

—. *Pan och Eros*. Stockholm, 1912.

—. *Sveriges rikes uppkomst*. Stockholm, 1941.

—. "The Foundation of the Swedish Kingdom." *VSNR* 10 (1928–29), 113–31.

Nielsen, Hans F. *Old English and the Continental Germanic Languages: Survey of Morphological and Phonological Interrelations*. 2nd ed. Innsbruck, 1985.

Niles, John D. *The Idea of Anglo-Saxon England 1066–1901: Remembering, Forgetting, Deciphering, and Renewing the Past*. Oxford and Malden, MA, 2015.

Nilesen, Valdemar. "Grundtvig set fra Sverige." *GS* 11.1 (1958), 30–35.

Nilsson, L. G. *Anglosaxisk (fornengelsk) grammatika*. 2 parts. Copenhagen, 1866, 1870.

—. *Anglosaxisk (fornengelsk) läsebok för Nybegynnare*. Lund, 1871.

—. *Judith, Fragment af ett fornengelskt Qväde*. Copenhagen, 1858.

—. *Några fornengelska andeliga quäden på grundspråket.* Lund, 1857.
Neuhaus, Johannes. "Sillende=vetus patria=Angel, i Angelsaksernes og Oldsaksernes Mund Navnet på det gamle Hjemland." *NTfF*, 4th ser. 5 (1916–17), 125–26.
Noack, Bent. "Den oldengelske digtning og Grundtvig." *GS* 41.1 (1989–90), 141–53.
—. *Helvedstorm og himmelfart: stykker af oldengelsk kristen digtning.* Copenhagen, 1983.
—. *Menneskevordelse og korsdød: stykker af oldengelsk kristen digtning.* Fredericksberg, 1996.
Nordstrom, Byron J. *Scandinavia since 1500.* Minneapolis, 2000.
Nordström, Patrik. "Knut Stjerna (1874–1909)." In Anne-Sofie Gräslund, ed. *Svenska arkeologer.* Acta Academiae Regiae Gustavi Adolphi 158. Uppsala, 2020. Pp. 119–29.
Nye, Robert. *Beowulf.* 2nd ed. Swedish translation by Birgitta Gahrton, afterword by Lena Törnqvist. Stockholm, 2007.
Olesen, Jens E., and E. I. Kouri, eds. *The Cambridge History of Scandinavia. Volume II, 1520–1870.* Cambridge, 2016.
Olrik, Axel. *Danmarks Heltedigtning, en oldtidsstudie*: I, *Rolf Krake og den ældre Skjoldungrække.* Copenhagen, 1903. Translated into English by Lee M. Hollander as *The Heroic Legends of Denmark.* London, 1919; repr. New York, 1976.
—. *Danmarks Heltedigtning, en oldtidsstudie*: II, *Starkad den gamle og den yngre Skjoldungrække.* Copenhagen, 1910.
—. *Nogle Grundsætninger for Sagnforskning; efter forfatterens død udg. af Dansk Folkemindesamling ved Hans Ellekilde.* Danmarks Folkeminder 23. Copenhagen, 1921. Translated into English by Kirsten Wolf and Jody Jensen as *Principles for Oral Narrative Research.* Bloomington, 1992.
—. Review of Gudmund Schütte, *Oldsagn om Godtjod: bidrag til etnisk Kildeforsknings metode med særligt henblik på folk-stamsagn.* Copenhagen, 1907. *Folklore* 19 (1908), 353–59.
Olsen, Lars-Henrik. *Bjovulf: Et sagn fra Danmarks oldtid.* Copenhagen, 2002.
—. *Nordiske heltesagn.* 2nd ed. Viborg, 2005.
Osborn, Marijane. "Bruder's *Beowulf.* Ein heldisches Spiel." *Geardagum* 26 (2006), 5–52.
Óskarsson, Þórir. "From Romanticism to Realism." In Daisy Neijmann, ed. *A History of Icelandic Literature.* Lincoln and London, 2006. Pp. 251–307.
Paulli, R. "Andreas Bussæus." *DBL.* 3rd ed., 1979–84. https://biografiskleksikon.lex.dk/Andreas_Bussæus. Accessed 19 June 2020.
—. "Hans Gram – filolog." *DBL.* 3rd ed., 1979–84. https://biografiskleksikon.lex.dk/Hans_Gram_-_filolog. Accessed 17 June 2020.
Pedersen, Ole. *Nordiske guder og sagnhelte: Fortællinger.* Illustrated by Lene Hahne. Aarhus, 1986; 2nd ed., 2001.

Pedesern, Vibeke A. Indledning til "Bjovulfs Drape eller det Oldnordiske Heltedigt." http://www.grundtvigsværker.dk/tekstvisning/14379/0?keywords=Schaldemose#{%220%22:0,%22k%22:0}. Accessed 4 July 2023.

Pekonen, Osmo, and Clive Tolley. *Beowulf. Suomennos, johdanto ja selitykset.* Juva, 1999.

—. *Widsith: Anglosaksinen muinaisruno.* Jyväskylä, 2004.

Petersen, Carl S. "F. Rønning." *DBL.* 3rd ed., 1979–84. https://biografiskleksikon.lex.dk/F._Rønning. Accessed 13 June 2021.

Pons-Sanz, Sara M. *The Lexical Effects of Anglo-Scandinavian Linguistic Contact on Old English.* Studies in the Early Middle Ages 1. Turnhout, 2013.

Pope, John C. *The Rhythm of Beowulf: An Interpretation of the Normal and Hypermetric Verse Forms in Old English Poetry.* New Haven, 1942.

Porthan, Henrik Gabriel. "Försök at uplysa Konung Ælfreds Geographiska Beskrifning öfver den Európeiska Norden." *Kongl Vitterhets Historie och Antiquitets Academiens Handlingar* 6 (1800), 37–106.

Posselt, Gert. "Finnur Magnússon." *Den Store Danske.* https://denstoredanske.lex.dk/Finnur_Magnússon. Accessed 14 August 2023.

Pound, Ezra. "The Music of Beowulf." Unpublished manuscript, 1928. https://uw.digitalmappa.org/57. Accessed 17 July 2021.

Rausing, Gad. "*Beowulf, Ynglingatal* and the *Ynglinga saga.*" *Fornvännen* 80 (1985), 163–78.

Ringbom, Håkan. "Enkvist, Nils Erik." *Biografiskt lexikon för Finland.* https://www.blf.fi/artikel.php?id=8301. Accessed 7 August 2023.

Robinson, Orrin W. *Old English and its Closest Relatives: A Survey of the Earliest Germanic Languages.* Palo Alto, 1992.

Rooth, Erik. "Ernst Kock." *SBL.* https://sok.riksarkivet.se/sbl/Presentation.aspx?id=11698. Accessed 22 July 2022.

Rosenblad, Jes. "Ludvig Schrøder." *DBL.* 3rd ed., 1979–84. https://biografiskleksikon.lex.dk/Ludvig_Schrøder. Accessed 31 March 2023.

Ross, A. S. C., and E. G. Stanley. Review of Collinder, *Beowulf. EGS* 6 (1957), 110–12.

Rossel, Sven H. "From Romanticism to Realism." In Sven H. Rossel, ed. *A History of Danish Literature.* Lincoln and London, 1992. Pp. 187–91.

Rubow, Paul V. "Fr. Schaldemose." *DBL.* 3rd ed., 1979–84. https://biografiskleksikon.lex.dk/Fr._Schaldemose. Accessed 4 July 2023.

Rudelbach, Andreas Gottlob. Review of Grundtvig's *Phenix-Fuglen. Zeitschrift für Lutherische Theologie und Kirche,* vol. 2 (1842), 192f.

Rydahl, John. *Bjovulf: Den gamle dragedræber.* Illustrated by Gitte Skov. Frederiksberg, 2012.

Rytter, Henrik, trans. *Beowulf og striden om Finnsborg.* Oslo, 1929.

—, and Sigmund Skard, trans. *Den guddomlege komedien.* Oslo, 1965.

Råsled, Bengt. *Landet vädermark, Beowulfs Swiorice: utveckling i Beowulfs Swiorice och övriga Götland speglad genom historia, forntidsgeografi, folk-*

vandringar, internationella relationer, makt, samhällsutveckling och embryon till det blivande Sverige. Del. 2. Mjölby, 2014.

Rønning, Frederik. *Beovulfs-Kvadet: en literær-historisk undersøgelse*. Copenhagen, 1883.

—. "Den oldengelske digtning." *Historisk Månnedsskrift for Folkelig og Kirkelig Oplysning* 4 (1885), 1–36.

—. *N. F. S. Grundtvig: et bidrag til skildring af dansk åndsliv i det 19. Århundrede*, 4 vols. Copenhagen, 1907–14.

—. "N. F. S. Grundtvig og den oldengelske Litteratur." *Historisk månedsskrift for folkelig og Kirkelig oplysning* 4 (1885), 321–66; 5 (1885), 1–41; 129–87.

Sandred, Karl Inge. "Domesday Book 1086–1986." *Ortnamnssällskapets i Uppsala Årsskrift* (1986), 86–96.

—. "Wulfstans resa 800-talets slut." *Gutar och Vikingar*. Ed. Ingmar Jannson. Stockholm, 1983. Pp. 417–23.

Sandved, Arthur O., trans. *Canterbury-fortellingene: i utdrag*. Oslo, 2002.

—, trans. *Det gjenvundne paradis*. Oslo, 2005.

—, trans. *Det tapte paradis*. Oslo, 1993 and 2005.

—. "Drømmen om Kristi Kors: Et kristent dikt i før-kristen form." *Kirke og Kultur* 86 (1981), 203–12.

—, trans. *Joseph Andrews*. Oslo, 1999.

—, trans. *Julian av Norwich: Visjoner av Guds kjærlighet*. Oslo, 2000.

—, trans. *Kong Arthur og hans riddere utvalgte fortellinger*. Oslo, 2007.

—, trans. *Kong Henrik VI. Første, Annen, og Tedje del*. Oslo, 1996.

—, trans. *Kong Henrik VIII*. Oslo, 2013.

—, trans. *Kong Lear*. Oslo, 2013.

—, trans. *Peter Plogman*. Oslo, 1990.

—, trans. *Vers fra vest: Gammelengelske dikt it utvalg*. Oslo, 1987.

Schaldemose, Frederik. *Beo-Wulf og Scopes Widsið, to angelsaxiske Digte, med Oversættelse og oplysende Anmærkninger*. Copenhagen, 1847.

Schiern, Frederik E. "Om Navnet Lodbrog hos Angelsaxerne." *Annaler for Nordisk Oldkyndighed og Historie* 18 (1858), 8–11.

Schrøder, Ludvig. *N. F. S. Grundtvig: Den nordiska folkhögskolans fader: En levnadsskildring*. Translated into Swedish from the author's manuscript. Stockholm, 1900.

—. *Om Bjovulfs-Drapen: Efter en række Foredrag på Folkehøjskole i Askov*. Copenhagen, 1875.

Schultz, Sigurd. "Niels Skovgaard." *DBL*. 3rd ed., 1979–84. https://biografiskleksikon.lex.dk/Niels_Skovgaard. Accessed 5 July 2023.

Schumacher, Jan Henrik. "Drømmen om korset - og angelsaksisk spiritualitet." *Ung Teologi* 36.2 (2003), 73–89.

Schück, Henrik. *Folknamnet Geatas i den fornengelska dikten "Beowulf"*. Upsala Universitetets Årsskrift, program 2 (1907).

—. *Studier i Beowulfsagan*. Upsala Universitets Årsskrift, program M.M. (1909).
Schütte, Gudmund. *Oldsagn om Godtjod: bidrag til etnisk Kildeforsknings metode med særligt henblik på folk-stamsagn*. Copenhagen, 1907.
—. Review of Olrik, *The Heroic Legends of Denmark*. *SS* 6 (1920–21) 210–21.
—. "Tendensdigtning i Heltesagnet." *DS* 31 (1934), 145–65.
—. "Vidsid og Slægtssagnene om Hengest og Angantyr." *AfNF* 36 (1920), 1–32.
—. *Vor Folkegruppe Gottjod: de gotiske, tyske, nederlandske, angelsaxiske, frisiske og nordiske Stammer i etnologisk Fremstilling*. Copenhagen, 1926.
Shetelig, Haakon. *Det norske folks liv og historie gjennem tidene. I. Fra oldtiden til omkring 1000 e. kr.* Oslo, 1930.
Shippey, Thomas A. "Kemble, *Beowulf*, and the Schleswig-Holstein Question." In Alice Jorgensen et al., eds. *The Kemble Lectures on Anglo-Saxon Studies*. Dublin, 2009. Pp. 64–80.
—. *Laughing Shall I Die: Lives and Deaths of the Great Vikings*. London, 2018.
—, and Andreas Haarder, eds. *Beowulf: The Cultural Heritage*. London and New York, 1998.
Sjöberg, Karin. "Bringsværd, Tor Åge." *Författarlexikon*. https://www.alex.se/lexicon/article/bringsvard-tor-age. Accessed 16 July 2023.
Skovgaard-Petersen, Karen. "The Literary Feud between Denmark and Sweden in the Sixteenth and Seventeenth Centuries and the Development of Danish Historical Scholarship." In Jean R. Brink and William F. Gentrup, eds. *Renaissance Culture in Context: Theory and Practice*. Aldershot, Hants, England; Brookfield, VT, 1993. Pp. 114–20.
Skyum-Nielsen, Erik. "Nyoversættelsen af 'Beowulf' er en prægtig gave." *Information*, 23 December 2018.
Spaans, Ronny. "Henrik Rytter, 1877–1950." *Norsk Oversetterleksikon* https://www.oversetterleksikon.no/2017/05/18/henrik-rytter-1877-1950/. Accessed 20 July 2023.
Stanley, Eric G. *The Search for Anglo-Saxon Paganism*. Cambridge and Totowa, NJ, 1975.
Steager, Jeanne P., trans. "Epic Laws of Folk Narrative." In *The Study of Folklore*, ed. Alan Dundes. Englewood Cliffs, NJ, 1965. Pp. 129–41.
Steenstrup, Johannes C. H. R. "Harald Harefod og Hardeknud 1035–42." In *Det danske Folks Historie*, vol. 1. Copenhagen, 1927. Pp. 414–37.
—. "Nogle Studier fra Vikingetiden." *Historisk Tidsskrift udg af den Danske Historiske forening*, 9th ser., 3 (1925), 148–64.
—. *Normannerne*. Vol. 3. Copenhagen, 1882.
Stenroth, Ingmar. *Gudar eller människor: Den nordiska renässansen i svensk konst*. Stockholm, 2012.
Stephens, George. "The King of Birds; or, the Lay of the Phœnix: An Anglo-Saxon Song of the Tenth or Eleventh Century." *Archæologia* 30 (1844), 256–322.

Stevick, Robert D. "Mathematical Proportions and Symbolism in 'The Phoenix'." *Viator* 11 (1980), 95–121.
—. "The Form of *The Phoenix*: A Model of Its Number, Proportion, and Unity." In Robert L. Surles, ed., *Medieval Numerology: A Book of Essays*. New York and London, 1993. Pp. 39–52.
Stjerna, Knut. *Esssays on Questions connected with the Old English Poem of 'Beowulf.'* Trans. and ed. by John R. Clark Hall. Coventry, 1912; repr. 1970.
Stjernquist, Berta. "Birger Nerman." *SBL*. https://sok.riksarkivet.se/sbl/Presentation.aspx?id=8838. Accessed 10 July 2022.
Strand, Tor H. "Bøheringen Beowulfs Kongesaga i Nytt lys." *T. A. Kronikken* (1958).
—. "Heltediktet *Beowulf*." *Affenposten*. Oslo, 15 and 16 July 1953.
—. *Norrønafolket*. Oslo, 1956.
Suhm, P. F. *Symbolæ ad Literaturam Teutonicam Antiquorem*. Copenhagen, 1787.
Sundén, Karl F. *Den fornengelska dikten Widsið*. Göteborg, 1929.
—. Essay I. The predicational categories in English. Essay II. A category of predicational change in English. Uppsala, 1916.
Svionum, See Fast, Carl Otto.
Sørensen, Knud. "Torsten Dahl." https://auhist.au.dk/fileadmin/user_upload/Binder1-Torsten_Dahl_nekrolog.pdf. Accessed 13 August 2023.
Sørensen, Søren, A. *Det gamle Skirinssal. I. Stedets Beliggenhed*. Christiania, 1900.
—. "Om Skiringssal." *Norsk historisk Tidsskrift*. 4th ser., 5 (1909), 358–97.
von Sydow, Carl Vilhelm. "Beowulf och Bjarke." *SNF* 14.3 (1923), 1–46.
—. "Draken som skattevaktare." In *Festskrift till Evald Kristensen = Danmarks Folkeminder* 17 (1917), 103–15.
—. "Geografi och naturbeskrivning i Beowulfsången." *Forhandlingar vid Svenska Filolog. och Historikermötet i Göteborg den 19–21 Augusti 1912* (1913), 74–75.
—. "Grendel i anglosaxiska ortnamn." *NB* 2 (1914), 160–64.
—. "Hur mytforskningen tolkat Beowulfdikten," *Folkminnen och Folktankar* 11 (1924), 97–134.
—. "Scyld Scefing." *NB* 12 (1924), 63–95.
—. "Tors färd till Utgård. II. Skryme-episoden." *DS* 7 (1910), 145–81.
Tarkiainen, Kari. "Collinder, Björn." *Biografisk lexikon för Finland*. https://www.blf.fi/artikel.php?id=8303. Accessed 20 July 2023.
—. "Porthan, Henrik Gabriel." *Biografisk lexikon för Finland*. https://www.blf.fi/artikel.php?id=2599. Accessed 8 August 2023.
Thornbury, Emily V. *Becoming a Poet in Anglo-Saxon England*. Cambridge Studies in Medieval Literature 88. Cambridge, 2014.

Tiemroth, Jens Henrik. "Johannes Steenstrup." *DBL*. 3rd ed., 1979–84. https://denstoredanske.lex.dk/Johannes_Steenstrup. Accessed 10 August 2023.

Tjerneld, Andreas. "Sundén släkt." *SBL*. https://sok.riksarkivet.se/sbl/Presentation.aspx?id=34713. Accessed 25 February 2023.

Toldberg, Helge. "Grundtvig og de engelske Antikvarer." *Orbis Litterarum* 5 (1947), 258–311.

Tolley, Clive. English version of his "Introduction" to his and Pekonen's Finnish translation of *Beowulf*. Unpublished.

—. English version of his "Introduction" to his and Pekonen's Finnish translation of "Widsith." Unpublished.

—. "From Anglo-Saxon England to Modern Finland: Linguistic, Cultural and Poetic Challenges in Translating *Beowulf*." Unpublished lecture.

Tómasson, Sverrir. "'Iarlar árhvatir / iörð um gátu': þýðingar Benedikts Gröndals Sveinbjarnarsonar úr fornensku." In *Skorrdæla: gefin út í minningu Sveins Skorra Höskuldssonar*, ed. Sverrir Tómasson. Reykjavík, 2003. Pp. 179–86.

Torfadóttir, Jóna Guðbjörg. "Í orðastað Alfífu." *Skírnir* 178 (Spring 2004), 35–57.

Townend, Matthew. "Pre-Cnut Praise-Poetry in Viking Age England." *RES* 51 (2000), 349–70.

Tveitane, Mattias, "Vá Drottenn kann allar Tungur." *Maal og Minne* (1964), 106–12.

Unger, C. R. "Fragment af en allitereret angelsaxisk Homili, hvori nævnes nogle af Nordens hedenske Guddome." *Annaler for nordisk Oldkyndighed og Historie* (1846), 67–81.

Varila, Mari-Liisa. "Beowulf seurueineen. Nowell Codexin mysteeri." In Leila Koivunen and Janne Tunturi, eds. *Papyruksesta PDF: ään. Tutkielmia kirjan historiasta*. Turku, 2008. Pp. 25–40.

—. "Biography." https://research.utu.fi/converis/portal/detail/Person/1038293. Accessed 25 May 2023.

—. Personal email to Bjork received 25 May 2005.

Vasbo, Vibeke. Personal correspondence with Bjork 21 July 1992.

—. *The Song of Hild*. English translation of *Hildas sang* (1991) by Gaye Kynoch. Durham, 2018.

Vind, Ole. *Grundtvigs historiefilosofi*. Copenhagen, 1999.

Wadstein, Elis. "Ett engelskt fornminne från 700-talet och Englands dåtida kultur." *Nordisk Universitets-tidskrift* 1 (1900–01), 129–53.

Wasberg, Gunnar Christie. *Store norske leksikon*. https://snl.no/Curt_Weibull. Accessed 21 July 2022.

Wawn, Andrew. "Early Literature of the North." In Peter France and Kenneth Haynes, eds. *The Oxford History of Literary Translation in English*, vol. 4: 1790–1900. Oxford, 2006. Pp. 274–85.

—. *The Vikings and the Victorians: Inventing the Old North in 19th-Century Britain*. Cambridge, 2000.
Weibull, Curt. *Om det svenska och det danska rikets uppkomst*. Lund, 1921.
Weinreich, Torben. "Lars-Henrik Olsen." *Den Store Danske*. https://denstoredanske.lex.dk/Lars-Henrik_Olsen. Accessed 14 July 2023.
Wieselgren, Per. *Författarskapet till Eigla*. Lund, 1927.
—. "Tideräkningsfrågan i norsk niohundratalshistoria." *Historisk Tidskrift* 49 (1929), 35–66.
Wilmont, Barry. *Bjowulf: et heltedigt fra Danmarks sagntid*. With a foreword by Ebbe Kløvedal Reich. Copenhagen, 1983.
Worley, Will. "Robert Nye Dead: Poet and Novelist Dies, Aged 77." *The Independent*. 2 July 2016. https://www.independent.co.uk/news/people/poet-and-novelist-robert-nye-dies-aged-77-a7116231.html. Accessed 13 July 2023.
Wright, Charles D. *The Irish Tradition in Old English Literature*. Cambridge, 1993.
Zeruneith, Zeld. trans. *Beowulf: En gendigtning med efterskrift og noter*. Copenhagen, 2018.
—. *Beowulf: The Tragedy of a Hero: A Reading*. Translated into English from the author's Danish manuscript by Paul Russell Garrett. Sorø, 2023.
—. *De sidste tider: Hedenskab heroisme kristendom: en anglesaksisk overgangshistorie. Gendigtning ved Suzanne Brøgger*. Copenhagen, 2017.
Ørum, Henning, ed. *Kommentarer til oldengelsk poesi*. Intro. by Graham D. Caie. Copenhagen, 1979.

Acknowledgments

This book had its gestation in and has been through various stages of development since about 1993, when John D. Niles and the Old English Colloquium at UC Berkeley invited me to give a paper for their conference on Anglo-Saxonism scheduled for March 1994. I thank Jack for that invitation and for his and Allen J. Frantzen's including a more fully developed version of my paper in their *Anglo-Saxonism and the Construction of Social Identity* (1997). Several other individuals and institutions have supported my work on this book since my initial foray into the field it explores. I thank especially Liselotte Larsen, librarian of Grundtvig-Biblioteket at Vartov in Copenhagen, for helping me track down several references both in person and via email, Professor Emeritus James Massengale, UCLA, for help with Grundtvig's music, Sven H. Rossel, Universität Wien, and Maria-Claudia Tomany, St. Cloud State University, for scrutinizing parts of the text and offering a number of helpful suggestions for improving the translations in my chapter on the OE *Phoenix*, and Anders Christensen of Dansk Folkemindesamling in Copenhagen for help in identifying the sources for Grundtvig's melodies. A number of other friends and colleagues have come to my aid in various ways along the way: James Neel, Michael McVeigh, Clive Tolley, Simon Keynes, Vibeke Vasbo, Keld Zeruneith, Suzanne Brøgger, Johan Elsness, Catherine Saucier, Zachary Bush, Erik Hansen, Stephen Laker, John Ole Askedal, Mari-Liisa Varila, Rob Lloyd Jones, Johan Sandberg McGuinne, John Rydahl, Gitte Skov, Þóra Björnsson, Leena Saarinen, Andy Orchard, Marijane Osborn, Tom Shippey, and Caroline Palmer. The Interlibrary Loan department of the Hayden Library at Arizona State University has given me invaluable support at all stages of my work.

In addition to the above, I must thank the Manchester Cluster for Anglo-Saxon Studies; the Department of Anglo-Saxon, Norse, and Celtic, University of Cambridge; and Lady Margaret Hall, Oxford University; all had me give talks on the project in 1997 when I was a visiting scholar at St. Catharine's College, Cambridge, and I benefited from feedback in all three settings. The Manchester Cluster for Anglo-Saxon Studies also invited me back to talk about Grundtvig's work on *Brunanburh* and his Phoenix ballads for the Fifth G. L. Brook Symposium in 2001, and the Medieval Research Colloquium, University of California, Davis, had me present on Grundtvig's edition of the OE *Phoenix* itself in 2001 as well. In 2006, I gave the plenary address on aspects of the project for the annual meeting of the Viking Society for Northern Research, University College London, delivered the biannual Fell-Benedikz Lecture, University of Nottingham, on "Ballads, Brunanburh, and Grundtvig's *Beowulf*," and gave the plenary address on Grundtvig's translations from OE for the Rocky Mountain Medieval and Renaissance Association. In 2008, I delivered the plenary address on N. F. S. Grundtvig's appropriations of OE literature for the annual meeting of MEMESAK (the Medieval and Early Modern English Studies Association of Korea) at Yonsei University. Finally, in 2009 and 2016 respectively, I presented papers on Scandinavia and Old English Studies at the Burdick-Vary Symposium, University of Wisconsin–Madison, and the International Congress on Medieval Studies, Western Michigan University. All these public presentations of my ideas have helped give them focus.

To help me focus them even more, two institutions granted me funding for this project and two others (*Klaeber's Beowulf* [Toronto, 2008] and *The Oxford Dictionary of the Middle Ages* [Oxford, 2010]): the Institute for Advanced Study, Princeton, where I was in residence from 2004 to 2005, and the National Endowment for the Humanities, which awarded me a Senior Fellowship for the years 2006–07. More recently, Arizona State University granted me sabbatical leaves in 2012 and 2019 to conduct research on this and other scholarly endeavors, and funds from the ASU Foundation made possible the indexing and the open access publication of this volume. My gratitude goes to all four institutions.

Portions of this book have appeared earlier in different form, and I wish to thank the original publishers for permission to revise for inclusion here the essays they published: the University Press of Florida for "Nineteenth-Century Scandinavia and the Birth of Anglo-Saxon Studies" in Allen J. Frantzen and John D. Niles, eds., *Anglo-Saxonism and the Construction of Social Identity* (1997), pp. 111–32 (see chapter 1); and the University of Toronto Press for "N. F. S. Grundtvig's 1840 Edition of the Old English *Phoenix*: A Vision of a Vision of Paradise" in Katherine O'Brien O'Keeffe and Mark Amodio, eds., *Unlocking the Wordhord: Anglo-Saxon Studies in Memory of Edward B. Irving, Jr.* (2003), pp. 217–39 (see chapter 3).

Appendix A

A Bibliography of Contributions to Old English Studies in the Scandinavian Languages, Finnish, and Neo-Latin Written in Scandinavia to 2023

(A bibliography based on GR. Its format is that of GR's, and items not in GR are marked with asterisks.)

I. Introduction: Studies in English

Most of the work done on Scandinavian scholarship on OE has focused on N. F. S. Grundtvig:

1940: Kemp Malone, "Grundtvig's Philosophy of History," *Journal of the History of Ideas* 1, 210–11;

1941: —, "Grundtvig as *Beowulf* Critic," *RES* 17, 129–38;

1941: Franklin Cooley, "Grundtvig's First Translation from *Beowulf*," *SS* 16, 234–38 [reprint of Grundtvig's 1815 free-verse translation of lines 1–52];

1949: David J. Savage, "Grundtvig: A Stimulus to Old English Scholarship," *Philologica: The Malone Anniversary Studies*, ed. Thomas A. Birby and Henry B. Woolf (Baltimore), pp. 275–80 [GR 836];

1975: *Andreas Haarder, *Beowulf: The Appeal of a Poem* (Copenhagen);

1983: *—, "Grundtvig and the Old Norse Cultural Heritage," *N. F. S. Grundtvig: Tradition and Renewal*, ed. Christian Thodberg and Anders Pontoppidan Thyssen (Copenhagen), pp. 72–86 [partially on Grundtvig's 1820 translation of *Beowulf*];

1989/90: *S. A. J. Bradley, "Grundtvig, Anglo-Saxon Literature, and 'Ordets Kamp til Seier'," *GS* 41.1, 216–45;

Appendix A

1993: *Bent Noack, "Grundtvig and Anglo-Saxon Poetry," and S. A. J. Bradley, *"'The First New-European Literature': N. F. S. Grundtvig's Reception of Anglo-Saxon Literature," *Heritage and Prophecy: Grundtvig and the English-Speaking World*, ed. A. M. Allchin et al. (Aarhus), pp. 33–44 and 45–72, respectively;

1993: *Fred C. Robinson, *The Tomb of Beowulf and Other Essays on Old English* (Oxford), pp. 299–303 [on Grundtvig's OE poem about Beowulf preceding his 1861 edition of the poem];

1993: *S. A. J. Bradley, "Grundtvig's Palm Sunday 1867 and the Anglo-Saxon Descent into Hell," *GS* 44.1, 198–213;

1996: *—, "'Stridige Stykker snild jeg forbandt': Grundtvig's Creative Synthesis of Anglo-Saxon Sources," *GS* 47.1, 97–127;

1998: *—, *N. F. S. Grundtvig's Transcriptions of the Exeter Book* (Aarhus);

1999: *—, "The Recovery of England's 'skrinlagt fortid': A Progressive Report," *GS* 50.1, 138–61;

2000: *—, "Det er hvad jeg kalder at oversætte Digte: Grundtvig as Translator," *GS* 51.1, 36–59;

2002: *—, "Grundtvig's *Land of the Living* and Anglo-Saxon Scholarship," *GS* 53.1, 157–83;

2004: *—, "Before Irenaeus: The Making of Grundtvig the Medievalist," *GS* 55.1, 234–54;

2007: *Marijane Osborn and Bent Christensen, "'Skjöld': A Song by N. F. S. Grundtvig," *American Notes & Queries* 20.3, 35–43";

2016: *S. A. J. Bradley, "Grundtvig's *I Kveld*: Reflections of an Anglo-Saxonist," *GS* 67.1, 142–81.

Three other essays broaden or shift the focus:

1926: Gösta Langenfelt, "Swedish Explorers into Anglo-Saxon," *Scandinavian SSN* 9, 25–30 [on late nineteenth- and early twentieth-century scholars such as Axel Erdmann, Erik Björkman, and Eilert Ekwall];

1940: Franklin Cooley, "Early Danish Criticism of *Beowulf*," *ELH* 7, 45–67 [on Grímur Thorkelin, Grundtvig, Rasmus Rask];

1943: Frederik Gadde, "Viktor Rydberg and some *Beowulf* Questions," *Studia Neophilologica* 15, 71–90.

See also **ca. 1955:** *Jorge Luis Borges, "Thorkelin y el *Beowulf*" (translated into English by Joe Stadolnik as "Thorkelin y el *Beowulf* / Thorkelin and *Beowulf*," *PMLA* 132.2 [2017], 462–70) for a sympathetic view of Thorkelin as a tragic figure;

1967: *Hans Aarsleff, *The Study of Language in England 1780–1860* (Princeton; repr. Minneapolis, 1983), for observations on Grundtvig and Thorkelin;

1990: *Allen J. Frantzen's *Desire for Origins: New Language, Old English, and Teaching the Tradition* (New Brunswick and London) for intermittent commentary on Grundtvig and Rask;

1996: *Robert E. Bjork, "Grímur Jónsson Thorkelin's Preface to the First Edition of *Beowulf*, 1815," *SS* 68, 290–320 [Latin original of Preface with a facing-page translation by Taylor Corse and Bjork and an introduction and notes by Bjork];

1997: *—, "Nineteenth-Century Scandinavia and the Birth of Anglo-Saxon Studies," *Anglo-Saxonism and the Construction of Social Identity*, ed. Allen J. Frantzen and John D. Niles (Gainesville, FL), pp. 111–32 [on Hans Gram, Jacob Langebek, Erasmus Nyerup, Frederick Hammerich, Thorkelin, Ludvig Müller, George Stephens, Rask, Frederik Rønning, and Ludvig Schrøder] (revised and expanded as chapter 1 of this book);

1997: *—, "Digressions and Episodes," *A Beowulf Handbook*, ed. Robert E. Bjork and John D. Niles (Lincoln and London), esp. pp. 196–99 [on Langebek, Thorkelin, Grundtvig, Schrøder, and Pontus Fahlbeck];

1997: *Marijane Osborn, *"Translations, Versions, Illustrations," *A Beowulf Handbook*, esp. pp. 343–50;

1998: *T. A. Shippey and Andreas Haarder, eds., *Beowulf: The Critical Heritage* (New York) [translations of and commentary on Langebek, Thorkelin, Grundtvig, Gísli Brynjúlfsson, Schrøder, Guthbrandur Vigfússon, Rønning, and Axel Olrik];

2003: *Robert E. Bjork, "N. F. S. Grundtvig's 1840 Edition of the Old English *Phoenix*: A Vision of a Vision of Paradise," *Anglo-Saxon Studies in the New Millennium: Essays in Memory of Edward B. Irving, Jr.*, ed. Katherine O'Brien O'Keeffe and Mark Amodio (Toronto and Buffalo), pp. 217–39 (revised and expanded as chapter 3 of this book);

2008: *Magnús Fjalldal, "To Fall by Ambition – Grímur Thorkelín and his *Beowulf* Edition," *Neophilologus* 92, 321–32;

2012: *Pétur Knútson, "The Intimacy of *Bjólfskviða*," *Beowulf at Kalamazoo: Essays on Translation and Performance*, ed. Jana K. Schulman and Paul E. Szarmach (Kalamazoo), pp. 186–206;

2015: *John D. Niles, *The Idea of Anglo-Saxon England* (Oxford), pp. 204–15 [on Thorkelin and Grundtvig];

2018: *Lea Grosen Jørgensen, "Reconstructing the Past and the Poet: Grundtvig and the Anglo-Saxon Phoenix," *GS* 69, 17–35;

2020: *Kirsten Wolf, "Grímur Thorkelin, Rasmus Rask, and the Origins of Philology," *The Oxford Handbook of Victorian Medievalism*, ed. Joanne Parker and Corinna Wagner (Oxford), pp. 114–24;

2020–21: *Robert E. Bjork, "On N. F. S. Grundtvig's Becoming an Old English *Scop, Leoðwyrhta, Woðbora*, Poet," *GS* 71, 25–51.

II. General Bibliography

A. Bibliography

1977: *Bentzen, Ruth. *Et Udvalg af Bibliografiske Hjælpemidler til Studiet af Old- og Middelengelsk Litteratur* (Copenhagen).

B. Neo-Latin/Danish/Norwegian

COLLECTIONS IN OE

1772–86: Langebek, Jacobus. *Scriptores rerum danicarum medii ævi*, 6 vols. (Copenhagen). [Collection of documents relating to Denmark, Norway, and provinces: vol. 1, pp. 6–9, *Genealogy* from *A-S Chronicle*, "Langfeðgatal fra Noa til varra Konunga," p. 9, n. R, p. 44, n. E., and p. 2, table I [about Wanley]; vol. 2, pp. 106–23, "The Voyages of Ohthere and Wulfstan"; pp. 412–22, "Battle of Brunanburh"; vol. 5, pp. 1–231, miscellaneous OE material. Two later vols., by others, appeared in 1792 and 1834 and an index in 1878.] [GR 271]

1787: Suhm, Peter F. *Symbolæ ad Literaturam Teutonicam Antiquiorem ex Codicibus manu exaratis, qvi Havniæ asservantur*. Preface by Erasmus Nyerup

(Copenhagen). [Edition of "For an Unfruitful Land" and 4th West-Saxon Gospel from Junius's 1665 Dordrecht edition.] [GR 3957]

1835: Müller, Ludvig C. *Collectanea Anglo-Saxonica, maximam partem nunc primum edita et vocabulario illustrata* (Copenhagen; repr. Amsterdam, 1970). [Edition of Ælfric's "The Letter of Christ to Abgarus," the "Vindicta Salvatoris," Ælfric's homily "Dominica III in Quadragesima," "Maxims I," "Maxims II," "The Battle of Brunanburh," "The Battle of Maldon," *Riddles* 5 (shield) and 43 (book or Bible), and "Christ I," lines 1–29.] [GR 281]

Collections of Essays

1873–74: Munch, P. A. *Samlede Afhandlinger*, vols. 1 and 2 (Christiania). [Reprints a number of earlier articles touching marginally on several OE works: "Brunanburh," *Beowulf*, AS *Chronicle*, *Juliana*, "Widsith," Alfredian Bede and Orosius.] [GR 413]

Grammars with Readers

1817: Rask, Rasmus K. *Angelsaksisk Sproglære, tilligemed en kort Læsebog* (Stockholm). Trans. by Benjamin Thorpe as *A Grammar of the A-S Tongue, with a Praxis* (Copenhagen, 1830; 2nd ed. 1865; 3rd ed. 1879); Rvw: *Foreign Quarterly Review* II (1831) 227–28; *GM* 101, part I (1831) 240–42; [H. Wheaton] *NAR* 33 (1831) 325–50; 2nd ed. Rvw: *Ath* (1865[1]) 274 [GR 274]. [1st ed. omits Rask's dedicatory epistle to Johan Bülow, and 3rd ed. omits Rask's introduction. See Bjork, "Nineteenth-Century Scandinavia," in I. above.]

Historical, Linguistic, Cultural Studies

1751: *Gram, Hans. *Prove af Danske Ord og Talemaader af det Engel-Saxiske Sprog forklarede*. In *Det Københavnske Selskabs Skrifter* 5, 127–208. [Uses OE to elucidate 117 modern Danish words and expressions.]

1808: Grundtvig, N. F. S. *Nordens Mytologi, eller Udsigt over Eddalæren* (Copenhagen), 205 pp. Go to http://www.grundtvigsværker.dk/. Repr. 1818, pp. xxi, 177. [Numerous references to OE.] 2nd ed. as *Nordens Mytologi eller Sindbilled-Sprog, historisk poetisk undviklet og oplyst*, 1832, pp. xxiv, 635. 3rd ed.: 1869, pp. xxiv, 586. Repr. in *Udvalgte Skrifter* (Copenhagen, 1904), vol. 1, pp. 241–372. [GR 462]

1840: Munch, Peder A. *Nordens gamle Gude- og Helte-Sagn, i kortfattel Fremstillung* (Christiana). Translated into English by Sigurd B. Hustvedt as *Norse Mythology: Legends of Gods and Heroes* ... *In the revision of Magnus Olsen* (New York, 1926), pp. xvii, 392. [GR 466]

1862: *Jessen, C. A. E. *Undersøgelser til nordisk oldhistorie* (Copenhagen). [See esp. pp. 45 on "The Voyages of Ohthere and Wulfstan," 46–47 on Alcuin, 47–50 and 55 on *Beo*, 50–51 on "Widsith," and 51–55 on Bede.]

1876–82: Steenstrup, Johannes C. H. R. *Normannerne* (Copenhagen), 4 vols. [GR 6009]. [See esp. vols. 2 (1878) and 3 (1882).]

1909–12: Grønbech, Vilhelm. *Vor Folkeæt i Oldtiden* (Copenhagen), 4 vols. Rvw: A. Olrik *DS* (1909), 199–203 [vol. 1]; B. Kahle *EStn* 43 (1909), 428–32 [vol. 1]; S. Larsen *Tilskueren* (1910), 231–44 [vol. 1]; E. Ekwall *Beibl* 31 (1920), 1–9; L. M. Hollander *JEGP* 9 (1910), 269–78, and 14 (1915), 124–35; G. Neckel *EStn* 47 (1913–14), 108–16. Translated into English by William Worster as *The Culture of the Teutons* (Oxford, 1932). 2 vols. Rvw: T. B. *Folklore* 43 (1932), 442; *TLS* (26 May 1932), 393. *Translated into German by Ellen Hoffmeyer as *Kultur und Religionen der Germanen* (Darmstadt, 1937–39), 2 vols. [GR 490]

1927: La Cour, Vilhelm. "Vort Folks Oprindelse og ældste Historie." *Det danske Folks Historie: Skrevet af danske Historikere*, vol. 1 (Copenhagen), pp. 263–354, esp. pp. 276–327. [GR 498]

1927: Steenstrup, Johannes C. H. R. "Det danske Folk i Vikingetiden og Danevældens Tidesalder." *Det danske Folks Historie: Skrevet af danske Historikere*, vol. 1 (Copenhagen), pp. 357–439. See esp. "Harald Harefod og Hardeknud (1035–1042). Danevældens Ophør. Betydningen for England af de Danskes Bosættelse og Styrelse," pp. 432–37. [GR 6055]

1967: *Lund, Niels. *De danske vikinger i England: Røvere og bønder* (Copenhagen).

1973: *Birkeli, Fridtjov. *Norske steinkors i tidlig middelalder: et bidrag til belysning av overgangen fra norrøn religion til kristendom*. Det Norske Videnskaps-Akademi i Oslo, II. hist.-filos. Klasse n.s. 10. (Oslo). [References to stone crosses in the British Isles throughout.]

1974: *—. "Norske steinkors i tidlig middelalder," *Historisk Tidsskrift* (Oslo), 53, 183–84.

1974: *Johnsen, Ingrid Sanness. "Den runologiske plassering av innskriften fra Caistor-by-Norwich." *AfNF* 89, 30–43. [Includes an English summary, pp. 41–43.]

Appendix A

1975: *Johnsen, Arne Odd. "Om misjonsbiskopen Grimkellus," *Historisk Tidsskrift* (Oslo) 54, 22–34. [Includes an English summary, pp. 33–34.]

1976: *Kroman, Erik. *Det Danske Rige i den Ældre Vikingetid* (Copenhagen). [Discussion of AS historical sources, pp. 36–41. Includes an English summary.]

1976: *Moltke, Erik. *Runerne i Danmark og deres Oprindelse* (Copenhagen). Rvw: E. Antonsen *JEGP* 77 (1978) 308–09. [References to AS futhark and to numerous runic inscriptions in England.]

1977: *Pollestad, Kjell Arild. "St. Svithun, Stavangers Vernehelgen." *St. Olav: Katolsk Tidsskrift for Religion og Kultur* 89.2–3, 5–6.

1980: *Antonsen, Elmer H. "Den ældre fuþark: en gudernes gave eller et hverdagsalfabet?" *Maal og Minne*, 129–43.

1980: *Kisbye, Torben. "De danske stednavne i England." *Maal & Maele* 2, 6–15.

1981: *Westergaard, Kai-Erik. *Skrifttegn og symboler: noen studier over tegnformer i det eldre runealfabet*. Osloer Beiträge zur Germanistik 6 (Oslo). Rvw: E. Antonsen *JEGP* 83 (1984), 100–03; J. Knirk *SS* 56 (1984), 397–98.

1987: *Hødnebø, Finn. "Hvem var de første vikinger?" *Maal og Minne*, 1–16. [OE sources for the word "viking" discussed, pp. 3–5.]

1997: *Lund, Niels. *De hærger og de brænder: Danmark og England i Vikingetiden*, 2nd ed. (Copenhagen). Rvw 1st ed.: R. Malmros *Historisk Tidsskrift* 94.2 (1994), 405–06; E. Roesdahl *Historie/Jysk Samlinger* (1994 – 2), 139–41.

2004: *Grønvik, Ottar. "Ordet norr. víkingr m. – et tidlig lån fra anglofrisisk område?" *AfNF*, 119, 5–15. [On OE *wīcian, wīcing*.]

2009: *McGuire, Brian Patrick. *Da Himmelen kom nærmere: Fortællinger om Danmarks kristning 700-1300*. 2nd ed. (Copenhagen). [Chapter 2 on Beowulf and Grendel, pp. 40–52, and chapter 3 on Alcuin and Willibrord, pp. 54–67.]

Scholars and Scholarship

1885: Rønning, F. "N. F. S. Grundtvig og den oldengelske literatur." *Historisk Månnedsskrift for Folkelig og Kirkelig Oplysning* 4, 321–66. [GR

813] [On the Grundtvig-Thorkelin debate; Grundtvig and Rask; and Grundtvig's first trip to England.]

1885: *—. "N. F. S. Grundtvig og den oldengelske literatur." *Historisk Månnedsskrift for Folkelig og Kirkelig Oplysning* 5, 1–41. [On Grundtvig's second trip to England.]

1885: *—. "N. F. S. Grundtvig og den oldengelske literatur." *Historisk Månnedsskrift for Folkelig og Kirkelig Oplysning* 5, 129–87. [On Grundtvig's third trip to England.]

1932: Bang, Jacop P. *Grundtvig og England. Studier over Grundtvig* (Copenhagen). Rvw: H. J. *NTVKI* (1933), 246–47. [GR 822]

1990: *Schjørring, Jens Holger. "Grundtvig og den oldengelske digtning." In *Grundtvigs billedsprog og den kirkelige anskuelse* (Frederiksberg), pp. 113–38.

1992: *Grell, Helge. *England og Grundtvig. Grundtvigs møde med England og dets betydning for hans forfatterskab* (Aarhus).

OE POETRY: SURVEYS, CRITICAL ANALYSES

1885: Rønning, F. "Den oldengelske digtning." *Historisk Månnedsskrift for Folkelig og Kirkelig Oplysning* 4, 1–36. [Brief survey of OE poetry (pp. 1–7) followed by an assessment of OE poetic characteristics (pp. 7–19) and a translation of *Judith* (pp. 19–36)] [GR 882]

1901: *Hansen, Adolf. "Oldengelsk Litteratur." In *Illustreret Verdens-Litteraturhistorie*, vol. 3 (Copenhagen), pp. 5–19.

1979: *Ørum, Henning, ed. *Kommentarer til oldengelsk poesi*. Intro. by Graham D. Caie (Copenhagen). 187 pp. [Danish and English linguistic and literary commentary on "The Finnsburg Episode," "The Wanderer," "The Seafarer," "The Battle of Brunanburh," "Deor," *The Phoenix*, "The Dream of the Rood."]

2017: *Zeruneith, Keld. *De sidste tider: hedenskab heroisme kristendom: en angelsaksisk overgangshistorie* (Copenhagen). [Focusing on *Beowulf*, Zeruneith treats OE literature as transitional between heathendom and Christianity.] Rvws: Mikkel Bruun Zangenberg, *Weekendavisen*, 17 November 2017, p. 7; Bo Tao Michaëlis, *Politiken*, 2 December 2017, p. 13; Erik Skyum-Nielsen, *Information*, 6 January 2018, p. 9; Mark Bradshaw Busbee, *Dansk Kirketidende*, 170 (June 2018), pp. 18–19.

OE Poetry: Studies of Themes and Topics

1873: Hammerich, Frederik. *De episk-kristelige Oldquad hos de gothiske Folk* (Copenhagen). Rvw: G. L. *LitZbl* 26 (1875), 257–59; E. Wilken *GgA* (1875), 1438–40. [Contains text and alliterative verse translation of "The Dream of the Rood," pp. 15–20, a translation of "The Grave," pp. 92–93, and selected translations from "Cædmon's Hymn," "The Ruthwell Cross," *Genesis A and B*, *Exodus, Daniel, Christ and Satan, Judith, Christ I, Andreas, Guthlac B, The Phoenix*, "Soul and Body II," "The Wife's Lament," and "The Meters of Boethius" interspersed throughout a discussion of the poems, pp. 13–91] [GR 919]

1903: *Larsen, Henry. *Krist og Satan: nogle Blade af gammel kristelig digtning særlig hos Angelsakserne (Cædmon)* (Copenhagen). In *Skrifter til Oplysning og Opbyggelse* IV 5–6 H. Rvw: August Kristensen, *Højskolebladet* 1 (1904), 50–55. [Contains alliterative verse translations of "Cædmon's Hymn," pp. 94–95, large sections of *Genesis A* and *Genesis B* to the birth of Cain and Abel interspersed throughout a discussion of the poems, pp. 102–34, "Christ and Satan," pp. 135–66, "The Ruthwell Cross," pp. 168–69, and "The Dream of the Rood" to line 68a, pp. 172–76]

1912: Schütte, Gudmund. "De ældste gottoniske Sagnhelte," *DS* 9, 174–83. [GR 974]

1979: *Haarder, Andreas. *Det episke liv. Et indblick i oldengelsk heltedigtning* (Copenhagen; e-book 2022). Rvws: Lundgreen-Nielsen, *DS* (1980), 158–60.

1982: *Neumann, Hans. *Olgerdiget – et bidrag til Danmarks tidligste historie* (Haderslev). [See pp. 123–25]

1998: *Bøye, Merete. "Hallen og havet som eskatologiske modsætninger i den angelsaksiske poesie og hos Grundtvig," *GS*, 120–41.

OE Poetry: Prosodic Studies

1863: Jessen, Edward. "Oldnordisk og oldtysk Verselag," *TfPP* 4, 249–92, esp. 278–83. [GR 1261]

Individual Texts, Authors, Genres

Battle of Brunanburh: Studies

1817: Grundtvig, N. F. S. "Om Bruneborg-Slaget og et Riim i den Anledning," *Dannevirke* 2, 65–96. Go to http://www.grundtvigsværker.dk/. [GR 1487. Pp. incorrectly noted as 65–79]

1907: Olrik, Axel. *Nordisk Aandsliv i Vikingetid og tidlig Middelalder* (Copenhagen). See p. 77. German trans by William Ranisch as *Nordisches Geistesleben in heidnischer und frühchristlicher Zeit* (Heidelberg, 1908). 2nd ed.: rev. by Hans Ellekilde, 1927; English trans by Jacob W. Hartmann and H. A. Larsen as *Viking Civilization* (New York, 1930; repr. 1971). See p. 151. [GR 1916]

"The Battle of Maldon": Studies

1892-93: Jespersen, Otto. "Små randnoter til engelske texter." *NTfF* ser. 3, 1, 126–30. [GR 1570]

"The Dream of the Rood": Studies

1903: *Larsen, Henry. *Krist og Satan: nogle Blade af gammel kristelig digtning særlig hos Angelsakserne (Cædmon)* (Copenhagen). In *Skrifter til Oplysning og Opbyggelse* IV 5–6 H. [Contains alliterative verse translation of "The Dream of the Rood," pp.172–76.]

1981: *Sandved, Arthur O. "Drømmen om Kristi Kors, et kristent dikt i før-kristen form." *Kirke og Kultur* 86, 203–12. [Contains a metrical prose translation, pp. 209–12]

2003: *Schumacher, Jan Henrik. "Drømmen om korset - og angelsaksisk spiritualitet." *Ung Teologi* 36.2, 73–89. [Includes Arthur O. Sandved's translation of the poem.]

Genesis A and B: Study and Translation

1903: *Larsen, Henry. *Krist og Satan: nogle Blade af gammel kristelig digtning særlig hos Angelsakserne (Cædmon)* (Copenhagen). In *Skrifter til Oplysning og Opbyggelse* IV 5–6 H. [Contains alliterative verse translations of "Cædmon's Hymn," pp. 94–95, large sections of *Genesis A* and *Genesis B* interspersed throughout a discussion of the poems, pp. 102–66, 172–76.]

Appendix A

JUDITH: TRANSLATION

1885: Rønning, F. "Den oldengelske digtning." *Historisk Månnedsskrift for Folkelig og Kirkelig Oplysning* 4, 19–36. [Brief survey of OE poetry (pp. 1–7) followed by an assessment of OE poetic characteristics (pp. 7–19) and a translation of *Judith* (pp. 19–36).] [GR 882]

THE PHOENIX: EDITION AND TRANSLATION

1840: Grundtvig, N. F. S. *Phenix-Fuglen: et Angelsachsisk Kvad* (Copenhagen), 71 pp. Go to http://www.grundtvigsværker.dk/. [First edition of *The Phoenix* containing Lactantius's "De Ave Phoenice" running below the text and a free-verse translation after it, pp. 44–63, followed by a "Dansk Efterklang," a verse rumination on the poem, pp. 63–70, and "Jeg gik mig ud en Sommerdag," a poem inspired by the OE poem, pp. 70–71. For an analysis of the edition, see Bjork 2003 in I above.] [GR 4017]

THE RUTHWELL CROSS: STUDIES AND TRANSLATIONS

1836–37: Magnusen, Finn. "Om Obelisken i Ruthwell og om de Angelsaxiske Runer." *Annaler for nordisk Oldkyndighed* 1, 243–337. [GR 4240]

1903: *Larsen, Henry. *Krist og Satan: nogle Blade af gammel kristelig digtning særlig hos Angelsakserne (Cædmon)* (Copenhagen). In *Skrifter til Oplysning og Opbyggelse* IV 5–6 H. [Contains alliterative verse translation of "The Ruthwell Cross," pp. 168–69.]

WULF AND EADWACER:

1917: Larsen, Henning. "Sigrdrífa-Brynhild." *SSN* 4, 65–73 [See p. 67.] [GR 5128]

WIDSITH:

1862: *Jessen, C. A. E. *Undersøgelser til nordisk oldhistorie* (Copenhagen), pp. 50–51.

1903: Olrik, Axel *Danmarks Heltedigtning, en oldtidsstudie:* I. *Rolf Krake og den ældre Skjoldungrække* (Copenhagen), 352 pp. Rvw: R. C. Boer *Museum* 11 (1903), 102–06; W. Golther *LGRPh* 28 (1907), 8–9; A. Heusler *AfdA* 30 (1906), 26–36; E. Mogk *Zeitschrift für Volkskunde* 14 (1904), 250–52; K Mortenen *NTVKI* (1903), 410–14; L. Pineau *Rev crit* 56 (1903), 487–88; W. Ranisch *AfNF* 21 (1905), 276–80.[GR 1891]. Translated into English and revised in collaboration with the author by Lee M. Hollander, as *The Heroic Legends of Denmark* (New York, 1919), pp. xviii, 530. Rvw: G. T. Flom *JEGP* 19 (1920), 284–90; A. F. Major *YBVS* 6–16 (1914–24), 66–68; W. E. Mead *Nation* 110 (1920), 520–21; G. Schütte *SS* 6 (1920–21), 210–21. [Sixteen mentions of "Widsith"]

1911: Boer, R. C. "Om Hervararsaga." *Aarbøger for nordisk Oldkyndighed og Historie* 3, 1–80, esp. pp. 38–62, 69–74. ["Widsith" is mentioned on pp. 39–44, 46, 55, 58, 61, 65, 69.] [GR 5001]

1920: Schütte, Gudmund. "Vidsid og Slægtssagnene om Hengest og Angyntyr." *AfNF* 36, 1–32. [GR 5023]

1926: Schütte, Gudmund. *Vor Folkegruppe Gottjod: de gotiske, tyske, nederlandske, angelsaxiske, frisiske og nordiske Stammer i etnologisk Fremstilling* (Copenhagen), vol. 1, 299 pp. Rvw: G. Indrebö *Zeitschrift für Ortsnamenforschung* 8 (1932), 175–76; R. Much *AfdA* 47 (1928) 160–66; M. Schönfeld *APS* 3 (1928) 86–89, vol. 2 in typescript. English trans. by Jean Young, *Our Forefathers, the Gothonic Nations: A Manual of the Ethnography of the Gothic, German, Dutch, A-S, Frisian and Scandinavian Peoples*, 2 vols. (Cambridge, 1929–33), 483. [See esp. sections 214–25.] Rvw: S. B. *NTVKI* 12 (1936), 409–10; W. E. Collinson *MLR* 25 (1930), 231–34; F. C. Dauchin *LanM* 28 (1930), 281; E. Ekwall *Antiquity* 4 (1930), 527–28; G. T. Flom *JEGP* 33 (1934), 571–76; S. Gutenbrunner *AfdA* 54 (1935) 95–97; A. G. van Hamel *Museum* 41 (1934), 157–59; G. Knudsen *DS* 31 (1934), 84–88; K. Malone *MLN* 50 (1935), 106–08; A. Mawer *EHR* 45 (1930), 641–42; F. Mossé *Rev germ* 22 (1931), 194–95, and ibid. 25 (1934), 247–48; G. Neckel *DLitztg* 55 (1934), 268–71; F. R. Schröder *GRM* 22 (1934), 66; M. S. S[erjeantson] *SBVS* 11 (1928–36), 103–05; *TLS* (22 Aug. 1929), 644. [GR 2080]

1925: Steenstrup, Johannes C. H. R. "Nogle Studier fra Vikingetiden," *Dansk Historisk Tidsskrift*, 9th ser., 3, 148–64, esp. pp. 156–57. [GR 5031] [On the names *Lidwicingum* and *Wicingum* in the poem]

1934: Schütte, Gudmund. "Tendensdigtning i Heltesagnet." *DS* 31, 145–65. [Comments on *Beowulf* and "Widsith."] [GR 2150]

1958: *Schyman, Iwan. "Widsith" in *Värmlandsnäs från forntid till nutid*, vol. 2, *Norra delen*, pp. 49–50 (Säffle)

1978: *Skovgaard-Petersen, Inge. "Widsith og Uffesagnet." In *Danmarks historie*, ed. Aksel E. Christensen, et al. vol 1, pp. 29–31 (Copenhagen)

Appendix A

1982: *Neumann, Hans. *Olgerdiget – et bidrag til Danmarks tidligste historie* (Haderslev). [See pp. 118–22.]

ÆLFRIC: GENERAL

1964: Tveitane, Mattias. "Vá Drottenn kann allar Tungur," *Maal og Minne*, 106–12. [Skeat no. 13; Thorpe no 36, lines 14–15.] [GR 5207]

Orosius' HISTORIA: VOYAGES OF OHTHERE AND WULFSTAN: EDITIONS

1800: Porthan, Henrik Gabriel. "Försök at uplysa Konung Ælfreds Geographiska Beskrifning öfver den Európeiska Norden." *Kongl Vitterhets Historie och Antiquitets Academiens Handlingar* 6, 37–106. [Text of "The Voyages of Ohthere and Wulfstan" from Barrington's *The Anglo-Saxon from the Historian Orosius by Ælfred the Great* together with a translation in parallel columns, introduction, and notes.] [GR 5660]

1815: Rask, Rasmus. "Ottars og Ulfstens korte Rejseberetninger med dansk Overesættelse, kritiske Anmerkninger og andre Oplysninger." *Det Skandinaviske Litteraturselskabs Skrifter* 11, 1–132. Printed separately, Copenhagen 1816, pp. [iv], 132, and repr. in his *Samlede tildels forhen utrykte Afhandlinger* I (Copenhagen, 1834), ed. H. K. Rask, pp. 289–382. [GR 5665]

Orosius' HISTORIA: STUDIES

1803: Nyerup, Rasmus. *Historisk statistisk Skildring af Tilstanden i Danmark og Norge i ældere og nyere Tider*, 1 (Copenhagen), pp. 32–37. [GR 5661]

1819: Grundtvig, N. F. S. "Sciringesheal," *Dannevirke* 4, 187–92. Go to http://www.grundtvigsværker.dk/ [GR 5666]

1837: Brømel, A. "Om Norges Fiskerier i Fortiden," *Urda* 1, 119–32. [GR 5669]

1842: —. "Inledning til en historisk Fremstilling af Forfædrenes Vikinge- og Søtoge," *Urda* 2, 301–21, esp. 310–11. [GR 5670]

1862: Jessen, Edward. "Verdenshjönernes navne i sagaerne," *TfPP* 3, 113–16. [GR 5605]

1862: *—. *Undersøgelser til nordisk oldhistorie* (Copenhagen). [See esp. p. 45 on "The Voyages of Ohthere and Wulfstan."]

Appendix A

1889–90: Steenstrup, Japetus J. S. "Nogle Bemærkninger om Ottar's Beretning til Kong Alfred om Hvalros- og Hvalfangst i Nordhavet paa hans tid." *Danske Historisk Tidsskrift.* ser. 6, 2, 95–110. [GR 5676]

1898: *Bugge, Alexander. "Vore forfædres opdagelsesreiser i polaregnene." *Kungsjaa* 11, 497–509. [Contains a summary of Ohthere's voyage, pp. 497–98. Translated into Icelandic and emended by Jón Jónsson, "Landaleitir formanna i Norðurhöfum," *Tímarit hins íslenzka bókmenntafélags* 23 (1902), 138–57.]

1900: Sørensen, Søren, A. *Det gamle Skirinssal*: I. *Stedets Beliggenhed* (Christiania). [GR 5679]

1909: Kjær, A. "Hvad var Skíringssalr?" *Norsk historisk Tidsskrift*, 4th ser., 5, 267–83. [GR 5686]

1909: Sørensen, S. A. "Om Skiringssal," *Norsk historisk Tidsskrift*, 4th ser., 5, 358–97. [GR 5688]

1911: Nansen, Fridtjof. *Nord i Tåkeheimen. Utforskningen av jordens nordlige strøk i tidlige tider* (Copenhagen), pp. vii, 603. [Translated into English by Arthur G. Chater as *In Northern Mists: Arctic Explorations in Early Times* (New York, 1911), 2 vols. See esp. vol. 1, pp. 169–81, in chapter titled "The Awakening of Mediæval Knowledge of the North."] [GR 5690]

1911: Nielsen, Y. *Det halve Kongerige. Over Nordland og Finnmarken til Boris Gleb* (Christiania). [GR 5691] [Brief mention of the voyage of Ohthere in Orosius.]

1916–17: Neuhaus, Johannes. "Sillende=vetus patria=Angel, i Angelsaksernes og Oldsaksernes Mund Navnet på det gamle Hjemland." *NTfF*, 4th ser. 5, 125–26. [GR 5694]

1920–21: Jónsson, Finner et al *Konungs skuggsjá. Speculum regale.* Udgivet efter håndskrifterne af det Kongelige Nordiske Oldskriftselskab, 2 vols. (Copenhagen). See vol. 2, p. 112. [Note on *horschwælum* by O. Nordgård.] [GR 5696]

1930: Shetelig, Haakon. *Det norske folks liv og historie gjennem tidene. I. Fra oldtiden til omkring 1000 e. kr.* (Oslo). [See pp. 250–54 for a retelling and discussion of Ohthere's voyage. Alfred the Great is also mentioned on pp. 180 and 192, *Beowulf* on pp. 155 and 163, and Brunanburh on pp. 345 and 357.] [GR 5706]

Appendix A

1932: Larson, Sofus. *Jomsborg, dens Beliggenhed og Historie* (Copenhagen). [See esp. pp. 8–10, 14–15, 51.] [GR 5708]

1963: *Ilsøe, Harald. *Udlændinges rejser i Danmark indtil år 1700* (Copenhagen). [Annotated bibliography, pp. 1–6.]

1969: *Christensen, Aksel E. *Vikingetidens Danmark på oldhistorisk baggrund* (Copenhagen). [See pp. 27–28, 197.]

1971: *Anonymous. *Stednavne i tekster* (Copenhagen). [See pp. 17–18.]

1979: *Nyberg, Tore. *Skt. Peters efterfølgere i brydningstider. Omkring Pavedømmets historie, Rom og Nordeuropa 750-1200* (Odense). [See pp. 94–95.]

1982: *Neumann, Hans. *Olgerdiget – et bidrag til Danmarks tidligste historie* (Haderslev). [See pp. 126–27.]

1985: *Jørgensen, Ove. *Alfred den Store. Danmarks geografi. En undersøgelse at fire afsnit i Den gamle engelske Orosius* (Odense). Rvw: N. Lund, *Historisk Tidsskrift* 88.2 (1988), 410–11.

ANGLO-SAXON CHRONICLE: STUDIES

1916: Brynildsen, R. K. "Om tidsregningen i Olav den Helliges Historie." *Avhandlinger fra Universitetets Historiske Seminar* Utgit av Halvdan Koht 2.2 (Kristiania), 37–120, esp. chapter 7 (Olav i England 1009–1012), pp. 66–73, 80. [GR 6039]

1950: *Hald, Kristian. *Vore Stednavne* (Copenhagen). [Æthelweard's *Chronicle* mentioned, p. 202.]

C. *Swedish*

COLLECTIONS IN OE

1857: Nilsson, Lars Gabriel. *Några fornengelska andeliga quäden på grundspråket. Med svensk öfversättning och åtföljande glossarium* (Lund). [Sampling of texts of hymns and prayers from *E. Thomson's *Godcunde Lár & Theówdóm: Select Monuments of the Doctrine and Worship of the Catholic Church in England before the Norman Conquest: Consisting of Ælfric's Paschal Homily and Extracts from his Epistles, etc., the Offices of the Canonical Hours, and 3 Metrical Prayers and Hymns. In Anglo-Saxon and partly in Latin* (London,

1849), pp. 121–31, 134–40, 142–52, 212, and 216–25 with facing-page translation, notes, and glossary.] [GR 291]

1866 & 1870: —. *Anglosaxisk (fornengelsk) grammatika*, part 1 (Copenhagen), pp. 1–48, part 2 (Copenhagen, 1870), pp. 49–121. [Contains free translations of "Cædmon's Hymn," pp. 10–11, and *Beowulf*, lines 407–18 and 473–79, pp. 14–15.]

1871: —. *Anglosaxisk (fornengelsk) läsebok för Nybegynnare* (Lund). [Contains selections from the New Testament and *Judith*, lines 15–46a, with a new Swedish translation, pp. 12–14.] [GR 299]

1872: —. *Anglosaxisk läsebok* (Lund). [Contains selections from the New Testament and *Judith*, lines 15–46a, with a new Swedish translation, pp. 12–14.]

HISTORICAL, LINGUISTIC, CULTURAL STUDIES

1886–89: Rydberg, Viktor. *Undersökningar i germanisk mytologi* (Stockholm). Rvw: F Detter *AfNF* 6 (1890), 108–12; E. H. Meyer *AfdA* 14 (1888), 55–70, and 17 (1891), 265–69. English trans. by Rasmus B. Anderson as *Teutonic Mythology* (London, 1889). Rvw: *Ath* (1889[II]), 121–22; *Nation* 49 (1889) 357. [GR 477]

1980: *Ambrosiani, Kristina. "Spår av Nordiska bosättningar under Vikingatiden på de Brittiska öarna," *NTVKI* 56, 282–88.

1980: *Hellberg, Staffan. "Vikingatidens víkingar," *AfNF* 95, 25–88.

1982: *Ambrosiani, Kristina. "Vikingatida kammar i öst og väst: ett diskussionsinlägg," *Fornvännen* 77, 180–83. [Mentions Southampton, p. 182.]

1982: *Hellberg, Staffan. "Viking 'härnad, röveri': en kommentar," *Gardar* 13, 71–73. [Includes an English summary, p. 73.]

1990: *Sandred, Karl Inge. "Det anglosaxiska London i ny belysning," *Ortnamnssällskapets i Uppsala Årsskrift*, 63–69. [Includes an English summary, p. 69.]

1996: *Andersson, Thorsten. "Götar." In *Från götarna till Noreens kor. Hyllningsskrift till Lennart Elmevik på 60-årsdagen 2 februari 1996*, ed. Eva Brylla, Svante Strandberg, and Mats Wahlberg (Uppsala).

Appendix A

OE Poetry: Comprehensive Discussions

1923: Kock, Ernst A. "Notationes Norroenæ Anteckningar till Edda och Skaldediktning." *LUÅ* n.s. 1:19, no. 2, 1–107. [GR 896]. [Eighteen articles in which OE poems are frequently cited to illuminate passages in Eddic and Skaldic verse.]

OE Poetry: Themes and Topics

1903: Schück, Henrik. "Sigurdsristningar." *NTVKI*, 193–225. [GR 949] [Allusions to *Beowulf*, *Deor*, Franks Casket.]

1978: *Lönnroth, Lars. *Den dubbla Scenen: Muntlig diktning från Eddan till ABBA*, 2nd ed., Stockholm, 2008). See pp. 31–32 and 65–66 on *Beowulf*. Rvws: Peter Hallberg, *Samlaren* 100 (1979), 328–34; Hans Kuhn, *SS* 53.4 (1981), 475–79.

2017: *—. *Det germanska spåret. En västerländsk litteraturtradition från Tacitus till Tolkien*. (Stockholm), pp. 34–42 on OE poetry other than *Beowulf* and 43–52 on *Beowulf*. Rvws: J. Wickström, *Historisk Tidskrift* 138 (2018), 350–52; Mikael Males, *Samlaren* 139 (2018), 316–17.

OE Poetry: Textual Criticism

1891: Erdmann, Axel. "Bidrag till Ini-stammarnes historia i fornnordiskan." *AfNF* 7, 75–85. [GR 1081] [Contains a note on pp. 77–78 dealing with *ealdorlege*, Guthlac 1234; *feorhlege*, Elene 458, *Beowulf* 2800; *aldorlege*, Daniel 139.]

OE Poetry: Style and Language

1917: Kock, Ernst. "Domen över död man," *AfNF* 33, 175–77. [GR 1167] [On certain stylistic parallels in *Beowulf*, *Exodus*, *Judith*.]

1922: —. *Fornjermansk Forskning*. *LUÅ* n.s. 1, 18, no 1. [GR 1170] [On parallels in poetic style and diction between OE and other Germanic literatures.]

1929: —. "Asyndetiska adjectivattribut i fornjermansk diktning," In *Studier tillägnade Axel Kock* = *AfNF* 40, 190–93. [GR 1177]

Prosodic Studies

1915: Högberg, J. E. *Metriske Studier i forngermansk Alliterationspoesie* (Lund), 31 pp. [GR 1318]

Appendix A

INDIVIDUAL TEXTS, AUTHORS, GENRES

BRUNANBURH: STUDIES

1922: Kock, Ernst. *Fornjermansk Forskning. LUÅ* n.s. 1, 18, no. 1. [GR 1170] [on lines 55–56].

1927: Wieselgren, Per. *Författarskapet till Eigla* (Lund), 275 pp. [GR 1506] [See esp. pp. 78–84 on the likenesses between the OE poem and chapters 52 to 55 of *Egilssaga*.]

1929: —. "Tideräkningsfrågan i norsk niohundratalshistoria," *Historisk Tidskrift* 49, 35–66. [GR 1508] [See esp. pp. 46–48.]

Cædmon, "Cædmon's Hymn": STUDIES

1874: Rydberg, Viktor. "Skalden Kadmon och Ruthwell-korset," *Göteborgs Handels- och Sjöfartistidning* (24 Sept.). Repr. in *Skrifter af Viktor Rydberg* 14 (Stockholm, 1910), 516–23. [GR 3212]

1922: Kock, Ernst. *Fornjermansk Forskning. LUÅ* n.s. 1, 18, no. 1, 37. [GR 1170]

DEOR: EDITION

1828: Magnusen, Finn. *Priscae Veterum Borealium Mythologiae Lexicon* (Copenhagen), pp. 582–83. [Text of stanzas 1, 2, and 7 of "Deor," repr. from Conybeare's *Ilustrations of Anglo-Saxon Poetry* with Latin translation of stanzas 1 and 2.] [GR 3422]

EXODUS: STUDIES

1917: Kock, Ernst. "Domen över död man," *AfNF* 33, 175–77. [GR 1167]

1922: —. *Fornjermansk Forskning. LUÅ* n.s. 1, 18, no. 1, 18. [GR 1170]

FINNSBURG FRAGMENT: STUDIES

1997: *Herschend, Frands. "Striden i Finnsborg," *Tor* 29, 295–333. [Contains text and translation in parallel columns of the Finnsburg Fragment and the Finnsburg episode in *Beowulf*, pp. 297–300.]

Appendix A

THE FRANKS CASKET: EDITIONS AND TRANSLATIONS

1900–01: Wadstein, Elis. "Ett engelskt fornminne från 700-talet och Englands dåtida kultur," *Nordisk Universitets-tidskrift* 1, 129–53. Rvw: T. von Grienberger *ZfdPh* 33 (1901), 409–21. [Study and translation of the runic inscription.] [GR 3662]

GENESIS A AND B: STUDIES

1922: Kock, Ernst. *Fornjermansk Forskning. LUÅ* n.s. 1, 18, no. 1, 8. [GR 1170]

GUTHLAC A AND B: STYLE AND LANGUAGE

1917: Kock, Ernst. "Domen över död man," *AfNF* 33, 175–77. [GR 1157]

JULIANA: STUDIES

1919: Kock, Ernst. "Bidrag till eddatolkningen," *AfNF* 35, 24. [On lines 242ff.] [GR 3891]

RIDDLES:

1912: Kock, Ernst A. "Två textförklaringar." In *Festskrift till K. F. Söderwall* (Lund), pp. 307–08. [On *Riddle* 26:17.] [GR 4108]

1918: —. "En misskänd ordfamilj." In *Studier tillägnade Esaias Tegnér* (Lund), pp. 298–303. [On *æfter dome* in *Beowulf*, lines 1719–20, 2177–80; *Riddle* 73:10.] [GR 2443]

ALFRED:

1910: Björkman, Erik. "Några anekdoter om konung Alfred den store i kritisk belysning," *Finsk Tidskrift* 69, 332–48. [GR 5431]

WIDSITH: STUDIES

1929: Sundén, Karl F. *Den fornengelska dikten 'Widsið'* (Göteborg), 43 pp. Rvw: F. Holthausen *Beibl* 42 (1931), 341–42. [Study of "Widsith" together with a rhythmic prose translation of the poem from Holthausen's 1905–06 edition of *Beowulf*, pp. 25–30.] [GR 5035]

Appendix A

1997: *Herschend, Frands. "Striden i Finnsborg," *Tor* 29, 295–333. [Contains translation of lines 18–49 of "Widsith," pp. 325–26.]

Orosius' HISTORIA: VOYAGES OF OHTHERE AND WULFSTAN: STUDIES

1896: Wiklund, K. B. "Om kvänerna och deras nationalitet," *AfNF* 12, 103–17. [GR 5678]

1918: Kock, Axel. "Är Skåne de gamles Skadinavia?" *AfNF* 34, 71–88. [GR 2001; also listed as GR 5695]

1925: *Nerman, Birger. *Det svenska rikets uppkomst* (Stockholm), pp. 111 and 263. [Considers Wulfstan's listing of lands belonging to the Swedes as proof that the Swedish kingdom existed during the second half of the ninth century.]

1926: Lindqvist, Sune. "Hedeby och Birka," *Fornvännen* 21, 1–26. [GR 5701] *[æt Hæþum (Hedeby) mentioned on p. 11.]

1938: Ekblom, Richard. "Den forntida nordiska orienteringen och Wulfstans resa till Truso," *Fornvännen* 33, 49–68. [GR 5713]

1954–55: Ellegård, Alvar. "De gamla nordbornas väderstrecksuppfattning," *Lychnos*, pp. 1–20. [Includes English summary.] [Attack on Ekblom GR 5631.] [GR 5727]

1953–57: Envkist, Nils E. "Porthans 'Forsök at uplysa Konung Ælfreds Geografiska Beskrifning åfver den Europeiska Norden' [Ohtheriana vii]," *Årsskrift utgiven av Åbo Akademi* 38–41, 103–22. [Includes English summary, pp. 120–22.] [GR 5729]

1958: Ekblom, Richard. "Wisle 'tager från Ilfing (Elbing) dess namn'," *Scando-Slavica* 4, 121. [GR 5730] [This article cannot be located. Ekblom did publish an essay titled "King Alfred and Bearings in the Borderland between the West Slavs and the Balts" in *Scando-Slavica* 4 (1958), 117–26, and pp. 120–22 do concern the Vistula and the Elbing, but the discussion is in English.]

DOMESDAY BOOK

*Sandred, Karl Inge. "Domesday Book 1086–1986," *Ortnamnssällskapets i Uppsala Årsskrift* (1986), 86–96. [Includes English summary.]

Rushworth Gospels

1883: Svensson, Jacob V. *Om språket i den förra (merciska) delen af Rushworth-Handskriften.* I. *Ljudlära.* Uppsala diss. (Göteborg), pp. vi, 68. [GR 5851]

D. Icelandic

Historical, Linguistic, Cultural Studies

1978: *Benediktsson, Hreinn. "Lo. *mikill: mykill.*" *AfNF* 93, 48–62. [OE mycel]

2018: *Jakobsson, Sverrir. "Kennileiti sjálfsmyndar: Miðaldaorðræðan um Aðalstein Englandskonung," *Gripla* 29, 167–202. [King Athelstan in ON-Icel texts with a summary in English, p. 201.]

Individual Texts, Authors, Genres

The Battle of Brunanburh: Studies

1889: Jónsson, Jón. "Rannsóknir í fornsögu Norðlanda," *Tímarit hins íslenzka bókmenntafjelags* 10, 70–104. [GR 1494] [See footnote, pp. 82–85.]

1911: —. "Uinuaed=vínheiðr," *AfNF* 27, 94–95. [GR 1501]

Widsith: Studies

1936: Einarsson, Stefán. "Wídsíð = Víðförull," *Skírnir* 110, 164–90. [GR 5052] *[Contains an alliterative verse translation of "Widsith," pp. 185–89.]

1951: —. "Víxlkveðandi í Wídsíþ (?), Sturlungu og á Finnlandi," *Skírnir* 125, 109–30. Translated into English as "Alternate Recital by Twos in Wídsíth (?), Sturlunga and Kalevala," *Arv* 7 (1951), 59–83. [GR 5080]

Ælgifu of Northampton: General

2004: *Torfadóttir, Jóna Guðbjörg. "Í orðastað Alfífu," *Skírnir* 178 (Spring), 35–57 at 37. [Summary in English, p. 57.]

Brynjúlfsson, Gísli: Studies

2006: *Ísaksson, Sigurjón Páll. "Þýðingar úr fornensku. Fyrri hluti: Frá Abgarus konungi." *Gripla* 17, 167–92. [Part one of a study of Gísli's translations from OE. This part concerns *De Abgaro Rege.* Summary in English, pp. 91–92.]

2007: *—. "Þýðingar Gísla Brynjúlfssonar ur fornensku," *Gripla* 18, 89–109. [Part 2 on Gísli's translations of OE. Summary in English, p. 109].

GRÖNDAL, BENEDIKT SVEINBJARNARSON: STUDIES

2003: *Tómasson, Sverrir. "'Iarlar árhvatir / iörð um gátu': þýðingar Benedikts Gröndals Sveinbjarnarsonar úr fornensku," *Skorrdæla: gefin út í minningu Sveins Skorra Höskuldssonar* (Reykjavík), pp. 179–86.

Orosius' HISTORIA: STUDIES

1902: Jónsson, Jón. 'Landaleitir formanna i Norðurhöfum' *Tímarit hins íslenzka bókmenntafélags* 23, 138–57. [Recounts Othere's voyage to the Beormas, pp. 139–42.] [GR 5680]

ANGLO-SAXON CHRONICLE: STUDIES

1895: Jónsson, Jón. 'Um Erík blóðöx' *Tímarit hins íslenzka bókmenntafélags* 16, 176–203. [GR 6017] [AD 948]

E. Finnish

VOYAGES OF OHTHERE AND WULFSTAN

1906–08: Grotenfelt, Kustavi. "Mikä oli muinanen Kvenland, 'terra feminarum'?" *Historiallinen Arkisto* 20, 91–103. [GR 5683]

III. Beowulf Bibliography

A. Latin/Danish/Norwegian

EDITIONS

1815: Thorkelin, Grímur Jónsson. *De Danorum rebus gestis secul. III et IV. Poëma Danicum dialecto Anglo-Saxonica* (Copenhagen), pp. xx, 299. Rvw: G-s [=G.W. Gumælius] *Iduna* 7 (1817), 133–59; N.F.S. Grundtvig *GgA* (8 Jan. 1818), 41–47, and in *Nyeste Skilderie af Kjöbenhavn* nos. 60ff. (1815), cols. 945, 998, 1009, 1025, 1030, 1045, 1106, 1121, 1139 [with responses to Grundtvig by Thorkelin, ibid. cols. 1057–61, 1073–80]; Pem [= P. E. Miller] *Dansk-Litteratur-Tidende* (1815), pp. 401–32, 437–46, 461–62; N. Outzen *Kieler Blätter* (1816), III, 307–27; 'Pia' *Ergänzungsblätter zur Jenaischen allgemeinen Literatur-Zeitung* nos. 45, 46 (1816), 354–66; B. Pontoppidan *Nyeste Skilderie*... nos. 75, 85 (1815); [W. Taylor] *Monthly Review* 81 (1816), 516–23. [GR 1632] [Text and Latin translation in parallel columns. For discussion of reviews of Thorkelin's edition, see Haarder's *Beowulf: The Appeal of a Poem* in I above. For facing-page translation of and discussion of Thorkelin's preface, see Bjork, "Thorkelin's Preface" in I above.]

1847: Schaldemose, Frederik. *Beo-Wulf og Scopes Widsið, to angelsaxiske Digte, med Oversættelse og oplysende Anmærkninger* (Copenhagen; 2nd ed., 1851). 188 pp. Rvw: P. A. Munch, in Lange's *Norsk Tidsskrfit for Videnskab og Litteratur* 2 (1848) 133–38. [Kemble's text with Danish translation in parallel columns, pp. 1–148, plus commentary on the geographical, historical, and mythic elements in the poem, pp. 149–75; text and translation in parallel columns of "The Finnsburg Fragment," pp. 161–64, and of "Widsith," pp. 176–82, with commentary.] [GR 1634]

1861: Grundtvig, N. F. S. *Beowulfes Beorh eller Bjovulfs-Drapen det Old-Angelske Heltedigt* (Copenhagen), pp. lviii, 210. Rvw: [C. W. M.] Gr[ein] *LitZbl* 13 (1862), 488–90. Go to http://www.grundtvigsværker.dk/. [GR 1636]

CULTURAL & HISTORICAL / AUTHORSHIP & DATE

1841: Francke, E. C. T. "Om Folkevandringernes Inflydelse paa det gamle Skandinaviens (navnligen Danmarks) Religion og Mythologie" *[Dansk] Historisk Tidsskrift* 1.2, 273–392; see esp. pp. 342ff., 365ff., and 381–83 for commentary mainly on Scef. [GR 1773]

1844: Grundtvig, N. S. F. *Brage-Snak om Græske og Nordiske Myther og Oldsagn for Domer og Herrer* (Copenhagen). Go to http://www.grundtvigsværker.dk/. [Includes a brief discussion of *Beowulf*, pp. 322ff.] [GR 1662]

1852–54: Brynjúlfsson, Gísli. "Oldengelsk og Oldnordisk," *Antiquarisk Tidsskrift* 4 (Copenhagen), 81–143. [Argues for the poem's links with Danish and Icelandic, not German, legend, and for OE being a South Scandinavian instead of a West Germanic language.] [GR 1783]

1858: Schiern, Frederik E. A. "Et Par Anmærkninger til Beowulf," *Annaler for Nordisk Oldkyndighed og Historie* 18, 3–8. [GR 1789] [On Ongenþeow.]

1858: —. "Om Navnet Lodbrog hos Angelsaxerne," *Annaler for Nordisk Oldkyndighed og Historie* 18, 8–11. [On *Beowulf* and *The Anglo-Saxon Chronicle*.] [GR 1790]

1862: *Jessen, C. A. E. *Undersøgelser til nordisk oldhistorie* (Copenhagen). [See esp. pp. 47–50 and 55 on *Beowulf*, 50–51.]

Appendix A

1875: Schiern, Frederik E. A. "Om nogle gamle Navne." *Nyere historiske Studier* 1, 65–74. [GR 1803] [On a number of names in *Beowulf*, including Ongenþeow, Hygelac, Wealþeow, and Merewioingas.]

1883: Rønning, F. *'Beovulfs-Kvadet': en literær-historisk undersøgelse* (Copenhagen), 175 pp. Rvw: [R.] Heinzel *AfdA* 10 (1884), 233–39; *LitZbl* 35 (1884), 94; *Nordisk Revy* (1883), cols 170–71. [GR 1816] [A refutation of *Liedertheorie* as applied to *Beowulf*.]

1890: Bugge, Sophus. "Bidrag til nordiske Navnes Historie," *AfNF* 6, 225–45. [On names of Danes, Weahltheow, etc.] [GR 1844]

1890–92: —, and Axel Olrik 'Røveren ved Gråsten ... og ... Beowulf,' *Dania* I (1890–92), 233–45 [On lines 2231–71.] [GR 1847]

1892: Olrik, Axel "Er Uffesagnet indvandret fra England? Bemærkninger til Müllenhoffs Beovulf," *AfNF* 8, 368–75. [GR 1851]

1894: *—.* "Skjoldungasaga i Arngrim Jonssons Udtog," *Aarbøger for nordisk Oldkyndighed og Historie* 9, 83–164.

1894: *—. Kilderne til Sakses Oldhistorie: II. Norröne sagaer og danske sagn* (Copenhagen), pp. 177–83.

1896: Bugge, Sophus. *Helge-Digtene i den aeldre Edda* (Copenhagen), 355 pp. Rev. ed.: English translation by William H. Schofield as *The Home of the Eddic Poems: with Especial Reference to the Helgi-Lays* (London, 1899), 403 pp. [Of marginal relevance to OE.] [GR 935]

1901: Lehmann, Edvard. "Fandens Oldemor," *Dania* 8, 179–94. Translated into German as "Teufels Grossmutter," *Archiv für Religionswissenschaft* 8 (1905), 411–30. [GR 1883]

1903: Olrik, Axel *Danmarks Heltedigtning, en oldtidsstudie*: I. *Rolf Krake og den ældre Skjoldungrække* (Copenhagen, 1903), 352 pp. Rvw: R. C. Boer *Museum* 11 (1903), 102–06; W. Golther *LGRPh* 28 (1907), 8–9; A. Heusler *AfdA* 30 (1906), 26–36; E. Mogk *Zeitschrift für Volkskunde* 14 (1904), 250–52; K Mortenen *NTVKI* (1903) 410–14; L. Pineau *Rev crit* 56 (1903) 487–88; W. Ranisch *AfNF* 21 (1905) 276–80 [GR 1891]. Translated into English and revised in collaboration with the author by Lee M. Hollander, as *The Heroic Legends of Denmark* (New York, 1919), pp. xviii, 530. Rvw: G. T. Flom *JEGP* 19 (1920), 284–90; A. F. Major *YBVS* 6–16 (1914–24), 66–68; W. E. Mead *Nation* 110 (1920) 520–21; G. Schütte *SS* 6 (1920–21), 210–21.

Appendix A

1904: Hansen, Andreas Martin. *Landnåm i Norge. En Utsigt over Bosætningens Historie* (Christiania), 154–207, esp. pp. 162–63. [GR 1896]

1907: *Schütte, Gudmund. *Oldsagn om Godtjod: bidrag til etnisk Kildeforsknings metode med særligt henblik på folk-stamsagn* (Copenhagen), 204 pp. Rvws: A. Olrik *DS* 4 (1907), 193–201, abstracted in English by A. Nutt for *Folklore* 19 (1908), 353–59; A. F. Major *Saga-Book* 5.2 (1908), 411–12.

1907: Olrik, Axel. *Nordisk Aandsliv i Vikingetid og tidlig Middelalder* (Copenhagen). See p. 73. German trans as *Nordisches Geistesleben in heidnischer und frühchristlicher Zeit* (Heidelberg, 1908) by Wilhelm Ranisch. 2nd ed.: rev by Hans Ellekilde, 1927; English trans by Jacob W. Hartmann and H. A. Larsen as *Viking Civilization* (New York, 1930) pp. 246. [GR 1916]

1908: —. "Episke Love i folkedigtningen" *DS* 5, 69–89. [Mentions *Beowulf*, p. 79.] A slightly different version in German, "Epische Gesetze der Volksdichtung.," *ZfdA* 51 (1909–10), 1–12 [GR 1921]. *Translated into English from the German version by Jeanne P. Steager, "Epic Laws of Folk Narrative." In *The Study of Folklore*, edited by Alan Dundes (Englewood Cliffs, NJ, 1965), pp. 129–41.

1910: —. *Danmarks Heltedigtning, en oldtidsstudie*: II, *Starkad den gamle og den yngre Skjoldungrække* (Copenhagen), 322 pp. [First mention of the connection between Pekko and Beow, pp. 254–55.] Rvw: R. C. Boer *Museum* 19 (1912), 171–74; M. Cahen *Rev germ* 8 (1912), 203–06; W. Golther *LGRPh* 32 (1911), 393–95; A. Heusler *AfdA* 35 (1911), 169–83; L. Pineau *Rev crit* 71 (1911) 212–13; H. Ussing *DS* 7 (1910) 193–203. [GR 1934]

1915: Kier, Christian Ludwig. *Beowulf: Et Bidrag til Nordens Oldhistorie* (Copenhagen), 192 pp. Rvw: E. Björkman *Beibl* 27 (1916), 244–46. [GR 1976] [For further discussion, see E. Hjärne "Vagi fluvius och Vatà. En historisk ortnamnsstudie," *NB* 5 (1917), 53–89.]

1916: Logeman, Henri. "Bøigens oprindelse.," *DS* 13, 168–88, esp. pp. 174–79. [GR 1980] [On Grendel.]

1918: Clausen, H. V. "Kong Hugleik," *DS* 15, 137–49. [GR 1999]

1919: Schütte, Gudmund. *Hjemligt Hedenskab* (Copenhagen), 239 pp. [GR 2015] [*Beowulf* mentioned on pp. 44, 88, 127, 168, and 219.] [Revised, abridged, and translated into German as *Dänisches Heldentum* (Heidelberg, 1923), 154 pp.]

1919: Severinsen, P. "Kong Hugleiks Dødsaar," *DS* 16, 96. [GR 2016]

Appendix A

1920: La Cour, Vilhelm. "Lejrestudier," *DS* 17, 49–67. [GR 2022]

1920: Schütte, Gudmund. "Vidsid og Slægtssagnene om Hengest og Angantyr," *AfNF* 36, 1–32. [GR 2030]

1921: La Cour, Vilhelm. "Lejrestudier: Mindesmærkerne," *DS* 18, 147–66. [GR 2034]

1921: Olrik, Axel. *Nogle Grundsætninger for Sagnforskning; efter forfatterens død udg. af Dansk Folkemindesamling ved Hans Ellekilde*. Danmarks Folkeminder 23 (Copenhagen), 199 pp. Rvw: W. Golther *LGRPh* 43 (1922), 237–39. [GR 2037] English trans. by Kirsten Wolf and Jody Jensen. *Principles for Oral Narrative Research* (Bloomington, 1992), 244 pp.

1922: Boer, R. C. "Studier over Skjoldungedigtningen," *Aarboger for Nordisk Oldlsynighed og Historie* 22, 133–266. [GR 2039]

1922: Knudsen, Gunnar. 'Udlejre' *DS* 19, 176–77. [GR 2043]

1922: Schütte, Gudmund. "En gammel Kulturvej fra Lilleasien til Skandinavien," *DS* 19, 40–54. [GR 2046] [On p. 52, suggests that Herebeald = Baldr.]

1923: Hagen, Silvert N. "Yrsa og Rolf Krake," *DS* 20, 180–82. [GR 2051]

1924: La Cour, Vilhelm. "Lejrestudier: Navnet," *DS* 21, 13–22. [GR 2061] [Cf. August F. Schmidt, "Lejrskov," *DS* 23 (1926), 77–81.]

1926: La Cour, Vilhelm. "Skjoldungefejden," *DS* 23, 147–56. [GR 2077] [Reply to Boer, "Studier over Skjoldungedigtningen."]

1926: Schütte, Gudmund. *Vor Folkegruppe Gottjod: de gotiske, tyske, nederlandske, angelsaxiske, frisiske og nordiske Stammer i etnologisk Fremstilling* (Copenhagen), vol. 1, 299 pp. Rvw: G. Indrebö *Zeitschrift für Ortsnamenforschung* 8 (1932), 175–76; R. Much *AfdA* 47 (1928), 160–66; M. Schönfeld *APS* 3 (1928), 86–89, vol. 2, in typescript. English trans by Jean Young, *Our Forefathers, the Gothonic Nations. A Manual of the Ethnography of the Gothic, German, Dutch, A-S, Frisian and Scandinavian Peoples*, 2 vols. (Cambridge, 1929–33), 483 pp. [See esp. sections 214–25.] Rvw: S. B. *NTVKI* 12 (1936), 409–10; W. E. Collinson *MLR* 25 (1930), 231–34; F. C. Dauchin *LanM* 28 (1930), 281; E. Ekwall *Antiquity* 4 (1930), 527–28; G. T. Flom *JEGP* 33 (1934), 571–76; S. Gutenbrunner *AfdA* 54 (1935), 95–97; A. G. van Hamel *Museum* 41 (1934), 157–59; G. Knudsen *DS* 31 (1934), 84–88; K. Malone *MLN* 50 (1935), 106–08; A. Mawer *EHR* 45 (1930), 641–42; F. Mossé *Rev* *germ* 22 (1931), 194–95, and ibid. 25 (1934), 247–48; G. Neckel *DLitztg* 55 (1934), 268–71; F. R. Schröder *GRM* 22 (1934), 66; M. S. S[erjeantson] *SBVS* 11 (1928–36), 103–05; *TLS* (22 Aug. 1929), 644. [GR 2080]

1927: —. "Daner og Eruler," *DS* 24, 65–74. [GR 2090]

1930: —. "Geaterspørgsmaalet," *DS* 27, 70–81. [GR 2124]

1933: —. "Daner, Sveer, Geater i episk Rang," *DS* 30, 36–42. [GR 2139]

1934: —. "Tendensdigtning i Heltesagnet," *DS* 31, 145–65. [GR 2150] [Comments on *Beowulf* on pp. 147, 155, 156, and 158–60 and alludes to "Widsith" on pp. 148 and 156.]

1935: Brix, Hans. "Bjarkemaalet." In *Analyser og Problemer: Undersögelser i den ældre danske Litteratur* II (Copenhagen), 5–32. Rvw: M. Kristensen *DS* 32 (1935), 85–86; P. V. Rubow, *DS* 32 (1935), 79–85. [GR 2154]

1940: Schütte, Gudmund. "Episoderne med Hygelac og Ongentheow," *DS* 37, 49–58. [GR 2196]

1942: —. "Skjoldungsagnene i ny Læsemåde," *DS* 39, 81–100. [GR 2201]

1945–48: Boberg, Inger M. "Er Skjoldungerne Hunnerkonger?" *APS* 18, 257–67. [GR 2216]

1949: Kuhn, Hans. "Kappar og berserkir," *Skirnir* 123, 98–113. Published in German in slightly different form as "Kämpen und Berserker," *Frühmittelalterliche Studien* 2 (1968), 218–27. [GR 2220] [*Beowulf* cited passim.]

1968: Starcke, Viggo. "*Fyder* eller *Göter*: Hven var Geaterne, Beowulfs Folk?" *Berlingske Tidendes Kronik* (6 June), p. 7. [GR 2326]

1972: *Bæksted, Anders. "Bjovulf." In *Guder og helte i Norden*. Illustrated by Palle Bregnhøi. 3rd ed. (Copenhagen), pp. 336–44.

1981: *Reich, Ebbe Klovedal. *De første: 30 fortælinger om Danmarks fødsel*. Illustrated by Ib Spang Olsen. 2nd ed. (Copenhagen), pp. 167–87. [Loose paraphrase of first part of poem.]

1984: *Friis-Jensen, Karsten, and Claus Lund, trans. *Skjodungernes Saga. Kong Skjold og hans slægt Rolf Krake, Harald Hildetand, Ragnar Lodbrog*. Introduction and notes by Claus Lund (Copenhagen), 154 pp.

1985: *Kragh, Bodil. *"Heorot revisited": håbløshed og heltemod : brugen af Beowulf – som litteratur og i litteratur – i det tyvende århundrede, med hovedvægt på J.R.R. Tolkiens forfatter*skab. (Odense).

1991: *Christensen, Tom. *Lejre: syn og sagn* (Roskilde), 111 pp. English trans by Faith Ingwersen. *Lejre: Fact and Fable* in John D. Niles, *Beowulf and Lejre* (Tempe, 2007), pp. 13–101. [A discussion of the English translation is included in a review of *Beowulf and Lejre* by R. Dance *MÆ* 77 (2008), 121–23.]

2005: *Christensen, Arne Søby. "Beowulf, Hygelac og Chlochilaichus: Om beretningskronologien i *Beowulf*," *Historisk Tidsskrift* 105.1, 40–79. English summary, pp. 78–79.

2007: *Råsled, Bengt. *Landet söder om Vänern: Makt och samhällsutvweckling i Västergötland speglad genom arkeologin, historien och myten.* (Göteborg), pp. 49–51, 221.

2008: *—. *Götland: Språkområdet Götland och dess forntida "internationella relationer"* (Göteborg), pp. 36–47.

2014: *—. *Landet vädermark, Beowulfs Swiorice: utveckling i Beowulfs Swiorice och övriga Götland speglad genom historia, forntidsgeografi, folkvandringar, internationella relationer, makt, samhällsutveckling och embryon till det blivande Sverige.* Del. 2 (Mjölby). [Basing his argument partially on those of Carl Otto Fast, Råsled advances the "Kinnekulle" hypothesis that the poem is connected to the area around Kinnekulle mountain on the eastern shore of lake Vänern in Västergötland.]

2021: *Egerkrans, Johan. *Drakar*. Illustrated by Egerkrans. (Stockholm), pp. 80–87.

Textual Criticism

1868–69: Bugge, Sophus. "Spredte iagttagelser vedkommende de oldengelska digte om *Beowulf* og *Waldere*," *TfPP* 8, 40–78, 287–307. [GR 2361]
1930: Pedersen, Holger. "Oldengelsk *fæmne*." In *A Grammatical Miscellany Offered to Otto Jespersen on his Seventieth Birthday*, ed. N. Bøgholm et al. (Copenhagen), pp. 55–68. [GR 2495] [On line 2034.]

Literary Interpretations

1815: Grundtvig, N. F. S. "Et Par Ord om det nys udkomne angelsaxsiske Digt," *Nyeste Skilderie af Kjøbenhavn*, nos. 60, 63, 64, 65, and 66. Go to http://

www.grundtvigsværker.dk/. [Listed in GR 1632] [Primarily a response to an anonymous review of Thorkelin's first edition of *Beowulf*. English trans by Mark Bradshaw Busbee. *GS* 66.1 (2015), 7–36.]

1817: —. "Om Bjovulfs Drape eller det af Hr. Statsraad Thorkelin 1815 udgivne angelsachsiste Digt," *Dannevirke* 2, 207–89. Go to http://www.grundtvigsværker.dk/. [GR 2709] [Here on pp. 284–85 Grundtvig identifies Hygelac (Hilac) as Chochilaicus (Cohilac) of Gregory of Tours and thus provides the only datable reference (ca. 515–20 CE) in the poem. In "Et Par Ord," no. 65, col. 1030, Grundtvig mentions the possibility of the connection between Hygelac and Chochilaicus.]

1841: —. "Bjovulfs Drape eller det Oldnordiske Heltedigt," *Brage og Idun* 4, 481–538. Go to http://www.grundtvigsværker.dk/. [GR 2711] [Review of several editions of the poem.]

1875: Schrøder, Ludvig. *Om Bjovulfs-Drapen: Efter en række foredrag på folkehøjskole i Askov* (Copenhagen). [GR 2715] [Offers elaborate symbolic reading of the poem.]

1917: Fog, Reginald. "Trolden 'Grendel' i *Bjovulf*: En Hypothese," *DS* 14, 134–40. [GR 2747] [Argues that Grendel symbolizes infectious disease.]

1919: —. "Bjarkemaals 'Hjalte'," *DS* 16, 29–36. [GR 2751] [Includes letter by Axel Olrik.]

1965: Haarder, Andreas. "Et gammelt indlæg i en ny debat: Grundtvigs vurdering af *Beowulf* som kunstværk.," *GS*, 7–36. [GR 2927] [Basis for Haarder, *Beowulf: The Appeal of a Poem* (1975), chapter 4 and appendix 1.]

2023: *Zeruneith, Keld. *Beowulf: The Tragedy of a Hero: A Reading*. Translated from the Danish original by Paul Russell Garrett (Sorø).

Scholars and Scholarship

1888: Molbech, K. F., and L. Schrøder. *Christian Molbech og Nikolai Frederik Severin Grundtvig; en Brevvexling* (Copenhagen), pp. 213–18. [GR 3177] [On the publication of early English texts.]

1946: Toldberg, Helge. *Grundtvig som Filolog* (Copenhagen). [GR 3187]

1947: —. "Grundtvig og de engelske Antikvarer," *Orbis Litterarum* 5, 258–311. [GR 3188] [With English summary.]

Appendix A

1948: —. "Grundtvig belyst af en modern anglist," *GS*, 98–102. [GR 3190]

1950: —. *Grundtvigs Symbolverden* (Copenhagen), esp. chapter 6. [GR 3192]

1960: Malone, Kemp. "Gundtvigs oversættelse af *Beowulf*," *GS*, 7–25. [GR 3193]

1968: Haarder, Andreas. "Syv *Beowulf*-anmeldere," *GS*, 65–75. [GR 3195] [English translation in Haarder, *Beowulf: The Appeal of the Poem* (1975), chapter 1.]

1971: Paulsen, Asta. "Bjovulf" *Vartovbogen* (Copenhagen), pp. 33–53. [GR 3017] [On Grundtvig's engagement with *Beowulf* with a summary of the poem, pp. 35–45]

B. Swedish

CULTURAL AND HISTORICAL STUDIES

1884: Fahlbeck, Pontus. "Beovulfskvädet såsom källa för nordisk fornhistoria," *ATfS* 8.2, 1–88. Rvw: *Acad* 29 (1886), 12. [GR 1819] [Contains summary of *Beowulf*, pp. 4–21.]

1903: Stjerna, Knut. "Hjälmar och svärd i *Beovulf*." In *Studier tillägnade Oscar Montelius* (Stockholm), pp. 99–120. [GR 1892] [Translated into English by John R. Clark Hall as "Helmets and Swords in *Beowulf*" in *Essays and Questions Connected with the Old English Poem of "Beowulf"* (Coventry, 1912), pp. 1–32.]

1903–05: —. "Arkeologiska anteckningar till *Beovulf*," *Kungl. Vitterhets Historie och Antikvitets Akademiens Månadsblad* 32–34, 436–51. [GR 1903] [Translated into English as "Archaeological Notes on *Beowulf*" in *Essays and Questions*, pp. 33–49.]

1904: —. "Skölds hädanfärd." In *Studier tillägnade Henrik Schück* (Stockholm), pp. 110–34. [GR 1904] [Translated into English as "Scyld's Funeral Obsequies" in *Essays and Questions*, pp. 97–135]

1905: —. "Svear och Götar under folkvandringstiden," *Svensk Förminnesföreningens Tidskrift* 12, 339–60. [GR 1905] [Translated into English as "Swedes and Geats During the Migration Period" in *Essays and Questions*, pp. 64–96.]

Appendix A

1905: —. "Vendel och Vendelskråka," *AfNF* 21, 71–80. [GR 1906] [Translated into English as "Vendel and the Vendel Crow" in *Essays and Questions*, pp. 50–62.]

1906: —. "Drakskatten i *Beovulf*," *Fornvännen* 1, 119–44. [GR 1912] [Translated into English as "The Dragon's Hoard in *Beowulf*" in *Essays and Questions*, pp. 136–68]

1907: Schück, Henrik. *Folknamnet Geatas i den fornengelska dikten "Beowulf."* Upsala Universitetets Årsskrift, program 2, p. 45. Rvw: V. O. Freeburg *JEGP* 11 (1912), 279–83; A. Mawer *MLR* 4 (1908–09), 273. [GR 1917]

1907: —. "Studier i Ynglingtal," *Upsala Universitetets Årsskrift*, program M.M., 97–135. [GR 1918]

1908: Levander, Lars. "Sagotraditioner om Sveakonungen Adils," *ATfS* 18.3, 1–55, esp. 1–5. [GR 1920A]

1908: Stjerna, Knut. "Fasta fornlämningar i *Beovulf*," *ATfS* 18.4, 1–64. [GR 1922] [Translated into English as "The Double Burial in *Beowulf*" and "Beowulf's Funeral Obsequies" in *Essays and Questions*, pp. 169–240.]

1909: Schück, Henrik. *Studier i Beowulfsagan*. Upsala Universitets Årsskrift, program M.M. p. 50. Rvw: V. O. Freeburg *JEGP* 11 (1912), 488–97. [GR 1927]

1910: —. *Sveriges förkristna konungalängd*. Uppsala Universitetets Årsskrift, program M.M., 1–37. [GR 1941]. See p. 4.

1910: von Sydow, Carl Wilhelm. "Tors färd till Utgård. II. Skrymeepisoden." *DS* 7, 145–81, at 156. [GR 1942] [On Grendel's glove as the earliest example of the giant glove motif.]

1913: Brate, Erik. "Betydelsen av ortnamnet Skälv," *NB* 1, 102–08. [GR 1954] [On Scylfingas.]

1913: Fahlbeck, Pontus. *Beowulfskvädet såsom källa för nordisk fornhistoria*. N. F. Kungl. Vitterhets Historie och Antikvitets Akademiens Handlingar, 13, no. 3 = 33, no. 2 (1924), 17. Rvw: F. Klaeber *EStn* 48 (1914–15), 435–37. [GR 1956]

1913: Nerman, Birger. *Studier över Svärges hedna litteratur* (Uppsala), pp. xiii, 212, at pp. 16–17, 26–27, 69–73, 95. [GR 1959]

1913: —. *Vilka konungar ligger i Uppsala högar?* (Uppsala), 15 pp., at pp. 8–10. [GR 1960]

1913: von Sydow, Carl Wilhelm. "Geografi och naturbeskrivning i Beowulfsången," *Forhandlingar vid Svenska Filolog och Historikermötet i Göteborg den 19–21 Augusti 1912*, 74–75. [GR 1962] [Mentioned in a brief article of the same title in *Göteborgs handels-och sjöfartstidning* 192 (20 Aug. 1912), p. 7.]

1914: —. "Grendel i anglosaxiska ortnamn," *NB* 2, 160–64. [GR 1969]

1915: Lindroth, Hjalmar. "Är Skåne de gamles Scadinavia?" *NB* 3, 10–28. [GR 1977]

1915: Nerman, Birger. "Baldersagans älsta form," *Edda* 3, 1–10. [GR 1978] [On lines 2425–62.]

1917: Björkman, Erik. "*Bēowulf* och Sveriges historia," *NT*, 161–79. [GR 1982]

1916–17: Fredborg, Emil Äng. *Det första årtalet i Sveriges historia* (Umeå h.a. läroverks årsredogörelse). [GR 1984]

1917: Lindqvist, Sune. "Ottarshögen i Vendel," *Fornvännen* 12, 127–43 at pp. 127–29. [GR 1985] [On the excavation of Ottar's (Ohthere in *Beowulf*) mound in Vendel.]

1917: Nerman, Birger. "Ottar Vendelkråka och Ottarshögen i Vendel," *Upplands Fornminnesförenings Tidskrift* 7, 309–34 at pp. 315, 319–21, 323–26, 332. [GR 1986]

1917: —. "Ynglingasagan i arkeologisk belysning," *Fornvännen* 12, 226–61, at p. 245. [GR 1987]

1917: von Sydow, Carl Wilhelm. "Draken som skattevaktare." In *Festskrift til Evald Kristensen* = *Danmarks Folkeminder*, 17, 103–15 at pp. 107, 114–15. [GR 1991]

1918: Björkman, Erik. "Beowulfforskning och mytologi," *Finsk Tidskrift* 84, 250–71. [GR 1995]

1918: —. "Fe. Scedeland, Scedenig," *NB* 6 (1918), 162–68. [GR 1996]

1918: —. "Sköldungaättens mytiska stamfäder," *NT*, 163–82. [GR 1997]

1918: Kock, Axel. "Är Skåne de gamles Skadinavia?" *AfNF* 34, 71–88. [GR 2001]

1918: Lindroth, Hjalmar. "Skandinavien och Skåne," *NB* 6, 104–12. [GR 2002]

1918: Montelius, Oscar. "Ynglingaätten," *NTVKI*, 213–38. [GR 2003]

1918: Noreen, Adolf. "Skandinavien och Skåne." In *Studier tillägnade Esaias Tegnér* (Lund), pp. 43–48. [GR 2004]

1918: von Sydow, Carl Wilhelm. "Sigurds strid med Fåvne. En studie rörande hjältesagans förhållande till folkdiktningen," *LUÅ* 14, no. 16, pp. vi, 51, at pp. 5–7. [GR 2005]

1919: Arne, T. J. "Gravar från 'Vendeltid' vid Lagerlunda i Kärna socken, Östergötland," *Fornvännen* 14, 1–20, esp. 19–20 on Beowulf's burial mound. [GR 2006]

1919: Björkman, Erik. "Skialf och Skilfing," *NB* 7, 163–81. [GR 2008] [Eilert Ekwall adds a note on Björkman's research on names, "Erik Björkman som namnsforskare," pp. 182–85.]

1919: Linderholme, Emanuel. "Vendelshögens konunganamn i socknens 1600-talstradition," *NB* 7, 36–40. [GR 2011]

1919: Lindroth, Hjalmar. "Äro *Scadinavia* och *Skåne* samma ord?" *AfNF* 35, 29–47. [GR 2012]

1919: Neuhaus, Johannes. "Om Skjold," *AfNF* 35, 166–72. [GR 2014]

1920: Kock, Axel. "Vidare om *Skåne* och *Skadinavia*," *AfNF* 36, 74–85. [GR 2024]

1920: Langenfelt, Gösta. "Sverige och svenskarna i äldre engelsk litteratur," *NTfF* 9, 51–62. [GR 2025]

1920: Noreen, Adolf. "Yngve, Inge, Inglinge m.m.," *NB* 8 (1920), 1–8. [GR 2029]

1920: von Sydow, Carl Wilhelm. "Iriskt inflytande på nordisk guda- och hjältesaga," *VSLÅ*, 19–29. [GR 2031] [At p. 29 on the influence of the Celtic Finn cycle of tales on *Beowulf*.]

Appendix A

1921: Lindqvist, Sune. "Ynglingaättens gravskick," *Fornvännen* 16, 83–194. [GR 2036] [On burial customs in *Beowulf*, see pp. 119–36, and with a German summary, pp. 261–75.]

1921: *Weibull, Curt. *Om det svenska och det danska Rikets Uppkomst* (Lund). Rvw: Vilhelm LaCour *Historisk Tidsskrift* 7 (1929), 497. [Frequent references to *Beowulf*.]

1923: Brate, Erik. "Sinfjotle," *SNF* 14, no. 2, 1–8. [GR 2048] [See p. 2 on Fitela in *Beowulf*.]

1923: Koht, Halvdan. "Var 'Finnane' alltid Finnar?" *Maal og Minne*, 161–75. [GR 2052] [On line 580.]

1923: Lindqvist, Ivar. *Galdrar. De gamla germanska trollsångernas stil undersökt i Samband med en Svensk runinskrift från folkvandringtiden.* Göteborgs högskolas Årsskrift, 29, pp. viii, 193. See chapter 10 on the Heruli, esp. pp. 132, 138–39, 143, 145, 147, and 150. [GR 2054]

1923: Lindqvist, Sune. "Hednatemplet i Uppsala," *Fornvännen* 18, 83–118, esp. pp. 110–12. [GR 2055] [Comparison of architecture of Heorot with that of Scandinavian wooden churches.]

1923: von Sydow, Carl Wilhelm. "Beowulf och Bjarke," *SNF* 14, no. 3, 1–46. Rvw: A. K. Cyriax *Folklore* 39 (1928), 102–07; A. Heusler *AfdA* 43 (1924), 52–54; F. Holthausen *Beibl* 34 (1923), 357–58 [reply to this review by H. Hecht, item 2062]; S. B. Lijegren *Neophil* 10 (1924–25), 73–74; K. Malone *JEGP* 23 (1924) 458–60. [GR 2058]

1923: —. "Beowulfskalden och nordisk tradition," *VSLÅ*, 77–91. [GR 2059] Summary pp. 90–91. [Argues against Sarrazin's theory that *Beowulf* is an OE translation of a Danish original from the Lejre region.]

1924: —. "Hur mytforskningen tolkat Beowulfdikten," *Folkminnen och Folktankar* 11, 97–134. Rvw: A. K. Cyriax *Folklore* 39 (1928), 102–07. [GR 2064]

1924: —. "Scyld Scefing," *NB* 12, 63–95. [GR 2065] [Disputes the mythic underpinnings of Scyld.]

1924: Wessén, Elias. *Studier till Sveriges hedna mytologi och fornhistoria, UUÅ* no. 6, 198 pp. Rvw: S. Lindquist *Fornvännen* 19 (1924), 235–36; *Svenska Historiska Tidskrift* 44 (1924), 295–96; C. C. Uhlenbeck *APS* 3 (1928–29), 172–75. [GR 2066] [*Beowulf* is mentioned throughout the text.]

Appendix A

1925: Nerman, Birger. *Det svenska rikets uppkomst* (Stockholm). [Frequent allusions to *Beowulf*. See especially chapter 5, "Beowulf," pp. 57–136.] [GR 496] *[See also Nerman's "The Foundation of the Swedish Kingdom," *VSNR* 10 (1928–29), 113–31, especially 119–22, for an abbreviated version of the book's argument. (GR 2113). Nerman revised the book for a popular audience under the title *Sveriges rikes uppkomst* (1941). See pp. 65–70 on *Beowulf*.]

1925: Wadstein, Elis. "Norden och Västeuropa i gammal Tid," *Populärt vetenskapliga föreläsningar vid Göteborgs Högskola*, n.s., 22, pp. 10–32, 159–67, 323–36. Rvw: W. van den Ent *Museum* 36 (1929), 17–20; V. La Cour *Dansk Historisk Tidsskrift* ser. 9, 4 (1925–26), 376–80; C. C. Uhlenbeck *APS* 2 (1927–28) 287–88. [GR 2073]

1926: Strömholm, D. "Försök över Beowulfdikten och Ynglingasagan," *Edda* 25, 233–49. [GR 2081]

1927: Wessén, Elias. *De nordiska folkstammarna i Beowulf*. KVHAA 36:2 (Stockholm), 85 pp. Rvw: F. Holthausen *Beibl* 39 (1928), 303–06; K. Malone *Speculum* 5 (1930), 134–35; R. E. Zachrisson *SN* 1 (1928), 87–88. [GR 2093] [On the Heruli, Danes, Scyldings, Heathobards, Froda and Healfdan, the Geats, Theodorik the Great, and *Beowulf*.]

1927: —. "Nordiska namnstudier," *UUÅ* no. 3, 1–118. Rvw: R. E. Zachrisson *SN* 1 (1928), 85–87. [GR 2094]

1929: *Svionum [Carl Otto Fast]. *Beowulf, germanernas äldsta epos* (Stockholm), 33 pp.

1930: *—. *Västgöta-Dal. Daner och Anglo-sachsare* (Stockholm).

1931: *Boethius, Gerda. *Hallar, tempel och stavkyrkor: Studier till kännedomen om äldre nordisk monumentalarkitektur*. (Stockholm), pp. 70–71. [Maintains that Heorot was a building of the same kind as a Nordic stave church.]

1933: *Svionum [Carl Otto Fast]. *Götaland, den forngermanska diktningens landskap*. (Göteborg; repr. 1984).

1936: Lindqvist, Sune. *Uppsala Högar och Ottarshögen*. (Stockholm), pp. xii, 363, plates 25. With a summary in English. See esp. pp. 251–58, 297–301 in text, pp. 347–48 and 351 in summary. Rvw: T. D. Kendrick *Antiquity* 11 (1937), 247–48. [GR 2168]

1938: Arbman, Holger, et al. *Vendel i Fynd och Forskning: Skrift med Anledning av Vendelmonumentets tillkomst.* (Uppsala). Rvw: F. Holthausen *Beibl* 51 (1940), 5–6. [GR 2177]

1944: *Fast, Carl Otto. *Svenska rikets ursprung.* (Göteborg; repr. 1984), 152 pp. [Mention of *Beowulf* throughout.]

1947: Johansson, Gust. *Beowulfsagans Hrones-Næsse: Lekmannafunderingar angående det Gamla Götland.* (Göteborg), 245 pp. Rvw: F. P. Magoun *Speculum* 27 (1952), 225–26. [GR 2214]

1948: Lindqvist, Sune. "Sutton Hoo och *Beowulf*," *Fornvännen* 43, 94–109 with an English summary, pp. 109–10. [GR 2218]

1950: *Fast, Carl Otto. *Vänerbygdens sägner* (Stockholm), pp. 35–39.

1955: Johansson, Gust. *Beowulfsagans Götar* (Göteborg). [GR 2251]

1958: Harding, Erik. "Om *Beowulfs* Geatas och några andra problem," *Språkvetenskapliga problem i ny belysning eller bidrag till nordisk och germansk språkhistoria*, H. 8, Bilaga 3. [GR 2265]

1958: Schyman, Iwan. "Beowulfs land är Brosjöområdet i Värmland." In *Värmlandsnäs från forntid till nutid*, vol. 2, *Norra delen*, pp. 28–48 (Säffle). [GR 2267]

1961: Langenfelt, Gösta. "*Beowulf* och Fornsverige: Ett försök till datering av den fornengelska hjältedikten, del 1," *Ortnamnssälskapet i Uppsala Årsskrift*, 35–55; del. 2 (1962), 23–36. [GR 2286]

1964: Johansson, Gust. *Beowulfsagans historiska fragment* (Göteborg). [GR 2296]

1964: *Stenberger, Mårten. *Det forntida Sverige.* Stockholm; 3rd ed. 1979 with afterword by Bo Gräslund, p. 535.

1972: Areskoug, Malte. "De nordiska folknamnen hos Jordanes," *Fornvännen* 67, 1–15. [GR 2350]

1978: *Lönnroth, Lars. *Den dubbla scenen: Muntlig diktning från Eddan till ABBA* (Lund). See especially pp. 31f. and 65f.

1992: *Gannholm, Tore. *Beowulf. Gutarnas nationalepos samt Gutasagan.* (Visby). [An elaboration of Gad Rausing's hypothesis that the *Geatas* in

Appendix A

Beowulf came from Gotland. See "Beowulf, Ynglingatal and the Ynglinga saga: Fiction or History?" *Fornvännen* 80 (1985), 163–78.]

1999: *Johnson, Rakel. "Att ge eller inte ge: det är frågan: om gåvoinstitutet i Eddan och Beowulf>." In Barbro Ryder Liljegren, ed., *Europa* (Göteborg), pp. 185–93. [On the gift as construed by Marcel Mauss in the *Poetic Edda* and *Beowulf*.]

2001: *Hiller, Anders. *Om Beowulf: Baowoolf – Boithulf – Botholf – och så Båtel* (Stockholm). [Supplies more evidence to support Gannholm's theory that Beowulf came from Gotland.]

2007: *Ney, Agneta. "Hallkvinnor och sjömonster: forntida kvinnogestalter i text och bild." In Marlene Hugoson, ed., *Bodil Lajv: Festskrift till Bodil Nildin-Wall den 18 januari 2007* (Uppsala), pp. 33–39.

2012: *Lindqvist, Jan. *Från Beowulf till Blyton: barn- och ungdomsklassiker på engelska*. (Stockholm). [Synopsis of the poem with references, pp. 1–16.]

2012: *Kuusela, Tommy. "Varulven i fornnordisk tradition." In Ella Odstedt, *Varulven i Svensk folktradition*. Expanded ed. by Per Faxneld and Per Norström (Tallinn), pp. 320–52. [*Beowulf* mentioned on pp. 339 (Grendel) and 345 (Wylfingas).]

2017: *Harrison-Lindbergh, Katarina. "Beowulf" and "Beowulfkvädet." In *Nordisk mytologi från A till Ö* (Stockholm), pp. 73–74.

2017: *Lönnroth, Lars. *Det germanska spåret. En västerländsk litteraturtradition från Tacitus till Tolkien*. Stockholm, 2017). See esp. pp. 43–52. Rvw: J. Wickström *Historisk Tidskrift* 138 (2018), 350–52.

2017: *Ney, Agneta. *Bland ormar och drakar: hjältemyt och manligt ideal i berättartraditioner om Sigurd Fafnesbane* (Lund). [Contains a brief discussion of Sigmund as a dragon slayer in *Beowulf*, pp. 75–79.]

2017: *Lundqvist, Hans H. *Vikingarnas ursprung. Beowulf sprider nytt ljus* (Stockholm).

2018: *Gräslund, Bo. *Beowulfkvädet: Den nordiska bakgrunden* (Uppsala). Rvws: R. E. Bjork, *SS* 90.2 (2020), 247–49; A. Cooper, *JEGP* 120.1 (2021), 130–31. Translated into English by Martin Naylor as *The Nordic Beowulf* (Leeds, 2022).

2018: *Eriksson, Kristina Ekero. *Gamla Uppsala: Människor och makter i högarnas skugga* (Stockholm). [*Beowulf* mentioned on pp. 74, 155, 172–74, 184, and 197.]

TEXTUAL CRITICISM

1918: Kock, Ernst A. "En misskänd ordfamilj" in *Studier tillägnade Esaias Tegnér* (Lund), pp. 298–303. [GR 2443] [On æfter dome in *Beowulf*, lines 1719–20, 2177–80; Riddle 73:10.]

1919: Jungner, Hugo. "Uppsala-och Vendel-konungarnas mytiska ättefäder," *Fornvännen* 14, 79–102. [GR 2446] [See p. 88 on *eaforheafodsegn* and p. 94 on *Wendla leod*.]

1921: Kock, Ernst A. "Bidrag till eddatolkningen," *AfNF* 37, 105–35. [GR 2453] [See p. 105 on *wið earm gesæt*, line 749.]

1954: Collinder, Björn. "Beowulfskolier," In *Festskrift tillägnade Elias Wessén* (Lund), pp. 16–25. [On lines 303b–6a, 1030–3a, 1114–18a, 1144–45, 2155–59, 2249–52a, 2255–57a, 3069–75, 3143–48a.] [GR 2611]

C. Icelandic

CULTURAL AND HISTORICAL

1899: Jónsson, Jón. "Liserus – Beów," *AfNF* 15, 255–61. See pp. 258–61. [GR 1877]

1915: Jónsson, Jón. "Ætt Haralds hilditannar," *AfNF* 31, 26–46, at p. 28. [GR 1975]

1963: *Guðnason, Bjarni. *Um Skjöldungasögu* (Reykjavík). [Mentions *Beowulf* on pp. 3, 61, 80, 165, 175, 221; with English summary, pp. 306–25.]

D. Finnish

MANUSCRIPT STUDIES

2008: *Varila, Mari-Liisa. "Beowulf seurueineen. Nowell Codexin mysteeri." In *Papyruksesta PDF: ään. Tutkielmia kirjan historiasta*, ed. Leila Koivunen and Janne Tunturi (Turku), pp. 25–40.

Appendix A

E. Norwegian

1949: *Brøgger, Niels Christian. *Nordens demring: Nordiske myter og sagn.* Foreword by A. W. Brøgger. Illustrated by Knut Yran (Oslo), pp. 184, 189–235, 243–45.

1953: Strand, Tor H. "Heltediktet *Beowulf,*" *Affenposten* (Oslo), 15 and 16 July. [GR 2245]

1956: —. *Norrønafolket.* (Oslo), p. 181. See pp. 157–61. [GR 2258]

1958: —. "Bøheringen Beowulfs Kongesaga i Nytt lys." *T. A. Kronikken.* [GR 2268]

Appendix B

A Bibliography of Translations of Old English Literature into the Scandinavian Languages, Finnish, Sámi, and Neo-Latin Written in Scandinavia to 2023

(A bibliography based on GR. Its format is that of GR's, and items not in GR are marked with asterisks.)

I. General

A. Neo-Latin

1733: Bussæus, Andreas. *Periplus Ohtheri, Halgolando-Norvegi, ut et Wulfstani, Angli, secundum narrationes eorundem de suis ... jussa Ælfredi Magni ...* Appended to his *Are Frodes Schedæ* (Copenhagen), 28 pp. [Text of "The Voyages of Ohthere and Wulfstan" with facing-page Latin translation by Christopher Ware and notes.] [GR 5654]

1773: *Langebek, Jacob. *Periplus Otheri Norvegi et Wulfstani sive eorum narrationes de suis in septentrionem et in mari Balthico navigationibus* in *Scriptores rerum Danicarum* 2 (Copenhagen). [Introduction pp. 106–07 and OE and Latin translation in parallel columns, pp. 108–23, with extensive, detailed notes to the text.]

1828: Magnusen, Finn. *Priscae Veterum Borealium Mythologiae Lexicon* (Copenhagen), pp. 582–83. [Text of stanzas 1, 2, and 7 of "Deor" reprinted from Conybeare's *Ilustrations of Anglo-Saxon Poetry* with Latin translation of stanzas 1 and 2.] [GR 3422]

B. Danish

1815: Rask, Rasmus. "Ottars og Ulfstens korte Rejseberetninger med dansk Oversættelse, kritiske Anmærkninger og andre Oplysninger." *Det Skandinaviske Litteraturselskabs Skrifter* 11, 1–132. Also printed separately (Copenhagen, 1816) and reprinted with corrections in *Samlede tildels forhen* *utrykte Afhandlinger af R. K. Rask* 1 (Copenhagen, 1834), ed. posthumously by H. K. Rask, pp. 289–384. [Facing-page translation with introduction, notes, and extensive commentary.] [GR 5665]

1817: Grundtvig, N. F. S. "Om Bruneborg-Slaget og et Riim i den Anledning," *Dannevirke* 2 (1817), 65–96. Go to http://www.grundtvigsværker.dk/. [Contains a literal prose translation of "The Battle of Brunanburh" (pp. 73–79) as well as "Kæmpevise om Bruneborg-Slaget" (pp. 79–87), a heroic ballad about "Brunanburh" followed by "Efter-Klangen" (pp. 88–96), a verse rumination on the ballad. The first poem is reprinted in Grundtvig's *Nordiske Smaadigte* (Christiana, 1838), pp. 119–24, and both poems are reprinted in *N. F. S. Grundtvigs Poetiske Skrifter* 4 (Copenhagen, 1883), ed. Svend Grundtvig, pp. 355–67.] [GR 1487, pp. incorrectly noted as 65–79].

1820: *—. "Brudstykke" [Finnsburg fragment] in parallel OE/Danish format, pp. XL–XLV of his introduction to *Bjowulfs Drape. Et Gothisk Helte-Digt fra forrige Aar-Tusinde af Angelsaxisk paa Danske Riim* (Copenhagen). Go to http://www.grundtvigsværker.dk.

1820: *—. See II.B., below. (Translation of "The Finnsburg Fragment").

1836–37: *—. *Sang-Værk til den danske Kirke* (Copenhagen). Go to http://www.grundtvigsværker.dk/. [Hymn 124 is a free rendition of antiphon 1 in *The Advent Lyrics*; hymn 158 is a free rendition of antiphons 8 and 9; hymn 243 is a free rendition of *Christ and Satan*, lines 398–596 (Harrowing of Hell) ; hymn 244 is a verse paraphrase of parts of *Christ II*; hymn 245 is a rendition of *Christ II*, lines 720–44 (the six leaps of Christ); and hymn 355 is a rendition of *Christ II*, lines 600ff. Hymns 243 and 244 have been translated into modern English in *Living Wellsprings: The Hymns, Songs, and Poems of N. F. S. Grundtvig*, trans. and ed. Edward Broadbrige (Aarhus, 2015), pp. 94–97 and 106–08. For an earlier translation of hymn 243, see *A Book of Danish Verse* (New York, 1922), trans. S. Foster Damon and Robert Silliman Hillyer, selected and annotated by Oluf Friis, pp. 51–55.]

1840: —. *Phenix-Fuglen: et Angelsachsisk Kvad.* (Copenhagen). Go to http://www.grundtvigsværker.dk/. [First edition of *The Phoenix* with dedicatory poem, foreword, introduction, and textual notes. Contains Lactantius's "Carmen de ave phoenice" running below part I of the text and a free-verse translation of the OE after it, pp. 44–63, followed by "Dansk Efterklang," a verse rumination on the poem, pp. 63–70, and "Jeg gik mig ud en Sommerdag," a poem inspired by the OE poem, pp. 70–71. Translation, "Efterklang," "Jeg gik mig ud," and dedicatory poem ("Kongen döde under Vinters Hjerte") reprinted in *N. F. S. Grundtvigs Poetiske Skrifter* 6 (Copenhagen, 1885), ed. Svend Grundvig, pp. 297–366.] [GR 4017]

1840: *—. "Fugl Fønix." In *Viser og Sange for danske Samfund* 1, 60–64. Go to http://www.grundtvigsværker.dk/. [Heroic ballad summarizing the contents of the Old English *Phoenix*. Reprinted in *N. F. S. Grundtvigs Poetiske Skrifter* 6 (Copenhagen, 1885), ed. Svend Grundtvig, pp. 294–97.]

1846: Unger, C. R. "Fragment af en allitereret angelsaxisk Homili, hvori nævnes nogle af Nordens hedenske Guddome," *Annaler for nordisk Oldkyndighed og Historie*, 67–81. [Text and literal translation in parallel columns of *De falsis diis*.] [GR 5285]

1846: Schaldemose, Frederik. See II.B below (translation of "The Finnsburg Fragment" and "Widsith").

1853: Stephens, George. *Tvende Old-Engelske Digte med Oversættelser og Tillæg* (Copenhagen). [Edition of "Letter of Christ to Abgarus" from Ælfric's *Lives of the Saints* XXIV ("Abdon and Sennes") with English, Danish, ON translations; ON, OSwed, OHG, MHG, MDutch versions of letter; edition of OE versified homily for third Sunday in Lent with English, Danish, and ON translations.] [GR 290]

1864: *Kragballe, Chr. M. *Anglerfolkets Kirkehistorie af Beda den Æværdige* (Copenhagen; reprinted 2021 as *Anglernes kirkehistorie: anno 731*). [Translation of Latin version of Bede's *Historia Ecclesiastica* with introduction and notes. Contains literal translation of "Bede's Death Song," p. xiv.]

1873: Hammerich, Frederik. *De episk-kristelige Oldkvad hos de gothiske Folk* (Copenhagen; repr. 2019). German trans. by A. Michelsen. Rvw: G. L. *LitZbl* 26 (1875), 257–59; E. Wilken *GgA* (1875), 1438–40. [Begins with a picture and analysis of "The Ruthwell Cross" and contains text and alliterative verse translations of parts of "The Dream of the Rood," pp. 15–20, a translation of "The Grave," pp. 92–93, and selected translations from "Cædmon's Hymn," "The Ruthwell Cross," *Genesis A* and *B*, *Exodus*, *Daniel*, *Christ and Satan*, *Judith*, *Juliana*, *Elene*, *Christ I*, *Andreas*, *Guthlac B*, *The Phoenix*, "Soul and Body II," and "Meters of Boethius" interspersed throughout a discussion of the poems, pp. 13–96.] [GR 919]

1876–82: Steenstrup, Johannes C. H. R. *Normannerne* (Copenhagen), 4 vols. [vol. 3 (1882) contains alliterative verse translations of "The Battle of Brunanburh," pp. 76–77, and of "Conquest of the Five Buroughs," p. 80, and a prose retelling of "The Battle of Maldon," pp. 229–37.] [GR 6009]

1885: Rønning, F. "Den oldengelske digtning." *Historisk Månnedsskrift for Folkelig og Kirkelig Oplysning* 4, 1–36. [Brief survey of OE poetry (pp. 1–7) followed by an assessment of OE poetic characteristics (pp. 7–19) and a translation of *Judith* (pp. 19–36).] [GR 882]

1903: *Larsen, Henry. *Krist og Satan: nogle Blade af gammel kristelig digtning særlig hos Angelsakserne (Cædmon)* (Copenhagen). In *Skrifter til Oplysning og Opbyggelse* IV 5–6 H. Rvw: August Kristensen, *Højskolebladet* 1 (1904), 50–55. [Contains alliterative verse translations of "Cædmon's Hymn," pp. 94–95, large sections of *Genesis A* and *Genesis B* to the birth of Cain and Abel, pp. 102–34, "Christ and Satan," pp. 135–66, "The Ruthwell Cross," pp. 168–69, and "The Dream of the Rood," pp.172–76, interspersed throughout a discussion of the poems.]

1910: *Bugge, Alexander. Translation of "The Battle of Brunanburh." In *Norges Historie fremstillet for det norske Folk*, ed. A. Bigge et al., vols. 1, 2 (Oslo), pp. 177–78.

1936: Dahl, Torsten. *Den oldengelske Krønike i Udvalg* (Copenhagen). [Selections from *The Anglo-Saxon Chronicle* from the Viking period in translation with introduction and notes. Includes a prose version of "The Battle of Brunanburh," pp. 34–36, and a paraphrase of "The Battle of Maldon," pp. 40–41.] [GR 5994]

1979: *Haarder, Andreas. "En oldengelsk gåde" and "Slaget ved Maldon" in *Det episke liv. Et indblik i oldengelsk heltedigtning* (Copenhagen; e-book 2022), pp. 125, 130–39. [Free-verse translations of Riddle 27 and "The Battle of Maldon." The book also contains translations of selections from "The Fates of Men," *Beowulf*, "Maxims I," "The Ruin," "The Wanderer," and "The Seafarer" throughout.]

1983: *Noack, Bent. *Helvedstorm og himmelfart: stykker af oldengelsk kristen digtning* (Copenhagen). [Alliterative verse translations of *Genesis A*, lines 1–91, pp. 5–11; *Genesis B*, pp. 12–67; *Christ and Satan*, lines 398–441 and 455–67, pp. 68–72; and *Christ II*, pp. 73–100.]

1983: *Lund, Niels. *Ottar og Wulfstan. To rejsebeskrivelser fra vikingatiden*. With commentary by Lund, essays by Ole Crumlin-Pedersen, Peter H. Sawyer, Christine E. Fell (Roskilde). Translated by Christine E. Fell as *Two Voyagers at the Court of King Alfred* (York, 1984). [Text and translation in parallel columns.]

1983: *Wilmont, Barry. *Bjowulf: et heltedigt fra Danmarks sagntid*. With a foreword by Ebbe Kløvedal Reich, a translation of "The Fight at Finnsburg," and an afterword by Wilmont. Lithographs by Wilmont. Pages are not numbered (Copenhagen).

1991: *Lund, Niels. *Sangen om slaget ved Maldon og andra kilder til Sven Sveskægs og Olav Tryggvessons kampe i England i 990erne* (Copenhagen). ["The Battle of Maldon," extracts from Byrthferth of Ramsey's *Life of St. Oswald, The Anglo-Saxon Chronicle,* Æthelred's agreement with the Vikings (994), Æthelred's confirmation of bishop Æscwig to the seat at Risborough, Ælfgar's will, Æthelflæd's will, Ælfflæd's will, Æthelric of Bocking's will, Æthelred's confirmation of Æthelric's will; obituary notice from New Minster, Winchester; obituary notice from Ely; extracts from John of Worcester's *Chronicon ex chronicis,* Henry of Huntingdon's *Historia Anglorum,* the Ely Book, *Chronicon Abbatiæ Rameseiensis, Symoneonis Monachi Opera Omnia*].

1991: *Vasbo, Vibeke. *Hildas sang,* 2 vols. (Copenhagen; 2nd ed. 1992; 3rd ed. 1993). [Paraphrase of "Æcerbot," vol. 2, p. 451; trans of part of "The Finnsburg Fragment," vol. 2, p. 515, "Wulf and Eadwacer," vol. 2, pp. 611–12, and Bede's story of Hilda's life and death, vol. 2, pp. 650–53.] English translation by Gaye Kynoch as *The Story of Hild* (Durham, 2018).

1996: *Noack, Bent. *Menneskevordelse og korsdød: stykker af oldengelsk kristen digtning* (Fredericksberg). [Alliterative verse translations of *The Advent Lyrics,* pp. 7–37; "The Dream of the Rood," pp. 38–48; the "Pater Noster," p. 49; and "Cædmon's Hymn," p. 50.]

2017: *Brøgger, Suzanne. In Keld Zeruneith. *De siste tider: hedenskap heroism kristendom: en angelsaksisk overgangshistorie* (Copenhagen), pp. 317–32. [Verse translations of "Cædmon's Hymn," "The Wanderer," "The Seafarer," "Deor," "The Wife's Lament," "The Husband's Message," "The Ruin."]

C. Norwegian

1981: *Sandved, Arthur O. "Drømmen om Kristi Kors, et kristent dikt i før-kristen form." *Kirke og Kultur* 86, 203–12. [Contains a metrical "Riksmål" prose translation of "The Dream of the Rood," pp. 209–12, which is reprinted in *Vers fra vest,* pp. 63–71.]

1987: *—. *Vers fra vest: gammelengelske dikt i utvalg* (Oslo). [General introduction plus introductions to and "Riksmål" verse translations of "Cædmon's Hymn," pp. 31–33, "Bede's Death Song," pp. 34–36, "The Ruin," "The Wanderer," and "The Seafarer," pp. 37–62, "The Dream of the Rood," pp. 63–71, and "The Battle of Brunanburh," pp. 117–22, and introductions

Appendix B

to and prose translations of *Genesis B*, pp. 72–91, *Judith*, pp. 92–103, and "The Battle of Maldon," pp. 104–16. Concludes with an introduction to and verse translations of 14 brief Middle English lyrics, pp. 125–33.]

D. Swedish

1800: Porthan, Henrik Gabriel. "Försök at uplysa Konung Ælfreds Geographiska Beskrifning öfver den Európeiska Norden," *Kongl Vitterhets Historie och Antiquitets Academiens Handlingar* 6, 37–106. [Text of "The Voyages of Ohthere and Wulfstan" from Barrington's *The Anglo-Saxon from the Historian Orosius by Ælfred the Great* together with a translation in parallel columns, introduction, and notes.] [GR 5660]

1857: Nilsson, Lars G. *Några fornengelska andeliga quäden på grundspråket.* (Lund). [Sampling of texts of hymns and prayers from *E. Thomson's *Godcunde Lár & Theówdóm: Select Monuments of the Doctrine and Worship of the Catholic Church in England before the Norman Conquest: Consisting of Ælfric's Paschal Homily and Extracts from his Epistles, etc., the Offices of the Canonical Hours, and 3 Metrical Prayers and Hymns. In Anglo-Saxon and partly in Latin* (London, 1849), pp. 121–31, 134–40, 142–52, 212, and 216–25, with facing-page translation, notes, and glossary. "Gloria Patri," "Pater Noster," "Credo in Deum Patrem Omnipotentem," "Precationes A," "Precationes B."] [GR 291]

1858: —. "Judith, Fragment af ett fornengelskt Qväde" (Copenhagen; repr. 2009). [M.A. thesis at University of Copenhagen. Thorpe's text from *Analecta Anglo-Saxonica* (1834) with facing-page translation in "rhythmic prose" instead of alliteration, no introduction, brief textual notes, and glossary.] [GR 3848]

1866: *—. *Anglosaxisk (fornengelsk) grammatika*, part 1 (Copenhagen), pp. 1–48; part 2 (Copenhagen, 1870), pp. 49–121. [Contains free translations of "Cædmon's Hymn," pp. 10–11, and *Beowulf*, lines 407–18 and 473–79, pp. 14–15.]

1871: —. *Anglosaxisk (fornengelsk) läsebok för nybegynnare* (Lund). [Contains selection of *Judith*, lines 15–46a, with a new Swedish translation, pp. 12–14.] [GR 299]

1872: *—. *Anglosaxisk läsebok* (Lund). [Contains selection from *Judith*, lines 15–46a, with a new Swedish translation, pp. 12–14.]

1900–01: Wadstein, Elis. "Ett engelskt fornminne från 700-talet och Englands dåtida kultur," *Nordisk Universitets-tidskrift* 1, 129–53. Rvw: T.

Appendix B

Von Grienberger *ZfdPh* 33 (1901), 409–21. [Study and translation of the runic inscription on the Franks Casket.] [GR 3662]

1907: *Schütte, Gudmund. *Oldsagn om Godtjod: bidrag til etnisk Kildeforsknings metode med særligt henblik på folk-stamsagn* (Copenhagen), 204 pp. Rvw: A. Olrik *Folklore* 19 (1908), 353–59. [Alliterative verse translation of "Widsith," pp. 198–201.]

1929: Sundén, Karl F. *Den fornengelska dikten 'Widsið'* (Göteborg). 43 pp. Rvw: F. Holthausen *Beibl* 42 (1931), 341–42. [Study of "Widsith" together with a rhythmic prose translation of the poem from Holthausen's 1905–06 edition of *Beowulf*, pp. 25–30. Introduction, pp. 3–24; translation, pp. 25–30; commentary, pp. 30–43.] [GR 5035]

1941: *Bengtsson, Frans G. "Om den strid som stod vid Maeldun och vad därav kom," vol. 1, chapter 1 in section 2 in *Röde Orm. Sjöfarare i västerled* (Malmö). English translation as *The Long Ships: A Saga of the Viking Age* by Michael Meyer (London, 1954), pp. 189–211. [Prose retelling of "The Battle of Maldon" from the Vikings' point of view with translations of lines 29–41, 45–61, 93–95, 96–99, and 311–12.]

1962: *Jansson, Sven B. F. "Deors klagan" (Deor) and "Sjöfararen" (The Seafarer). In Hildeman, Karl-Ivar, ed. *Medeltidens litteratur: Episk diktning m.m.*, ed. Karl-Ivar Hildeman; Vol. 4 of *Litteraturens klassiker*, ed. Lennart Breitholtz (Stockholm; repr. 1996, 2000), pp. 17–22. [Alliterative verse translations.]

1983: *Sandred, Karl Inge, trans. "Wulfstans resa 800-talets slut." *Gutar och Vikingar*, ed. Ingmar Jannson (Stockholm), pp. 417–23. [Introduction, pp. 417–18; translation, pp. 418–21; notes, pp. 421–23].

1991: *Hansson, Gunnar D. *Slaget vid Maldon och sju elegier* (Gråbo). [Verse translations of "The Battle of Maldon," "The Ruin," "The Wanderer," "The Seafarer" (facing-page), "Deor," "The Wife's Lament," "The Husband's Message," "Wulf and Eadwacer" with commentary by Hansson and a translation of parts of chapter 5 of Andreas Haarder's *Det episke liv*, pp. 36–48 (see I.B, above).]

1992: *Borgehammar, Stephan, trans. Ælfric's "På en kyrkas invigningsdag," *Från tid och evighet: Predikningar från 200-tal till 1500-tal*, ed. Stephan Borgehammar (Skellefteå), pp. 191–200, commentary pp. 200–02. [Translation of Ælfric's "In dedicatione ecclesiae" from *The Catholic Homilies*, vol. 2, pp. 574–95.]

1992: *Herschend, Frands. See II.D. below (translations of "The Finnsburg Fragment" and "Widsith").

E. Finnish: "Waldere"

2005: *Himes, Jonathan, Osmo Pekonen, and Clive Tolley, trans. *Waldere: Anglosaksinen muinaisruno* (Jyväskylä). [Alliterative verse translation.]

"Widsith"

2004: *Pekonen, Osmo, and Clive Tolley, trans. *Widsith: Anglosaksinen muinaisruno* (Jyväskylä). [Alliterative verse translation.]

F. Icelandic: "Battle of Brunanburh"

ca. 1853: Brynjúlfsson, Gísli. In Sigurjón Páll Ísaksson. "Þýðingar Gísla Brynjúlfssonar ur fornensku." *Gripla* 18 (2007), 95–96.

ca. late nineteenth century: Gröndal, Benedikt Sveinbjarnason. In Sverrir Tómasson, "'Iarlar árhvatir / iörð um gátu': þýðingar Benedikts Gröndals Sveinbjarnarsonar úr fornensku," Sverir Tómasson, *Skorrdæla: gefin út í minningu Sveins Skorra Höskuldssonar* (Reykjavík, 2003), pp.179–86 at pp. 181–83.

"Widsith"

1936: *Einarsson, Stefán. "Wídsíð = Víðförull." *Skírnir* 110, 185–89. [Alliterative verse translation.]

II. Beowulf

A. Neo-Latin

1815: Thorkelin, Grímur Jónsson. *De Danorum rebus gestis secul. III et IV. Poëma Danicum dialecto Anglo-Saxonica* (Copenhagen), pp. xx, 299. Rvw: G-s [= G. W. Gumælius] *Iduna* 7 (1817), 133–59; N. F. S. Grundtvig *GgA* (8 Jan. 1818), 41–47, and in *Nyeste Skilderie af Kjöbenhavn* nos 60ff. (1815) cols. 945, 998, 1009, 1025, 1030, 1045, 1106, 1121, 1139 [with responses to Grundtvig by Thorkelin, ibid. cols. 1057–61, 1073–80]; Pem [=P. E. Miller] *Dansk-Litteratur-Tidende* (1815), 401–32, 437–46, 461–62; N. Outzen *Kieler Blätter* (1816) III, 307–27; 'Pia' *Ergänzungsblätter zur Jenaischen allgemeinen Literatur-Zeitung* nos. 45, 46 (1816), 354–66; B. Pontoppidan *Nyeste Skilderie* ... nos 75, 85 (1815); [W. Taylor] *Monthly Review* 81 (1816), 516–23. [Text and Latin translation in parallel columns, preface, notes, and glossary. Preface reprinted with facing-page English translation in *Robert E. Bjork, "Grímur Jónsson Thorkelin's Preface to the First Edition of *Beowulf*, 1815," *SS* 68 (1996), 290–320.] [GR 1632]

B. Danish

1815: *Grundtvig, N. F. S. "Et Par Ord om det nys udkomne angelsaxiske Digt," *Nyeste Skilderie af Kjöbenhavn* (July 29). Go to http://www.grundtvigsværker.dk/. [Contains free-verse translation of lines 1–52. Reprinted in Franklin Cooley, "Grundtvig's First Translation from *Beowulf*," *SS* 16 (1941), 234–38.] [Listed in GR as a review of Thorkelin.] Translated into English by Mark Bradshaw Busbee in *GS* 66.1 (2015), 7–36.

1819: —. "Stykker af Skjöldung-Kvadet eller Bjovulfs Minde," *Dannevirke* 4, 234–62. Go to http://www.grundtvigsværker.dk/. [Free rhymed-verse translation of lines 53–319 (through the coastguard episode).] [GR 1658]

1820: —. *Bjowulfs Drape. Et Gothisk Helte-Digt fra forrige Aar-Tusinde af Angel-Saxisk paa Danske Riim* (Copenhagen). Go to http://www.grundtvigsværker.dk/. [Free rhymed-verse translation of entire poem and also contains the first Danish translation of 'The Finnsburg Fragment' in parallel OE/Danish format, pp. XL–XLV.] Rvw: [Hans Gardthausen] *Ergänzungsblätter zu Jenaischen Allgemeinen Literatur-Zeitung (April 1822)* Num. 80, Sp. 249–51, and [Jacob Grimm] *Göttingische gelerthe Anzeigen* (2 January 1823), 1–12. [GR 1659]

1847: Schaldemose, Frederik. *Beo-Wulf og Scopes Widsið, to angelsaxiske Digte, med Oversættelse og oplysende Anmærkninger* (Copenhagen, 1847; repr. 1851 [2nd ed.]; repr. 2022. Chinese ed. 2010), 188 pp. Rvw: P. A. Munch, in Lange's *Norsk Tidsskrfit for Videnskab og Litteratur* 2 (1848), 133–38. [Kemble's text with Danish translation in parallel columns, pp. 1–148, plus commentary on the geographical, historical, and mythic elements in the poem, pp. 149–75; text and translation in parallel columns of "The Finnsburg Fragment," pp. 161–64, and of "Widsith," pp. 176–82, with commentary.] [GR 1634]

1865: *Grundtvig, N. F. S. *Bjovulvs-Drapen, et høinordisk heltedigt, fra Anguls-Tungen fordansket* (Copenhagen). Go to http://www.grundtvigsværker.dk/. [Second, "improved" edition of *Bjowulfs Drape*, 1820.]

1904: Hansen, Adolf. "Et Brudstykke af *Beowulf*," *Dansk Tidsskrift* 7, 468–73. [Alliterative verse translation of lines 491–924.] [GR 1704]

Appendix B

1910: —. *Bjovulf* (Copenhagen), pp. xv, 119. Rvw: A. Olrik *DS* 7 (1910), 112–13; V. J. von Holstein Rathlou *Tilskueren* (June 1910), 557–62. [Alliterative verse translation, posthumously ed. with an introduction and a translation of "The Finnsburg Fragment" by V. J. von Holstein Rathlou.] [GR 1714]. Reprinted as *Bjovulf og Kampen i Finsborg* (Copenhagen, 2019), 122 pp.

1914: Konstantin-Hansen, Thora. *Bjovulf: et angelsaksisk Heltedigt. Frit gengivet for Børn.* Illustrated by Niels Skovgaard (Copenhagen; 2nd ed. 1952), 70 pp. [Prose retelling for children of Part I of the poem.] [GR 1720]

1960: *Albeck, Gustav. "Grundtvigs ældste Udkast till Digtet om Kong Skjold," *GS* 47–53.

1983: *Wilmont, Barry. *Bjowulf: et heltedigt fra Danmarks sagntid.* Illustrated by Wilmont. With a foreword by Ebbe Kløvedal Reich and a translation of "The Fight at Finnsburg" and an afterword by Wilmont. Pages are not numbered (Copenhagen).

1984: *Haarder, Andreas. *Sangen om Bjovulf.* Drawings by Viggo Kragh-Hansen (Copenhagen; repr. 2001 with a foreword by Thomas A. Shippey). [Alliterative verse translation with introduction and commentary.]

1986: *Pedersen, Ole. *Nordiske guder og sagnhelte: Fortællinger.* Illustrated by Lene Hahne (Aarhus, 2nd ed. 2001). [Prose retelling of Beowulf's fight with the Grendel kin, pp. 110–17.]

2002: *Olsen, Lars-Henrik. *Bjovulf: Et sagn fra Danmarks oldtid.* Illustrated by Niels Bach. (Copenhagen). [Prose re-telling for young adults from age 12 to 14.]

2003: *—. *Nordiske heltesagn.* Illustrated by Thomas Dreyer (Viborg; 2nd ed. 2005). [Retelling for young adults from age 12 up of the stories of over 40 Nordic heroes including Scyld Scefing, pp. 13–16, and Beowulf, pp. 49–71.]

2004: *Barkow, Henriette. *Beowulf og hvordan han bekæmpede Grendel – et angelsaksisk epos.* Danish translation of Barkow's adaptation *Beowulf: An Anglo-Saxon Epic* (2003) by Jakob Kjær. Persian translation by Sajida Fawzi. Illustrated by Alan Down (London). [Danish and Persian retelling for children 9 to 14 of Beowulf's fights with Grendel and his mother.]

2012: *Rydahl, John. *Bjovulf: Den gamle dragedræber*. Illustrated by Gitte Skov (Frederiksberg). [Retelling for children 9 to 12 of the whole of *Beowulf*.]

2018: *Zeruneith, Keld. *Beowulf: En gendigtning med efterskrift og noter* (Copenhagen). Rvw: Erik Skyum-Nielsen, *Information* (23 November 2018). [Prose translation from text in R. D. Fulk, Robert E. Bjork, and John D. Niles, eds., *Klaeber's Beowulf* (Toronto, 2008), with notes and an afterword.]

C. Norwegian

1921: Rytter, Henrik. *Beowulf og striden um Finnsborg frå angelsaksisk* (Oslo). ["Nynorsk" translation in alliterative verse, with foreword, notes, and a brief bibliography.] [GR 1723]

1976: *Dietrichson, Jan W. *Beowulf-kvadet*. (Oslo). ["Riksmål" prose translation with a foreword and introduction.]

1999: *Bringsværd, Tor Åge. *Beowulf: han som ville bli husket*. Illustrated by Arne Samuelsen (Oslo). ["Riksmål" prose retelling for children with commentary and notes, pp. 73–85.]

D. Swedish

1817: *Gumælius, Gustaf Wilhelm. "Recension. De Danorum rebus gestis [...]." In *Iduna*, 133–59 at pp. 138–40 [attempts translating some passages into *fornyrðislag* meter.]

1889: Wickberg, Rudolf. *Beovulf, en fornengelsk hjeltedikt* (Västervik; 2nd ed., as *Beowulf, en fornengelsk hjältedikt* with updated introduction, Uppsala, 1914; repr. 2013, 2022). 2nd ed., vol. 5 of Askerbergs populärvetenskapliga bibliotek. Rvw: E. A. Kock *AfNF* 32 (1916), 223–24. [Translation of text from manuscript in free alliterative verse with an introduction and notes.] [GR 1685]

1902: Björkman, Erik. "*Beowulf*, Fornengelsk Dikt." *Världslitteraturen i urval och öfversättning*, ed. Henrik Schück (Stockholm), pp. 463–501. [Detailed prose summary of lines 1–2207, pp. 463–70, followed by a brief essay on *Beowulf* by Henrik Schück, pp. 471–74, anticipating his more fully developed 1909 arguments in *Studier i Beowulfsagan*. Björkman's "prosaic," line-by-line translation of lines 2208–17, 2232–2310, 2313–3182 with footnotes to the translation mostly by Schück follows on pp. 475–501.] [GR 1700, pp. incorrectly noted as 463–74]

1954: Collinder, Björn. *Beowulf översatt i originalets versmått*. With linoleum cuts by Per Engström (Stockholm; 2nd ed. 1955, 3rd ed. 1959, 4th ed. 1963, 5th ed. 1983; 1st paperback ed. 1988, repr. 1992, 2nd paperback ed. 1998). Rvw: A. S. C. Ross and E. G. Stanley *EGS* 6 (1957), 110–12. [Alliterative verse translation.] [GR 1750]

1958: Lindqvist, Sune. *Beowulf Dissectus. Snitt ur fornkvädet jämte svensk tydning* (Uppsala). [Excerpts and translation in parallel columns, with a commentary. Summary in English, pp. 137–42.] [GR 1753]

1962: *Collinder, Björn. *Beowulf*. Selections from part 2. In Hildeman, Karl-Ivar, ed. *Medeltidens litteratur: Episk diktning m.m.* Vol. 4 of *Litteraturens klassiker*, ed. Lennart Breitholtz (Stockholm; repr. 1996, 2000), pp. 9–16.

1997: *Herschend, Frands. "Striden i Finnsborg," *Tor* 29, 295–333. [Contains text and translation in parallel columns of "The Finnsburg Fragment" and the Finnsburg episode in *Beowulf*, pp. 297–300, and translation of lines 18–49 of "Widsith," pp. 325–26. English abstract, p. 295, and summary, pp. 331–32.]

2000: *Birgitta Gahrton, *Beowulf*. Swedish translation of Robert Nye, *Beowulf* (Stockholm; 2nd ed. 2007 with afterword by Lena Törnqvist). [Retelling for children aged 12–15.]

2011: *Birgit Lönn, *Beowulf*. Swedish translation of Rob Lloyd Jones, *Beowulf* (Stockholm). [Retelling for children ages 7+.]

2022: *Gräslund, Bo. *Beowulf: En nordisk berättelse från 500-talet: Rudolf Wickbergs tolkning från fornengelska i bearbetning av Bo Gräslund* (Stockholm). [Revised translation based on R. D. Fulk, Robert E. Bjork, and John D. Niles, eds., *Klaeber's Beowulf* (Toronto, 2008), with introduction, notes, and an afterword.]

E. Icelandic

1983: *Björnsson, Halldóra B. *Bjólfskviða*, ed. and with a foreword by Pétur Knúttson Ridgewell. Illustrated by Alfreð Flóki (Reykjavík). [Alliterative verse translation posthumously edited from Björnsson's three manuscripts.]

F. Finnish

1927: Dillström, R. "*Beowulf,*" *Laivastolehti* 2, 35–40, 73–78, 137–44, 176–80, 201–04, 243–46, 284–89, 316–21, 349–56. [Alliterative verse translation of lines 1–1472 and lines 2961–81 with commentary.] [GR 1733]

1999: *Dillström translation completed by Matti Järvinen (Helsinki; repr. 2019).

1999: *Pekonen, Osmo, and Clive Tolley. *Beowulf. Suomennos, johdanto ja selitykset* (Helsinki; reissued 2007). [Alliterative verse translation.]

G. Sámi

2019: *McGuinne, Johann Sandberg. *Beowulf: dïhte staalehke alma* (Trøndelag). [Translation into South Sámi of Rob Lloyd Jones's retelling of *Beowulf* for children.]

Index

Aalborg, University of 119
Aarhus 145
 University of 113, 125
Aarsleff, Hans 245
Abel, biblical figure 112, 116, 233
Adam, biblical patriarch 60, 111, 113
Adam of Bremen, *Gesta* 133
Addison, Joseph 182
The Advent Lyrics 63, 218, 220, 230
"Æcerbot" 219
Ælfflæd 219, 235
Ælfgar 219, 235
Ælfgifu of Northampton, wife of Cnut the Great 121
Ælfric 41
 De falsis diis 230
 "Dominica III in Quadragesima" 42
 "In dedicatione ecclesiae" 230
 "The Letter of Christ to Abgarus" 39–40, 42–3, 218
Aeschylus, *Oresteia* 156
Æscwig, Bishop of Dorchester 219, 235
aesthetics 6–7, 11–12, 17–18, 40, 77, 79, 87, 97, 108, 143, 148, 151, 217, 232, 244–5
Æthelflæd 219, 235
Æthelred II, King of England 3, 219, 235, 238
Æthelric of Bocking 219, 235
Alcimus Avitus, *Carmina de spiritalis historiae gestis* 41
Alcuin 122
Aldhelm 114–15, 118
Alfred the Great, King of Wessex 33, 132, 134–6, 220
alliteration 11–13, 16–17, 40, 50, 109–10, 122, 128–9, 160, 163, 181, 187, 196–7, 204, 208, 211, 227–30, 232–3
Anderson, Hans Christian 41
Andreas 13, 40, 120–1, 125, 219
Andrew, saint 121
Angantyr 126–7, 144
Anglo-Saxon Chronicle 7, 11, 36, 105–6, 125, 219, 222, 235
Angul, brother of Dan 32, 82, 90, 104
Annales Lindisfarnenses et Dunelmenses 105
Annales regni Francorum 37
Apuleius 180
Arbuthnot, John 182
Arnold, Matthew 107, 182
Artemidorus 79
Asser, *Life of Alfred* 105
Athelstan, King of England 124
Athens 153
Atlantis 30
Atwood, Margaret 200
Augustine, saint, Bishop of Hippo 58–9, 79, 156

Bagby, Benjamin 69
Balder, Norse god 84, 113, 160, 175
Barkow, Henriette 189
Barrington, Daines 22
"The Battle of Bråvalla" 127
"The Battle of Brunanburh" 36, 42, 105, 121, 124–5, 130
 Danish translations 4, 7–11, 60, 64, 72–3, 218–19, 221–3
 Icelandic translations 218–19, 222
 Norwegian translations 16, 219, 222
"The Battle of Maldon" 42, 120, 125, 144, 226, 238–41

"The Battle of Maldon" (*continued*)
  Danish translations   119, 219, 233–5
  Norwegian translations   219
  Swedish translations   219, 235
Bay, Rudolph   71
Bede, saint   59, 118, 156, 219, 241
  Bede 3   125
  Ecclesiastical History   104–5, 115, 218, 230, 244
"Bede's Death Song"   1, 16, 218–19
Bengtsson, Frans G.   237–41
Beowulf   14–15, 34, 36, 47, 82, 86, 101–5, 108, 110, 113, 115–21, 125, 134, 136, 140–1, 144, 149, 180, 217, 227–8, 231, 237
  and archaeology   156, 159–61, 164, 166–8, 170, 172–4, 176, 198, 201–3, 225
  authors of   142
  and burials   143, 160–1, 164, 167–8, 186
  and Beow, Anglo-Saxon deity   1, 146, 169, 174, 210
  cultural and historical aspects   156–74
  date and origins   106–7, 159–61, 164, 177
  dragon   107, 116, 119, 121, 146, 150, 153, 158, 160, 162–3, 165–6, 174, 194–6, 215–16
  "*Electronic Beowulf*"   139
  Finnsburg episode   124, 127
  and Gaelic Finn cycle   165–6
  Grendel   47, 51, 103, 107, 116, 119, 146, 150, 155, 162–3, 174, 181, 186, 188, 194, 199, 211
    as Cain, race of   121
    as Catholic Church   66
    in children's book   190, *191*
    as sloth or lethargy   153
    song about   169–70
    as street name   178
    as water troll   165–6
  Grendel's mother   103, 107, 116, 121, 146, 156, 162–3, 165, 194, 201, 206
  Grundtvig's translation and writing on   7, 31–2, 35, 51, 57, 60, 65–7, 69–72, 76, 94, 96, 115–16, 139, 148–50, 152–3, 170, 172, 174, 179–80, 182–4, 186, 188, 198, 223–4, 244
  Hrothgar   69, 71, 103, 121, 145–6, 148, 152–3, 156, 169, 186, 190, 200–1, 216
  "The Jute Theory"   145–6, 157–8, 161, 164, 176, 180
  on kings, Danish   144
  and *Liedertheorie* (ballad theory)   142
  literary interpretations   148–56
  manuscript   49, 203
  meaning of   116–17
  and Nordic tales   162–5
  and Nowell Codex   176–7
  and orality   115, 120, 142, 154, 203
  and Pekko, Finnish deity   1, 210
  and place-names   147–8, 159–62, 165, 173–4, 176
  poetic style   115, 142–3, 149–50
  and Romantic Nationalism   31–2, 139
  and Scyld Scefing   84–4, 165, 183, 188, 199–200, 214
  in songs   68–72, 169–70
  Thorkelin's edition and translation   1, 4, 24–5, 31, 38–9, 65–6, 76–7, 139–40, 148, 174, 179–80, 192
  Tolkien on   6–7, 11, 150, 152, 154
  translations
    for children   18, 179, 183–4, 188–90, *191*, 200–1
    Danish   1, 4, 18, 24–5, 31, 38–9, 51, 65–7, 72, 76–7, 94, 96, 107, 139–40, 148, 150, 152, 174, 178–93, 223–4
    Finnish   18, 178–9
    Icelandic   15, 18, 178–9, 212–15
    Norwegian (including *Riksmål*)   16, 18, 178–9, 204–8
    Saami   18, 179, 208–12, 215–16

Swedish   18, 172, 174, 178–9, 193–203
   tribes, origin of   145–7, 157–62, 166–70, 172–4, 180, 198
   and Västergötland School   169–70
Bergman, Ingmar   117, 119
Bernadotte, Jean Baptiste Jules   26
Bettelheim, Bruno   188
Biar, Norse god   174
Birka   130
Björkman, Erik   194–6
Björnson, Björnstjerne   112
   Sigurd Jorsalfar   26
Björnsson, Halldóra B.   15, 18, 212, 213, 214–15
Blicher, Steen Steensen   114
Boccaccio, Giovanni, *The Decameron*   114
Boer, Richard Constant   124
Boethius   156
Boethius, Gerda   176
Boniface (Winfred), saint   58
Borgehammar, Stephan   230
Borges, Jorge Luis   140
Bosworth, John   22
Bosworth, Joseph   4
Böthvar Bjarki, legendary Norse hero   165, 174
Bradley, S. A. J.   152
Bragi Boddason, "Ragnarsdrápa"   127
Brandl, Alois   129
Brandt, C. J.   43
Braunius, Georgius   133
Bråvalla, battle of   174
Bringsværd, Tor Åge   207–8
Brink, Bernhard ten   129
Brøgger, Niels Christian   175–6
Brøgger, Suzanne   18, 217, 218, 228, 237
Brynild   188
Brynjlfsson, Gísli   43
Brynjúlsson, Gísli "the younger"   140–1, 222
Bugge, Alexander   130, 222
Bugge, Sophus   159
Bülow, Johan   45

Bureus, Johannes   23
burials/burial mounds   28, 53, 143, 160–1, 164, 167–8, 170, 186, 199
Busbee, Brad   150, 152
Bussæus, Andreas (Anders Buss)   32–3, 129, 220
Byron, George Gordon Lord, "Childe Harold"   108
Byrthferth of Ramsey, *Life of St. Oswald*   219, 235

Cable, Thomas   69
Cædmon   50, 59, 86, 110–13, 115
   "Cædmon's Hymn"
      Danish translation   13, 40, 219–20
      Norwegian translation   16, 219
      Swedish translation   218
   Genesis   4
Cain, biblical figure   112, 116, 121, 233
Carlyle, Thomas   118
Caroline Amalie, Crown Princess of Denmark   77
Cassiordorus   166
Cervantes, Miguel de   180
Chambers, R. W.   15, 129, 152, 176, 244
Charlemagne, Frankish emperor   132
Charles XII, King of Sweden   238
charms   120, 241–2
Chater, Arthur G.   131
Chaucer, Geoffrey, *The Canterbury Tales*   15, 114
Christ, Jesus   45, 47, 112–14, 117, 120–2
   as judge   123
   as phoenix   74
   as warrior, Germanic   123
   See also Cross; Harrowing of Hell
Christ I   13, 40, 42, 219
Christ II   63, 218–19, 230
Christ and Satan   13, 40, 63–4, 111, 113, 218–19, 230, 233

Index

Christian VIII, King of
    Denmark   76, 81–2, 84, 91
Christiana   230
Christiansen, Arne Søby   149
Christiansen, Tom   147–8
Christine de Pizan   206
Chronicon Abbatiae Rameseiensis   219, 235
Clark, George   152
Clark Hall, John R.   159–60, 182, 198, 224–5
Claudian   79
Claussen, Peder   24
Clement I, Pope   74
Clement of Alexandria   111
Cnut (Canute) the Great, King of
    England, Denmark, and
    Norway   3, 104, 107, 121
Collinder, Björn   172, 196–7, *198*, 207, 210
Conrad, Joseph, *Youth*   114, 117
Constantin-Hansen, Thora   183–4, 186
Constantinople, Hagia Sophia   153
Conybeare, John Josias   139
Copenhagen   6, 49, 172, 183, 185
    British attack on   24–5, 71, 75–6
    "Det Norske Selskab"   29
    University of   12–13, 23, 33, 35, 42–3, 75–6, 105, 108, 124–5, 139–40, 149, 182, 222, 233
Cour, Vilhelm la   103–5
"Credo in Deum Patrem
    Omnipotentem"   218, 231
Cross (Holy)   45, 59, 72, 91
    as embodiment of Christ   122–3
    See also "The Dream of the Rood";
    "The Ruthwell Cross"
Crumlin-Pedersen, Ole   221
Crusell, Bernhard Henrik   26
Cynewulf   109

Dahl, Torsten   222–3
Dan, legendary founder of
    Denmark   32, 82, 91, 104
Daniel   13, 40, 219, 233

Dante Alighieri, *Divine Comedy*   204
"De falsis diis"   218
"Deor"   14, 115, 118, 125, 217, 230
    Danish Neo-Latin
        translations   218, 220, 235, 237
    Danish translations   217, 220, 226, 228
    Swedish translations   219, 227
Dickens, Charles, *David
    Copperfield*   108
Dietrichson, Jan W., 16, 206–7
Dillström, Johan Rudolf   208–10, *209*
Domesday Book   106
Donaldson, E. Talbot   192
Doomsday   58
Down, Alan   190
dragons   112, 223
    in *Beowulf*   107, 116, 119, 121, 146, 150, 153, 158, 160, 162–3, 165–6, 174, 194–6, 215–16
"The Dream of the Rood"   111, 113, 120–1, 123
    Danish translations   13, 40, 219–20
    Norwegian translations   15–16, 18, 122, 219
Dumas, Alexandre   180
"Durham"   125

Earle, John   94
Edinburgh, Advocates Library   49
Edwin, King of Northumbria   118
Egeria   123
Egils saga Skalla-Grímssonar   7, 124, 133
Eidsvoll   24
Einarsson, Stefán   14–15, 129, 229
Elene   123, 125
Eliot, T. S.   198
Ellekilde, Hans   145
Ely   219, 235
Ely Book   219, 235
Emonds, Joseph Embley   40
Enkvist, Nils Erik   221

Erik Bloodaxe, King of Norway and of Northumbria   124
Eriksberg   168
Ettmüller, Ludvig   31, 180
Eumenides   156
Euripides   156, 197
Eve, biblical matriarch   112–13
Exeter   49–50
The Exeter Book   4, 73, 76–8, 86
   contents *see* Christ I; Christ II; "Deor"; *Guthlac B*; "The Husband's Message"; *Judgment Day 1*; "Maxims I"; *The Phoenix*; Riddles; "The Ruin"; "The Seafarer"; "Soul and Body II"; "The Wanderer"; "Widsith"; "The Wife's Lament"; "Wulf and Eadwacer"
   importance of   49–50
Exodus   13, 40, 219, 233

Faarlund, Jan Terje   40
Fahlbeck, Pontus   146, 157–8, 161, 164, 169
Fast (Svionum), Carl Otto   168–70
"The Fates of Men"   115, 219
Fawz, Sajida   190
Fell, Christine E.   221
Fenrir, legendary wolf   163
"The Fight at Finnsburg"   182, 225
"The Finnsburg Fragment"   14, 114, 124, 127, 144, 217, 241–42
   Danish translations   218–19, 223–5
   Swedish translations   220, 225–6
First Grammatical Treatise   2
"The Five Buroughs"   219
Fogelberg, Bengt Erland, "Tor" sculpture   27
Fornmanna sögur   2
Frank, Roberta   152
"The Franks Casket"   109, 117–18, 133, 219
Frederik VI, King of Denmark   76, 84

Frederiksstad   162
Freyja, Norse goddess   59
Fridleifs saga   127
Frigg, Norse goddess   230
Friðþjófs saga   21
Frode I, legendary Danish king   189

Gahrton, Birgitta   200
Gannholm, Tore   170, 172
Garrett, Paul Russell   154
Gay, John   182
Gelstad, Otto   191–2
Genesis A   13, 40, 112, 215, 219, 233
Genesis B   112
   Danish translations   13, 40–1, 219, 233
   Norwegian translations   16, 219, 233
Gering, Hugo   224
Gibson, Edmund   7, 9
"Gloria Patri"   218, 231
gnomic verse   102, 120
Goethe, Johann Wolfgang von   192
Gog and Magog, biblical giants   30
Good Friday   122–3
Gospel of Nicodemus   111, 113
Gothenburg   172
   University of   119, 128, 163, 194, 227
Gram, Hans   33, 34, 35, 37–8, 41, 49
Gräslund, Bo   170, 172–4, 194, 201–3
"The Grave"   13, 40, 219
Greenfield, Stanley B.   152
Gregory of Tours   149
Gregory I the Great, Pope   51, 231
Grendel *see under* Beowulf
Grendel's mother *see under* Beowulf
Grettissaga   162
Grieg, Edvard   26
Grimm, Jakob   5–6
Grønbech, Vilhelm   97, 101–3
Grundtvig, N. F. S.   8, 12–14, 17, 22, 26, 47–8, 95, 141–3, 220, 223
   on "The Battle of Brunanburh"   4, 7–11, 60, 64, 72–3, 221

Grundtvig, N. F. S. (*continued*)
    on *Beowulf*, translation and writing on   7, 31–2, 35, 51, 57, 60, 65–7, 69–72, 76, 94, 96, 115–16, 139, 148–50, 152–3, 170, 172, 174, 179–80, 182–4, 186, 188, 198, 223–4, 244
    Christenhedens Syvstjerne   58
    Dannevirke journal   11, 37, 75
    death   94
    and *The Exeter Book*   49, 73, 76–7, 86
    Grønbech, compared to   101–2
    hymns and songs   62–4, 68–72, 111–12, 244
    on Logos   60–2
    "Maskeradeballet i Danmark 1808"   45
    nationalism of   31–2, 40–3, 59, 77, 82–6, 94–5, 139, 154, 230
    Nordens Mytologi   28, 61, 65, 70
    OE poem (1820) by   51–7
    The Phoenix (*Phenix-Fulgen*) edition and translation   1, 6, 11, 60, 73, 76, 230
        concluding poem   91–4
        dedicatory poem   82–5
        edition   77–9, 94
        introduction   79–81
        reception   95–6
        structure   77–8
        translation   86–91, 94
    on phoenix as rebirth   74–6, 79–81, 88, 90, 94
    "Phønix-Gaarden"   75–6
    preaching by   13
    promotion of OE literature   3–6, 24, 46, 49–51, 72–3, 94, 230, 244
    Prospectus   4, 42, 49, 76, 85–6
    "Rasmus Christian Rask"   44
    as reformer, educational   72
    on *Revelation*   57–9
    "Skjold"   116
Grundtvig, Stener   96
Grundtvig, Svend   143
Gudrun   188
Gumælius, Gustaf Wilhelm   193

Gunnlaugr ormstunga   3
Gustav IV Adolf, King of Sweden   25
Guta saga   172
Guthlac, saint   109
Guthlac B   13, 40, 219
Guðnason, Bjarni   175

Haarder, Andreas   18, 113–19, 121, 144, 149–50, 152, 186–8, 192–3, 234–6
Hammerich, Frederik   13–14, 40–1, 94, 96, 230–1, 233, 244
Hansen, Adolf   107–8, 182–5, 187, 224–5
Hansen, Oskar   182, 225
Hanson, Howard, "Lament for Beowulf" choral work   68
Hansson, Gunnar D.   227–8, 236–7
Harald Bluetooth, King of Denmark and Norway   238, 240
Harald I Harefoot, King of England   105
Harald Wartooth, semi-legendary King of Denmark   174
Hardicanute, King of Denmark and England   105
Hardy, Thomas   114
Harrowing of Hell   63, 111–13, 122, 184
Heaney, Seamus   192, 196
Hedeby   130, 133–6, 147
Heiberg, Ludvig Johan   69
Helgakviða Hundingsbana II   144
Heliand   113
Helsingør   33
Hengest   104, 126–7, 149, 223–5
Henry of Huntingdon
    "Battle of Brunanburh" translation   7, 9
    Historia Anglorum   219, 235
Heraclitus   60
Herder, Johann Gottfried   45–7, 61–2
Herodotus   79
Herschend, Frands   18, 124, 225–6
Hervararsaga   124, 127

Hesiod 79
Heusler, Andreas 110
Hickes, George 40
Hilda, saint, Abbess of Whitby 113, 241–3
Himes, Jonathan 229
Historia Brittonum 147
Hitler, Adolf 117, 119
Hlöðskviða 144
Hoffmeyer, Ellen 101
Hørup, Henning 96
Hollander, Lee M. 144
Holstein Rathlou, Viggo J. von 182
Holthausen, Ferdinand 205, 224, 228
Homer
 Iliad 32, 115, 152, 184, 191–2
 Odyssey 32, 152, 156, 184, 191–2
homilies 4, 42–3, 51, 218, 220, 230
Howley, William, Archbishop of Canterbury 4
Hrothgar *see under Beowulf*
Hughes, Thomas 22
Hume, David 85
"The Husband's Message"
 Danish translations 217, 220, 237
 Swedish translations 219, 236–7
Hygelac (Chlochilaicus) 149
hymns and songs 62–4, 68–72, 111–12, 169–70, 244
"Hyndluljóð" 127

Ingemann, B. S. 71–2
Ingwersen, Niels 127
Irenæus 111
Isaac, biblical patriarch 60
Isaacsson, Lanae 243
Isidore of Seville 30
Íslendingasögur 14

Jack, George 207, 210
Jansson, Sven B. F. 227–8, 235
Järvinen, Matti 208–9
Jensen, Jody 145
Jensen, Johannes V., "Stæren" 116
Jerusalem 123
 Solomon's temple 153

Jespersen, Otto 102
Johansen, Steen 96
Johansson, Leif 185
John of Worcester, *Chronicon ex chronicis* 219, 235
John the Baptist, saint 111
John the Divine, saint 57
Jonah, biblical patriarch 60
Jónsson, Jón 124, 129–30, 174–5
Jordan, Richard 129
Jordanes 30, 166
Jørgensen, Ove 133–6
"Judgment Day 1" 215
Judith
 Danish translations 13, 40, 219, 231–2
 Norwegian translations 16, 219, 233
 Swedish translations 1, 12–13, 218, 231
Julian of Norwich, *Revelations of Divine Love* 15, 122
Junius, Francis 112
The Junius Codex 49

The Kalendar of Abbot Samson of Bury St. Edmunds 106
The Kalevala 197
"Kálfsvísa" 127
Känne 173
kappatöl (list of heroes) 14
Kemble, John M. 5–6, 31–2, 47, 140, 180–2, 245
kennings 108, 115, 169, 232
Kier, Christian Ludwig 145–7, 169
Kiernan, Kevin 106, 139, 244
Kjær, Jakob 190
Klaeber, F. 168, 198, 210, 212
Knittelvers 67
Knútsson, Pétur 215
Kock, Ernst 110
Kragballe, Christian Malta 231, 244
Kragh-Hansen, Viggo 188
Kraki, Hrólfr 175
Kroman, Erik 105

Lactantius, *De Ave Phoenice* 77–9

Laetus, Erasmus, *Res Danicae*   30
Laholm   162
Landnámabók   129
Langebek, Jacob   35, 36, 37, 49, 105, 220, 222
Langland, William, *Piers Plowman*   15
Larsen, Henry Vincent Christian   64, 111–13, 122, 230, 233
Laurentius Petri   230
Lawrence, William W.   129
"The Lay of the Last Survivor"   118
"The Lay of Vafðrúðnir"   14
Layamon, *Brut*   4
Leeds   124
Leif Erikson   132
Lejre   147–9, 155, 175, 180
Leo X, Pope   153
Leo, Heinrich   31–2, 146, 157, 180
Lindisfarne   122
Lindqvist, Sune   158, 167–8, 194, 198–9
Ling, Pehr Henrik   28
Lloyd Jones, Rob   179, 200–1, 215
Logos   60–2
Loki, Norse god   165
London   5, 85, 175, 189
Society of Antiquaries   4, 49
Lönn, Birgit   201
Lönnrot, Elias   26–7
   Kalevala, edition of   27
Lönnroth, Lars   119–21, 245
Lund, Christen Andersen   45
Lund, Niels   18, 105–6, 221, 235
Lund, University of   110, 157–8, 161, 164, 170, 193–4
Luther, Martin   59, 111, 153

Madden, Sir Frederic   5
Magna Carta   24
Magnus, Johannes, *Historia de omnibus gothorum suedonumque regibus*   30
Magnússon, Finnur (Finn Magnusen)   226, 228, 235

Malone, Kemp   3, 15, 129, 134, 148, 150, 152
Malory, Thomas   15
"Maxims I"   42, 219
"Maxims II"   42
McGuinne, Johan Sandberg   215–16
McGuire, Brian Patrick   106–7
"Meters of Boethius"   13, 40, 219
"Metrical charm 1"   241
Midgard Serpent   163
Milton, John
   Paradise Lost   15, 112, 237
   Paradise Regained   15
Möller, Hermann   129
Montelius, Oscar   158
Mörk, Jacob, and Anders Törngren, *Adalriks och Giöthildas äfwentyr*   23
Moses, biblical patriarch   60
Much, Rudolf   15
Müllenhoff, Karl   129, 165, 182
Müller, Ludvig Christian   48
   Collectanea Anglo-Saxonica   41–2
Munch, Peter   12

Nansen, Fridtjof   130–33, *131*
Napoleon Bonaparte   24–6, 29
nationalism   158, 174, 176, 244
   of Grundtvig   31–2, 40–3, 59, 77, 82–6, 94–5, 139, 154, 230
   and historical writing, tradition of   30
   post-Napoleonic   38–48
   Romantic Nationalism   7, 24–9, 32–9, 59, 103, 105–6, 133, 139, 154, 204, 230
Nazis/Nazism   103, 128, 163, 167–9, 175, 178; *see also* World War II
Nennius   127
Nerman, Birger   158, 166–7
Neumann, Erich   156
The Nibelungenlied   115
Nielson, Hans F.   40
Niles, John D.   148
Nilsson, Lars Gabriel   12–13, 231–2
Niðhögg, legendary serpent   163

Njals Saga 21
Noack, Bent 230, 233
Norna-Gestr 14
Nutzhorn, H. 67–8, 71
Nye, Robert 179, 200
Nyerup, Rasmus 37–8, 47

Odense 133
  University of 47, 113
Odin, Norse god 14, 45, 59, 90, 161, 199, 230
Oehlenschläger, Adam, *Nordiske Digte* 27–8
Ohthere 33
Ólafr Tryggvason, King of Norway 14, 120, 234–5
  opera about 26
Olai, Ericus, *Chronica regni Gothorum* 30
Olaus Magnus, *Historia de gentibus septentrionalibus* 21
Olav Tryggveson's Saga 11
Olrik, Axel 126–7, 143–5, 164, 182, 184, 205
  laws, nine epic 145
Olsen, Lars-Henrik 188–9
orality 45
  Finnish 27
  OE 114–15, 120, 142, 145, 154, 203
  oral-formulaic theory 115
Origenes 230
Orosius, *Historiae adversum paganos* 22
  OE translation *see* Orosius
Orosius 33, 121, 129, 132–5, 167
Örvar-Odds saga 127
Oslo 135, 241
  University of 15, 122, 130, 164, 175–6, 206
Ovid 79

The Parker Chronicle 147
Pascal, Blaise 118
"Pater Noster" 218, 220, 231
Pedersen, Ole 188
Pekko, Finnish god 1, 210

Pekonen, Osmo 209–12, 229
The Phoenix
  Danish translations 1, 6, 11, 13, 40, 60, 73, 76–96, 218–19, 230
  Grundtvig's edition and translation 1, 6, 11, 60, 73, 76–96, 230
picture stones 172
Pliny the Elder 79, 125, 172
Poetic Edda 21, 37, 115, 119
Pope, Alexander 182
Pope, John C. 69
Porthan, Henrik Gabriel 130, 221
Pound, Ezra 68–9
"Precationes A" and "B" 218, 231
Procopius 166, 172
prosopopoeia 120
Pytheas of Massalia 132

Ragnarok 175
Ragvaldsson, Nils 30
Rask, Rasmus 41–2, 44–8, 61, 102, 130, 133, 221, 244–5
Rausing, Gad 170, 172–4
Reich, Ebbe Kløvedal 185
Renaissance, Nordic 23
Revelation, Book of 57–9
Reykjavík 222
riddles 42, 80, 120, 215, 219
Riddles 42, 215, 219
Ridgewell, Pétur Knútsson 212
Robinson, Fred C. 152
Rolf Krake, semi-legendary Danish king 175, 188
Rome, St Peter's 153
Rønning, Frederik 47–8, 107, 141–3, 146, 231–2, 244
Rooth, Erik 110
Roskilde 111, 176, 221
Ross, A. S. C. 196
Rousseau, Jean-Jacques 29
Rudbeck, Olof, *Atland, eller Manheim* 30
"The Ruin" 94, 118
  Danish translations 219–20, 235, 237

"The Ruin"(*continued*)
　Norwegian translations　16–17, 219, 236
　Swedish translations　219, 236
"The Rune Poem"　102, 104, 125
runes　21, 23, 42, 44, 47, 172, 227; *see also* "The Rune Poem"
"The Ruthwell Cross"　13, 40, 219
Rydahl, John　190
Rytter, Henrik　16, 204–7

St. Andrews, University of　130
Samuelsen, Arne　207–8
Sandred, Karl Inge　221
Sandved, Arthur O.　15–18, 122, 233, 235
Sawyer, Peter H.　221
Saxo Grammaticus, *Gesta Danorum*　21, 30, 82, 104, 156, 174, 198
Schaldemose, Frederik　146, 180–2, 186, 224, 228
Schiller, Friedrich　58
Schrøder, Ludwig　11, 150–4, *151*
　and historical songs　67–8, 71
Schück, Henrik　158, 161–3, 194–5
Schumacher, Jan Henrik　122–3
Schütte, Gudmund　15, 125–7, 144, 228
Scott, Walter　180
　The Pirate　21
Scyld, son of Dan　82–4, 91
"The Seafarer"　108, 110, 118, 120
　Danish translations　13, 219–20, 235, 237
　Norwegian translations　16, 219, 236
　Swedish translations　219, 236
Sergius I, Pope　123
Setesdal　176
Shakespeare, William　161, 197, 204
　Hamlet　85, 117, 119
　Henry VI　15
　Henry VIII　15
　King Lear　15
　Pericles　108
　The Tempest　108

Shelley, Percy Bysshe　107, 182
Shippey, T. A.　113, 144, 149, 152
Siebs, Theodor　129
Sievers, Eduard　110, 129
Sigrid　188
Sigurd Fafnesbane, legendary Germanic hero　162, 188
Simeon of Durham　124
Sir Gawain and the Green Knight　206
Skando-Saxon　42, 141
Skard, Sigmund　204
Skov, Gitte　190, 191
Skovgaard, Joakim, "Christ in the Realm of the Dead" painting　64, *65*, 111, 184, 244
Skovgaard, Niels　184, 187
Skúlason, Einarr, *Geisli*　113
Sneedorf, J. S.　23
Snorri Sturluson　127, 156, 168, 198
　Edda　14, 160, 165
　Gylfaginning　160, 165
　Heimskringla　21, 23, 297
　Ynglingasaga　147, 167, 175
The Song of Roland　115, 237
Sophocles　197
"Soul and Body II"　13, 40, 219
Spelman, John　33, 220
Stafafelli　124, 130, 174
Stalin, Joseph　117, 119
Stammbaum model　38
Stanley, E. G.　196
Steenstrup, C. H. R.　105, 124, 22, 233–4
Steffens, Henrik　180
Stephens, George　12, 42–44, 48, 95, 140–1, 230–1
Stevns　172–3, 178
Stjerna, Knut　158–61, 164, 167
Stockholm　42, 168, 178
　National Museum　166–7, 170
　University of　227
Stolberg, Friedrich Leopold zu, Count　39
Strand, Tor H.　175–6
stress, law of initial and terminal　126–7
Strindberg, August　23

Suhm, Peter Frederik 37–8, 49, 149
Sundén, Karl Fritiof 15, 128–9, 228
Sutton Hoo 168, 174
Svanhild 188
Svaning, Hans, *Refutatio calumniarum cuiusdam Ioannis Magni* 30
Sveinbjarnarson, Gröndal 222
Sven Aggeson 146
Sven Tveskæg 235
Swedberg, Jesper 23
Swedenborg, Emmanuel 23
Swift, Jonathan 182
Swinburne, Algernon 107–8, 182
Sydow, Carl Wilhelm von 164–6
Sydow, Max von 165
Symoneonis Monachi Opera Omnia 219, 235

Tacitus 79, 125, 156, 172
  Germania 119
Tartu, University of 124
Tavares, Victor 200
Tegnér, Esaias
  Frithiof's Saga 21, 26
  "Svea" 28
Telemark 176
Tennyson, Alfred Lord 107, 182
Tertullian 74, 111
Thjódólf of Hvinir, *Ynglingatal* 147
Thor, Norse god 27, 28, 31, 47, 59, 165, 175, 188, 230
Thoreau, Henry David, *Walden* 237
Þorgilsson, Ári, *Íslendingabók* 33
Thorkelin, Grímur Jónsson 25, 29, 96–7
  Beowulf edition and translation 1, 4, 24–5, 31, 38–9, 65–6, 76–7, 139–40, 148, 174, 179–80, 192
  and nationalism 38–9, 139, 244
Thorpe, Benjamin 6, 12, 42, 46, 86, 96, 245
A Thousand and One Nights 114
Tolkien, J. R. R., on *Beowulf* 6–7, 11, 150, 152, 154
Tolley, Clive 209–12, 229
Trautmann, Moritz 224
Travares, Victor 215

Troilus and Creseyde 206
Turku 176, 210, 221
Tvillingrigerne (Twin Realms) 28

Undset, Sigrid 243
Unger, C. R. 12, 230
Uppsala 240
  burial mounds 161, 164, 167–8
  University of 124, 158, 161, 166–7, 170, 194, 197, 225

Vafþrúðnismál 111
Varila, Mari-Liisa 176–7
Vasbo, Vibeke 241–3, 242
Venantius Fortunatus 123
Vendel 159–60, 167
The Vercelli Book 49
Villemoes, Peter, naval officer 28
"Vindicta Salvatoris" 42
Virgil, *Aeneid* 25, 120
Víðförull 14
Völsunga saga 144
Völundarviða 3, 215
Völuspá 37, 111, 127
Vos, Reinecke 180
"Voyages of Ohthere and Wulfstan" 33, 36, 121, 130, 156, 217
  Danish Neo-Latin translations 217, 220
  Danish translations 218–19, 221
  geography of 134–6
  Nansen on 131–3
  Neo-Latin translations 129, 217, 220
  Swedish translations 217, 220–1

"Waldere" 14, 114, 220, 229
"The Wanderer" 110, 118, 120
  Danish translations 219–20, 236–7
  Norwegian translations 16, 219, 236
  Swedish translations 219, 236
Ware, Christopher 33, 220
Webster, John 198
Weibull, Curt 160, 163–4
Weibull, Lauritz 164

Index

Weyland, legendary Germanic smith 118, 188, 226
Weyse, C. E. F., "Der vanker en ridder" song 69
Wickberg, Rudolf Mauritz 174, 193–4, 201–3
"Widsith" 14–15, 103–4, 110, 115, 120–1, 124–7, 129, 136, 144, 175, 217, 228
   Danish translations 218–19, 228
   Finnish translations 220, 228–30
   Icelandic translations 219, 228–9
   names in 128–9
   Swedish translations 15, 128–9, 219, 228–9
Wieselgren, Per 124
"The Wife's Lament" 13, 156, 219–20, 236
Wilfrid of York, saint 163
William IV, King of Great Britain 4
William of Malmesbury 114–15
Willibrord, saint 58, 106
Wilmont, Barry 184–7, 225
Winchester, New Minster 219, 235
Winfred *see* Boniface, saint
Wolf, Kirsten 145
World War II 103, 163, 167, 175; *see also* Nazis/Nazism
Worm, Ole 23
Worster, William 101
Wrenn, C. L. 198, 210
Wright, David 225
"Wulf and Eadwacer" 121, 219, 236, 242
Wulfstan of Hedeby 167

Ynglingatal 167

Zeruneith, Keld 18, 108–10, *109*, 154–6, 186, 191–3

ANGLO-SAXON STUDIES

Please see the Boydell & Brewer website
for details of earlier titles in the series.

Volume 24: The Dating of *Beowulf*: A Reassessment, *edited by Leonard Neidorf*

Volume 25: The Cruciform Brooch and Anglo-Saxon England, *Toby F. Martin*

Volume 26: Trees in the Religions of Early Medieval England, *Michael D.J. Bintley*

Volume 27: The Peterborough Version of the Anglo-Saxon Chronicle: Rewriting Post-Conquest History, *Malasree Home*

Volume 28: The Anglo-Saxon Chancery: The History, Language and Production of Anglo-Saxon Charters from Alfred to Edgar, *Ben Snook*

Volume 29: Representing Beasts in Early Medieval England and Scandinavia, *edited by Michael D.J. Bintley and Thomas J.T. Williams*

Volume 30: Direct Speech in *Beowulf* and Other Old English Narrative Poems, *Elise Louviot*

Volume 31: Old English Philology: Studies in Honour of R. D. Fulk, *edited by Leonard Neidorf, Rafael J. Pascual and Tom Shippey*

Volume 32: 'Charms', Liturgies, and Secret Rites in Early Medieval England, *Ciaran Arthur*

Volume 33: Old Age in Early Medieval England: A Cultural History, *Thijs Porck*

Volume 34: Priests and their Books in Late Anglo-Saxon England, *Gerald P. Dyson*

Volume 35: Burial, Landscape and Identity in Early Medieval Wessex, *Kate Mees*

Volume 36: The Sword in Early Medieval Northern Europe: Experience, Identity, Representation, *Sue Brunning*

Volume 37: The Chronology and Canon of Ælfric of Eynsham, *Aaron J Kleist*

Volume 38: Medical Texts in Anglo-Saxon Literary Culture, *Emily Kesling*

Volume 39: The Dynastic Drama of *Beowulf*, *Francis Leneghan*

Volume 40: Old English Lexicology and Lexicography: Essays in Honor of Antonette diPaolo Healey, *edited by Maren Clegg Hyer, Haruko Momma and Samantha Zacher*

Volume 41: Debating with Demons: Pedagogy and Materiality in Early English Literature, *Christina M. Heckman*

Volume 42: Textual Identities in Early Medieval England: Essays in Honour of Katherine O'Brien O'Keefe, *Edited by Jacqueline Fay, Rebecca Stephenson and Renée R. Trilling*

Volume 43: Bishop Æthelwold, his Followers, and Saints' Cults in Early Medieval England: Power, Belief, and Religious Reform, *Alison Hudson*

Volume 44: Global Perspectives on Early Medieval England, *edited by Karen Louise Jolly and Britton Elliott Brooks*

Volume 45: Performance in *Beowulf* and Other Old English Poems, *Steven J. A. Breeze*

Volume 46: Wealth and the Material World in the Old English Alfredian Corpus, *Amy Faulkner*

Volume 47: Law, Literature, and Social Regulation in Early Medieval England, *edited by Anya Adair and Andrew Rabin*

Volume 48: The Reigns of Edmund, Eadred and Eadwig, 939–959: New Interpretations, *edited by Mary Elizabeth Blanchard and Christopher Riedel*

Volume 49: Emotional Practice in Old English Literature, *Alice Jorgensen*

www.ingramcontent.com/pod-product-compliance
Lightning Source LLC
Chambersburg PA
CBHW070749230426
43665CB00017B/2304